In the
BOAT *with*
LBJ

John L. Bullion

Republic of Texas Press
Plano, Texas

Library of Congress Cataloging-in-Publication Data

Bullion, John L.
    In the boat with LBJ. / John L. Bullion.
        p.   cm.
    Includes index.
    ISBN 1-55622-880-5 (pbk.)
    1. Johnson, Lyndon B. (Lyndon Baines), 1908-1973--Anecdotes.
    2. Johnson, Lyndon B. (Lyndon Baines), 1908-1973--Friends and
    associates--Anecdotes.   3. Bullion family--Anecdotes.   4. Johnson,
    Lyndon B. (Lyndon Baines), 1908-1973--Homes and haunts--Anecdotes.
    5. Presidents--United States--Biography--Anecdotes.   I. Title.

    E847.2.B85   2001
    973.923'092--dc21   2001031642
                                                                                    CIP

Republic of Texas Press is an imprint of Wordware Publishing, Inc.
No part of this book may be reproduced in any form or by
any means without permission in writing from
Wordware Publishing, Inc.

Printed in the United States of America

ISBN 1-55622-880-5
10 9 8 7 6 5 4 3 2 1
0106

All inquiries for volume purchases of this book should be addressed to Wordware
Publishing, Inc., at 2320 Los Rios Boulevard, Plano, Texas 75074. Telephone
inquiries may be made by calling:

(972) 423-0090

For Laura, the love of my life;
For Jack and Chandler, our children;
And for Nancy, my dear and best friend.

When many cares fill my mind,
your consolations cheer my soul.

— Psalm 94:19

Contents

What is man that thou shouldst remember him,
    mortal man that thou shouldst care for him?
Yet thou hast made him little less than a god,
    crowning him with glory and honour.
Thou makest him master over all thy creatures;
    all sheep and oxen, all the wild beasts,
The birds in the air and the fish in the sea,
    and all that moves along the paths of ocean.

— Psalm 8: 4-8

This is my ranch
    and I do as I damn please.

— needlepointed motto
at the LBJ Ranch

Prelude

Sometime late in the summer of 1940, my father met Lyndon Johnson. Soon afterwards, he began advising LBJ on his family's taxes. His professional association with the Johnsons did not end until the early 1990s, twenty years after the former president's death. Dad's friendship with Lady Bird Johnson has lasted into this century. The two still talk periodically about fond memories and business matters.

That enduring connection with the Johnson family helps explain why this book does not include a full narrative of the legal advice J. Waddy Bullion gave Lyndon Johnson. Dad regards most of the tactics he developed to help LBJ pay less and keep more as privileged, confidential information protected by the attorney-client relationship. The book will discuss, however, the major strategies my father and LBJ devised. And it will cover many more things as well.

What this memoir provides is a close look at Lyndon Johnson in private. You will hear LBJ unplugged, in spontaneous performances before small audiences. Some of the things he talked about were of obvious significance to the nation he served; others mattered most to himself and his family. All of them were important to him. Lyndon Johnson took himself and his life very seriously. As you will see, even what most people regard as comparatively unimportant pastimes like hunting deer and pulling practical jokes had meanings to him far beyond the casual. We Bullions—my father, mother, stepmother, sister, and I—witnessed this. Often we benefited from knowing LBJ. Occasionally we suffered from our contacts with him. What we shared were uniquely intimate perspectives on Lyndon Johnson and the ranch he loved.

Of course, to a certain extent these are our stories as well. To understand why we were where we were and reacted as we did, you'll have to know a little about the Bullion family history. I've tried to resist the temptation to go on for too long at these times. That's difficult, because I don't think of any of us as ordinary people. More precisely, I suppose, we're not famous beyond the orbits of our own personal and professional spheres. A good bit of this book is about the impact of a famous and powerful man upon the lives of the not-famous. Since we lack fame, you'll have to hear about us from me.

My father's stories make up most of Part I. With some detours, principally my account of the background and circumstances of my first meeting with LBJ, this section explains what it was like for Dad to work for him from 1940 until roughly late 1965. Dad called this being "in the boat."

Part II is my story. It is a detailed recollection of the experiences my father and I had at the ranch in late December 1965. During that time, the president of the United States and I hunted deer together. Mine is by far the fullest account of one of LBJ's favorite sports. As you will see, he defined this sport as testing his guests' manhood as well as hunting whitetails.

The Bullions' relationships with Lyndon Johnson during his final years are the subjects of Part III. A few of these stories take place close to the Potomac River. More central ones occur by the banks of the Colorado, the Llano, and the Pedernales. Other bodies of water include Lake LBJ and the Pacific Ocean. Those of you who are familiar with a fine old Baptist hymn will recognize one significance of Part III's title immediately. For those who are not, it's down by the riverside where people lay down their swords and shields and study war no more. Whether it was Lyndon Johnson's good fortune to be able to gladly set aside the tools and preoccupations of his trade after retirement is something these pages explore.

It won't spoil the suspense too much, I trust, to let you know right now that one of the book's main protagonists dies in the end. The Bullions' stories go on, but their brush with history in the form of Lyndon B. Johnson was mostly over after January 1973.

A few more words to introduce this book are appropriate here. Early on, I decided not to make it a formal, academic history. To make a bad pun: I wanted this book to be the Bullions' story, not his-story. This puzzled my colleagues in the department of history at the University of Missouri-Columbia, who have a hard time seeing me as anything but a historian. One of them, on hearing what I was doing, immediately assumed that Dad had provided me with some revealing new documents about the Johnsons' business interests. "Not at all," I told him. "Anyway, this is a memoir, not a monograph." In this book, I have kept my distance from the preoccupations and procedures of my profession.

At times, I have commented on things in this book from the perspectives of the men the young John Bullion and his middle-aged father became. In other places, I have referred to insights and information I have borrowed from historians and journalists. But mostly these are stories told to and by a young man.

One last comment, this one about stories. Although my family enjoys telling them and loves them for their own sakes, we also recount them because they teach us some things of value. Because we feel they should instruct as well as amuse, we're not shy about pointing to their morals. I've done a good bit of that in this memoir. I have tried, however, to avoid moralizing about them. Nothing is worse than demanding that others meet standards the self-appointed paragon of virtue can't or won't meet him or herself. To fault others for not being perfect: no one should do that unless he or she can cast the first stone. As you'll discover, I certainly can't claim that status. Nor can anyone in my family. Nor could Lyndon Johnson.

Enough said by way of prelude and prospectus. Let's start.

What happened, was this:

PART I

In the Boat

Countless are the things thou hast made, O Lord.
    Thou has made all by thy wisdom;
And the earth is full of thy creatures,
    beasts great and small.
Here is the great immeasurable sea,
    in which move creatures beyond number.
Here ships sail to and fro,
    here is Leviathan whom thou hast made
That it may sport in it.

—Psalm 104:24-26

CHAPTER 1

Washington Stories

My parents didn't set many rules for my sister Ann and me when we were growing up. We knew there were ten commandments, though we might have trouble listing them all and certainly would be pressed to explain them. And we learned from Froggy the Gremlin that "pals stick together" through thick and thin, a precept Dad and Mother approved of. But rules specific to the household at, first, 5736 W. Bryn Mawr and, after early 1954, 6131 Lupton Drive, Dallas, Texas, were few and far between. After a soft-drink binge of mine one afternoon while Mother and Ann were out somewhere, we kids were strictly limited to one Coke per day. That was my mother's one rule. My father devised two. Anything less than a perfect score on a spelling test was unacceptable. So was being late to breakfast on the weekends. The first he punished with a spanking, administered with an old-fashioned razor strop. The second meant you choked down one hundred percent of a large helping of ice-cold eggs and bacon. While these rules were enforced, Ann and I made do with one soft drink a day, drilled ourselves constantly on the spelling assignment for the week, and didn't risk riding our bikes before breakfast on Saturday and Sunday.

Having only three articulated rules didn't leave us free to do as we pleased every other way. Instead, it meant we learned by family custom, by explanation, and by observation. For instance, "Thou shalt not take the name of the Lord thy God in vain" became in real life "don't say God dammit." That was Mother's gloss on the commandment. Dad was free to say "God dammit" as often as he chose, and that was pretty frequent. I'm sure he was neither aware how much he said it, nor what a wide variety of people, animals, machines, and inanimate objects he routinely invited the Almighty to condemn. When we became adults, Ann and I joked that we thought God's last name was Dammit. Of

Waddy, Ann, and John Bullion, early 1950s.
Bullion Family Collection.

course, we didn't think that at the time. We saw swearing as a mark of maturity; nothing more, nothing less. Kids couldn't do it; grown ups could. It didn't even seem unfair. If we'd had the choice, we would have opted for two Cokes a day, or forgiveness for the occasional misspelling, well before the privilege of taking God's name in vain.

We also learned the rules of right living via stories. This method was as natural to our parents as it had been for Jesus of Nazareth. When it came to raising children, they followed Jesus' style of instruction to his first disciples, not Paul's abstract lectures to the early Church. To my folks, telling a story of love involving a Good Samaritan was more likely to have the desired effect than detailing faith, hope, and charity, then declaring which was the greatest of these. As they did this, they were continuing the tradition of their parents, all great storytellers who delighted in uncovering morals from their tales. We learned as they did.

It was through stories that I first became acquainted with Lyndon Johnson. I heard about LBJ well before I grasped that my father was one of his tax attorneys and a trusted adviser on family business. I'm sure my parents mentioned this to me; I just didn't know what a "client" was. And at first I didn't notice that Dad never spoke about his other clients in the way he spoke about the senator. In fact, he never talked about them at all. My father had a self-imposed rule: no discussion of any client's business at home. And he never talked about LBJ's business, either. But Johnson was famous enough, his manner colorful enough, and his usefulness for instilling one certain message on impressionable minds obvious enough, for Dad to bend his rule.

The story he told didn't have anything to do with business, either personal or the nation's. It had everything to do with work and with power. Which is why Dad told it to me, and more than once. Which is also why I still remember it vividly and have re-told it often myself to family, friends, students, and my own children. It's not surprising I'd relate it most frequently to those younger than I. The story of Congressman Johnson and the paper for Frank Knox, the Secretary of the Navy, is perfect for parental and generational sermonizing. It even starts with those classic words, "when I was young."

★ ★ ★

"After I graduated in June of '40 from law school," my father told me, "I went to Washington to work for the IRS. I had my mind on more than just working for the Revenuers. Your mother and I were engaged, and she and Grandma Lewis were planning the wedding, which was going to be in December in San Angelo. And the news from Europe was bad. In Texas, you could think we were at peace. Living in Washington put you at the center of things; you just know more there than people in the country. I knew we'd be at war soon, and I

Waddy Bullion, 1940.
Bullion Family Collection.

was thinking about how to get a commission in the Naval Reserve.

"During that time," Dad went on, "I did some work for LBJ on his taxes. When he wanted help or advice, I'd do that at night and on weekends. After I became an officer in February 1942, I worked for him during the day, but that was on Navy business. Somehow he'd got me and some other attorneys who were new officers to work with him on special investigations for the Secretary of the Navy, Frank Knox. We didn't even wear uniforms. That was so we'd be able to investigate whatever the Secretary wanted us to look into without superiors pulling rank on us. One time LBJ got an order from Knox for information about policies at the Navy's Bureau of Personnel. The Secretary wanted it right away. LBJ called me and a fellow named Jack Head to his office after business hours and told us he had to have a report on BuPers by 9:00 a.m. the following morning. He handed over some documents. It took me and Jack a couple of hours to read the papers, some more time to summarize them, and even longer to figure out the answers to the questions he wanted answered. Well after midnight, we wrote out our response. Then, because all the secretaries had gone home long before, we had no choice but to type it ourselves. Neither of us could type, so it was tiresome and slow going. We traded off through the night, both to relieve each other and to try to keep mistakes to a minimum. When morning came, we just weren't ready. Nine o'clock passed; we did well to get it to LBJ by eleven.

"We were proud of the job we'd done—typing and all. We were sure LBJ'd be pleased, and we thought the Secretary of the Navy would be impressed too. Not just with the job, but the effort. We hadn't shaved, we hadn't bathed, we were wearing yesterday's clothes, and nobody could see us without knowing we had put our assignment ahead of everything. The secretary let us right in to see The Man. He didn't say anything. 'Congressman, here's our report,' Jack said. LBJ held out his hand, and I gave it to him.

"Do you know what he did?" my father asked. "LBJ took the report. He held it up before us with both hands. Then he tore the pages in half. Turning to the side, he tossed them in the wastebasket. That done, he said, 'I told you boys I needed this at 9:00. At 9:00, not any later. I can't use it now. Get out of here. I got other things to do.'

"As quick as we were in the office, we were out. We were back in the hall before we knew it. LBJ never even looked at the report. He didn't care what our answers were. He didn't care how long we'd worked. He didn't want to hear about secretaries being at home. We

Congressman Johnson in his office, ca. 1944.
LBJ Library. Photo by unknown.

didn't do the job. To him, all the rest didn't matter. We'd failed; that's all that counted."

Dad didn't dwell on the moral of this story. I suppose he thought I could figure out most of it myself. I don't remember his saying very much, didactic or otherwise, after describing LBJ ripping the report and pitching it away. Turn in work on time. If you don't, nobody will be interested in excuses. So this episode revealed a general truth in his telling of it, not just something specific about the nature of Lyndon Johnson. Or so he intended, when I was young.

As I got older, it became clear to me that the story was about more than just punctuality. It was a warning that I would cross paths in my life with people who were powerful enough to insist on my meeting their standards, and hard enough not to care about good reasons for not quite succeeding. This story was about LBJ after all, the famous Majority Leader of the Senate often featured in the stories I read in *Time*.

After one retelling of it in the late 1950s, my father underscored this point. "John," he said, "to be a good administrator you have to be a son of a bitch." It was the first time I'd ever heard him refer to one of his clients that way. To this day, it remains one of the very few times Dad has said anything like this to me about people he worked for.

★ ★ ★

Mother never called LBJ an SOB. She had no trouble making clear her feelings about Lyndon Johnson in perfectly respectable language.

Not that she talked about him often. I don't recall her telling any stories about LBJ, or her life in Washington during the war, before she and my father separated in 1959. Because of that, I heard her recollections of Johnson later, when I was a teenager, not a young boy. I recognize now that her memories were also criticisms of Dad, and I suppose I knew that then. Invariably, they were inspired by discussion of LBJ in the *Dallas Morning News* (usually critical) or in *Time* (generally more favorable). Mother was on the side of the *Morning News*.

"Lyndon Johnson wanted me to work for him," she told me once, after reading a story on how busy he and his staff were. "He asked if I could help out, at night and on weekends, when mail got too heavy for his office to handle. What he wanted was typing letters to constituents. I was working full time at the Department of Agriculture, five days a week and most Saturdays. So I probably said I didn't think I could handle helping his staff on top of my job. I don't think he was happy, but he didn't try to change my mind."

"Couldn't you have used the extra money?" I asked. It was a natural question, considering how often my sister and I heard about the Depression from not just our parents, but from every adult whenever money came up for discussion during the fifties.

"He had no intention of paying me, John. He wanted work for free. Lyndon Johnson didn't pay wives who helped out."

Nor did he expect this to be purely volunteer labor, unforced by any sense of obligation, according to Mother. "Your father has never charged him a fee because he believes he owed his commission in the Navy to Lyndon Johnson. The work he's done for that man has been in return for services rendered. But I didn't owe him anything. He was trying to get something for nothing, and I wouldn't let him sweet talk me into it. Your father didn't try to persuade me, either."

I couldn't miss the note of pride in Mother's voice. During the late 1950s, you could hardly read about LBJ without learning more about his famous "treatment," the ways he could wheedle the unwary and pressure the unwilling to do his bidding. It hadn't worked on Billie Bullion. She wasn't going to be taken advantage of; she wasn't going to type after-hours for a notoriously demanding and critical boss. Left unspoken by her, but plain nonetheless, was the fact the treatment had worked on Waddy Bullion, and still was working.

This wasn't the first time I'd heard that Dad had never sent a bill to LBJ. I can't recall when he happened to mention this to me, or

Billie Bullion, 1940.
Lewis Family Collection.

what inspired a man usually tight-lipped about the details of his practice to say anything about it at all. He must have been joking about what he called the eleemosynary services a lawyer was expected to do, and tagged on to the end of this list providing free counsel and advice to the Majority Leader of the Senate. So I said to Mother that this was probably the most expensive commission anyone ever had, since high-priced talent was still paying for it nearly twenty years later.

Mother didn't comment on my observation. To her, it surely was beside the point, which was that Lyndon Johnson used people whenever and however he could. Maybe she felt my quip verged on being smart-alecky, a bright kid pretending to be obtuse. Whatever her reaction, she answered by downplaying what her estranged husband and

Thompson, Knight, Wright, & Simmons, the large Dallas law firm in which Dad was a senior partner, got in return for his work for Johnson.

When clients needed a passport in a hurry, Mother said, LBJ pulled strings for them. Little stuff, nothing major, was her clear implication. Neither of us guessed then that one day those pulled strings would get me a summer job fighting forest fires in Yosemite National Park. Little stuff can mean a lot to those on the receiving end. And, whether she was fully aware of it or not, Dad and his law firm reaped some major advantages from his work for Lyndon Johnson. I'll explain what those were later. I also know now that my mother completely misunderstood why my father did not charge his famous client. That explanation I'll save for later as well.

★ ★ ★

Politicians courting votes during the fifties kissed babies. Photographs of Johnson doing that made Mother laugh. "One evening," she said, "we were invited over to his place. It was a gathering of Texans in Washington for drinks, sandwiches, and talk. The first two were served by Lady Bird, with help from the other women present; the last, by Lyndon, with very little assistance from anyone else.

"This night, though, he had competition. Lynda Bird Johnson, who was still an infant, had colic. Colicky babies—like you were—can cry and cry, until they start howling. She could be heard throughout the house even with all possible doors shut. Despite everything all the women could do or think of, she kept crying. The only time she stopped was to catch her breath; once she did that, she tuned up again, louder than ever, drowning out her father. And despite our hope she'd just exhaust herself and go to sleep, she didn't. Finally, Lyndon yelled loud enough to be heard over his daughter, 'Dammit, Bird, do something to shut that kid up.' That didn't work, either. Guests began making their excuses. By the time we got our coats, it was clear it wouldn't be long until Lady Bird would be alone with a sick baby and a furious husband. How she handled that, I don't know."

Mother didn't care, either. Wives in the 1940s didn't look for any help with infants from their husbands in the usual course of events, and didn't expect much aid from them as the children matured. That Lyndon Johnson would be helpless when confronted with a squalling baby was par for the course. That he would blame his wife for not working a miracle and quieting a child with the colic seemed typical, too.

Lady Bird Johnson with Lynda, Summer 1944.
LBJ Library. Photo by unknown.

Nothing new there. There was no call for special sympathy; all women had to struggle with their mates' weaknesses.

But even if Mother had felt a twinge of empathy for Lady Bird's plight, she would have suppressed it. She firmly believed Bird put up with too much from Lyndon and accepted too passively his shortcomings as father and husband. She never speculated in my presence on why this was so. But she did make clear what she believed was the problem Mrs. Johnson faced with Mr. Johnson.

★ ★ ★

LBJ himself defined that problem. Soon after Dad arrived in Washington, Johnson told him that he paid attention to his constituents' opinions on all things except two: they couldn't tell him what kind of car he could drive, and they couldn't tell him which women he could sleep with.

At that time, according to Mother, hearing this shocked my father. It shocked her, too, as he described the scene to her. Devoutly religious mothers had dominated their childhoods. The combination of maternal example and exhortation, plus the ministrations of the First Baptist Church of Eden, Texas for Dad and Calvary Episcopal Church in the nearby town of Menard for Mother, had made them deeply committed Christians. Each was stunned that Lyndon Johnson would openly and unrepentedly talk about his penchant for adultery and compare sex with the most attractive women to owning the most expensive car in the district. Not sins, but matters of reputation and power, prestige and pride—that's what infidelities were to him. Here I must point out to readers of today that neither Dad nor Mother, nor I who heard the story from her in the late 1950s, nor, I'm sure, LBJ, saw his love for fast cars and willing women as private issues of personal morality with no bearing on his public performance as a political leader. Unlike latter-day politicians, he gloried in the never-published but wide-spread knowledge of his affairs. Telling my father about his determination not to let the voters' moral views check his sexual freedom was simply impressing a new audience with his power. It also served to spread the word further. Dad, for instance, told his wife. The result was not the one LBJ desired. She, like Queen Victoria, was "not amused."

This knowledge about Lyndon Johnson explained Mother's decision never to work for him. Her contempt for his morality made volunteering to type for him for free particularly offensive. The fact she would be typing deferential replies to constituents while knowing they couldn't instruct him on automobiles or mistresses no doubt strengthened her resolve to avoid his office at night and on weekends.

Her reaction to LBJ's comments to Dad also more than likely explains her coolness toward Lady Bird. Bird must have known. Not just about his extramarital adventures, and boasting about them, but also that he made them part of his political power and prestige. That she would put up with this humiliation meant she had come to some sort of terms with it. Whatever bargains she had made, whatever benefits she gained, they did not, to Mother's mind, entitle her to sympathy.

Most of all, though, what my mother detested in LBJ was his power to corrupt. It did not escape my notice that she said that my father had been shocked by his remark *at that time*. Mother lifted her eyebrows when she said it. She used this nonverbal means of communication in order to stick to her resolve never to explicitly criticize Dad in front of Ann and me. Too, she didn't want to give the impression that Lyndon Johnson was to blame for Dad's deficiencies as husband and parent.

Mother wanted me to understand that there are men in the world who will do more than just act immorally. They will deny moral commandments. They will suggest that these rules do not apply to them, or to you either. They will show how breaking these laws can be fun and result in attractive rewards. By their acts and words, they will make it clear that they believe only the naive, the unimaginative, or the limited in vision or circumstance actually lead lives governed by what they scorn as Sunday school morality. If you were smart enough, powerful enough, hardworking enough, special enough, you could and should do what you pleased and take what you could grab.

Mother saw men such as these from the perspective of the Episcopal liturgy. Lyndon Johnson did not resist the devices and desires of his own heart. He did those things which he ought not to have done, and did not those things which he ought to have done. As a result, there was no health in him. Periodically, as I went through high school and approached college, Mother would say to me, "John, be a man." By that, she did not mean be like the worldly wise and the worldly powerful. Because he was both, and gloried in each, LBJ should *not* be my model.

These stories are all I remember my parents telling me during the fifties about Lyndon Johnson. His name didn't come up frequently when Dad or Mother talked with me. As I've said, Dad almost never mentioned his clients or his life at the firm to Ann and me, and he talked less and less frequently about them with his wife as their marriage decayed. Most of Mother's observations about life were drawn from stories she told about people she knew in West Texas as a child, and moral precepts from the Bible and the Prayer Book.

Conversely, it was the infrequency of stories about LBJ that embedded them in my memory. Of course, they also stood out because he was a famous man. You could read about him in the newspapers and the magazines. That my parents knew this powerful man was impressive. That they knew things about him that were not reported was fascinating. Most intriguing of all, though, was the fact that I could see distinctions between printed versions of the senator from Texas and the man they described. Having an insider's knowledge was a pleasure, pure and simple.

One thing I don't remember feeling at that time was any curiosity about how Lyndon Johnson and my father met. Probably this was the result of a belief common to children: whatever happened before I was born was really of no interest to me. It wasn't until I was much older and a historian by profession that it ever occurred to me to ask Dad about this. The story didn't disappoint me, though it was predictable once he began to tell it.

By his last semester in law school, my father had decided he wanted to specialize in tax law. That practice had three principal attractions for him: it was intellectually challenging, because Congress, the IRS, and the courts were continually amending the Tax Code and thereby changing the rules of the game; it would provide a constant business, owing to the fact that taxes were numbered with death as certainties of human existence; and it promised to be remunerative, because the sort of people who needed advice on their taxes generally had the resources to pay well for it. The best place to learn the ropes of this practice was in the offices of the adversary, the Internal Revenue Service. And the best office to start there to master your trade was the Civil Division of the Chief Counsel's Office, which had oversight and final approval over arguments and supporting materials used in all civil litigation by the IRS. So my father applied for a job in that division.

Dad had done very well at the University of Texas School of Law. When he applied to the IRS, he ranked second in his class and was editor-in-chief of the Law Review, the highest honor a student can attain. The letters of support for his application from his instructors were, I'm sure, equally compelling. For their part, officials at the IRS were willing to hire him, at an annual salary of $2,000, pretty good money in 1940 (though not, as my father delighted in pointing out, as good as the FBI; beginning agents there got $3,200, which made the Bureau appealing to many young attorneys, including Dad's contemporary, Richard Nixon). But no one in 1940 was hired by a federal agency for such an important position as one in the Chief Counsel's Office without approval from his or her Congressman. Although Dad still voted in Eden, he had put his Austin address on the application. As a result, when Oscar Cox, the Assistant Counsel to the Treasury, picked up the phone to call Capitol Hill, he dialed the number of the Congressman for the Ninth District of Texas, Lyndon Johnson.

LBJ listened to Cox describe Dad's qualifications, then asked him to wait a moment. Cupping a hand over the phone, he asked his Congressional secretary, John Connally, "Do we know a Bullion in Austin?" Connally, who had been a class ahead of my father in law school, immediately said that Waddy Bullion was a fine man, an excellent law student, and a staunch Democrat. He predicted that Dad would be a wonderful tax attorney. "Okay, that's enough," said LBJ, who then uncovered the phone and told Cox that he was enthusiastically in favor of Bullion's getting a job at the IRS. That was that.

When my father came to Washington, John Connally advised him to rent a room in the basement of the Grace Dodge Hotel. There, in "the Catacombs," as he and other young Texans called their dwelling place, he began the process of working and making contacts. Connally told him the story of Johnson's approval. My father did not need to be told that had LBJ not been agreeable, he would have had no job at the IRS. Nor did he require much urging from his neighbor in the Catacombs to go over to the House Office Building, introduce himself to his Congressman, and say thank you. Dad did that about a month after his arrival. Johnson appeared both friendly in person and influential on Capitol Hill; a good man to know, an even better one to be close to. From LBJ's perspective, Waddy Bullion seemed to be everything John

LBJ and his office staff. John Connally is next to LBJ,
Walter Jenkins is on the far right, ca 1939/1940.
LBJ Library. Photo by NYA of Texas.

Connally had said he was and would be. The Congressman expressed a desire to discuss taxes, his own and others, on occasion; the neophyte IRS attorney was more than willing to serve as assistant and adviser on these matters. From this, their long association, which lasted from late summer 1940 until January 1973, flowered.

Obviously, my father's candidacy for a commission in the Navy was not harmed by his connection with an important member of the House Naval Affairs Committee. Mother always believed he would have been commissioned whether he knew LBJ or not. Perhaps so, but it's doubtful he would have begun his service investigating the Navy's procedures and practices for the Secretary of the Navy without his Congressman's intervention. She was right, however, about Johnson's influence in one regard. Once Carl Vinson, the chairman of the Naval Affairs Committee, discontinued LBJ's investigations, Dad's client had no more impact on his subsequent service. My father's next posting was to have been San Francisco, where he was to await transport to Guadalcanal. "What would you have done there?" I asked him recently. "Whatever they told me to do," was his blunt reply.

Before that could happen, though, Admiral Ernest J. King's office conducted a computer search of officers in the Navy for those qualified to brief the Commander-in-Chief of the Navy before he participated in meetings of the Joint Chiefs of Staff and the Combined Chiefs of Staff. The room-sized UNIVAC churned out Dad's name, and within a short time he was writing memoranda for King. LBJ had nothing to do with that posting. He also had nothing to do with my father's serving as the assistant to King's administrative aide for the remainder of the war. The admiral, a martinet of Johnsonian caliber with much greater power than a Congressman, flatly told Dad when he left the Navy in late 1945 that if he hadn't pulled his weight, he would have been gone. A war spent writing briefs that King ordered be no longer than one page on complicated strategic and tactical issues was hardly a bad war. Still, it had its own dangers. Failure to measure up to high standards under intense pressure meant a transfer to the South Pacific or the North Atlantic. Dad met that test.

Of the two men, Ernest King and Lyndon Johnson, King interested me most when I was a kid, by a wide margin. Those who commanded in World War II were heroes to practically every American. Pretty typically for boys then, I didn't just buy baseball cards; I bought cards depicting combat scenes and a variety of weapons and commanders as well. I loved hearing about King, and begged Dad for more stories. That King always arrived at his office at exactly 8:22 a.m. fascinated me. So did the reason for this regularity: he always went through morning colors on the yacht he lived on in the Anacostia River. By being on a ship and saluting the flag as it was ceremoniously raised each morning to the top of a mast, he qualified for sea pay—a significant sum for an admiral.

Admiral Ernest J. King, November 5, 1945. King inscribed this portrait to Waddy Bullion, and presented it to him at his discharge ceremonies.
Bullion Family Collection.

Dad's accounts of the admiral's rages at high-ranking officers were great fun. I especially liked hearing about the poor captain who disregarded my father's reminder to him that King had left directions never, ever to disturb him after he left the office. Frightened by the messages from Leyte Gulf in late October 1944, the captain brushed aside my father's advice to wait until morning and took the responsibility upon himself to warn the admiral immediately. He went to the yacht after midnight to inform him about the terrible pounding our fleet was taking. "Christ Jesus! Do you think I can walk on water?" the admiral yelled at the quaking officer. "What in the hell do you expect me to do about it?" Then King, who was in his nightshirt, stomped back to his bed—or berth, as he probably called it, since he was "at sea." The captain did not remain on duty in King's office for long.

I admired Dad for his good sense. I admired him, too, for meeting Eisenhower, Nimitz, Halsey, Spruance—in fact, every major British or American commander with the exception of Douglas MacArthur. And I reveled in the fact that Dad had a much higher security clearance than most of them. It meant a lot to me that he'd been in a position to tell Mother on the morning of June 6, 1944, "Be sure to listen to the radio today." That meant a lot to her, too; I could tell.

Being an insider on D-Day did not make Mother fond of King. In fact, I dimly remember that she did on one occasion call him an SOB, a name, as I've said, she never used to describe Johnson in front of me. Even if I had not heard her swear, I would have sensed the difference in her reaction to the two men. Johnson's demands merely enraged her. King scared her. Not only were the admiral's temper tantrums legendary and his exacting and uncompromising demands on the officers and sailors around him well-known, but his power over her husband was for all practical purposes unlimited. Consequences from his rages could include lengthy separations from young wives and infant sons, maiming the body, destroying the mind and spirit, and dying in combat. The telling and retelling of the story of the unwise captain did not amuse her, as it did Dad and me. She would grow white and silent, as if she could clearly see a telegram from the Department of the Navy arriving at some woman's door. But to her son, who knew nothing of war, this sort of power was the real stuff, the true essence of sending men into battle.

Next to this legendary figure from a glorious war, Lyndon Johnson paled in comparison. I could understand that he was important. I did not think he was a hero. I'd listen to what my folks said about him; I'd try to understand and absorb the morals they wanted to extract from these narratives; but I wouldn't ask for more information or more stories about LBJ.

★ ★ ★

It wasn't just Lyndon Johnson who interested me less than Admiral King and Lieutenant (junior grade) Bullion. I never asked my mother what she did at the Department of Agriculture. This surprises me today, and for a number of reasons I wish I'd been curious. But in the fifties, her life before she became a mother and housewife had no fascination for me. Equally surprising when I contemplate it, she never volunteered anything about her job. Long after her death in 1983, her sister Mary mentioned to me that she had been the secretary to the Librarian of the department—a very responsible and comparatively well-paid position. In today's bureaucracy, she would have been called an Executive Assistant.

My guess is that Mother avoided talking about her work at Agriculture because she believed it was a touchy one for Dad. Through no fault of his own, he had applied for a job at the IRS that depended on his Congressman's approval. His first assignment in the Navy was a reflection of that same politician's power. He did feel obliged to Lyndon Johnson, even though his successes were the result of his own intelligence and hard work. Determined not to appear critical of him before us, she avoided talking about their careers in Washington. She only slipped once. In a conversation with me before I married in 1976, she mentioned that Dad was troubled by the fact that her salary at Agriculture was higher than his as a naval officer. It was one of the few glimpses either parent gave me of a possible competition between them as a young married couple over the nature and pay of their respective jobs.

I realize now how reticent Mother was on other subjects, too. She told the story of Lyndon, Bird, and the howling Lynda with great relish, but she never balanced it with vignettes like the one I heard from Aunt Mary.

One Saturday morning in 1945, when Mary was visiting my parents, she answered a knock on the apartment door and opened it to discover a smiling Lyndon Johnson. He'd come to loan his car to John and Nellie Connally, whose place was just down the hall, and he thought he'd visit with the Bullions while he was there. Dad had the weekend watch at Admiral King's office. Undeterred by my father's absence, completely relaxed, totally happy, LBJ sprawled out on the floor and began rolling a ball back and forth with me. My aunt claims she couldn't tell who was chuckling and gurgling more, the prone Congressman or the nine-month-old propped against a couch. As we amused each other, he explained to the adults watching our play that Alice Glass was going to pick him up in a few minutes, and they'd spend

LBJ in a lighthearted moment with Lynda,
much like the one he enjoyed with me, 1945.
LBJ Library. Photo by unknown.

the day together. What she had planned, he didn't know, but they'd have fun. Just like he was having a good time with John here, he laughed. After a little bit, he raised himself up, tousled my hair, hugged and kissed Mother and Mary, and went down to the street. Soon after he left, Mary asked and my mother explained who Alice Glass was. Not only was she LBJ's mistress, she was the wife of one of his most influential constituents and trusted advisers—the publisher of the Austin newspaper.

Mary told me later that this tale of sinning in our nation's capital tickled her, though at that time she made appropriate noises of disapproval to her sister. Mother was perturbed that her home had been used as a way station on the tracks toward adultery, and that Johnson would be so frank about who he was seeing and his expectation of having a good time. I doubt she missed the *double entendre* of doing with Alice what he was doing with me—lying down and playing with balls. Evidently she did not bother to discuss the visit with her husband when he returned home from the Navy Department. The first time he heard the story was when I told it to him, over fifty years after Lyndon Johnson and I were together on the floor of an apartment in Arlington, Virginia.

★ ★ ★

I did not form my own opinion about LBJ from the Washington stories I heard. Nor did I adopt one parent's perspective on him and reject the other's. I didn't need to. From Dad's account, I learned what he was like to work for, and what demanding bosses were like in general. And I grasped—in theory, at least—the necessity of practicing workaday, career virtues of careful preparation, thoughtful analysis, punctuality in meeting deadlines, and realizing that the world and the boss were not interested in excuses, no matter what. Mother's stories were modern examples of her morality tales. To make unreasonable demands on people, to dominate and to domineer, and to flout the commandments by word and act were the marks of wickedness. And I accepted—again, at least in theory—the rightness of these moral positions. But I had no idea that I might one day have to reconcile the two systems of values; or that I might have to pick and choose virtues within them and then blend them into my own system; or that I might perhaps even be forced to choose between them. Very few boys of my age and upbringing in the 1950s could have articulated these issues, let alone dealt with them.

As a result, when I met Lyndon Johnson myself during that decade, I didn't measure him by either Dad's or Mother's standard. Where I met him, and with whom, had a greater impact upon me.

CHAPTER 2

West Texas Lessons

During the 1950s, Ann and I spent our summers in West Texas with our grandparents. Mother's parents, John and Hettie Lewis, lived in Menard, a town of a little over 2,000, the county seat of Menard County. Dad's folks, Tom and Florence Bullion, were twenty-one miles away in Eden. A little under 2,000 souls made their homes there, in a town that did not even have the distinction of being the center of government in Concho County.

Both counties suffered during the fifties from a terrible drought. I can remember whole summers without rain, white dust from the limestone gravel West Texans called caliche coating everything, and temperatures hovering for weeks at around one hundred degrees. Farmers and ranchers could not make ends meet, and our playmates regularly disappeared with their parents into Texas's cities.

Neither set of grandparents was still involved with livestock or crops. Big John and Grandma Lewis had quit ranching during the 1940s and moved to town. When a small liquor store he owned went under, he and Grandma lived off social security. Pop and Grandmommy Bullion had lost their land and stock in the early thirties. After the family packed up its personal effects and took them to a house in Eden, Pop got a job working for the Texas Highway Department. He held that job until 1940. That year, he bought a small restaurant with hard-earned savings. From then till his death in 1959, he was the owner and operator of Tom's Cafe. My Aunt Geraldine lived with them. She taught English at Eden High School during the school year and helped out at the cafe in the summer.

That Pop was the chief breadwinner in his family and Big John's social security check supported Grandma made no difference in the dynamics of the two households. My grandmothers were the dominant personalities. Big John was too aware (and well informed) about his shortcomings to dispute his position; Pop was simply too tired from the demands of running the cafe to make many decisions around the house. Seeing to it that Ann and I went to church and minded our manners were duties they gladly ceded to their wives. When we required disciplining, our grandmothers scolded and paddled. Big John and Pop had no interest in playing the part of the stern paterfamilias. They allocated to themselves a different role in our upbringing during those summers.

As near as I could tell, what they tried to do with Ann was spoil her rotten. Both men doted on my sister. There was no one-Coke-a-day rule for her at Tom's Cafe, and she could have ice cream cones for the asking at Bean's Drug Store in Menard. They were less openly indulgent to me. Although neither was harsh or stern, my grandfathers were determined that I would learn from them how to appreciate the pleasures and to fulfill the responsibilities peculiar to boys and men.

Given Big John's thoroughly deserved reputation in Menard during the thirties and forties for tireless womanizing, one might expect that he schooled me on flirting with girls and making moves on them. To the contrary, he never said anything to me about seduction or sex. Lyndon Johnson boasted about his conquests to everyone; John Lewis hid his from his grandson. Perhaps he felt remorseful. Perhaps he believed every man had to figure out relationships with women for himself. The only bit of advice he ever had for me was this: giving a woman something got you the opportunity to start talking to her. Then he offered me a dime to buy an ice cream cone for a girl I was admiring from afar. I was too shy to do that. Maybe that's why he decided I needed to learn how and what to drink. Alcohol would make me bolder. Besides, as they

John Lewis, early 1950s.
Lewis Family Collection.

grew older, women in Menard tended to switch from ice cream to harder stuff.

So Big John encouraged me to drink, first beer and later whiskey. "I don't want you running around in alleys, drinking rotgut," he'd say. "Ask me, and I'll give you good alcohol here." He claimed that's what his father had done for him. Some nights I'd share with him the shot of bourbon he insisted he needed to go to sleep. I rarely took more than a sip or two; even though Old Crow tasted smooth in my mouth, it burned uncomfortably all the way down. When we were out together in "town," as he called the square less than a mile from his house, he'd occasionally stop at a bar and buy us both beers. I was in my early teens at the time and didn't particularly like the taste of Lone Star or Falstaff. But bartenders never questioned his right to buy it for me, and no one paid any attention to how much or little I drank of it.

The other job Big John assigned to himself was to teach me how to shoot rifles and shotguns. We'd drive around highways and ranch roads outside town, road hunting. I shot at cans, bottles, telephone poles, trees, armadillos, rabbits, and all birds, except roadrunners, which were extremely bad luck to kill. My rewards for improving were a .410 shotgun and a .22 rifle of my own.

One summer afternoon, we spotted a deer. Excited, I shouted, and it fled. Big John was disappointed in me. "I wanted you to take a shot at him," he scolded. I responded by pointing out, "But Big John, they're out of season." "Don't worry about that," he said. No doubt he was right. If I could drink in Menard bars, no doubt the Menard Packing Plant wouldn't object to turning deer into venison sausage and steaks in July. To this day, I'm sure one of the most thankless jobs in the world is that of the state game warden in Menard County.

To do justice to my grandfather, I must say this was the only time we were tempted to hunt deer out of season. I'm going to put off telling you what I learned from him on a cold November day until later, when it will help you understand road hunts I made with Lyndon Johnson.

★ ★ ★

Pop wasn't much like Big John. For starters, he didn't hunt. There were no guns or rifles in the house at Eden. Pop didn't drink, either. He did sell beer in his cafe, and he defended his right to do so against a succession of Baptist preachers who regularly pleaded with him to stop supplying his customers with sin. When they pressed him on the subject, he pointed out the Good Book called for temperance, not

Tom Bullion, mid-1950s.
Bullion Family Collection.

abstinence. Therefore he was not morally bound to deny his customers alcohol. But Pop did not believe practicing temperance was a wise thing to do. Too many people could not control their drinking. Best not to start—that was his considered advice.

The most obvious contrast, however, between my grandfathers during the 1950s was not hunting or drinking. It was this: Pop was still working for a living. And how that man worked! Out of bed at 5:00 a.m.; open the cafe at 5:30 for early ranchers, motorists, highway patrolmen, and truckers; work through the lunch hour; home to nap between 2:30 and 4:00; back for dinner; close at 8:00; mop the floor; clean the kitchen; clear the cash register; balance the receipts; and home to bed. He was cook, waiter, cashier, janitor, and what passed as *maitre d'* when customers wanted to talk. In addition, he sold tickets and checked luggage for the Kerrville Bus Company, whose stop in Eden was at Tom's Cafe. I think he also did something for the Goodyear Tire Company. Drivers regularly came through Eden testing truck tires; they always stopped at Pop's place and brought their records up to date.

Pop was as famous in Eden for working long hours as Big John was infamous in Menard for chasing women. Yet, just as my Menard grandfather refused to talk to me about women, my Eden grandfather had no interest in introducing me to the manly obligation of work. He never sermonized on the moral lessons work taught people. To Pop, work was a necessity, not a virtue. And he never required me to do anything at Tom's Cafe. I hung out there for hours, but Pop never asked me to help out. He'd worked as a child, and he thought his grandson had better things to do while he was young.

What Pop passed on to me was his love for baseball. The summer I was ten, I arrived in Eden to discover that Tom's Cafe was sponsoring a Little League team. He sponsored the team out of town spirit, but I'm sure the real reason for his involvement was his determination I would play ball. Pop worried that I did too much reading. He knew that I played no organized sports in Dallas and intended to remedy that situation.

My triumphs at the ball park were rarely spectacular. There were enough modest ones, however, to raise me in the eyes of the team's sponsor and my peers to the boundary between mediocre and above average. Pop and I had both seen I could be what he called a mean man in the clutch. I'd also shown I could put failure out of my mind and bear down again after things didn't work out as I'd hoped. Lessons in life, taught on a dusty diamond during hot afternoons in a small Texas town, learned with other boys, coached by my grandfather.

My grandfathers may have been poles apart in their advice to me on drinking, but they both believed I should experience what it took to become a master at masculine pursuits such as shooting guns and playing baseball, and achieve a level of skill at each sufficient to make me proud of my accomplishment. And they also made sure I knew that politics and politicking were also subjects I should become knowledgeable about. Both were patriots. Both believed in the necessity of an informed citizenry. Both emphasized the duty of Americans to express their convictions and to vote their consciences. Both ran successfully for local office. Last, but far from least—indeed, Big John and Pop would have listed this first!—they were Democrats.

Although in the fifties I was years away from casting my first ballot, I already considered myself a Democrat due to family example and tradition. Mother voted Democratic, as did both grandmothers. Dad was a Democrat and, of course, worked for Lyndon Johnson. He loved to say that his father was even more of a Democrat than he was. Pop's proudest boast, Dad told me, was his vote for Al Smith in 1928, despite the insistence of those around him that this would mean Rule by Rome.

Big John couldn't make that claim, because he was one of those who fought popery by voting for Hoover. He had long since repented of his sin. Indeed, Big John confessed freely and often to all who would listen (and to those who had heard it before and tuned him out) that this was his worst mistake. Franklin Roosevelt became his political hero; Republicans were his bane. Every night I stayed in Menard we listened to the nine o'clock news together. It originated on a San Antonio station and was sponsored by a department store that proudly boasted it was "Joske's of San Antonio, by the Alamo!" The co-anchor of the broadcast was in Menard, across the room from me, brought to me courtesy of the shot of Old Crow we shared as we listened. President Eisenhower was dumb; Vice President Nixon was unspeakable; and Ezra Taft Benson, the Secretary of Agriculture, was evil incarnate.

"You see, John," my grandfather would preach to his namesake, "Republicans have never tried to understand the needs of ranchers and farmers. They think food gets grown in banks and makes it to the table by magic." For some days, the two Johns' hero was Tennessee's Governor Frank Clements, whose keynote address to the 1956 Democratic Convention lambasted Benson and borrowed from Tennessee Ernie Ford's song *Sixteen Tons* by describing the Eisenhower Administration's agricultural policy and its results as "Another Republican promise/And deeper in debt." We listened in excitement to the convention's balloting for the nomination for vice president, rooting for John Kennedy against Estes Kefauver.

Maybe Big John felt he was atoning for his apostasy in '28. Certainly, he was attracted by what he perceived as JFK's liberalism. Although he voted for LBJ and admired him as man and senator, Big John's real hero was Ralph Yarborough, a stalwart champion of the liberal wing of the Democratic Party in Texas, and a fervent opponent of the usually dominant conservative Democrats, whom he identified with someone whose politics he detested: Governor Allan Shivers. That man, he was certain, would sell Texas and Texans to the highest bidder. Shivers had no interest in the fate of ranchers, farmers, and working people: witness his public support for Eisenhower in 1952. Perhaps because Big John had run for office during the Depression, perhaps because as Tax Assessor of Menard County he tried to temper his duty with an appreciation for how hard-pressed his neighbors were, perhaps because he failed as a rancher himself soon after those bleak years, he had no patience with those whom he suspected held office without serving the people's best interests. Republicans did that; so did many Democrats. That such as these had power and position aroused strong feelings in him, passions he expressed freely in domino parlors, in bars, outside church, at the post office, and to his grandson every night at nine. For years, I kept a comb Big John gave me. One side read "Vote for Yarborough," the other, "Comb 'Em Out of Our Hair!"[1]

---

1   Those who know the history of Texas politics will notice I have not described Big John's attitudes toward the most prominent conservative Democrat of this era, Coke Stevenson. Stevenson ranched in Kimble County, which is adjacent to Menard County, and practiced law in Junction, its county seat, which is about forty miles southeast of Menard. Due to location and vocation, Big John knew

★ ★ ★

Pop was nowhere near as openly outspoken about politics as Big John. He rarely talked about state or national politics in my presence, and he confined his partisanship to acknowledging he had never cast a ballot for a Republican. I believe he was equally reticent around others. After all, those who make their livings selling food and drink to the public tend not to broadcast or force their views on their customers as well—at least not in West Texas during the fifties. Besides, Pop wasn't a fan of politics as he was of baseball. Policy differences and political infighting between Yarborough and Shivers didn't intrigue him. Nor did issues such as Texas's claim to regulate tidelands oil wells or the federal government's attitudes toward parity for cotton. He judged politicians as he judged men. Were they hard working? Did they understand his concerns? When they promised something, did they do their best to keep their pledge? Could you count on them? Did they follow the lessons taught by their parents and peers? Pop was by no means a harsh judge. Until he had reason to dislike or distrust anyone, he always assumed the best, not the worst. (Always excepting Republicans, whose choice of party automatically branded them as untrustworthy.)

On the rare occasions when some elected official did cause Pop to lose faith, though, he acted on his convictions. Two of these times became part of family folklore. The first involved politics at the state level, a contest between Allan Shivers and Ralph Yarborough for the Democratic Party's nomination for governor in 1954. The second was Concho County politicking, the 1958 race for the position of justice of the peace in Eden. One I only learned about much after the event. The other I not only witnessed; I participated in it.

When my uncle graduated in 1951 from law school at the University of Texas, Harris Melaskey, who practiced in Taylor, a small town in

him well enough to separate Stevenson's political beliefs from his judgment of the man himself. Moreover, Stevenson represented him during the 1930s when he was indicted for embezzling tax revenues. My grandfather went to Junction and said, "Coke, I can't be guilty. I just assess taxes; others collect, budget, and spend them. I've got no way to get my hands on any of that money." Stevenson thought for a minute, puffed on his pipe, and then replied, "John, I believe you. We'll win this case." A jury found Big John not guilty; the voters of Menard County re-elected him Assessor. Afterwards, he exempted his neighbor and attorney from any criticism for two very conservative terms as governor of the state during the 1940s and for becoming a Republican in 1952, acts that ordinarily called forth Big John's fiercest condemnations.

central Texas, hired him. It was a signal honor for Thomas. Mr. Melaskey's reputation as an attorney and his influence in the state Democratic Party extended well beyond Williamson County. To be associated with him conferred an instant prominence on my uncle in both pursuits. Thomas realized this soon after he moved to Taylor, when John Connally wandered into the office asking for a contribution for LBJ. "How much?" asked Melaskey. "Oh, twenty-five will do," Connally answered. Mr. Melaskey took out his checkbook and wrote a check for $25,000. "Jesus Christ," Connally gasped, "I was expecting twenty-five *hundred*, not thousand." Then he said it was sure good doing business with Melaskey & Bullion, and that he and the senator would remember this in the future.

Harris Melaskey was also generous in his financial support of the more conservative wing of the state party; to him, Ralph Yarborough was anathema. The firm's junior partner, who possibly could have managed a check for $250 and certainly would have been more comfortable with—*literally*—"twenty-five," donated his time instead. Thus he became the Williamson County manager of Shivers' campaign for re-election as governor in 1954.

LBJ talks with Harris Melaskey on the far left, September 13, 1968.
LBJ Library. Photo by Yoichi R. Okamoto.

Thomas proudly mentioned this fact to Pop. "You can do what you want to, and vote as you please," Pop responded, "but I'll vote for Yarborough, because he hasn't broken his word." Recovering swiftly from his surprise, my uncle spoke long and passionately about how the governor served the true interests of small businessmen, while Yarborough would tax people like the owner of Tom's Cafe to death. To no avail: Pop had concluded that Shivers had reneged on promises he made solemnly and repeatedly during his last campaign, and that meant he'd not have Tom Bullion's support ever again. His son persisted, arguing that Yarborough and men like him cared nothing for men like Tom Bullion, other than as a source for money. Finally, Pop told him to be quiet. "Never ask me to vote for Allan Shivers again" were his final words on the subject. That flash of anger and exasperation, so unlike my grandfather, burned the incident into the family's collective memory. Thomas stopped talking, but he never forgot. Nor did Waddy Bullion, who heard his brother's aggrieved report of how stubborn and just plain wrong their father was, and much later passed it on to me.

Four years later, Pop was involved in a campaign himself. He'd become convinced that a local justice of the peace was not doing a good job. After reasoning with this man did not work, and after discovering no one else was willing to run against him, Pop plunked down the filing fee and began a low-key campaign for the office. His family thought what finally convinced him to throw his hat into the ring was a friend's taunt: "Well, Tom, if you're so unhappy, you always could run yourself." "I guess I will," was his immediate reply.

Pop wasn't a vigorous campaigner. He simply talked quietly, one-to-one, with people he knew about his dissatisfactions with the incumbent. The single time he departed from this tactic occurred when he permitted me to write what I thought was an irrefutable list of his virtues as person and candidate, then publish my effort as a political advertisement in the *Eden Echo*, the town's weekly paper. I'm not boasting when I tell you the ad was one of the best things published that year in the *Echo*. The quality of the competition was not high, and, to borrow from the wisdom of Dizzy Dean, "It ain't braggin' if you can do it." And I not only composed this closely reasoned argument, I painfully typed and retyped the text, using two fingers on an old Underwood, until it was without typographical errors. I did not trust the *Echo*'s editor to correct any mistakes, and rightly so. I like to think that my reasons to vote for Tom Bullion helped Pop's cause. Whether they did or not, he won the Democratic primary, which amounted to winning the election, in August 1958.

All his family and friends were elated. I teased him, saying I wanted to be invited to the first wedding he conducted. "Remember, Pop, it starts Dearly Beloved, and it ends by you telling the groom to kiss the bride." Others, including Dad and Uncle Thomas, wanted to hear about what sorts of fines Pop would impose on those the local law caught speeding. He'd laugh and promise legal marriages and impartial justice. I'm sure he would have kept his word.

Pop would have approached being a JP the way be did everything else: quietly, responsibly, ready to work as long as it took, and determined to do his job as best he could. Added to these habits of a lifetime would have been a keen sense of obligation to keep his promises to the voters by improving on his predecessor's performance. He never betrayed to me any sign of a personal ambition to hold office. What I saw was a readiness to do his civic duty when others could not or *would* not. Obviously, that was the judgment of a thirteen-year-old grandson. Still, it remains my judgment over four decades later. But Pop never married any couples. He dealt with only a handful of citizens trapped by his friends on the Highway Patrol. Soon after the election, doctors in San Angelo discovered the cancer that was the cause of his back pains. Six months later, on March 7, 1959, he died.

★ ★ ★

At that time, I wasn't fully aware of the lessons my grandfathers were trying to teach me. Sure, I understood Big John enjoyed hunting and wanted me to enjoy it too. And I could easily figure out that Pop loved baseball. On the most basic level, my grandfathers wanted me to learn how to hunt deer and doves and how to play the game.

Beyond this, I know now what I imperfectly grasped then. While Pop and Big John were proud of the books I read, the stories I wrote, and the grades I made in school, they believed that such intellectual pursuits were only part of being a man. To understand that and to do well in the world, I had to be able to do physical as well as mental things. Why? In part, because my body wasn't as fully gifted as my mind, and I had to learn how to confront and overcome challenges that did not come easily to me. I had to toughen up, or I wouldn't be able to deal with all of life's problems. Hunting and baseball were the means of strengthening me psychologically as well as physically.

Also, in their culture men were judged by how well they handled themselves physically. My grandfathers never asked whether this was fair, or equitable, or socially useful, or just. It simply was a fact of life.

Moreover, the necessity of being powerful, physical, and manly extended into other areas as well, including those of politics and governance in this republic. Thus they saw being informed about and interested in politics as not merely a civic duty that every citizen shared, but an intensely masculine enterprise. Ralph Yarborough was a real man, fighting for "us against them," and keeping his word, just like real men did. Lyndon Johnson was a powerful senator, a man capable of running the entire country even though the electorate had committed the folly of elevating a Republican to the White House.

Indeed, Lyndon Johnson was a perfect example of the blending of political and physical prowess, in the most elemental and intimate senses of those terms. Aware of the potency of presenting himself in this way, he encouraged the spread of stories about his political deeds and his sexual exploits. My father would have disappointed him in this respect. Dad never discussed what little he heard or knew about LBJ's attitudes toward sex or his adventures in adultery with anyone except his wife. Mother was much less reticent. She passed along to both of my grandfathers LBJ's insistence that his constituents could not advise him about the women he bedded or the cars he drove. Without question, my mother didn't tell this story to improve LBJ's reputation. But whatever Pop and Big John thought about it—my guess is one disapproved, while the other applauded—each of them admired him for his sheer masculine power in politics. And both could readily see that I might well have to deal with such men during my life. So Lyndon Johnson was well worth going to see, whenever he might come to town or to a nearby city. Pop and I had that chance during the summer of 1958. My grandfather saw to it that we didn't miss our opportunity.

CHAPTER 3

Pressing The Flesh

In June of 1958, before his pain became unbearable, Pop learned that Lyndon Johnson would be speaking at a Democratic rally and barbecue in Brady, a town twice the size of Eden around thirty miles to the northeast. Right away he decided the two of us should go. Pop didn't tell me why we were doing this, and I didn't ask. Going to see LBJ, the famous Majority Leader of the Senate, the pre-eminent Democrat in the state, and the man my father had worked with for nearly twenty years, was reason enough for me.

By the morning of the rally, both the first-time candidate for office at age sixty-nine and his neophyte publicist of thirteen years were keenly looking forward to Johnson's speech. It would be exciting, we were sure, to witness a man at the height of power in the Senate, one who, according to report, was ready to pursue the presidency. And this story would be interesting to my friends in Dallas, though probably less entertaining than speculating about girls and the next school year.

The major source of my excitement about seeing Lyndon Johnson was literally that: *seeing* him. Television news was still in relative infancy. Most national news broadcasts were only fifteen minutes long. At some time during the fifties CBS expanded to half a hour, but my family so rarely watched anything but local news that I don't recall if this had happened yet. Anyway, local news for Pop and me was limited to the weather—continued hot and dry in the Concho River Valley, with no rain or relief in sight—and the baseball scores—Yankees win again, extend lead to five games. We never saw LBJ, except in still photographs in the newspapers and magazines. What did he look like? What did he sound like? Was he friendly or aloof in person? West Texans really didn't know the answers to these questions. As a result, there was more curiosity then about LBJ the senator than there would be later about LBJ the president. Within six years, television made that big a difference. I'm sure one reason Lyndon Johnson came to places such as Brady during the 1950s was to show himself to the folks, to connect directly with them, to shake hands and smile and speak, to be there in the flesh.

LBJ in Brady, July 1948.
LBJ Library. Photo by unknown.

★ ★ ★

People today might imagine my grandfather and I expected LBJ would be just folks, a man of the people, Mr. Smith goes to Washington. They'd be wrong if they did. We were acutely aware the most powerful wheeler-dealer in the nation wasn't like other men. He didn't run a cafe, or sell stuff, or ranch, or farm, or teach, or lawyer, or doctor. He ran the entire country, more or less. We craved a vivid presence, a person unlike us, who still thought we were important enough to come to Brady during the summer. We hungered for a show. And we positively lusted after the chance to tell those who weren't there about it later. LBJ appreciated the keenness of our appetites; he'd satisfy them. Somehow, some way, I was sure he'd show us the riveting power he had over men and events in our nation's capital.

One thing more, and it's not something Pop and I would have consciously thought about as he parked the car near the city park and we walked toward the raw lumber platform specially constructed for the occasion. We were patriots. We loved our country. We fervently believed it was the finest nation on earth. The USA had beaten the Nazis and Japan. Now we were engaged in a worldwide struggle with another terrible aggressor. We had to fight that enemy all over the world. We respected our leaders and believed they were doing their best to stand up to the communists. That did not mean we always agreed with them or voted for them. But even Pop and Big John would concede that Republicans, as awful as they might be on domestic issues, meant well in foreign policy. "Politics ends at the water's edge" is a phrase that elicits knowing snickers today. Then it was accepted as truth, at least in West Texas. That politicians are crooked as a dog's hind leg became an axiom only toward the end of the century. Earlier, the voters were more apt to give those who ran for office or represented them the benefit of the doubt. We did expect Lyndon Johnson to deliver a patriotic address, as well as giving the Republicans hell. And we were ready to believe he was being honest with us.

How did LBJ feel that day? At the top of his game, at the height of his power, the master of all before him. He was a confident, powerful speaker in Brady. He knew his audience, what they expected, what they desired, and how they'd react. He proved he was different. He flexed his power. He demonstrated his patriotism. And he was believed.

But less than a decade later, characteristics that distinguished Lyndon Johnson from his fellow citizens would be savagely parodied

LBJ in Fredericksburg, June/August 1948.
LBJ Library. Photo by unknown.

and attacked. He would be told yes, LBJ, you're different all right—you are meaner, crueler, less moral, less decent, inferior to the people in every way that matters, and a killer of women, children, and young men to boot. His thirst for power was portrayed as unforgivably evil. His patriotism was mocked, scorned, and labeled a pack of lies and a pathetically transparent catering to a military-industrial complex of interests. It was widely regarded, à la Samuel Johnson, as the last refuge of this particular scoundrel. No one took him at his word. Skill at wheeling and dealing was now the sign of an incorrigible, malevolent, and unprincipled tyrant. Television—a medium he did not perform well in—made his features tediously familiar, his voice a dull monotone, his accent thicker than in real life, and his body gross and obviously uncomfortable. When he came to most places as president, it was a different kind of event: sufficient cause for angry demonstrations that teetered perilously on the brink of violence.

Vietnam wore Lyndon Johnson down and drove him out; no question about that. I'm equally sure, however, that losing his understanding of American audiences and seeing his mastery over them disappear took a terrible toll on him. In the end, he couldn't speak in Brady anymore. I mean to say *couldn't*—he was incapable of speaking there. I'm not implying *wouldn't*, which suggests he chose not to go to Brady. His excuse might have been security, but in fact West Texans retained longer than many their traditional ideas of patriotism and accepted the necessity of fighting for freedom. LBJ didn't go there because he had lost his confidence. He was no longer sure even of West Texans in Brady's city park.

Pop and I arrived early enough to stake out a good place right in front of the speakers' platform. There weren't any chairs or benches; the crowd was expected to stand in the open area. No doubt this influenced the scheduling of political rallies and dances. Either they took place no later than mid-morning, or around eight at night. To do otherwise risked sun- or heat stroke. No planning committee worried about the prospect of rain during the fifties. Should that blessed event occur, the audience would have been happy to stand out in it. Indeed, rain might even have inspired Baptists to dance!

A clump of huge, broad live oaks shaded the speaker's platform. Just looking at this mott—a word adapted by West Texans from the Spanish term for "cover" to call a small grove of trees—made me realize that in the past more rain must have fallen. I'd been taught by Big John that mature, well-watered live oaks spread out, parallel to the ground. Their trunks were gnarled; their limbs, knotty. In contrast, younger, thirstier live oaks give the illusion of being taller, because they have not yet spread, and their branches remain thin and unformed. The shape of the trees in this park and the size of their limbs revealed that this mott had thrived centuries ago. Generous watering from the city's wells insured that it would continue to flourish.

Speakers in shade; crowd in sun. Nature constituted this hierarchy. Man-made distinctions abounded, too. While awaiting an introduction and a turn at the podium, speakers sat. We stood. Their individual voices, amplified and made powerful by microphones, surrounded the audience from horn-shaped loudspeakers on top of the light poles that circled the clearing. Voices of people in the crowd were feeble, the barely audible equivalent of muttered or whispered asides. Only *the* voice of *the* people, collectively expressed in laughter, cheers, or applause, could compete with the word projected from the podium. Moreover, speakers had the visible authority of patriotism: the boards in front of them had been festooned with red-white-and blue bunting; the lectern was flanked by the flags of Texas and the United States of America. We patiently waited for our patriotic lessons without any such symbols. Finally, speakers broadcast their wisdom from a platform that elevated them about six feet above us. They looked down. We looked up. They were meant to be seen. Our role was to see.

When Pop and I got there, we joined a rapidly thickening knot of men immediately in front of the platform early enough, though, for a clear view of the speakers. I didn't see any women around. I'm sure some were in the crowd, but they must have been a tiny minority.

The men had dressed carefully. With the exception of candidates for local office sprinkled throughout the audience, no one wore his Sunday-go-to-meetin' clothes: blue or brown suit, wide, flowered ties, handkerchief in breast pocket. Instead, pressed khaki pants, ironed shortsleeve shirts, and "town" hats, with much narrower brims than straw hats or Stetsons, was the dress of the day. Some wore dress boots; more had on laced shoes. It was the sort of outfit men who owned small businesses, or farmed, or ranched, wore to talk to the banker about a loan or to escort their ladies to San Angelo to shop at Cox, Rushing, & Greer and eat later at the Cactus Hotel's dining room. They were dressed for serious town business, not for church, a wedding, or a funeral.

As he looked down at us, did LBJ see us as *the* people? That's an important question, because I've already said I don't recall any women in the crowd, and I don't remember any Mexicans or Negroes, as those two peoples were called then in polite company, either. When historians today discern greatness in Johnson, they almost always associate it with his gift for seeing beyond the successful white male Protestants in front of him, and including within the people the poor who had only blue jeans to wear and couldn't take off from work to see him, the women who had pressed the shirts and the pants and stayed at home cooking dinner, and the ethnic minorities consigned by this society to the dirtiest and worst-paying jobs and the most wretched housing. That day in Brady, I don't know whether Lyndon Johnson looked beyond us. I do feel confident he saw the men before him as *voters*. Which they were. He also knew at least some of them had the personality or power to deliver other voters to candidates they favored, whether by persuasion or coercion. So he handled us with practiced care.

★ ★ ★

Before LBJ was introduced, I couldn't pick him out among the dignitaries and hangers-on that lined the platform. I'd never seen him in living color before, so my uncertainty was understandable. Pop wasn't sure himself, because it had been a long time between sightings of Johnson for him. And everyone up there was wearing a blue suit. I giggled to myself at the thought that they looked like pallbearers at a funeral, or a bunch of Baptist preachers on Sunday. Later at the lunch I realized that LBJ's presence had dictated the dress of all of the local officials and candidates. He wore a Sunday suit, which for a U.S. Senator, was an everyday, working-in-the-Capitol Building suit. The others wore their Sunday best both to honor and to imitate him.

Finally, some county commissioner introduced our senator, a man of the soil just like us, to the crowd. LBJ was tall, towering over the others on the platform, and perhaps the tallest person present. He looked broad from side to side, deep from front to back, and not fat but big. I was surprised by his voice. To this Texan's ears, Lyndon Johnson did not have a pronounced accent. He spoke his words precisely, with none of the drawl or soft slur that you could hear in West Texas. "Length" was not "lenth," "strength" was not "strenth," "guest" was not Pop's "guesss," when he said them. The plural "you" never became "y'all" that day, nor was "I" changed to "Ah." With something like a shock in its speed and surprise, I realized he sounded like Dallas attorneys I had met. Men who did business with people from outside the state on a regular basis didn't do "bidness" with them. They didn't come into Washington or New York on a load of wood, combing straw out of their hair and pulling goatheads or grassburrs off their pants legs. They were men of the world. Johnson came into Brady the same way. His language may have been colored by homey metaphors, but his accent was anything but Texan. Like his work clothes, it set him apart.

LBJ began by talking about his suit. He had several of them, but this one was special because it was part of an order he made just before his heart attack. "There I was, in an oxygen tent in the hospital, with Lady Bird by the side of the bed. We were talking about matters that we should decide on as soon as possible. She asked me what to say to the tailor about the blue suits I was having altered. I looked at her, and said, 'Tell him to keep working. One way or another, I'll need a blue suit.'" After our laughter stopped, he added with practiced timing, "So today I'm using it, and I sure am glad." More laughter from the crowd, who agreed with him.

This story was fresh to me and Pop when we heard it that day. Subsequently, I found out from reading biographies of LBJ that he told it

frequently in speeches and to cronies after his brush with death in
1955. None of these accounts fully describes why the story was funny.
To crowds like the one at Brady, dressed as they were, what made
them laugh was Johnson's implicit point that only politicians, preachers, or dead men had a use for a blue suit on a weekday, outside, in
Texas, during the hottest of hot spells. Like the proverbial mad dogs
and Englishmen, they were there, in their blue suits, in the noonday
sun. It was a way of poking fun at himself—you men aren't so foolish—and showing his common sense and his humor while confronting
a life-and-death situation. You laughed with him and admired him, all at
once. I'm sure, too, that LBJ would not have been in the least upset if
the crowd noticed that others wore blue suits as well, out of their obvious desire to defer to him and an equally obvious craving to be like him.
Among those who aspired to leadership or exercised it on a local scale,
he was *the* leader.

I don't remember anything about the substance of the speech. No
doubt this was a pretty typical talk, spiced with specific references to
the locale and comments about local officials and characters he had
known. A good old Democratic speech, as LBJ once characterized such
efforts: it attacked Republicans, praised his own party, promised a
better future, and wound things up pretty quickly. Then we could get
out of the sun and down to the business of shaking hands and eating
barbecue.

When Johnson ran for the presidency in 1964, I continually saw
him on TV and in still photographs plunging into crowds, reaching out
into the forest of hands. Reporters were fascinated by the spectacle.
Not only was it obviously dangerous—John Kennedy had been shot
during a motorcade, after all—but clearly LBJ regarded it as a competitive sport that displayed his toughness as a campaigner. We heard
about how his hands were bruised and bloodied. We also were treated
to estimates, openly encouraged by the man himself, of how many
hands he had shaken in an hour, afternoon, day, week, month, and campaign, to that date. His determination to touch and be touched was
described as compulsive, irresistible, and habitual. Some commentators traced its origins to Texas campaigning. Perhaps so. But I didn't
see anything like that after this speech.

Once LBJ had finished, and the county commissioner reminded
people when lunch would be served at a nearby livestock pavilion, the

senator simply went down the platform's steps, and stood on our level directly in front of the podium. An assistant hustled over to hold his coat and stand behind him. Then those who wanted to shake his hand began to line up. No one ordered us into single file or even suggested it. Men did it themselves. One at a time, they shook hands, said a few words, received a smile, a nod, a few words in return, and then moved off.

The sight reminded me of a lunch line at school, waiting for roast beef and mashed potatoes with gravy to be dropped on your plate. Clearly, I was anticipating the chunk of smoked brisket, the mound of potato salad, the heaping spoonful of pinto beans, and the slice of white bread Pop and I would soon get. This metaphor, though, was not particularly appropriate. The men who were waiting to shake hands with the senator were much less talkative and far better behaved than kids in a junior high lunch line. For that matter, they were quieter than they themselves would be less than an hour later in line for barbecue. Lunch was the proper time for howdying, hoorahing, arguing about politics, and talking about the weather. This was a more solemn and serious occasion. One focused on LBJ, how he looked, what he was saying to those in front. One thought about the mechanics of reaching out for a handshake and what to say to this famous and powerful man. I was mentally rehearsing my gestures and lines as Pop and I waited our turn. Certainly my grandfather had his mind on my meeting with Lyndon Johnson.

Pop didn't ask me if I wanted to shake hands. Without comment, he joined the line. I followed. Once there, he nudged me in front of him. Like others, we didn't talk. I didn't look back, so I have no memory of how many were behind us. My impression is that the line wasn't too long. Most of the crowd had left for lunch, voting with their feet for food over pressing the flesh and exchanging greetings with LBJ. The men ahead of us were the same ones who had been sufficiently interested in the event to arrive early and get places right below the platform. They looked familiar for other reasons too.

Many were in their fifties and sixties, like Pop. Like him, too, they carried themselves with a dignity befitting their years, experience, economic standing, and position in their communities. A sprinkling of them reminded me of Big John. Older, balder, and, to judge from the eagerness of their expressions, more openly fascinated by politics, they were a recognizable type: retired men who slapped down dominoes, sipped beer, whittled and smoked on courthouse squares, and argued about what was going on in the world. You didn't have to listen to them long to figure out that their memories were elephantine, their opinions were confident, and their decisions in politics had almost always been wise and farsighted. (To be fair, I should add that their omniscience in matters political was almost always balanced by wonderfully wry retellings of Godawful mistakes they had made in planting cotton, buying cattle, judging horses, repairing trucks and tractors, predicting prices, and depending on good weather. They also laughed about how the Almighty, in His wisdom, had seen fit to keep gold, uranium, and oil off their property.)

One such old-timer just ahead of us grinned as he shook hands with Johnson, and said, "The last time you came to town you came in a helicopter." LBJ's own smile widened, and he said, "That's right, I did." Caught for a moment by their own memories of the 1948 Democratic primary, that desperate struggle between Johnson and Coke Stevenson for the senatorial nomination that ended in LBJ's famous—or infamous, depending on whom you backed—victory by eighty-seven votes, the two nodded at each other. Then Johnson glanced over his shoulder to his aide, who swiftly handed him a short-brimmed Stetson. The silent command, the quick response, and the act of putting on the hat and tilting it back on his head had the effect of preventing any longer reminiscences. Long experience had taught LBJ how to hustle the garrulous along. A few more handshakes, brief expressions of appreciation and thanks, and it was my turn.

Up close, what impressed me most was Johnson's height, not his bulk. Since I was a short and skinny boy, I was used to looking up at most of my contemporaries and all adults. But even from my accustomed perspective, LBJ was tall. To concentrate on his face, I had to crane my neck, which meant I literally did not see how wide his torso was. The next things I noticed were his ears. They were not only long from top to lobe, they stuck out from his head like flaps of flesh. There was a slight smile on his lips, and his eyes widened as he looked at me. These facial expressions were not the result of suddenly seeing a boy in the middle of a line of mature men. It was the same routine I had observed as he greeted voters forty and fifty years older than I.

I'd also studied closely the etiquette of handshaking while I waited. Johnson held his hand out, but made no move to reach for or grasp at the other's hand. It was up to the voter to make connections. That wasn't hard to do. His right hand was huge; it couldn't be missed. As I touched it, I could feel that it was softer than most West Texas hands—the result of doing no manual labor more strenuous than shaking hands. Surprisingly, his grip was virtually nonexistent. My family had drummed into my head that few things were worse than what they called a wet-fish handshake. To greet another properly, you took firm hold, applied steady pressure, and pumped up and down two or three times. My sister and I had to practice this until whichever parent or grandparent testing us was satisfied with the grip and movement of our handshakes. LBJ's limp hand wasn't at all what I expected from a big, important man, to say the least. Instinctively, I grabbed his hand with my left hand and pressed it from both sides to get an approximation of a real handshake.

Later I realized that doing this both protected his fingers and knuckles from too hearty a grip from an enthusiastic citizen, and spared him some of the strain of squeezing the flesh of hundreds of voters in a short period of time. You didn't shake hands with Lyndon Johnson at a rally; you touched hands. Naturally, no one called this ritual touching hands. That wouldn't be manly. Moreover, it smacked of serfs touching their lord's glove as a symbol of deference, or—worse from the standpoint of most Protestant West Texans—it resembled Catholics kissing the Pope's ring, a sign of servility if ever there was one. Veterans of political rallies referred to the ritual more accurately, as "pressing the flesh." Only the inexperienced took the description of this as "shaking hands" at face value. Since this was my first handshake from a politician plying his trade, I was disconcerted.

The etiquette of handshaking also required the voter to speak first. Johnson waited expectantly for my greetings, just as he had from others. He must not have anticipated bursts of eloquence. Despite the fact that encounters such as these were not spontaneous, and the voters had a chance to rehearse their few lines, proximity to the mighty had the effect of discombobulating them. The best—that is, the most coherent—comments I heard while I waited were laconic: enjoyed your speech; keep up the good work; thanks for coming. When they deviated from this formula, even to stray onto such a familiar topic as the weather—one man I overheard stumbled over whether he should say it was hot as hell or not, and settled for comparing Brady's temperature to Hades'—their sentences became tangled. Once this occurred, it was well nigh impossible to straighten one's thoughts out, and speech tended to trail off into uncomfortable silence.

Uncomfortable for the citizen, I should say. LBJ's response didn't go further than a smile and a "thanks," or a "good to be here," or "it sure is," before his eyes switched toward the next person, and thereby signaled the first it was time to move on, and the second it was time to move up. No matter what was said to him, he reacted the same way.

It still pains me to remember that I didn't merely witness nervous stammering incoherence; I practiced it as well. "I certainly enjoyed your wonderful, er great speech, uhhh, you do a good, er, wonderful job for me, us." I can assure you that what I actually said was probably less clear than this version of it, because at the critical moment my voice, always an unpredictable instrument during my adolescence, began to rise and fall without any relation to what I was saying, or trying to say. Nervousness, plus experiencing the non-handshake, had literally unmanned me.

Pop rescued me. All of a sudden, I heard him say, "Don't you recognize this boy, Lyndon? This is John Bullion. He's Waddy Bullion's son."

LBJ swiveled so he could look at Pop. He nodded and grinned broadly then turned back to me. "Well, John," he said, "I'm real glad to see you. I think a lot of Waddy and"—here a sideways glance at my grandfather—"your whole family. Lemme get some things for you." Without looking, he snapped to the helper behind him, "Gimme one of those pens. And a knife." Without hesitating, his aide pulled a gold ball-point pen from one pocket and, after juggling LBJ's coat from his left to his right hand, extracted a small pocketknife from another. He slipped them into Johnson's left hand. "Here's a pen," he said to me. Then, grinning at me again, he asked, "Got a penny?" Dumbfounded by this turn of events, I just stared back.

Once more, Pop to the rescue. "I've got one," he said with a laugh. He dug it out of his wallet and passed it over to LBJ, who, also laughing, slipped it into his pocket. "Now our friendship won't be cut," he said to me. At that point, I recalled the old country superstition: if you give a friend a knife, always get a penny or something else of value in return, or the friendship will be cut off soon. "No it won't," I replied, "I'm proud of that." He handed over the knife, saying he hoped to see me again soon and telling me to say hello for him to my daddy and the rest of my folks. With that, he turned to Pop, and for the first time that I'd seen, thrust out his hand. Both of them were grinning from ear to ear. I walked away, stunned by the gifts and feeling like I was Lyndon Johnson's boy forever.

Which, the cynical would say, was how I was supposed to feel. For me, though, this interpretation is a bit extreme. I don't believe LBJ's principal motivation was trying to recruit a thirteen-year-old boy to work for him one day in the future. Mostly, he was showing his respect and affection for my father and, by extension, for Pop. At the same time, though, I don't doubt that he intended to make our meeting memorable for me. If I became another Waddy, he wanted me to remember getting a ballpoint pen and a knife, each with a facsimile of his signature on it, with U.S. Senate printed below, from him on a hot summer morning in Brady, Texas. And, of course, as Pop admired my new possessions, clicking the pen and opening the knife's blades, he had another reason to vote for LBJ.

More mysterious were my grandfather's motives. Obviously, he took me to the rally with the fixed intent of introducing me to Lyndon Johnson. Why? Was this another rite of passage, similar to playing third with a right-handed pull hitter coming up, or being at bat with two on and two out in a tight game? Was it merely taking advantage of the chance for me to meet a famous person? Did he want to show me what politics was like, just as the new candidate for justice of the peace and his self-styled campaign manager began the process? Did he want to be sure I'd see an unforgettable example of a real man, one at the peak of his powers, whom I might one day imitate? Or was Pop concerned by the widening rift between my parents, and determined that, no matter what happened, his grandson would have the chance to make contact with his son's most famous and influential client? It could have been all, or some, or none of the above. I don't know what impelled that great and good man, bone-weary from running Tom's Cafe and hurting from the cancer that was killing him, to drive thirty miles with me to a rally I never would have heard about had he not called it to my attention. Over forty years later, those questions linger in my mind.

The lunch crowd was much larger and included quite a few women, who had dressed for an indoor event and left standing outdoors to the men. They didn't gain much by this decision. The air cooling system for the Heart of Texas Coliseum couldn't overcome the heat of the sun outside and the bodies inside. The pavilion soon became more uncomfortable than the park.

Johnson spoke briefly after the peach cobbler. His subject was the necessity of electing good men in a democracy, a proposition that sparked no controversy. Nor did his rendering of what this meant in the real world: vote for Democrats. Way too wary to suggest how we would choose *between* Democrats, and thus providing no real guidance in a state where winning the Democratic primary equaled election, he confined himself to praising everyone moved by duty to campaign for office.

Then LBJ abruptly commanded, "Everyone who's running for office, stand up!" Obediently, every blue suit in the place leaped upright; weasels going pop! when the button of the box is pressed.

"Give them a round of applause," he demanded. We promptly obeyed, like children told to clap after a toy has been demonstrated, or a puppet show was over.

It was funny to me at the time. It still is, as I recall the immediate, kneejerk reaction of the supposedly independent and strong-minded leaders who sought to govern us, and the equally swift response of the sturdy citizens commanded to applaud. I remember with pride that Pop remained seated. He claimed later that he didn't think running for justice of the peace was the same as campaigning for the legislature or state-wide office. Less-important candidates shouldn't put on airs, he laughed to me. Personally, I don't believe Tom Bullion lept up at the command of anyone. He was too proud to do that, and too determined not to "put on airs" to boast about sitting afterwards. Still, that others could not resist standing and applauding on demand unforgettably demonstrated the power of the man who had just given me a pen and a knife. Strong men and proud women did his bidding without thinking, rising when he said rise, approving what he said approve, clapping when he said clap. If he felt nothing else, LBJ must have left Brady feeling confident of its unified support.

As for Pop and me, we left Brady pleased with what we'd seen and done. "We had a good time, Pop," I told him, "and I met Lyndon Johnson and got a pen and a knife." I thanked him for the day. He smiled and nodded his appreciation for my good manners. As he drove off, Pop fiddled with the radio, trying to find a station that would give us the Game of the Day. There was no more thinking or talking about LBJ on the way home. Baseball had our undivided attention.

Back in Eden and Menard, I showed off my gifts to Big John, my grandmothers, my aunt, and assorted friends. All were duly impressed. When Mother came to pick up Ann and me for the return trip to Dallas and another school year, she said she was happy, too. Typically, she also told me that the pen and the knife I'd been given weren't promises of future favors or success. I'd have to make my way, use my talents properly, and be my own man. Lyndon Johnson could command others, to be sure; but my job, she reminded me gently, was to learn to command myself. She didn't say more, and she didn't comment on LBJ or his

Grandma Lewis and Billie, Ann, and John Bullion, 1958.
Lewis Family Collection.

adviser, my father. Even so, I have far fewer questions about Mother's feelings than I have about Pop's thoughts as he planned to go to Brady.

In Dallas, my closest friends and some of the neighbors saw LBJ's gifts. Then these souvenirs went on my desk. After a few weeks, they migrated into a drawer. Time passed, and they were covered by other mementos and pushed toward the back. During periodic fits of cleaning, generally inspired by a desperate search for a lost ticket or misplaced library card, I pulled them out and relived the moment. Ultimately, like Ralph Yarborough's comb, they were gone, victims of my carelessness, chronic disorganization, and the absence in me of any passion to collect things.

Those tangible keepsakes simply weren't as important to me as the skills I absorbed and practiced during West Texas summers. I could handle weapons safely and confidently, and I had learned the drill and discipline of shooting well. I had experienced how challenging baseball could be, and I had played it capably in the Eden Little League. And I knew that if I was determined to risk drinking, I should avoid cheap beer and rotgut whiskey. I'd also learned to swallow Falstaff and Old Crow without too much wincing.

These were not trivial accomplishments in a country that cele-brated masculinity and elevated manliness. It was especially important for a skinny, short kid with glasses to know he was capable of doing these things.

Big John and Pop also pointed me toward broader worlds, the one by his interest in the politics of Texas and the nation, the other by his vote for Al Smith, his involvement in the politics of Eden, and his intro-duction of me to Lyndon Johnson. To modern eyes, they may appear limited, provincial men, suffused with the mores of manhood peculiar to their place, which was West Texas, and their times, which had been hard. But I knew they didn't expect me to duplicate their lives. I would return to my parents' home in a modern city and live in a time that was clearly much different from the thirties. The role my two grandfathers played was to make sure I developed and tested in West Texas the con-fidence to succeed in that wider, newer world.

By the end of the decade, I was looking forward to making my own way and leaving Texas. Lyndon Johnson, and people like him, would in large part define what that world would be. I was ready. My grandfa-thers had helped prepare me, and LBJ had hoped we would soon meet again.

CHAPTER 4

Growing Up Poor

What was this newer, wider world that Lyndon Johnson and men such as my father were trying during the 1950s to create for themselves and other Americans? How did they understand the present? What visions did they see, what dreams did they dream, about the future? Obviously, each had his own ambitions, strategies, and goals. That was true of every individual in that generation. But did they all believe in the same general principles? Did common experiences shape their definition of the new life?

To me, the last question is the crucial one. Kids like Lyndon and Waddy, those who spent their childhoods on ranches and farms and in small Texas towns during the 1920s and 1930s, grew up poor. They spent the years of their maturity comparing their present circumstances to those earlier times. What were the fifties like? One thing for sure, that decade was not rural Texas in the twenties and thirties. What should the future be for themselves, their families, and the nation? The simplest and most heartfelt answer was: *not like the Depression*!

This insight is hardly unique. No child of the fifties with Depression-era parents would be surprised by it in the least. We heard constantly about how hard our fathers and mothers had to work to get to where they were now, and how little was given them. And we were frequently warned to be thrifty and to take care of our possessions, because you could never know when the wolf would be at the door once more. "Willful waste makes woeful want," my Aunt Geraldine preached to me, stretching out the "woe" in "wooooooeful" until it sounded like a plaintive howl. She spoke for Dad and Mother on that subject, just more humorously. Auntie and I always laughed at her "woeful"; her smile and the long "o" communicated perfectly her amused awareness that I was not a boy of the thirties, even though I,

Tom, Florence, Waddy, and Geraldine Bullion, early 1920s.
Bullion Family Collection.

who was not growing up poor, was supposed to act as though I were. My father was much grimmer. He knew God damn well my sister and I weren't poor, and he was working God damned hard to make sure we'd never have to go through what he did to get a college education. Still, he wanted us to adopt the attitudes and skills he developed during the depressed thirties and apply them to our lives in the affluent fifties. What he learned then would always serve my sister and me well, no matter what the economic climate was or which careers we chose. With this in mind, he was fond of repeating to us the directions a neighboring stock farmer gave his young son about chopping cotton. "Pressley," the neighbor said, "take your time, hit it slow and steady, and get all the weeds." Then he'd tell Ann and me that ol' man Watson's advice was just as good for a lot of things as it was for working with a hoe in a cotton patch under a blazing sun. Of that, Dad was certain.

LBJ felt the same way. One of his first acts as president was to insist that staff at the White House turn out lights when they left rooms empty. I don't remember how much money the taxpayers saved because of this frugality, only that the new president proudly announced the amount. In an eerie foretaste of the savage attacks that would be launched against him over Vietnam, he was immediately parodied as Light Bulb Johnson. Commentators, used to what they presumed was Jack Kennedy's urbane, sophisticated modernity, evidently were as put off by 1930s style behavior as Ann and I occasionally were by exhortations that we act as if the Depression were back with us again. His feelings stung, LBJ stopped boasting about savings on the White House electric bill. He kept on turning out lights, though. I know, because my father approvingly remarked that he had never seen Lyndon Johnson fail to do this when everyone left a room at the White House and the LBJ Ranch. He did this despite the facts that he had risen to power during an era of unexampled prosperity and believed he was pouring the foundation for a Great Society in the future, one which would fight a victorious War on Poverty.

If the thirties had such a profound and enduring impact on my father and Lyndon Johnson, I guessed they must have had fascinating conversations about that decade. So recently I asked Dad what they said to each other about growing up poor.

My father didn't hesitate. With a slight smile on his face, he said, "Growing up poor among that crowd—the Johnsons, the Bullions, the Kellams, Bill Deeson, Glenn Stegall, Walter Jenkins, and the rest—was a given. You took it for granted," he went on. "It wasn't something you talked about with each other." Here he shrugged, then splayed his hands. "You see, we all had been poor country kids. Why would we have to explain anything about that to each other?"

This answer disappointed the hell out of me. There'd be no treasure trove of Johnson stories about early poverty comparable to the revealing ones he told to Doris Kearns Goodwin as she wrote *Lyndon Johnson and the American Dream*. In fact, there'd be no anecdotes at all! Aside from frustration, I felt surprise. My father had never hesitated to tell me stories about his childhood, whether I wanted to hear them or not. They weren't all bleak tales of hungers, fears, and grinding, desperate work, either. Nor did they all end with moralizing sermons. When the spirit moved him, Dad leavened his narratives with wonderful humor and affectionate asides about himself, family, and friends. So I quizzed him further.

"Did anyone ever joke about his childhood?" I asked. "You know, 'we were so poor that we...' and then fill in the blank."

No hesitation this time, either. "No, not that I recall," was his answer. A beat of time passed, then he spread his hands again and said, "As you know, life when we were growing up had its good times and funny moments, just like it always does. But," and here he smiled to soften his point, "that was despite hard times. There wasn't much funny to us about being poor."

I persisted. "So you and LBJ didn't talk about the good times ever. You didn't reminisce about them, as sort of moments of light and happiness?" I suppose I was thinking of the way country songwriters can cast a nostalgic glow over, say, the togetherness at even hard-candy Christmases.

Dad just shook his head. He was being diplomatic in ways he had not been when I was much younger and more impressionable. It was clear he and Lyndon shared no rosy moments from the thirties with each other. Equally evident from Dad's crossed arms was his feeling that there was no reason for anyone who lived through that time to be nostalgic or to sentimentalize it.

"One last question," I promised him. "I guess I'm right in assuming you and the president never quoted morals from your experiences as young men to each other, like," here I thought for a few seconds to formulate one myself and a smile spread across Dad's face, "I learned you had to work hard at Renfro's Drug in Brownwood, Texas."

The former top soda jerk at Renfro's grinned widely. "John," he said, "President Johnson wasn't interested at all in *where* or *how* his people learned to work. All he cared about," my father continued, "was *that* you worked hard, long, and well for Lyndon Johnson."

Another time, I asked Dad some more questions about the twenties and thirties. These dealt with the relationships between parents and children during those difficult years. I had noticed, I told him, some interesting similarities between the Bullions of Eden and the Johnsons of Johnson City. The most obvious was that both Lyndon and Waddy gave the major share of the credit for their success to the example and urgings of their mothers. As boy and man, LBJ never failed to praise his mother publicly and fulsomely. When he was a child, he proudly confessed to being a "Mama's Boy"; as an adult, he never mentioned his mother, according to Hubert Humphrey, without tears coming to his eyes. Then I reminded my father that he told me when I was quite young that Mother would always be my best friend. He was certain of this because, as he added, "Mine was."

As I recalled this to Dad, suddenly I remembered him, right after Pop died, staring into a glass of scotch and passing judgment on his father. "He was a good man," he told me, "but he never pushed us." He swallowed some scotch, then set the glass down. "Pop never tried to make us want to be better or get better." My father drained his drink. "That was Mother. She pushed us. She drove us." I don't remember him shedding a tear that day.

Florence Bullion and children, Waddy Bullion
in the center foreground, early 1920s.
Bullion Family Collection.

Without sharing this stark memory with Dad, I asked him, "Did you and LBJ discuss your mothers and their roles in your lives?" He thought for a while, then said, "I don't believe I ever heard him mention his mother. I know we never talked about her and Grandmommy and what they meant to us."

This surprised me. So did what Dad said next. "LBJ did frequently mention his father," he recalled. "He never said anything much,

LBJ's boyhood home in Johnson City, 1940-41.
LBJ Library. Photo by Austin Statesman.

generally just something like 'I'm a politician, like my father,' or 'my father was a politician, and so am I.'" Dad didn't remember any pride in these references. Johnson was simply pointing out that he was what his father was. These words called attention to a continuity in vocation and, perhaps, emphasis in their lives as well.

To others, LBJ expressed near hatred for Sam Ealy Johnson. The problem, as he saw it, was not his father's political career. It was Sam's drinking, which in turn contributed to a series of disastrous invest-ments. Johnson held his father responsible for the rapid collapse of the family's fortunes during the 1920s. The tears he wept after Sam's funeral in 1937 were not for a deceased parent; they welled up in his eyes because he feared his father's debts would pull him and Lady Bird under financially. When the attorney for the estate assured him the sit-uation could be managed and he'd be able ultimately to pay off what Sam owed, he could only mutter, "We'd better, buddy. We'd better."

Johnson's contempt for his father and his resentment at the predic-aments Sam constantly landed his family and his eldest child in lingered throughout his life. When he looked back on his past with Doris Kearns Goodwin after he left the White House, these feelings spewed out. With Dad, however, none of these emotions was discern-ible in his comments. To the contrary, in an undramatic but none-theless real way, Lyndon Johnson was identifying himself with Sam Ealy Johnson. They were both politicians.

LBJ's putting his father in that context has some significance for understanding how he remembered hard times during the 1950s. Before I get into that, though, let me observe that this sort of comment foreclosed any possibility that Dad might bring up Pop and the two men might start discussing their fathers. My dad was different from Pop. He couldn't claim, as LBJ could and did, that he and his father did the same thing.

So it was as if their backgrounds had nothing to do with their present relationship. Where they came from, what they experienced, seemingly had no relevance to their business together. Intent on that business, they never talked about what it had been like for them both with fathers who failed, mothers who aspired, land and stock that depended on the twin whimsys of weather and the marketplace, and times that were hard: growing up poor.

"What *did* they talk about?" a friend asked after I'd described my father's answers to these questions. She and I have worked together for almost a decade and a half, and in the course of those years we've learned a great deal about each other's experiences as young people. Our discussions serve as a framework of reference as we ponder together how to raise children in an era very different from the ones we grew up in. Because we've gained both pleasure and profit from our reminiscences, it is difficult for us to imagine that LBJ and my father never mentioned their pasts, beyond Johnson's periodic recital of the fact that he and his father were politicians. To repeat another of my friend's questions about this: "Why not?"

The obvious answer is, of course, that my friend and I are very different people from Lyndon Johnson. Years of working at a department of history have led us to believe that the past is worth examining because it does have an impact on the present and the future. How much and what type of impacts are open to debate; we both noticed while I chaired the department how my problems were the same ones my predecessors faced, and that my colleagues approached these difficulties from much the same angle their ancestors on the history faculty did. This didn't mean we concluded that all human experience past, present, and future was essentially cyclical in nature. Instead, we felt that the larger environment in which the department functioned—in this case, the University of Missouri-Columbia—had changed very little. To reach a conclusion such as this one, we had to be introspective personally and willing professionally to spend the time contemplating our own and the institution's histories.

During the 1950s, Lyndon Johnson was neither introspective nor ready to take the time to examine what had happened to him twenty and thirty years earlier. That had no relevance to a man who spent long hours each day being Majority Leader of the Senate and one of the most prominent politicians in the nation. He wasn't going to waste his time—or, for that matter, my father's, either—rehashing things long gone when they had business to do and decisions to make. Time was precious. There were always other people to see and things to finish. Move on; move forward; move up. Accustomed to adapting himself to the personalities of his clients, my father fell right into step with LBJ when they were together.

Dad would be quick to say that you should not conclude from this that Lyndon Johnson found the history of his times utterly useless. He didn't. What LBJ believed about the past was this: to profit from its study, you had to be careful to separate out the essential and valuable from the inconsequential and trivial. Put another way, you had to iso-late the aspects of the past that were most useful to you in the present, then use them as truisms to assist your decisions and to persuade others to your point of view. Where the twenties and thirties were con-cerned, this meant that he should focus on the politics and forget the personal. Those decades proved to his satisfaction the efficacy and desirability of government intervention in the economy. They also served as evidence—probably to his even deeper satisfaction—of the power of a gifted politician to change how his fellow citizens lived. When Johnson strayed off concerns about taxation in discussions with my father during the fifties, he almost always praised Franklin Roose-velt and the New Deal. "LBJ," my father has said to me many times, "was a real fan of the New Deal." He missed few chances to tell Dad that and to express his belief that FDR had been "on the right track" and did "great things for his country."

Johnson rarely went beyond these brief statements when he men-tioned the New Deal. My father recalls one of those occasions vividly. At some point in the mid-fifties, not long after Grandmommy had a mild heart attack, LBJ remarked that some form of federally subsidized health care for the elderly was a logical extension of Social Security. Surely what inspired him was the knowledge that my father had been visiting his mother in a San Angelo hospital. He must have assumed that Dad would have to help Pop out with the bills, and thus would lis-ten sympathetically to this thought. What is striking is the fact he made such a statement in the political milieu of the fifties. Mainstream politicians in that decade took their cue from the American Medical Association. National health insurance, or any other form of what we know today as Medicaid and Medicare, was socialized medicine, pure and simple. It should be resisted tooth and nail, or the liberties of the people and the quality of their medical treatment would suffer irreparable damage from the imposition of a communistic system. For LBJ to say what he did, even privately and presumably with the protection of the attorney-client privilege, placed him on a radical fringe in American politics insofar as health care was concerned.

It also reveals how much Lyndon Johnson knew about my father's background. He was aware that most of my father's clients in the oil business would have regarded "socialized" medicine in particular and the New Deal in general as anathema. Because he dealt with oilmen frequently himself, LBJ knew Franklin Roosevelt was no hero to them. They had voted for Eisenhower twice over Adlai Stevenson. Many of them were in the process of becoming Republicans in name as well as in fact in national elections. Perhaps Johnson even suspected that my father had liked Ike in '52 and '56. (Indeed he had!) But to LBJ even this apostasy did not signify Dad was uneducable on federal health care for the elderly. After all, Waddy had been poor. He had experienced firsthand how parental poverty could affect the lives of their children well after they became adults themselves. Knowing this, Lyndon Johnson felt his attorney and adviser would be susceptible to arguments in favor of that policy. There was no need to twist arms now, because national health care obviously wasn't on the immediate horizon. Nor was there any call to refer explicitly to experiences during the Depression. A master politician, Lyndon Johnson was as capable at subtly testing the appeals of arguments as he was at giving folks the full treatment. Obviously nothing in Dad's cautious and noncommittal reaction to his comment discouraged him about the future prospects for Medicare.

My father had a quite different view of history, in the abstract and in the personal, than LBJ did. For three years during the thirties, he taught American and World History at Eden High School, while he lived at his parents' house and saved enough money to pay tuition and feed, clothe, and house himself without working while he attended the University of Texas Law School. Mastering the facts and figures of secondary school history didn't take him very long. Determining what it meant and deciding how to teach it engaged his intelligence more.

Dad concluded that to teach history well and to understand it fully, you had to emphasize its predictive qualities. This insight was not merely a tactic he adopted for classroom use. He became convinced you could confidently forecast the broad outlines of the future by correctly remembering the past. Many years later, while I was writing my dissertation, I made the error of pooh-poohing this idea in his presence. His reaction was immediate: "Then why bother to study it?" My retort—"For the fun of it!"—cut short the argument without convincing my father, who turned away with a snort.

I do not intend to portray my father's understanding of the employment of the past to comprehend the present and predict the future as a naive faith that history always repeats itself. To him, the critical step in using past events in this fashion is best described by the word "correctly." Anyone studying history has to be, in his opinion, keenly aware of differing contexts. Much as a student in law school learns how to "distinguish" cases—that is, filtering out what is different about them to determine whether citing one as a precedent for the other is correct—someone who applies history's lessons to latter-day problems and opportunities must be always alert to the possibility of crucial differences between the two situations. My father never regarded the past as an infallible guide to what to do in the present. Sometimes, though, he failed to notice factors that distinguished two seemingly similar decisions. Dad's favorite example of this is the time his interpretation of the moral of Pop's loss of the Bullions' ranch made him overconfident about the lessons of the past.

The Bullions weathered the bad years of the 1920s in good shape. Indeed, Pop had prospered so much at raising cotton, hogs, cattle, and a few sheep that he paid all of Dad's expenses during his freshman year at Howard Payne College. He planned to do even better during the next decade. Sheep, he decided, were the wave of the future. Giving up the strategy of diversification, which had cushioned the family against slumps in any one market, he persuaded the Eden State Bank to loan him $32,000 so he could buy 2,000 ewes. He could hardly have chosen a worse moment in American history to plunge into wool. By June 1930 the price of ewes had plummeted from sixteen to two dollars a head. Pop signed them over to the bank, along with his land and everything else he owned.

Busted as stock farmers, the Bullions moved to Eden. Pop found work with the Highway Department; Dad hired on as a soda jerk at

Burleson's Drug Store. Nearly three years passed before the family's finances stabilized to the point where he could return to Howard Payne. By that time, he wryly recalled, "I had mastered a useful trade." His experience as a soda jerk landed him a job at Renfro's Drugstore #2. He never took a break, studying and working fall, winter, and summer until he had his degree.

Dad didn't practice his skills behind a soda fountain again. What stuck with him was his conclusion that risking everything even for what was apparently a sure route to riches was extraordinarily unwise. Caution should be his watchword; hedging bets and diversifying investments, his strategy; sticking to what he knew best, his guiding principle. Dad believed Pop was responsible for the family's disaster. Neither Pop nor he gave any credence to excuses like "times became hard" or "nobody could have guessed the stock market would crash." The fact that these statements were more or less true did not change the reality that bad times were made much worse by Pop's gamble. For the rest of his life, my grandfather referred to himself as "Knotty-headed Tom" around his sons, a constant admission of his great mistake. My father, for his part, vowed never to repeat that error.

Years later in the mid-fifties, Dad was advising a group of young entrepreneurs and engineers about setting up a new company. The soon-to-be CEO was impressed by the shrewdness of his attorney and grateful for the tax savings gleaned from his counsel when the enterprise went public and began selling stock. As a result, he took Dad aside one day. Closing his door, he said, "Waddy, I want you to sell all the stock you own, liquidate your investments in oil companies, put a second mortgage on the house, borrow against your share in the law firm, and sink every penny you can scrounge up into this company." Then he promised, "You won't regret it, Waddy, because we'll make you so rich you can practice law as a hobby from now on." My father had come to admire the energy and enterprise of his client, and to respect his intelligence and potential. He felt confident success was in the wings for this young man—as soon as this highly speculative company failed and he turned his talents to other pursuits. True to the principles he derived from Pop's experience, he politely declined the offer to be present at the creation of the totally new industry his client was excitedly describing.

So Dad said "no" to Erik Jonsson. He didn't invest a penny in the company Jonsson and his partners had just named Texas Instruments. Growing up poor had helped keep him from becoming very rich.

As the value of shares in TI rose meteorically, and as the stock split again and again, my father did not reproach himself over much. To be sure, he regretted not being fantastically wealthy, but he still believed that careful conservatism was the best investment policy almost all of the time. He did formulate a corollary to that general rule, however. His mistake with Texas Instruments, he believed, was his failure to give greater weight to his high estimation of Jonsson's talents. "Bet on the man, not on the company" became his new rule of thumb. This piece of his personal history had taught him that you wouldn't go far wrong very often when you invested your money with a person whom you trusted and respected. Since the late fifties, Dad has had no cause either to discard or modify that piece of wisdom.

In contrast, during the 1950s Lyndon Johnson regarded distilling lessons from unfortunate gambles and missed opportunities in the past as foolishness. Very much a creature of the here, now, and next, he lived in the present tense, with an eye cocked toward the future perfect. He did not believe the past molded people unless they short-sightedly or timidly let it. Nor did he think it could assist much in planning for the future. Its usefulness was limited to persuading others to agree with him. Whenever he recited chapter and verse from history, it was because he could portray experiences then as supporting his thoughts and desires now. Thus the thirties "proved" that the federal government could intervene successfully in the economy and help improve people's lives. That the Second World War actually ended the Depression was a reality that had no significance to him and probably didn't impinge on his consciousness. After all, he wasn't suggesting we fight a major war to achieve full employment. In much the same way, the ultimate fate of the appeaser at Munich "proved" that we had to stand up to aggressors immediately, or a more dangerous conflict would inevitably result. In this case, history was a handy club to wield against those who pointed out differences between Nazi Germany and North Vietnam. LBJ didn't try to understand the past, or to assess what relevance it might have for the present and future. He simply used it whenever he felt it might give him an advantage in political argument.

Why? The best explanation I've ever heard I owe to a former colleague who has spent most of his career teaching military history to the brightest and most promising young officers in the United States Army. At one point, he was seconded to the command of a major general, where he capably served as chief aide de camp. During this tour of duty, my friend frequently briefed members of the Joint Chiefs of Staff and the highest ranking officers in many foreign armies. Once I asked him how these men and women responded to arguments about policy and doctrine that were grounded in the experiences of armies in the past.

My friend looked out over his deck, toward a gap in some low, rolling hills in eastern Kansas, a topography he'd just described to me as similar to the terrain in central Germany that would invite a Soviet tank attack on NATO forces. As I followed his gaze, I was inspired to sharpen my question. "What would they say, for instance, if you told them, 'Don't do that, because it got the French in trouble in the Ardennes during 1940?'" He smiled and shook his head. "Mostly," he answered, "they wouldn't listen." Why? "Often people in command don't really believe that history applies to them." My friend elaborated by saying they believed the worst couldn't and wouldn't happen to them because they were too smart, too good, too wise, too lucky, too blessed, too favored by God, etc., etc., etc. "What it boils down to," he went on, "was the feeling that that was the French, but this is *me*! And I'm different!" Whenever he wanted to deflect them from a decision he felt would be mistaken, my friend always couched his arguments in terms of the current situation. He carefully left out the historical reasons underpinning his analysis.

I found that fascinating. My friend frequently told his students that he was teaching the officers of a defeated army. That army on the institutional, official level insisted it wanted to learn from Vietnam and other lost battles and integrate those lessons into planning for the years ahead. Military education accordingly focused on these topics. A number of skilled and dedicated historians—my friend was among the very best of these—dissected military history with an eye to contributing to the creation of new doctrine. Their students were taught the fresh results of their careful and pathbreaking research. Yet at the command level, history was in practice irrelevant.

My friend would recognize the Lyndon Johnson of the 1950s. He was one of the men over whom military historians despaired thirty years later. His past, LBJ determined, was irrelevant. He would not let it capture his attention even briefly, let alone influence his thoughts or deter him for one moment from acting as he pleased. He was a force, not an object; an actor, not a reactor. He was the sort of man who took his own time by the throat and wrenched it into shapes pleasing to him. He would shape history; it would not shape him. Like Franklin

Roosevelt, he could change the world. Lyndon Johnson defined himself that way.

So LBJ said nothing to my father about how they'd both grown up poor, the victims of their fathers' weaknesses and mistakes and the beneficiaries of their mothers' drive and ambitions. He surely never thought about admitting anything along those lines. Had the subject come up, if he had been pressed to say something, probably he would have protested, "I'm not a drunk. I am my own man. I'm LBJ!" He would not have wanted to hear, and he wouldn't have listened to, the prosaic wisdom Dad once heard from one of his friends. "Poor folks," she said, "have poor ways." She left unsaid but unmistakable her central point: for most folks of the thirties, poor ways lingered on and continued to influence, long after poverty itself was left behind—and the chance to get in on the ground floor as Texas Instruments rose toward the penthouse was before them.

Later in his life, Lyndon Johnson would find cause to examine the impact of growing up poor. But not then, not yet. Right now in the 1950s, he was a power everyone and everything else had to reckon with.

CHAPTER 5

In The Boat

Every biographer of Lyndon Johnson devotes pages to describing what it was like to work for a man who regarded himself as practically a natural force capable of rearranging the political landscape of his times. How he drove his staff, demanding long hours and high quality; how he praised and bullied, depending on circumstances and his judgment of which would be more effective; how he inspired and intimidated, uplifting by personal example or compelling by sarcastic exhortation—all this is the stuff of LBJ legend. Reactions of the staffers, ranging from anger to awe, flesh out these accounts. The evidence is sufficiently mixed for historians to come down on the side of their own reactions to Johnson. To some, his excesses were mitigated by the fact he and the staff were doing significant, indeed vital, work for the nation. To others, his behavior betrays the personality of a perfect tyrant, who would not rest until he dominated everyone and everything around him.

Interestingly, no historian has ever made a systematic survey of the early lives of the men who worked with LBJ from the 1930s until he became president in 1963. Maybe no one has researched the biographical sketches necessary for such a study because the results are so obvious. As my father said, youthful poverty was a given among the Kellams, Deesons, Jenkinses, *et. al*. Certainly I haven't filled this gap, if gap it indeed is. Still, I'm going to describe what I think the results would be, in order to highlight how Dad was similar to, and different from, Johnson's staff. That, in turn, will put his rather unique perspective on working for LBJ into context.

An analysis of the biographies of LBJ's crew would, I predict, reveal that they were white; that they came from rural backgrounds; that they had at least some education beyond high school; and that they were young when they began working for him, generally in their mid-

National Youth Administration of Texas Administrative Staff and District Directors, Austin, October 1, 1939. Members of LBJ's staff pictured are Ray Roberts (seated, second from left), Jesse Kellam (seated, fifth from left), and Bill Deeson (standing, second from right); note how young they were.
LBJ Library. Photo by unknown.

to late-twenties. To go on, these young people would be intelligent, hard working, and ready, willing, and able to seek their destinies far from home. Digging still deeper into the days of their youth, our researcher would find a common determination not to do manual labor, and to leave the farm, the ranch, the drugstore, restaurant, and small town behind. These people would also have fathers whom hard times in the twenties and thirties had baffled, stymied, driven into new jobs, impelled into risky enterprises, or outright defeated. Most, if not all, of them would believe they owed every success they achieved to their mothers.

This shouldn't surprise. Hard times in rural Texas had been especially hard on daddies. They were expected to be the breadwinners, the providers, and the widely competent and fully masculine figures who dominated their families. When providing became difficult and precarious, it became tough for them within their homes. If respect and love depended on a father's ability to deal with the economic world successfully, then the failure to do this inevitably resulted in loss of standing and self-esteem. When mothers insisted their sons could do better, they asked themselves, "Better than who?" and answered privately and personally, "My father." In this way, many times without meaning to, wives subverted their husbands' authority and weakened their reputation.

For some of LBJ's men, this was their first job. For all of them, it was a very meaningful job. Not just because being employed in the 1930s was a blessing in and of itself, and having a job after World War II provided a welcome measure of security. Working for Lyndon Johnson was meaningful because he could convince you that you would make a difference in the republic's future. This wasn't just sitting at a desk forty hours a week and fifty weeks a year until you retired. This meant you were helping make life better for everyone. When LBJ hired you, you had the real prospect of some political power to do good for others and a genuine opportunity to do well for yourself, both in terms of personal satisfaction and economic profit. In sum, those who took and kept these jobs were ambitious to succeed.

The points of similarity between the composite of Johnson's staff and my father should be obvious. They're the things this group didn't need to elaborate on and Lyndon Johnson refused to talk about. Poverty and parents head that list. Let's talk instead about the differences.

Working for LBJ was not Dad's first meaningful job. Serving on Admiral King's executive staff was. Assisting with decisions that profoundly affected the fate of the United States was not a novel experience for him.

Working for Lyndon Johnson did not expose Dad for the first time to a dominating, demanding boss. Three and a half years with King familiarized him with that species of human. In fact, the admiral was so demanding that my father did nothing whatsoever for LBJ between mid-1942, when his temporary duty with the Naval Affairs Committee ended, to late 1945, when he was honorably discharged from the Navy. "You worked your butt off for King," Dad recently told me. "If you did not, you were gone. Even if you did wear your rear down to a nub, if he got wind you were spending some time conducting private business for a congressman from Texas, he'd assume you weren't working hard enough for him. That meant you'd find yourself elsewhere in a hurry."

So, when Dad resumed advising LBJ in 1946, he was far more experienced at doing significant work for a driven, committed man than the rest of Johnson's staff when they began working. That history made him, I suspect, more confident than they were and less prone to being surprised or intimidated by the rich variety of Johnsonian manipulations of events and moods. I'd add to this confidence greater maturity. In 1946 Dad was thirty-two. He was older than many staffers were when they began their years with LBJ.

My father also had skills Johnson prized. LBJ didn't have to wonder about the potential usefulness of Waddy Bullion. Unless service in the Navy had blunted Dad's intelligence, LBJ could be certain he would continue to provide quality advice about taxes. For this reason, the congressman kept in social contact with the naval officer during the war and resumed discussing tax strategies with him in 1946. Dad wasn't in any doubt about where he stood with LBJ. Lyndon Johnson obviously valued his counsel so much that he sought him out when peace returned.

For this reason, plus his experiences in the Navy and with Ernest J. King, my father was far from being typical of the men who staffed LBJ's offices. What, then, were his reactions to working with The Man?

When Dad speaks about working for Johnson, he uses a nautical metaphor. Perhaps his choice of this figure of speech was inspired by his years in the Navy; in any event, he referred to working for LBJ as being "in the boat." Johnson's role was captain; those doing his bidding were stroking the oars or tending the sails.

As far as LBJ was concerned, according to my father, "if you couldn't pull your weight in the boat, you didn't stay there." Translated into the language of landsmen: "You had to come up to, and keep up to, his standards." He accepted no excuses and extended no sympathy to those who didn't achieve his expectations. "If you were not pulling your weight in the boat," Dad elaborated, "you got out of it and, I guess, walked home." Left unsaid was his obvious feeling that the captain couldn't care less whether the banished sank, swam, or strolled to shore.

Dad stayed in the boat from 1946 until 1973. He remained there because he pulled his weight. Indeed, he did better than that. In short order, he became one of the three attorneys LBJ relied on for tax advice. The other two, Carolyn Agger and Sheldon Cohen, were Washington-based lawyers, partners in high-powered and well-connected firms. Agger's presence in the District's legal scene was further enhanced by her marriage to Abe Fortas, one of the most prominent attorneys in the capital and another intimate adviser of LBJ. My father, Agger, and Cohen were all superb tax lawyers. They rarely worked together for Johnson. Instead, he consulted them separately on the same problem, and thus received a second and third opinion on each diagnosis. What distinguished Dad from the other two was this: his advice was free.

Initially, Dad did not charge LBJ because he began advising the congressman on taxes while he worked at the IRS. Revenuers cannot exact fees for any counsel they give taxpayers, for the good reason the citizenry is already paying them salaries for their professional expertise. But after he left the IRS in 1947, Dad continued this practice. He told Johnson he was used to doing this, and he wanted to keep on out of gratitude. Far from being immediately thrilled by the prospect of advice without a charge, LBJ was wary. He firmly believed in the truth of a classic adage of capitalism—you get what you pay for. To his mind, gift horses should have their teeth inspected. Someone who doesn't bill for services has no direct financial incentive to put much effort into maintaining quality. Opinions delivered for free could therefore be wholly whimsical, ill-informed, not clearly thought out, downright incompetent, or a combination of these undesirable traits. Johnson weighed my father's counsel closely against that given him by Agger and Cohen. He never found it wanting. By the 1950s, LBJ felt so confident about it that he would occasionally tease my father about how cheap his fees were. Once Dad responded by simply reminding him, "Free advice can be the most expensive advice anyone can ever have." Sobered by this truth, LBJ immediately conceded the wisdom of that statement. Then he got the last word by saying, "You know I value your advice, Waddy, despite its cost." Without question, LBJ was telling the truth. If my father had failed to maintain the high standard of his counsel, he would have found himself off the boat.

I can't describe any specifics about that advice, because Dad worked with Lady Bird on her taxes long after Lyndon's death, and he still regards many of the recommendations he made to the progenitor of the family's fortune as privileged information. He is willing to say that meeting LBJ's expectations could be challenging. In considering Johnson's present situation and future plans, my father had to be prepared to answer two questions. First, what were the most effective tax strategies? Second, which of those strategies would look best printed in the morning newspaper? Question number one fell within the boundaries of Dad's professional expertise. Question number two demanded that he weigh the political implications of various alternatives. That a master politician, a man absolutely confident in his judgments and instincts in politics would solicit my father's opinion on that issue speaks volumes.

My father tailored his presentation of tax strategies to fit LBJ's concerns. Tax attorneys take inspiration from a sentiment that Dad likes to express this way: "There's no law that says you have to pay more tax than you're legally required to pay." They are also fond of reminding themselves, their clients, and the Revenuers of Judge Learned Hand's *obiter dicta* from a federal appellate bench: "There is not even a patriotic duty to arrange one's affairs so they pay the greatest tax." The most gifted tax attorneys are the ones who take these laws most to heart and search the tax codes relentlessly, ingeniously, creatively, and aggressively for every omission, error, and loophole they can exploit for their clients' advantage. LBJ certainly wanted Dad to do all that for him; reductions in his tax bills delighted him. But he also wanted his personal tax strategies to be easily defensible to a skeptical public if need be. Thus Johnson was willing to pay a little more than he might legally have to if he believed that would better serve his political purposes. In particular, he wanted Dad to guard against courses of action that might leave him vulnerable to this accusation: he had gone so close to the line separating the legal from the illegal that he violated the spirit if not the letter of the law. As a result, Dad's job was to maximize the reduction of his taxes while minimizing the political risk.

This was not an easy thing to carry off, in large part because it seemed almost unnatural to my father. When at the peak of his powers—and he stayed there for a long time—Dad was highly creative and very aggressive. His clients admired those skills and were more than willing to do whatever they could to lower their payments as close as they could to the bare legal minimum. Because they trusted his genius and wanted to keep more of their money, they encouraged him to risk new strategies. Lyndon Johnson was a long way from being the most daring of the clients Dad, Agger, and Cohen regularly counseled. Political considerations made him more conservative than many. Not foolishly conservative, of course: LBJ wasn't interested in filling out Form 1040EZ and its equivalent for corporate taxation. For that, the advice of a first-year law student would have sufficed. What he wanted was as much money as he could legitimately wrest from the clutches of the federal government consonant with political prudence. He never found anyone better at this than Waddy Bullion, Carolyn Agger, and Sheldon Cohen.

★ ★ ★

Of course, anyone who spent time around LBJ swiftly concluded he was *sui generis*; after all, the man himself worked tirelessly to convince others he was one of a kind while they were closer to the norm. My father believed that the characteristic that most separated Lyndon Johnson from the mass of humanity was his amazing ability at one-on-one persuasion. Without question, when LBJ sat down face-to-face with someone and pulled out all the stops as he made his points, he was the best Dad had ever seen. That's saying something. Dad worked with and against some of the best lawyers in the nation, and his clients included some of the most forceful and articulate people in the business community. Moreover, my father himself was what the English call a "dab hand" at such matters. His tribute to Johnson was the expert and unforced acknowledgment by a master of the trade to the superior abilities of a genius at persuading an audience of one.

That Dad would believe this will astonish no one. The "Johnson treatment" was famous during the 1950s, and became even more widely known during the boom times of his presidency. Most accounts I've read emphasize LBJ's skilled use of nonverbal advantages. He was, as I've observed, big. He knew, as I've also said, how to use body language to move people to where he wanted them, whether in a line of handshakers at Brady or, I'm sure, seated in office chairs. He exuded masculine power. And, according to many observers, he underscored his arguments and presence by physically touching, grasping, jabbing, pointing, squeezing, and invading the personal space of those he worked on.

I have no doubt LBJ used all of these tactics. When I was with him for three days in December 1965, I was keenly aware of his powerful frame and how he employed it in close encounters. I can also testify to how expressive his features were and how they could convey in a split second disgust and contempt. His voice was a weapon in and of itself. By changing the inflection on words only slightly, he could change the most innocent of sentiments into vicious sarcasm. It's easy for me to see how one-on-one persuasion in his hands could swiftly become full-court bullying.

My father didn't experience any of this. What most struck Dad when he and Johnson were together alone was LBJ's intelligence. Johnson was, to borrow a Texanism, "whip smart." His mind coiled effectively and tightly around the target of his analysis, and his arguments exploded with an impressive crack! and concluded with a lethal sting. In over half a century of practicing law, Dad never met anyone smarter or quicker than Lyndon Johnson. Few even approached him in either raw intelligence or the capacity to apply it to different situations. LBJ never had to clarify for my father a first statement of his thoughts, concerns, and questions. Nor did he ever need a second explanation of Dad's advice and the rationales behind it. When it came to business, he was disciplined, focused, and very bright. To Dad, these attributes were what made him a master of one-on-one persuasion.

★ ★ ★

What did LBJ think about those in the boat? Dad has no pat, short answer. He approaches the question in a roundabout way.

Without question, Lyndon Johnson could be a charming, witty man whenever he chose. This happened often enough over the years, during time spent relaxing with drinks, food, and talk when the business at hand was tended to, for my father to grow to like him very much. And the reverse was true as well. Dad loves hearing and telling good stories; he is a receptive audience and an entertaining guest. In short, he's good company as well as an excellent attorney. LBJ came to appreciate that and enjoy the casual conversations they had together. But Dad never lost sight of the fact that Lyndon Johnson's attachment to him and the others in the boat was not very close. LBJ maintained a wide degree of remoteness from those who worked for him. He never permitted personal feelings to have an effect on his assessment of an individual's performance or his judgment on retention of that person in the crew. Sweet words, warm hugs, high praise, and unexpected gifts did not conceal from my father (or, I'd guess, anyone else) the cold, dispassionate ruthlessness that determined Lyndon Johnson's reactions to people. The best illustration of this characteristic was LBJ's relationship with his cook, Zephyr Wright.

More often than not, when LBJ consulted with Dad in Austin or at the ranch, he invited him to lunch or dinner. My father looked forward to these occasions, because Wright was one of the finest cooks he'd ever known. That she specialized in down-home cuisine was an extra pleasure. Dad loved the food his mother had prepared—fried chicken, pot roast, blackeyed peas with salt pork, red beans, mashed potatoes, turnip and mustard greens, okra and tomatoes, and Kentucky Wonder green beans—and he was overjoyed by Wright's mastery of these dishes. When she brought her meals to the table, Dad always complimented her highly. He sang her praises, ate multiple helpings, and

Zephyr Wright and Luci Johnson, September 8, 1965.
LBJ Library. Photo by Donald Stoderl.

asked for recipes. When he had the chance, he'd discuss cooking with her. "How did you do this? What seasonings did you use? Where did you learn this dish? My mother did such-and-such this way" were the sort of questions and comments he'd pepper her with.

Dad admired Wright as much as he did her cooking. She worked hard, thought carefully about what she was doing, had a wry sense of humor and a powerfully dignified manner. In these ways, as well as her genius in the kitchen, she reminded him of his mother. He thought they were women of similar character, talent, morality, and goodness.

Dad did not believe her employer judged her in the same way. When Lyndon Johnson looked at Zephyr Wright, he saw an excellent cook, nothing more, nothing less. She'd earned her way onto the boat, and she'd stay in the galley as long as she continued to do her job well. That she was an African American was of no significance. Nor was the strength of her character of much consequence. She was an employee, period. He was polite to her, he praised her food, and he might tease in passing about how she was to blame for his gaining weight. Still, Dad felt his mind and his attention were elsewhere.

This reaction interested my father. During the 1940s and 1950s, Dad represented a number of clients and worked with a few attorneys who employed African Americans as domestic workers. Most were women who cooked, cleaned, and cared for the kids; some were men who labored as butlers, valets, chauffeurs, and all-purpose major-domos. From both personal observation and casual talk with clients and colleagues, Dad concluded that many white employers conferred upon their black "help" special positions in their lives. This did not mean they did not share the racist stereotypes of their day. To the contrary. Almost all of my father's acquaintances were as convinced as the most prejudiced rednecks that blacks were intellectually inferior. Where they parted company with less-sophisticated bigots were their perceptions of African Americans' relationships with whites. In their opinion, blacks watched whites closely, reacted to their behavior quickly, and manipulated them shrewdly. They were certain African Americans were observant and intelligent enough to formulate general and specific guidelines for effective reactions to people and events. This talent, their bosses were convinced, had proven to be highly practical and useful for blacks. It could be equally practical and useful for their employers. Once they were persuaded they could rely on the judgment and trust the discretion of African Americans in their households, many whites Dad knew began to bare hopes and reveal fears to their domestic workers. They also invited advice and comments on their opportunities and predicaments and listened closely to the replies. Moreover, when the spirit moved them, they were not reluctant to praise their black confidantes' wisdom to other whites.

Those familiar with the role Mammy played in the book and movie *Gone With the Wind*, or with modern parodies of it, in the dealings between Chef and the kids in the cartoon series *South Park*, or in the adventures of Riddley Walker at Zenith House in Stephen King's Internet novel *The Plant* will recognize this relationship. Indeed, it was so glorified in *Gone With the Wind* during the thirties that the portrayals on pages and screen may have served as a prototype, inspiring the *nouveau riche* generation that followed to try to duplicate it in their homes. LBJ had right before him patterns of intimate relationships between white employers and black cooks and butlers he could have followed. No one would have been surprised or looked askance if this had occurred. But it was clear to Dad that Johnson thought of Zephyr

Wright as simply another of his employees. She cooked well, and she had a good job. To keep the job, she had to keep on cooking well. It was as plain as that.

Recently, I asked my father if Johnson's indifference to Wright's race and his determination to have only a businesslike connection with her revealed that he rejected the prevailing racism of whites in those days. Dad replied, "If you mean by 'rejected' that LBJ refused to judge people by the color of their skin, you're right. He didn't care about that. And," Dad went on, "I never saw any signs from him toward her of the self-serving paternalism white employers could adopt from their notions about the roles of masters and mammys." Then he repeated his belief that the relationship between Johnson and Wright was entirely straightforward, employer and employee. That was Dad's point. Zephyr Wright was in the boat, and that mattered more than her character or her color. Either she did the job, or she got out. Any other consideration was essentially inconsequential to LBJ.

Dad concluded by saying, "Imagine LBJ telling a story about how an employee was really wiser than he was. Or allowing an employee completely into his confidence on everything he did. That just wouldn't happen."

It wouldn't happen because he was captain of the boat. He judged all people in that boat equally as his inferiors, whether they were externally similar to him or obviously different. Of course, when he became president his colorblindness served him and the nation well. What helped nurture it, his arrogance and ambition, were irrelevant insofar as the common weal was concerned. For those in the boat, though, what lay at the root of his comparative freedom from prejudice could have unfortunate consequences. They had his support and attention only so long as they were useful. LBJ weighed them in terms of their present worth and future potential. From other aspects of their personalities, he kept himself coolly aloof at best, icily remote at worst.

What did LBJ expect his crew would gain from their labors for him? Obviously, he offered the excitement and satisfaction of meaningful work. It's also fair to say he expected they would learn things and meet people that would help them succeed, whether they stayed in the boat all their lives or left it voluntarily.

Saying this raises the question of what Lyndon Johnson meant by "success." No one can doubt that he defined success for himself as attaining the very pinnacle of political power in the United States. That ambition was as apparent to his contemporaries as it is to the historians who study him today. Along the way to the top, to succeed meant to control as much as possible the environments he operated in, both human and institutional. Certainly, part of his definition of success was personal wealth, which would provide security for his family and a firm base for his own activities. Above all else, success meant he would excel at everything he turned his hand to.

"Success" for his staff, "success" for his friends, had a different meaning. Waddy Bullion never doubted that LBJ wanted his friends to "do well." But, he added to me, "I'm not certain he wanted them to excel."

"So what?" was my first response. Although few of us like to confess it, we aren't necessarily overjoyed when a member of our family or someone who works with or for us succeeds beyond not only all expectation, but, especially, beyond our *own* performance. That's why, as Jesus once observed, prophets are without honor in their own country. Too many remember when our fellows were the carpenter's kids, and suspect that the new eminence may be undeserved, the result of pure luck. But when I pointed this out to Dad, he replied he was thinking of something else. When he began working for Johnson in the late forties, he didn't wonder if LBJ envied his friends' excellence after they attained it. He was concerned that Johnson didn't want them to excel *before* the event. Such being the case, would he take steps to thwart their rise to prominence?

Dad was never sure about this. This uncertainty still troubles him now, years after Lyndon Johnson's death. Back then, when they were in the boat together, he felt threatened.

No question, LBJ did not begrudge his people earning enough to secure their families' future. Any sensible man would want that for friends and co-workers. Johnson was not one of those people who perversely delight in the setbacks of those closest to them. Although he was gleeful at the defeats of his political opponents, Dad usually heard only sympathetic words from him about the personal misfortunes of those who worked with him. Indeed, he was generally willing to offer them advice and assistance.

Nor did LBJ want his friends merely to get by. My father believed he wanted them to do better than such a modest, though real, achievement. He was happy when they were comfortable. Not just for their sakes; after all, success could be portrayed to others as the result of his patronage and power. When those outside the boat perceived this, they'd want in it.

But for Lyndon Johnson's people to *excel* meant they might be exceeding his record in some arena of competition. That was so repellant to him that he even balked at calling Zephyr Wright what she was—a great cook. As far as Dad could observe, LBJ had no interest whatsoever in the craft and art of cooking. He never saw Johnson spend a moment salting and spicing or basting and tasting, pastimes my father deeply enjoyed. Still, at this stage of his career, he could not even concede another's greatness in an activity he never participated in. This did not bode well for those who gave him advice on subjects he had a keen personal interest in, namely enhancing his wealth without jeopardizing his career.

This revelation led Dad directly to another insight. The best way LBJ could win in his contests, the most foolproof way he could insure others would not excel, was to keep his people dependant on him and therefore under his control. Of course, you could fight this simply by quitting the job and leaving his employ. That wasn't easy to do. It was impossible if you wanted to keep reaping the benefits of association with Lyndon Johnson.

The trick, my father decided, was to be able to go along on, get off of, and return to the voyage when you chose. He would have to be in the boat, but not of the boat. Fortunately, he knew how to do this.

CHAPTER 6

Free Advice

Seizing the opportunities that shipping out with Lyndon Johnson offered did not come without a price. It could be a fearsomely expensive one, too. LBJ demanded levels of commitment and loyalty far beyond the ordinary.

To illustrate this as unforgettably as possible, he once told my father he wanted men so loyal that they'd be willing to kiss his ass in Garfinkel's window at noon and say that it smelled like roses. Dad never told me what response he made to what appeared to be an invitation to stand among the mannequins at the most fashionable Washington department store and do his duty. Perhaps LBJ didn't expect any answer. Certainly he seemed surprised when an employee at the family's Austin radio station, KTBC, did comment on a similar Johnsonian portrayal of loyal behavior.

LBJ did not substitute Scarborough's for Garfinkel's, as he was wont to do with other people in different cities (Macy's in New York; Neiman-Marcus in Dallas; and so on). Instead, when Jack Gwyn agreed that loyalty was very important, and if you hired a man, he owed you eight hours a day, Johnson replied that he had in mind the *"real loyalty"* of John Connally. He'd work the eight hours, then come right over at midnight and shine shoes if LBJ asked him to do that. Gwyn boldly responded, "Congressman, if anyone called me at midnight and told me to come over and shine his shoes, I'd tell him to go fuck himself." According to Gwyn, Johnson quickly said he was speaking metaphorically and wouldn't really ask anyone to do that. Unpersuaded by this swift backpeddling, Gwyn left KTBC soon afterwards. Much later, he explained his decision to Robert Caro by saying Lyndon Johnson didn't want loyalty as it was usually understood, but instead "a kind of total submission." If he had stayed at KTBC, continued Gwyn, he would have been required to become the sort of "shining" ideal John Connally was supposed to be.

My father avoided the trap, too. Not as did Jack Gwyn, by cutting himself off from LBJ. Dad not only stayed on board the boat, he flourished on it, rapidly becoming one of the most important and trusted members of the crew. He did this without performing at Garfinkel's or responding to late-night commands for cordovan polish. Now, my father is modest about this achievement. He'd be the first to tell you he avoided these fates because his relationship with Lyndon Johnson was different in important ways from the ones others in the boat had with their captain. That's the truth, as you'll see. But I'm not going to let his modesty mislead you into underrating what he accomplished. Dad figured out a way to reap the full benefits of working for LBJ without compromising his independence. Only someone with a keen and discerning intelligence could have devised this plan. Only someone with a confident and determined self-discipline could have executed it.

The first advantage Dad had in dealing with LBJ was his lack of any personal political ambitions. Being a congressman's, a senator's, or even a president's aide had no attraction to him. When Johnson asked him why, he simply said such jobs didn't pay enough. The truth of this LBJ had to concede, especially when my father pointed out that he had two children to educate. Beneath this economic argument, though, lay another significant one. Dad has never been interested in either the processes or the results of politics and legislating. Although he's given money to campaigns, he's never licked a stamp, made a phone call, or rung a doorbell for anyone. Nor was he ever ambitious to write laws or right wrongs by amending statutes. Important changes have been made in the Tax Code of the United States because of his efforts, but that's owing to the loopholes he either found by painstaking research or created by skilful argument, which in turn the Revenuers had to plug. Lyndon Johnson had considerable purchase on the hearts of men who were already fascinated by politics and government, or who developed a taste for those enterprises. He had no such foothold with my father.

Second, much in politics offended Dad's ethics. The bedrock his Southern Baptist faith rests on is the assurance that once God saves a sinner, that person is always saved. If the Lord can bind Himself so completely and eternally to those who cannot resist temptation and do not deserve such fidelity and commitment, then it behooves men and women in their lives to try their hardest to honor their agreements, no matter what. Just as Pop did, my father applied this principle to secular as well as spiritual obligations. Those whom Dad has respected most in his law practice have been people who have scrupulously kept their word. Put into the language of the marketplace, this ethic holds: a deal is a deal. He's often stated his admiration for Dallas contractors who suffered bankruptcy because they could not meet their contractual obligations, but once they were on their feet again fulfilled those original contracts to the letter, even though they were not legally bound to do so and lost money in the process. With equal frequency, he's expressed scorn for national, state, and local politicians who have been eager to befriend businessmen when they are trying to raise money for campaigns, then refuse to listen to or help out the same people after the election. In Dad's experience, that has happened too often for it to be merely the ingratitude of some individual politicians. The shifting allegiances of politics, the flip-flopping on issues, the welshing on promises, the readiness to cast aside or even attack friends, have always seemed suspect to him. Finally, my father was wary of the dangers posed by graft, even of the so-called "honest" variety. Throughout his career, he avoided representing local politicians who ran into tax problems as they skimmed the cream off the top of county contracts. None of this is to say he didn't like Lyndon Johnson personally or respect his abilities and accomplishments as a politician. He did both. As he told me recently, he was always impressed by Lyndon Johnson's intelligence and talent and admired his determination and his devotion to duty. "But," added Dad, "I looked askance at some of his methodology." The meaning of this caveat is clear: when politicians put the immediately expedient over the eternally moral, their ethical standards were not his.

Third, Dad did not owe his job to any influence of or intervention by Lyndon Johnson, even though his work for LBJ played an indirect but crucial role in his receiving an offer from Thompson, Knight, Wright, & Simmons. One of the young attorneys *cum* naval officers who worked with my father for Johnson on the Naval Affairs subcommittee was a man named Irving Goldberg. A Texan by birth, Goldberg had navigated his way from Port Arthur, a Gulf Coast town, to the Harvard Law School, and then to a commission. Probably because he managed the rare feat of combining in his mind and spirit the best of Texas and Harvard, the two became fast friends. After the war, they stayed in touch, Dad from Philadelphia, Irving from Dallas. When both of Thompson, Knight's tax attorneys resigned in a dispute over their share of the profits, one of the firm's partners asked Goldberg if he knew any bright young men specializing in tax law who might be interested in taking their place. Irving was aware my parents disliked Philadelphia and wanted to return to Texas. He recommended my father enthusiastically.

This decision had important implications for my father's relationship with LBJ, and not merely because that powerful man had nothing to do with his getting this chance. *How* he got this job was very important, to be sure. But *where* the job was—in Dallas—was significant, too.

Location was the fourth factor in Dad's retaining his independence from Lyndon Johnson.

My father and mother left the East Coast in 1947 and moved to Dallas. If Robert Caro is correct in saying that pre-1948 are the Texas years of LBJ's career and post-1948 are the Washington years—and I think this is as good a division of his life as any in terms of his major focus of attention—then the Bullions left the immediate vicinity of the Johnsons at crucial stages of the two men's careers. The distance between Dallas and the District of Columbia was much greater then. With no interstates, driving time was twice as long. Without jet planes, flights took substantially longer. In pre-area code days, long distance telephone calls were more difficult to place and much more expensive to pay for. Copiers and fax machines were unheard of; computers were the stuff of science fiction. There was no question of a midnight call for shoe shines. Distance prevented the small, nagging, cumulative contacts, requests, favors, and orders that cemented his boys to Johnson. To return to my father's nautical metaphor: he wasn't on the boat all the time, just occasionally, and then only for short cruises.

Finally, how Dad regarded making money and doing work was very crucial to his success at keeping LBJ at arms length. Doing well economically was extremely important to my father. In this, as in other things, he was typical of Texans raised during hard times. He knew what it was like not to have money. Having it was much better. This was the case for many reasons, not just what it could buy and the security it provided.

Before I married in 1976, as I was listing my intended's virtues for him, I joked that in addition to all Laura's other qualities, she was paid more than I was. This fact immediately perturbed him. "That has to change," he said. "No man wants his wife making more than he does. I was terribly unhappy," he confessed, "when I was in the Navy and your mother made more than I did by working at Agriculture." I teased him by saying, "You should have lived on a boat in the Tidal Basin. You could have gotten sea pay, just like the admiral did." Then I added, "As for me, well, I hope her salary keeps on rising faster than mine." He was not amused. It was one of those occasions when two generations suddenly and unexpectedly realize there is a space separating them, a gap created not by ideology or personality, but by culture and personal history. To be a real man, Dad had to be the sole breadwinner, the person who worked and brought his family first into economic security and then prosperity. The strong sense that this was his duty had been imprinted on his heart and mind. A career with Lyndon Johnson would not pay enough to allow him to meet that challenge.

Aside from the wages, my father also had no illusions about what working for LBJ would be like. Not only was he familiar with The Man, he had already worked for a demanding, unforgiving boss with a domineering personality and the habit of rigidly controlling his subordinates' lives. To be sure, he never regretted the three years he spent on Ernest J. King's staff. But that was wartime. Dad's country and his loved ones were in peril, and serving the admiral was therefore a duty and an honor. In peacetime, it would have been sheer hell. I'm positive the chief reasons my father declined the commission King offered him in late 1945 as a lieutenant commander in the Naval Reserve were his desires to stop being the admiral's boy and to get on with his own life. What could happen if he became entangled with the senator from Texas? He well might become Lyndon's boy, not Waddy Bullion.

Money was an absolute necessity, a positive good. Still, it had to be accumulated in ways that preserved Dad's ethics and independence. Otherwise, the pursuit of profit would lead him into great jeopardy. Although Dad never practiced much criminal tax law or tried many cases where the Revenuers were attempting to toss people into jail as well as take their money, he certainly was familiar with how greed and arrogance mixed could put people on the wrong side of bars. Even when somebody behaves in conformity with the law's letter, the power of anticipated riches can addle the shrewdest mind and plunge the strongest-willed people into situations they are helpless to extract themselves from. Sometimes, people have to resist the lure of easy money. Sometimes, they have to have the confidence in themselves to believe other, better chances will come along in due course.

Well before Dad became one of the most prominent attorneys practicing oil and gas tax law in Dallas, in Texas, and in the United States and Canada, he had confidence in his own abilities and in the future expansion of that area of law. Therefore he had the courage to act on the wisdom of this perception: There were some bills he shouldn't send, even though he had done first-class work and given excellent advice.

Dad never charged Lyndon Johnson a fee.

★ ★ ★

What this meant is best illustrated by a story Mother told me. She did not understand its significance, as we shall see. Rather, she intended it as a cautionary tale about the perils of alcohol, which it certainly is as well.

Dad was going to Washington on business and had arranged to do some things for LBJ while he was in town. Before he left Dallas, he met with Walter Jenkins, Johnson's right-hand man. Once they discussed the next day's agenda, the two men, who had known and liked each other since 1940, began an extended cocktail hour at Love Field, Dallas's airport. The plane left early in the evening, with a scheduled arrival at National Airport late around midnight. Already well fortified with scotch and certain they had no more work to do until morning, Dad and Walter took the precaution of filling flasks with more whiskey, the better to pass the four hours it then took to fly from Dallas to Washington. As often happens, the border dividing mellow sipping and witty storytelling from outright drunkenness and slurred, repetitive speech was crossed easily and—at least to the two participants—imperceptibly. By the time the plane landed, the friends had to support each other down the stairway, across the tarmac, and into the terminal. They weaved their way toward the baggage claim area. Suddenly, Dad felt his friend lurch to a stop and try to stand up straight. Then he saw what Walter saw. Striding briskly toward them through the terminal was the Majority Leader of the United States Senate.

LBJ was smiling, with hand outstretched. The smile vanished and the hand clenched when he got close. "God Dammit!" Johnson bellowed. "You boys are drunk! I want you to get right to work, and you're too drunk to stand up or see straight. What in the God damn hell were you thinking? How am I going to get any God damn work out of you? You God damn better sober up pretty damn fast."

LBJ's rage and his voice filled the corridor. The marble walls, ceilings, and floor echoed with his anger. The apologies a stuttering, shuddering Walter was trying to stammer out were completely drowned out. Passersby fell silent, too, and moved slowly and cautiously, lest they draw his attention and wrath onto them. Finally,

LBJ with Walter Jenkins, December 1959.
LBJ Library. Photo by Frank Muto.

Johnson paused for breath after snapping, "What do you have to say for yourselves, dammit!"

Dad looked at him, drew himself up to his full height, grasped his briefcase and the bag that a wary porter had brought up, and said, "You're right. I am drunk. In fact, I am so drunk that I cannot work this evening. I will not work tonight. Let me remind you that our meeting is scheduled for nine tomorrow morning. I will be there, and I will be ready to go to work for you then. Good night." With that, my father turned away and went out the door to the taxi stand.

He left behind a speechless Lyndon Johnson. Mother did not know what torments Walter Jenkins went through when LBJ regained his tongue and reminded Walter that he was paying him to be sober, ready, and willing whenever that was required. Dad, if he ever heard, never said. All he reported was that the next day it was business as usual, he was Waddy and the senator was Lyndon as always, and nothing more was said about the aborted effort to pick up my father at midnight and have him give legal advice.

The benefits of working with LBJ under these conditions went far beyond the minor ones Mother scornfully referred to as expedited passports for desperate clients and, for that matter, interesting summer employment for me in Yosemite. "I got plenty of business out of working for LBJ," Dad said. "After all, I didn't keep it a secret. I made sure people knew I was a tax attorney for the Senate Majority Leader." So did Thompson, Knight. The firm was more than willing for one of its rising stars to contribute his time *gratis* to LBJ. Its partners raised no objections to this, or to assigning junior associates to help Dad with research and secretaries to type memoranda, contracts, and affidavits. The upside of these eleemosynary services, in terms of the firm's and Dad's burgeoning reputations and the additional clients that resulted, more than made up for their expense. Indeed, as recently as 1998, the firm was still boasting of Dad's association with LBJ. T-shirts given to those students fresh out of law school whom Thompson & Knight hoped to recruit had this fact emblazoned on them.

I'm certain people occasionally expected LBJ to open doors for them in Washington. I know what my father's response was, from the stories he's told me about managing relationships with other Very Important Persons. Dad was willing to make the introductions, but past that point clients and partners had to present their own arguments to those they were trying to persuade. He would not serve as supplicant, advocate, or middleman in these negotiations. In this way, he guarded his independence in matters political. If he acted this way when dealing with VIPs with much less power and far weaker cravings for total domination than Lyndon Johnson, clearly he took particular care in approaching The Man. My father didn't mind pulling strings to get passports within a week for the forgetful about to go on vacation in Europe, or to find me a summer job. Beyond those comparatively small favors, he wouldn't go. He did nothing that might make him beholden to LBJ and place him within that grasp.

Their arrangement served both Waddy and Lyndon well from 1940 until Johnson's death in 1973. When he introduced my father to foreign dignitaries, LBJ never failed to smile and say, "This fella has worked for me for many years, and never sent me a bill!" One of my favorite photographs of the president and Dad captured the two men smiling, while

Johnson said this to a somewhat puzzled-looking Shah of Iran. Only once did Dad consider changing this arrangement. In early 1967, he swore to me that when LBJ left the White House, he God damn sure would start paying. But this never happened. My father thought better of it. I'll discuss why when the story reaches the final years of Johnson's life.

LBJ, the Shah of Iran, and Waddy and Wilma Bullion, June 11, 1968.
LBJ Library. Photo by Yoichi R. Okamoto.

★ ★ ★

When I asked Dad about the nature of his relationship with Lyndon Johnson, he quickly said, "I counted him as a friend of mine." Then he paused and slowly added, "I wanted him to count me as a friend of his." Despite that poignant uncertainty, I believe Waddy Bullion was one of the few men Lyndon Johnson regarded as his friend.

Ironically, however, the friendship between these two men points to one of the tragedies of LBJ's life. Lacking a firm sense of ethical or moral behavior in his world, bereft as far as I can tell of any assurance of salvation, determined to succeed beyond the dreams of most, certain that success depended on dominating others, he would not apply to his own life the lesson of friendship held out by my father. It wasn't necessary to reduce those around him to total submission to gain their respect and compel their commitment to hard work in the common cause. Making friends were not signs of weakness. Nor did being friends create commitments that always restricted freedom of action when circumstances required it. You could be a friend and still retain your independence. What Waddy Bullion did for him should have demonstrated all this to him.

Yet LBJ could not bring himself while he was still pursuing and amassing political power to say clearly and unambiguously, "Waddy, I count you as one of my friends." His inability to say those words to Dad is revealing. He couldn't believe he didn't need to always dominate. He didn't understand that friendship could accomplish wonders too. Among those wonders was telling him to fuck himself when that was the right thing to say, or reminding him that the meeting was scheduled for the morning, not midnight, when he wanted the impossible. Few, if any, in the boat could do that. Their automatic assent to his moods and perceptions endangered Lyndon Johnson before he reached the White House. Once in the Oval Office, where it is difficult for anyone to oppose the prevailing wisdom or the wishes of the president, the dangers were doubled.

CHAPTER 7

Buying Land

Although Dad worked closely with Lyndon Johnson on his personal and corporate taxes during the 1950s, the two rarely discussed the tax advantages of some types of investments over others. Many clients preferred to consult with Dad before they paid their money and took their chances; LBJ did not. He did not want my father advising him on overall investment strategies. He intended to choose where he'd put his money himself. Waddy Bullion would tell him how to reduce his obligations to the Internal Revenue Service and the State of Texas *after* he made his choices.

No doubt there were several reasons for this. A major one, I suspect, was LBJ's determination to avoid investing in oil and gas companies. What inspired this decision was politics, pure and simple. Making money off of oil would hardly damage Johnson in Texas elections. Lone Star voters would not be surprised to learn that anyone aspiring to office had stock in both major and independent companies, held oil leases on tracts of land, or lent money and influence directly to operators who were drilling wells in new locations. Candidates could, and did, say that they were investing in the state's major industry and ask what was wrong with that. "Plenty!" a few liberals and other cranks would answer, but the majority of voters simply shrugged. In national politics, however, the naysayers were in far greater numbers and wielded considerably more clout. By and large, they didn't begrudge too much Johnson's efforts in the Senate to defend oil and gas interests. He was, after all, a senator from Texas, and had to help important economic interests in his state, no matter how tarnished their reputation. But personally profiting from investments in oil would seriously damage his presidential aspirations. So LBJ stayed away from buying stock or speculating in leases and wildcat enterprises in this industry.

In contrast, most of Dad's investments were in oil and gas companies. Because he represented most of the majors when they required help in state and federal tax litigation, and because he was on retainer to many of the independent companies who looked for oil from the Arctic Circle to Venezuela, he could assess with an expert's eye their prospects for the future. Most important from his perspective, he had done business with the CEOs and upper-level managerial staffs of corporations large and small. It was the perfect opportunity to assess the ability and energy of those directing exploration and exploitation of oil and gas resources, and then reach judgment on who were the best to bet on. Dad took advantage of his knowledge of the companies and the men when he had money to invest. Or he tried to. Sad to say, he never made what oilmen called "a big strike." Although more scientific than they once were, exploration and drilling still contain a large element of chance. Markets for oil and gas can be highly volatile as well. More have gone bust than have boomed. Because of Dad's ability to pick shrewd, hardworking individuals, he profited more often than he lost. His luck never boomed, though.

Had Lyndon Johnson been interested in investing in oil and gas operations, he would have been constantly picking my father's brain about the men and the companies. It's just as well he steered clear of oil and gas. I don't think he would have been happy with my father's suggestions. Modest, consistent success was not what he wanted. Nor was he inclined to shrug off losses as bad luck. Someone would be to blame. That person would have been Dad. There's no telling how that would have affected their relationship. But, of course, Johnson stayed far away from such investments. Thus he and Dad had little to talk about regarding investment strategies.

The major focus of the Johnson family's investments was the Texas Broadcasting Corporation, the corporation they established that owned and operated their radio and television stations in Austin and controlled the shares they held in other stations elsewhere in Texas. Dad did not advise them on these purchases. During the 1950s, he had little expertise in communications and almost no contacts within that burgeoning Texas industry. Besides, the Johnsons had already found an adviser with both advantages — Don Thomas, a senior partner in the Austin law firm of Clark, Thomas.

LBJ began consulting with Thomas at the beginning of the fifties, which meant he was a comparative Johnny-come-lately on the boat. No matter, his amazing string of unbroken successes in predicting which way the communications market would go recommended him to the Johnsons. He advised them on their heavy investments in the industry and swiftly established himself as the person who knew the most about the family's private business interests. My father enjoyed working with Don immensely. He was highly intelligent, exceptionally well informed, quick to grasp the essentials of a problem, and imaginative in finding solutions to it. At times, such people can be difficult colleagues to work with. Don Thomas was the rare soul who complemented first-rate professional abilities with a pleasant, quiet, self-effacing personality. If he had a passion, it was his determination to remain behind the scenes and out of the public's eye. Others could take the bows; Thomas's satisfaction came from knowing that those who he respected admired his brilliance. To Dad, he was the ideal teammate. For Lyndon Johnson, he became that rarest of birds, a personal friend. "No one," Dad told me recently, "was closer personally than Don to LBJ, except, of course, Lady Bird." Then he looked directly at me, and repeated with an intense emphasis: "*No one.*"

It surprises my father that those who have written about LBJ have consistently failed to recognize what a significant role Don Thomas played in the Johnsons' lives. "Sure," he says, "Don was very unassuming and tried to stay out of the limelight. Still, his influence as friend and adviser ought to be obvious to anybody who knows much about Lyndon Johnson." I know why contemporaries and historians overlooked Thomas's contributions. They don't believe he deserved much credit for the success of the Texas Broadcasting Corporation. That success, they argued, was due to LBJ. More specifically, it came about not as the result of Johnson's business acumen, but as the inevitable outcome of his position as the most powerful man in the Senate.

Whether Johnson pulled strings at the Federal Communications Commission to get favorable rulings on requests for licenses was the subject of much speculation in the 1950s and 1960s. The FCC's decision to keep KTBC the only VHF television station in Austin well past the time it would be reasonable to expect that other licenses would be granted inspired the *New York Times* and the *Wall Street Journal* to assign reporters to investigate that issue. To this day, no one has uncovered conclusive evidence of interference by LBJ in the usual

LBJ, Lady Bird Johnson, and Don Thomas look
at art in the LBJ hangar, December 30, 1966.
LBJ Library. Photo by Robert Knudsen.

administrative processes at the FCC. Johnson also ostentatiously refused to participate in any senatorial debates on communications policy or to vote on any pending legislation.

Despite the absence of any smoking gun, few observers at the time and none of his biographers credited LBJ with scrupulous ethics in the matter of the FCC and KTBC. Instead, they assumed that he covered his tracks very well. My feeling is he didn't need to do very much. Those at the FCC knew who he was and what he was like. They could also predict what he wanted. The rest followed naturally, unprompted by the beneficiary. Still, these dealings had the distinctive aura of the sort of "honest graft" that my father avoided throughout his professional career. He lacked both the expertise and the inclination to make the obvious even plainer to the FCC. Probably for both reasons, Johnson kept him out of the loop when investment decisions had to be made about radio and television stations.

Once the stations were acquired, the licenses granted, and the monopoly secured for the immediate future, Dad had no problems with helping Don Thomas devise strategies to help LBJ reduce the taxes on his property. Although the bulk of Dad's practice dealt with oil and gas taxation, he was equally well thought of as an adviser on other types of corporate taxes and on individuals' estate planning. For instance, he helped work on Texas Instruments' taxes until he retired. Even after his retirement, he remained Erik Jonsson's personal tax attorney. Lyndon Johnson and the Texas Broadcasting Company benefited just as TI and Jonsson did from his energy and insights.

The details of Dad's activities in this area remain privileged. One particularly important piece of information regarding them is in the public record, however, which permitted my father to discuss a general strategy guiding certain investments. I can supplement this with what I know about similar arrangements made by the Bullion family during the 1960s and 1970s. The one type of investment Dad and Lyndon Johnson had in common was land.

★ ★ ★

Johnson began thinking about acquiring ranch land in Texas's Hill Country during the late 1940s. He focused his attention on acreage between the tiny crossroads towns of Hye and Stonewall in Gillespie County, near where he was born and lived until he was five. What particularly caught his eye was a 243-acre spread known locally as the Martin Ranch.

The Martins had owned this land since around 1900. While Lyndon was still a boy, Clarence Martin, the heir to the place, married Sam Ealy Johnson's sister Frank. Uncle Clarence and Aunt Frank worked the place for years. When they began feeling the effects of a hard life on aging bodies during the mid-1930s, the two asked their son Tom and his wife Lela to leave California, live on the ranch, and take care of them. In return, after both of the elder Martins died, Tom and Lela would inherit the property. This arrangement was agreeable to both parties. For some reason, Tom and Lela did not return to the ranch until 1940, four years after Clarence died. Once there, they fulfilled their part of the bargain. They ranched and looked after Aunt Frank. Unfortunately, Tom himself died in 1948. Within a year, Johnson's aunt went to court to break the agreement with Lela Martin.

The surviving records don't describe what inspired this litigation. The best guess is LBJ promised Aunt Frank an annual annuity plus the

LBJ on the ranch, Christmas 1953 or 1954.
LBJ Library. Photo by unknown.

use of the house the Johnsons had owned for years in Johnson City for the remainder of her life. In return, she'd sell the ranch to him. To persuade Lela to go along, he was willing to pay some compensation for her loss of the land. When she refused, Aunt Frank took her daughter-in-law to court. A decision in favor of Frank Johnson Martin was rendered in 1951. Soon afterwards, her nephew bought the ranch.

Why did Lyndon Johnson decide to buy a ranch? Why did he want to buy the Martin place?

Buying ranch land and building large houses on it were things wealthy and powerful Texans tended to do after the Second World War. Most of them came from rural backgrounds, so it's entirely possible that the idea of returning to their roots was appealing. More precisely, returning *in triumph* was attractive. The houses they built were considerably larger than typical ranch houses were. They also boasted more creature comforts and were clearly constructed with an eye toward frequent and large-scale entertaining. There's every reason to believe Johnson shared these feelings. I'll describe the house they built in the early fifties on their new property later; for now, suffice it to say its dimensions and amenities fit what I've just said. And it's no accident, I think, that LBJ wanted to own a ranch close to where he grew up. He knew the neighbors and loved the country. He could also have the undeniable pleasure of re-establishing his family as property owners in Gillespie County. Some might even say that he could take pride in besting his father's record. Sam lost his land; Lyndon could buy ranches.

Ranches: there's a crucial word. Why didn't Johnson and other prominent Texans simply buy enough land to build an attractive country place, where they could escape from the pressures of the city and their careers, and still have room to entertain when it suited their fancies? Why become involved in the business of cattle raising and stock farming?

One reason is straightforward. Those who put ranch land on the market do not want to sell their property in bits and pieces. Unless the seller is desperate, that causes more trouble than it's worth. It leaves the owner stuck with the least attractive and less marketable tracts. All or nothing is the prevailing rule in rural real estate transactions.

Once someone owns a ranch, letting the pastures remain ungrazed and the fields unplowed are not realistic options. Brush grows swiftly. Weeds choke out grass. Ungrazed foliage and groundcover create hazardous fire conditions. And the market value of the land visibly and rapidly declines. That does not, however, discourage the county tax assessor and collector. Land that is only being used as the site of a "show place" bears a much heavier tax burden than acres in agricultural production. Finally, whatever financial losses that occur as the result of ownership are much more difficult to deduct from the federal tax bill.

So the only questions LBJ had to answer when he took possession of the Martin place were these: Did he want to sell grazing and planting leases to ranchers in the area? Or did he want to ranch the land himself? Some wealthy investors in rural land opted for the first choice. I'm positive Johnson didn't think twice. Just as he was the dominating captain of his boat, he'd be the sole boss of his ranch. He wasn't about to turn that over to anyone else for any price, let alone the limited sums he'd get from leasing the use of his land to neighbors.

As a result, he had to choose which cattle and which machines, which feed and which seed. Because the Johnsons' wealth was not infinite, he was necessarily drawn into calculations of utility and price, and ultimately into the figuring of profit and loss. In other words, he became a rancher. I say this because the ranchers I've known I number among the most constantly economically motivated and concerned people of my acquaintance. To be sure, they do enjoy the pleasures of lives lived in tune with nature, in sync with the annual rhythms of the land. This blessing does not, however, mean they don't worry about the bottom line. Ranchers don't pass a day without continuously assessing situations and making decisions on the basis of pure economics. They know the cost of everything and are practiced at calculating margins of profit on it all. They don't miss many reports on commodity prices on the radio, and they see not only a steer but so many cents per pound on the hoof. They always keep in their heads a running tab of actual expenses and potential gains. Lyndon Johnson understood this aspect of ranch life, and he relished doing it as well as he could.

Obviously, LBJ was not a typical Central Texas rancher during the 1950s. His ranch was neither his sole nor his principle source of income throughout his life. He was not dependent on wringing regular profits out of his land, and he could afford more improvements and sustain more losses than the typical rancher.

It is also true that ranching meant more to him than just another business enterprise. To the extent that someone like him could relax, he relaxed there. While there with him, at a time when he was being sorely pressed by world events, I could see how driving around the Hill Country replenished his formidable energies and renewed his drooping spirits. He also appreciated the advantages he gained from entertaining people. It was an interesting place to visit, and his guests prized their invitations.

Still, despite his relative security as a rancher against fluctuations in agricultural markets, and despite the intangible but very real benefits his ranches blessed him with, I want to stress that LBJ did not view his operations in Gillespie County as nonprofit enterprises or as hobbies. To the contrary. According to Dad, he was keenly interested in making the ranch pay for itself. Till then, reducing its losses while improving the land and the stock enabled him to keep score on his own performance and satisfy himself of his skills as a rancher. And, while he was taking pride in these achievements, with my father's and Don Thomas's help he found ways the ranch could assist in the development of other investments.

★ ★ ★

Now, why was the Martin ranch attractive to Lyndon Johnson?

Reviewing LBJ's purchases of ranches in Gillespie and neighboring counties reveals a distinctive pattern. Dad could map its outlines by the late 1950s. It became even more apparent during the next decade. Johnson was particularly interested in buying land that fronted on the Pedernales River. The Martin place was the first of these acquisitions.

River frontage guaranteed his stock would have access to a reliable source of water. These were important considerations at any time; they were even more compelling during the long drought of the fifties. It also provided an easy opportunity to pump state-regulated amounts of water out of the Pedernales to irrigate fields. And having a river flow by or through one's land increased its value by adding to its scenic beauty. Moving water is refreshing, not only because of its ripples and eddies and gurgles, but because the motts of live oaks and cottonwoods that flourish along the banks please the eye. A ranch with the house overlooking a river was a more pleasant place to live and a more valuable one to own.

Without question, it was the Pedernales and the trees near it that made Lyndon Johnson determined to get his hands on the Martin place. Not one hundred yards from the river, directly across from a low-water ford where men and animals could safely cross the stream in good weather, grew a sizable mott of mature live oaks. They covered enough area to provide ample space for a large ranch house, and they were numerous enough that a sufficient number could be saved to shade that house against the afternoon sun. The Johnsons regarded it as a perfect location.

That perfection was improved upon by LBJ's realization that the place was within his grasp, even though Uncle Clarence and Aunt Frank had committed themselves to deed it to their son and his wife. Since neither my father nor anyone else was privy to the details of Lyndon's campaign to acquire this property, what follows is speculation on my part. It is, however, speculation that is grounded in my experiences in rural Texas communities.

Had Tom Martin not passed in 1948, it is highly unlikely LBJ would have had a chance to buy the place. Texas ranching families are clannish. The ones I've known have wanted to keep land within the immediate family. By "family" they generally mean the sons of the succeeding generations. Daughters are expected to marry and move away, or go to town and find a job. Daughters-in-law are further removed from this understanding of what is at the core of the family. Unsurprisingly, daughters-in-law without children are still more remote from the

LBJ and Aunt Frank, December 1959.
LBJ Library. Photo by Frank Muto.

center. That Aunt Frank would have favored her nephew over her son is nearly inconceivable. That would have gone against all of the folkways of her place and time. But would she prefer Lyndon's claims to the land over those of Lela? That's well within the realm of possibility, and that's what Lyndon depended upon. He was a male Johnson, after all. Thus the land would stay in the hands of her biological family.

By itself, this relationship probably would not have guaranteed Aunt Frank would decide in Lyndon's favor. My strong suspicion is that, for whatever reasons, she disliked Lela. In the intimate world bounded by Hye, Stonewall, and Johnson City, this antagonism would be well-known. Certainly Lyndon, who wanted to learn everything about everybody around him, would have been aware of it. He understood the consequences for him. This would be the weight that tipped the scales in his favor.

LBJ being LBJ, he couldn't resist slipping his finger onto the scales as well. Aunt Frank was seventy-seven years old in 1948, an age at which living in town became increasingly attractive to rural Texans.

LBJ and Lela Martin, September 1957.
LBJ Library. Photo by unknown.

You had neighbors to gossip with; you had more comforts (perhaps even indoor bathrooms); you could get to church and store easier. In the event of sudden illness, people were close by to aid you quickly, and the doctor was just down the street. When Lyndon offered her a place in Johnson City and an income she could live on, he was allowing her to escape the isolation of the ranch and the company of Lela. From Aunt Frank's perspective, this was a perfect exchange. From her nephew's, it was better than perfect. He'd get the land he wanted intensely, and her age made it unlikely he'd have to pay the annuity and forego the use of his boyhood home for very long. Lela wouldn't stand a chance.

As things turned out, she didn't. Even though she fought this scheme in court, she couldn't prevail against the advantages Texas law gave to property owners and the bias Texas juries had in favor of prominent people such as Senator Johnson. He waited patiently for the land he coveted, resisting any temptation he might have felt to buy a less attractive spread. In 1951 his tenacity was rewarded. The land was in his possession. He and Lady Bird began building their house beside the Pedernales. At the same time, LBJ began his career as rancher.

Johnson's first act was to rename the ranch after himself. From now on, it would be the LBJ Ranch. Then by word and act, he so stamped his identity on the place that his neighbors in the Hill Country began calling it the LBJ Ranch as well.

Those unfamiliar with ranch country will not realize how extraordinary this is. Yet my father has owned some land in Cooke County in North Texas since the mid-1960s that he and everyone else still refers to as "the Christian place," after the family who ranched it during the first half of the twentieth century. Similarly, he has owned "the old Cogburn place" for nearly twenty-five years. Until recently, my stepsister, sister, and I held joint title to a small ranch colorfully called after the outlaw Sam Bass, who kept his *remuda* in a stone corral there while hiding out between bank robberies. If we referred to any or all of these ranches as the Bullion place, residents of the nearby communities of Era and Leo wouldn't know what we were talking about. It's taken years to accustom them to calling the main Bullion spread, where Dad sited the house we call "The Barn," by the name he gave it: the W ^{2} Ranch.

Further south in the Hill Country, even Lyndon Johnson continued to call ranch land he acquired after 1951 by the names of original owners. For instance, his favorite place to hunt deer was "the Scharnhorst." Everyone, including him, continued to refer to outlying parts of the Martins' former property by their name. That the acres surrounding the Johnsons' new home were transformed almost instantly into the LBJ Ranch was compelling testimony to his personality, his prestige, and his power. Those who lived in Gillespie County had no choice. They knew they damned well had to learn its name and where it was. It was Lyndon Johnson's place.

But Lyndon Johnson's name could not be found on the title to the LBJ Ranch. On the advice of Dad and Don Thomas, the Texas Broadcasting Corporation, not LBJ, bought this land. When the house was completed, it too became the property of the corporation. Lyndon and Lady Bird Johnson rented the house from Texas Broadcasting.

At the ranch in September 1954.
LBJ Library. Photo by unknown.

I don't know how much it cost the Johnsons to rent the ranch. My guess is, not very much. Dad did pass on to me how the rent for the house was calculated. LBJ determined the daily rate for a room for two people in a hotel in Fredericksburg, Texas, the largest town in the area. The rent for the ranch house was roughly the equivalent of that sum. Moreover, Texas Broadcasting charged the Johnsons this rate only when they were actually in residence in Gillespie County. When the family was in Washington or elsewhere, no rent was billed at all.

Nominal rent as an advantage paled in comparison to others. Dad and Don Thomas had devised the means for substantial savings on taxes for Lyndon Johnson. Their plan was also perfectly calculated to take advantage of the profits generated by Texas Broadcasting and maximize the long-range profitability of the Johnson ranches, while making these reductions in his taxes possible. It proved how the imagination and ingenuity of skilled lawyers can turn an apparent problem into a golden opportunity.

The problem was the source of the funds the Johnsons needed to buy the ranch and build the house. By far, their most profitable investment was KTBC, their television station in Austin. The money LBJ needed had to come from it. But the Texas Broadcasting Corporation owned KTBC, and the only way he could get his hands on these profits for his personal use was for the corporation to make a formal distribution of money to shareholders. Doing that would be easy. The catch was this: the Tax Code defined a distribution as income, so the Johnsons would have to pay personal income tax on it. They also would have to pay corporate income tax on the same money, because it was part of Texas Broadcasting's profit for that year. Obviously, the IRS would love to tax the same income twice. No taxpayer would want to, least of all Lyndon Johnson. For him to invest in ranch lands, my father and Thomas had to show him how to avoid paying a double tax.

The solution was elegant and simple. The Texas Broadcasting Corporation would buy the land and own the house and all other outbuildings. As its officers, the Johnsons could take money from KTBC's profits and spend it on other corporate investments without making a distribution. They could get into ranching without paying a double tax on their earnings. Moreover, Texas Broadcasting would finance all future improvements on their land and their stock. The Johnsons could expand and improve their holdings without risking any increase in their personal income tax.

Even better, the corporate taxes Texas Broadcasting paid were lowered by this arrangement. The ranches were unprofitable for the rest of Lyndon Johnson's life. At times of heavy investment in fences, corrals, barns, cattle, erosion control, land clearing, and a dam across the Pedernales, they hemorrhaged red ink. These losses reduced the amount of profit the corporation had to declare at the end of each tax year, which lowered the amount Texas Broadcasting owed to the Internal Revenue Service. That resulted in two further advantages. The first and most obvious was fiscal. The second and more subtle was political. Let's talk about money first.

During the 1950s and 1960s, any and all deductions from corporate profits were welcome. The Texas Broadcasting Corporation was enjoying flush times, thanks chiefly to its Austin television station. If economics professors at the University of Texas needed an example of how monopolies prosper, they only had to look in their own living rooms.

Lyndon and Lady Bird had shrewdly refused to affiliate with any of the national networks. ABC, NBC, and CBS were all interested in

LBJ on the LBJ Ranch dam across the Pedernales, September 1954.
LBJ Library. Photo by unknown.

penetrating the Austin market, but the only way they could get a foot in the door was by offering KTBC its choice of their programs at favorable rates. The Johnsons picked the most popular shows from each. Viewers in Travis and adjacent Central Texas counties had an all-star lineup of programming every day of the week. As a result, consumer pressure for other TV stations in town was minimal and restricted to complaints about which days and times favorite programs came on.

The Johnsons charged advertisers top dollar, considering the size of the market. Later investigations by the national press illustrated this point by comparing advertising charges on stations in Rochester, Minnesota, a city of similar population and viewer profile, with KTBC's bills. In a competitive market, Rochester's stations received an average $325 per hour for advertising on network shows. KTBC charged $575 per hour for the same programs. The station got it, too. National and local companies had no choice.

Bottom line: KTBC could easily cover the ranch's losses and still generate a handsome profit. Part of that profit was the tax savings generated by the deductions created by the expenses of ranching in Blanco County. It was a beautifully reciprocal arrangement, one that made possible the new buildings on the LBJ Ranch and its sustained development.

The political payoff was substantial too. For understandable reasons, Lyndon Johnson was sensitive to charges that he was enjoying huge windfall profits that were generated by KTBC's monopoly of the Austin market. It was to his advantage to reply that those profits, though substantial, were by no means as great as his critics in the press claimed. He was not gouging consumers in Austin, and he could prove it by pointing to the Texas Broadcasting Corporation's overall profits. Omitted from this discussion and buried in the fine print was the reason why those profits were less than one might expect for a monopoly. LBJ was investing heavily in rural land and in improvements to his ranch.

The final advantage of my father's and Thomas's plan involved improvements. Improving ranch land can be an expensive proposition. Generally owners make them with an eye toward the long-term profitability of a ranch, because initial expenses are great enough to cause the operation to lose money in the present and immediate future. This fact of ranch management can make owning a ranch particularly difficult for people who have substantial incomes outside of their agricultural properties. To prevent those folks from lowering their personal income taxes by deducting losses from operating a ranch, the IRS has ruled that agricultural property must show a profit once every five years. If it does not, it becomes a hobby in the Revenuers' eyes, and no costs can be deducted. This rule posed no threat to LBJ. Ownership of the land by a corporation that always made money protected him against the periodic profit requirement.

Thus LBJ could be utterly unconcerned about the status of deductions on his personal income tax. Texas Broadcasting insulated him against the necessity of showing even a minimal book profit on the ranch every fifth year. As he made the old Martin place into what he wanted it to become, he was under no compulsion to cut corners and economize on expenses periodically. So long as the Texas Broadcasting Corporation would carry the ranch without strain, it was his to do with every year as he pleased.

Various students of Lyndon Johnson have characterized the LBJ Ranch as an avocation and even as a toy. Most of them would agree with Robert Dallek that he did not intend it to be a money-making proposition. None of this is wholly incorrect. In fact, these descriptions quite rightly call attention to the many intangible benefits Johnson gained from his house and his ranch.

That said, though, it's advisable to remember that LBJ himself would have bristled at the idea that this was a hobby. Dad and Don

Thomas had perfectly informed him about the consequences if the IRS started regarding the ranch that way, of course. Aside from that, to him words like "hobby," "toy," "pastime," and "avocation" smacked of a lack of seriousness. Lyndon Johnson was a serious man, one who knew the value of a dollar and wanted to make as many bucks as he could while leading the life and seeking the destiny he chose. I'm confident that he planned that his land in Gillespie County would be profitable. He didn't expect this to happen overnight. He knew that major expenditures would have to be made on the land, the stock, the buildings, and the machines necessary to do well from ranching. Thanks to KTBC and the Texas Broadcasting Corporation, he could afford to be patient and do it right.

★ ★ ★

Time's passage also drew the attention of Johnson and men such as Dad to the steady appreciation of the value of rural land in a rapidly urbanizing state. During the fifties, LBJ bought land with the intention of ranching it. He had no thought, according to my father, of speculating in ranches, buying low and selling high. By the sixties, however, he had begun to see the potential for a new investment strategy in rural real estate. Was there serious money to be made if the Texas Broadcasting Corporation purchased tracts of land, invested in the construction of small houses on them, and sold lots and homes to people who wanted a weekend retreat or a retirement home in the Hill Country? Later in that decade, Lyndon Johnson was ready to take the plunge.

The LBJ Ranch would never meet that fate. It might become a profitable line in Texas Broadcasting's annual report, but not by being broken up or by losing the characteristics that gave it a value beyond the merely economic to Johnson. Retaining those characteristics was one of the criteria by which he judged his success as a rancher. If that meant occasionally passing up immediate opportunities to make more money, so be it.

Nowhere is this determination of Lyndon Johnson more apparent than in the way he treated deer hunting on his ranches. I'll turn to that now.

CHAPTER 8

Hunting Deer

W hen Lyndon Johnson bought ranches in the Hill Country, he could not help but become involved in the business of deer hunting. Whitetails already grazed that land, eating food that otherwise would be his cattle's. If he did not reduce their numbers by arranging to kill some each year, natural increase by itself would guarantee they would eat more than their share of grass and foliage. And natural increase would be only part of his problem. If he did not allow hunting on his property, the sanctuary he'd created there would attract unwanted four-legged immigrants during hunting season.

Ranchers whose land abutted state and national parks were well aware that soon after the first shots were fired in November, the game migrated in large numbers into posted regions. Crafty ranchers set their deer blinds along routes into the parks. This strategy helped, but not enough for the good of either the public grasslands, which were stripped clean, or ultimately the condition of the deer, whose health and strength declined as they became too numerous for their environment to support. I personally witnessed this in Yosemite. In the mid-sixties, deer were overrunning the park, endangering the fragile ecological balance in its alpine meadows and visibly becoming scrawnier themselves. The Park Service was compelled to respond by shooting a significant percentage of Yosemite Valley's deer population in late 1965. So LBJ really had no choice. Even had he been philosophically opposed to hunting—which he definitely was not—to keep from being overrun with deer, and to protect his grass and cattle, he had to permit hunting on his ranches.

Who would be the hunters and under which circumstances would they hunt? LBJ rejected the notion of selling deer leases to outsiders. Thanks to KTBC, he could manage without the extra money.

LBJ with unidentified guest after a successful hunt, ca. 1959.
LBJ Library. Photo by Frank Muto.

Whitetails on his spreads could serve the purposes of pleasure and politics. Hunting them would be exclusively reserved for himself, his family, his friends, and his guests. Indeed, Johnson decided that men who visited his place in Gillespie County during the late fall could not fully experience ranch life without hunting. He made these expeditions essential parts of his hospitality, features of trips to the ranch he let them understand they were supposed to enjoy.

★ ★ ★

Whether the men LBJ invited were enthusiastic or not, whether they had hunted before or never, they knew they were expected to hunt deer during their visit. And they wouldn't just hunt. Their host was determined they'd have a good time. He defined what that would be: going home knowing that soon they would receive the mounted head of the buck they killed at the LBJ Ranch from taxidermists in Fredericksburg or Johnson City. That trophy would also bear on it an engraved flattened strip of gold, detailing the time, the place, and the name of the owner of the land. It would be both gift and reminder from Lyndon Johnson to those who hunted with him. Ideally, it would inspire fond memories and lasting gratitude in the hunter. No doubt LBJ also expected it would spark hope for a similar invitation in the breasts of all who enviously heard the story of deer hunting on the ranch, studied the trophy on the wall, and wanted one of their own.

The admirers of the head and horns might not be aware of another aspect of these hunts. Even the hunters themselves might be ignorant of it. It was easy for LBJ to turn the killing of a whitetail buck into a test of manhood. Johnson himself did not hunt with guests, so his own prowess at the sport was left implied. The unspoken message, delivered as he soliloquized on the beauties of the Hill Country, the condition of the stock, the length of the grass, and the habits of deer, was one of expertise and excellence. Could you measure up to him?

At a successful hunt, there was no contest. A guest shot his deer, then went on with LBJ to other pleasure or business. Missed shots created a different atmosphere. Once that happened, the contest was joined, and the stakes were one's manhood. Johnson's goal would become humiliation, not hospitality; the underlining of inferiority at men's work, not a relaxed sharing of men's sport. Under these conditions, deer hunting at the LBJ Ranch became the country mouse's revenge over his city cousin's impotent pretensions and posturings.

Hunting whitetails on Johnson's ranches was different from deer hunts on other Hill Country ranches. The difference, however, was of degree rather than kind. All ranchers wanted to create conditions conducive to the killing of deer. None aimed at giving the wild animals a fair chance; each wanted to give the hunter more advantages than the hunted. To landowners, deer hunting wasn't sport. It was what rangers in Yosemite called "management of the deer population." What made managerial strategy on Lyndon Johnson's spread unique was his determination to provide his hunters with every possible advantage over the game.

First, LBJ decided that his guests would roadhunt. There'd be no shivering in blinds or sitting in trees for him and those he was guiding. That was too uncomfortable, time-consuming, and silent for his personality. Roadhunting allowed conversation; indeed, it encouraged talk. Driving enabled passengers to keep warm during cold snaps and pleasantly shaded on sunny days. If the deer didn't happen to be in one place, you could speed on to where they were.

Deer generally avoided open pastures and territory adjacent to well-traveled roads during the day. What good would it do to drive in comfort if the guests didn't spot their quarry, let alone get within range? None. In fact, it would do damage. Hunts without game were generally blamed on the guide or the land owner. Anyway, LBJ wanted his visitors to go home with a trophy, not just fading memories of the quiet beauties of rolling country, waving brown grass, and outcroppings of rock, mesquite, and live oaks. To solve the difficulties created by a commitment to daytime road hunting, he and his hands had to do more than merely entice deer into a killing ground. The whitetails must be confined there.

Accordingly, Johnson had his men build high fences around the favorite pastures and fields for deer, so high even they couldn't leap over them. Once in, they were captives. The next step was clearing many of the brush patches in the enclosed areas, thereby affording the deer less cover. Networks of roads crisscrossed the fields. Feed was regularly brought in by truck. The game in the enclosures soon grew used to the sounds of cars and trucks and associated the vehicles with salt, range cubes, hay, and cottonseed cakes.

LBJ took steps to improve hunting in other ways, too. He wanted deer on his ranches to be larger and more impressive-looking than Hill Country whitetails typically were. So he acquired larger bucks and does, kept them separate from the deer already on his property during breeding seasons, and waited patiently for the results. While they were being fruitful and multiplying, and as the bucks matured and grew larger racks, he restricted hunting to the indigenous whitetails. After he built up a good breeding herd with substantial numbers of trophy bucks, Johnson could legitimately boast his deer were bigger and better than others' wildlife.

How did he get the original breeding stock? When I asked my father, I found out he did not know for sure. The animals were not included on the ranch's accounts as an investment, and Johnson never

LBJ next to a deer fence on the ranch, December 28, 1967.
LBJ Library. Photo by Michael Geissinger.

mentioned spending money on bucks or doe to his tax attorney. My father surmised from the absence of evidence to the contrary that the larger whitetails had been given to him. Ranchers eager to get on the Senate Majority Leader's good side must have gone to considerable trouble to corner, capture, and tranquilize the most imposing deer on their land, then haul them to the LBJ Ranch. Whether he was surprised by the first gift, whether he had already hinted he would like to improve his "stock," or whether he made his desires so unmistakable that they amounted to commands, is unknown. Whatever the circumstances, the outcome was everything he hoped for: impressive heads and antlers for his guests.

At the end of the process of managing the animals and the environment they would be hunted in, LBJ came to regard the whitetails on his ranch as his property. After all, they couldn't get off his place and therefore couldn't be said to be roaming freely. Nor could their reproductive habits be said to be as serendipitous and whimsical as was the case with wild animals. To use a phrase familiar to cattle owners, he was "breeding up" the herd by bringing in superior stock. In his mind, such planned improvement of the deer on his land apparently equaled the domestication of them. Domestication in turn meant they were no longer wild and owned by no one, but were his.

This conviction was reinforced by his success at turning some of his prime breeding stock nearly into pets. To his delight, LBJ discovered that deer, like goats, loved tobacco. Favorites among his herd were offered this treat and rapidly learned to take it from their master's hands. During the 1960s, guests at the ranch were amazed to see Clarence, a huge buck who performed very well as a stud, come to Johnson's whistle and nose his pockets for cigarettes and snuff. (Apparently, Clarence relished nicotine after mating as much as some humans do.) Both parties to this transaction came out ahead. Clarence momentarily satisfied his craving; LBJ gleefully showed off to appreciative audiences. Without question, this increased the buck's value to his owner. Of course, had Clarence not done his primary duty to the president's satisfaction, soon he would have become a rack on someone's wall. The degree to which Lyndon Johnson became sentimental about anything or anyone was strictly limited. Like everyone else on board, Clarence had to pull his weight to stay in the boat.

LBJ and Clarence, September 25, 1966.
LBJ Library. Photo by Robert Knudsen.

I'm not sure whether the complete enclosure of these animals, the successful training of the Clarences among them, and the systematic generation of larger bucks and doe meant they in fact had become his legal property. My father wasn't certain on this point, either. He inclined toward the position that the deer remained wild in the eyes of the law. Lyndon Johnson, however, firmly believed they were his property. Nobody argued with him. Guests who hunted on his land did not have to purchase the licenses the law said they had to have to hunt wild animals. Game wardens who worked in the Hill Country were not so foolhardy as to insist on this punctilio on the LBJ Ranch.

★ ★ ★

A practiced eye could assess at a glance just how artificial the set-up on Johnson's pastures was. Big John would have noticed the high deer fences immediately and observed how unusually open the pastures were during his first swing through them. Anybody who had ever driven around a ranch would have been struck by how much more comfortable roadhunting was from a Lincoln Continental than from the bed of a Chevy pickup. West Texas ranchers would have quickly seen how relatively unfazed by vehicles these deer were and how much they grazed during the day within sight of a road and figured it out without puzzling much.

That Johnson regarded the whitetails as his legal property was not apparent at first sight, or even from later looks. This information had to be given to you by LBJ. Even so, that they were absolutely under his control would be obvious to old hands. So would something else: Johnson wisely restricted the amount of hunting on his properties. These deer had a false sense of security, because he rotated hunting grounds and reserved them for guests he meant to impress and, in some cases, to test. They were used to men as well as pickups and cars.

All this made for ideal hunting conditions for Johnson's visitors. Hunting his deer on his land was not quite like hunting his cattle. Cattle, after all, weighed more, and were clumsier, slower, and easier to shoot. Otherwise, LBJ's domestic and wild animals were quite similar.

The visitors who hunted Johnson deer did not have a practiced eye. This was not coincidental. Inviting someone like, say, Waddy Bullion to go hunting would have been pointless. Dad would have recognized the special arrangements and the wildlife's unusual behavior and known all this was atypical of ranch life and deer hunting. Besides, shooting a buck on the LBJ Ranch wasn't going to change my father's attitude toward or make him any more obliged to Lyndon. Neither purpose of these hunts, therefore, would be served.

Greenhorns, however, would believe this was a normal hunting trip in Central Texas and would buy into the notion it was proof of manliness. No rancher would swallow either proposition. What would impress them was the effort and expense that had gone into creating this shooting park with live targets. The high fences, the cleared ground, the elaborate road network, the bigger deer, the highly restricted hunting—these were proofs of wealth to them.

They couldn't afford to go so far to insure a successful hunt on their land. If LBJ could and did—fine, more power to him. Which, of course, these arrangements were meant to reinforce as well.

I haven't checked LBJ's calendars to see how many people he took hunting with him during the 1950s and 1960s. I do know the vast majority have not recorded their experiences. Nor did Johnson himself refer to these expeditions very often. This leads me to conclude that most of the hunts were unremarkable. Successful ones went quickly. LBJ allowed his guests one trophy buck. When it was shot, the hunt was over. The hunters and their guide did not dawdle over the kill. Ranch hands field dressed the carcass and hauled it into town so the meat could be processed and the head mounted. Whenever good bucks were not sighted within two or three hours, evidently LBJ would call a halt. For whatever reason, the deer hadn't drifted within range on that day, and there was no profit in spending more time driving around. He had the perfect excuse: these were, after all, wild animals, and they couldn't be delivered on a schedule. I have no doubt his cowboys were quizzed pretty closely after unsuccessful hunts and asked to explain what in the hell went wrong, but these sessions would be held after guests departed.

What percentage of guests resented their host's insistence that they kill a deer, what numbers enjoyed it, how many endured it for the sake of endearing themselves to LBJ—these are things we'll never know. To my knowledge, only two accounts of hunts at the ranch and their aftermaths have made their way into print. Neither shows Johnson at his best. Both revolve around events that went awry during the pursuit of a trophy buck.

In November 1959, Robert Kennedy traveled to Gillespie County. His brother had sent him to Texas to ask LBJ face-to-face whether he was running for the presidency. The answer was no, which surely did not sound convincing to Bobby or Jack. Johnson went on to volunteer that he would neither assist nor oppose a Kennedy candidacy; the brothers probably believed only one of those promises was sincere. Finally, Johnson stated his view that a third nomination for Adlai Stevenson would be unwise, a sentiment all of them could wholeheartedly agree upon. This sparring out of the way, LBJ insisted his visitor go hunting.

Robert Kennedy accepted this offer. Why he said yes is unknowable. No one but these two men knew exactly how Johnson made his invitation; only RFK could say how he assessed his host's motives for making it. If he interpreted LBJ's words as a challenge to Kennedy toughness and masculinity, he would have immediately accepted that dare. He was too competitive to back down, and he had enough confidence in his athletic abilities to be sure he would kill a deer. If he instead understood Johnson to be simply trying to be a good host and suspected feelings might be wounded by a refusal, then his agreeing to go hunting may be a sign of how far he was willing to go to keep himself and his brother on LBJ's good side.

What follows is a three-sentence description of the hunt in the first volume of Robert Dallek's biography of LBJ. Dallek based it on an interview a television producer had with A.W. Moursund, Johnson's longtime business partner who owned land nearby and was a frequent guest at the LBJ Ranch. "Bobby was knocked to the ground and cut above the eye by the recoil of a powerful shotgun Johnson had given him to use. Reaching down to help the thirty-four-year-old Bobby up, Lyndon said: 'Son, you've got to learn to handle a gun like a man.'" Dallek concluded that "the incident was an indication of Johnson's small regard for Jack Kennedy's claim on the White House."

This conclusion is accurate so far as it goes. Dallek goes on to point out that Johnson regarded both Kennedys as boys rather than men, and Jack as a not very serious boy at that. Seen in the context of deer hunting, though, the incident reveals a darker aspect of LBJ's personality that extended beyond his contempt for the brothers' youth, lack of experience, and unjustified presumption that together they could win the presidency.

Why did Johnson hand over a powerful shotgun to an obviously novice hunter? The most plausible excuse he might have given was that the scattering of shot made it more likely that a beginner would hit what he was aiming at, and the weight and velocity of the slugs would

The Judge (A.W. Moursund) and Lyndon "anticipatin"
getting their limit—come deer season, November 1954.
LBJ Library. Photo by unknown.

knock the prey to the ground and wound it mortally. The hunt, by definition, would be successful.

In reply, I can say that the comparatively short range at which a
shotgun was effective meant that a shot from a rifle with a telescopic
sight from that distance would be relatively easy too. Robert Kennedy's hand-eye coordination was certainly equal to skiing, sailing, and
throwing and catching footballs in weekend games. Surely, then, he
could make an easy shot at an unmoving target while resting the rifle
on the car. Besides, if he missed under these conditions, that would
serve as obvious proof of his shortcomings as a full-grown man. There
was no reason I can think of for giving him a powerful shotgun other
than this: giving one to a person who had never shot such a weapon

before or seen it fired had the potential for inflicting humiliation and pain on the unprepared. It did exactly that to Kennedy.

I've never fired one of those guns, but I have witnessed their powerful impact on both the shooter and the shot.

One summer in Yosemite, rangers at the Crane Flat Campground were having a great deal of trouble with a huge, aging, grumpy brown bear. He had progressed beyond raiding garbage cans at night to tipping them over in broad daylight. Worse, he was standing his ground rather than lumbering off at the approach of people. We firefighters had lured him into a culvert-shaped cage with fresh meat. Then we marked him as a potentially dangerous bear by spray-painting his sides orange through slits in the trap. That done, we hitched the cage to a pickup and took him miles away. There we turned him loose. But not long afterwards, an orange and brown bear was sighted around Crane Flat. Park policy mandated the killing of bears that returned to campgrounds after being trapped and moved. The rangers assumed these beasts would hold a grudge against those who fooled, confined, and painted them, then expected that they would give up tasty garbage for roots and insects. Such bears were only a short step removed from attacking campers. So the district ranger checked a ten-gauge shotgun out of the park's armory. Then he set up some targets so each ranger could test-fire the weapon. I was having lunch and wandered over to watch.

The district ranger warned everyone about the gun's recoil. He had them dry-fire it first, both so they could learn the pull on the trigger without shells in the chamber, and so he could be sure they held the stock as tightly as they could to their shoulders. Then he loaded the gun. Despite these precautions and despite all they could do, big men were being rocked backward two and three steps after they fired. A slighter man, roughly the size of Robert Kennedy, was knocked down. The gun would have done the same to me. And if I hadn't already been impressed by its power, I was later that day, after the district ranger killed the bear with it. Because the fire crew were the lowest-ranking employees, we got the job of moving the remains to the park's dump. The ranger hadn't made a particularly good shot. He'd missed the heart, lungs, and head. But the slugs had torn the whole side of the bear's paunch off. It died instantly from the shock and trauma of the wound.

Robert Kennedy had been handed a weapon that was probably powerful enough to punch a hole clear through a whitetail deer, if not literally tear it in half. He might have been warned about the recoil—"this gun sure kicks, so hold her tight"—but he couldn't have had the actual experience of firing the weapon or seeing it in action. Under these circumstances, being laid flat on the ground and having the stock fly dangerously upward toward mouth, nose, and eyes were certainly probable and maybe inevitable outcomes. So was the opportunity to rub salt into the wounds to both pride and flesh with the comment, "'Son, you've got to learn to handle a gun like a man.'"

What Lyndon Johnson knew and his guest didn't, was that this was not just *a* gun. It was among the most powerful weapons ranchers handled. Experienced hunters—and strong ones, too—had trouble controlling a ten-gauge shotgun. To hand it to a small man who didn't know what he was shooting was an act of calculated meanness—mean because it was meant to hurt, calculated because it was meant to prove the power and superiority of a real Texan over the effete and underachieving sons of a New England family.

A year later, John Kennedy was a guest at the LBJ Ranch. The passage of those twelve months had, of course, dramatically changed the relationship between the Kennedys and Johnson. Now the elder brother was president-elect; the younger one was clearly going to be highly influential in the new administration, whatever his formal role might be; and Lyndon Johnson was vice president, holding an office a former vice president and fellow Texan, John Nance Garner, had memorably described as "not worth a bucket of warm spit."

LBJ was eager to assure the new president of his loyalty and friendship, so he extended the full hospitality of the Hill Country to him. This included deer hunting. I'm convinced Johnson would have proposed this in any event; to his mind, going hunting made visits especially memorable. Even if he had been reluctant, though, he would have had no choice. Neglecting to ask Jack, or readily acceding to any reluctance by gracefully withdrawing the invitation, after insisting that Robert Kennedy hunt, might have looked strange. It could be interpreted as an absence of real friendliness to the president. It might also inspire questions about LBJ's real motives for taking Bobby out and giving him a shotgun. There would be no shotguns on this expedition. Johnson supplied Jack with a rifle.

Later, this hunt became the raw material for public controversy. In the first draft of his detailed study of John Kennedy's assassination, William Manchester began the work with an elaborate and critical recounting of that morning at the ranch. It featured two contrasts in

LBJ and JFK, November 16, 1960.
LBJ Library. Photo by Art Kowert.

character: JFK, cool, rational, detached, intelligent, urbane, a man who
was repulsed by the act of shooting what were in effect tame deer, but
unwilling to offend his host; LBJ, excited, emotional, viscerally
enthralled with the thrill of killing, a man so caught up in shooting deer
that he slaughtered two himself in front of Kennedy and later forced
the president to put the mounted head of his victim upon the wall of the
Fish Room in the White House.

As narrative, this was heavy-handed and obviously slanted. But
Manchester went beyond mere narration. He used the hunt to symbol-
ize and highlight the differences between a cultured civilization that
produced a man who regarded killing as senseless, and an environment
that warped another man into dealing out and then celebrating violent
death. The author meant to compel readers to remember rifles with

telescopic sights in Gillespie County and Dallas, and to identify a peaceful, defenseless buck with a president in Dealey Plaza.

Unsurprisingly, those who vetted this manuscript decided this was a bit much, especially at the beginning of what the Kennedys hoped would be the definitive and final description of the assassination. Some of their objections were literary; there were simply better ways to start the book. Some of their criticism took politics into consideration; this rendition would obviously offend the Oval Office's current occupant.

Persuaded by their comments, Manchester agreed to shorten his account of the hunt and bleed off much of the symbolism he suffused it with. Although he was unwilling to delete it entirely from the final version of *The Death of a President,* he did move it to pages 118-119, embedding it in a discussion of the visit the president and his wife planned to make to the LBJ Ranch on November 23.

None of this made Lyndon Johnson like it any better. "All of it . . . ," he complained, after first receiving reports on Manchester's work while it was in galleys then reading sections of it himself, "makes me look like a son of a bitch." If LBJ exaggerated, he didn't by much.

★ ★ ★

In the revised text, Manchester did concede Johnson "was determined to be cordial, and [hunting deer] was the finest treat his ranch could offer." He also commented that if LBJ "had dreamed that his hunting invitation might give offense, he would never have mentioned it." Because he could not conceive that it would, Johnson interpreted Kennedy's reluctance as a polite desire to avoid causing his hosts extra trouble. Thus he thought the new president "needed cajoling." Hunting "was a local custom [Johnson] explained, taking his new chief's arm in his tactile way. This was something you just *did.* An eminent guest was expected to join in the ritual."

Let's pause for a moment and read this as LBJ did. Hunting was "the finest treat his ranch could offer"—it didn't have anything worth a damn to a classy guy like Jack. He didn't dream the invitation might be offensive—how insensitive and boorish he was, how limited his perspectives, not to realize that Kennedy (as Manchester explained in the paragraph above the concessions to Johnson) thought "shooting tame game was not sport," and "tried to bow out gracefully," because "to him all killing was senseless." Jack did such things "gracefully"; Lyndon, though "gracious" in his invitation, would "never understand" his leader's "scruples," perhaps even think him "squeamish," and became as a result "dogged" in his insistence.

Even before he read Manchester's account of the actual shot, LBJ's blood must have been boiling. The words the author used were clearly chosen to diminish him in contrast to his predecessor, who was everything he was not. Lyndon Johnson was fully aware of what these passages implied. To him, they proved Manchester was "a fraud." This so-called historian was simply a cat's-paw for the Kennedys, who were using *The Death of a President* to attack him.

Setting aside his dismissal of Manchester, which was manifestly unfair, and his suspicions of Bobby, when in reality the Kennedys were as perturbed as he was by the book's portrayal of JFK's successor, Johnson's reading of the prose was careful, his interpretation of its implications was acute, and his anger at the signals about his nature understandable. To quote him quoting Manchester: "'[I] lumbered out of the room as [Jacqueline Kennedy] came in'? Well, now, lumbering—I don't know, I guess that's their way of saying I walked out. But [Manchester] didn't see me walk out [and] he doesn't know whether I lumbered or trotted or walked or anything else." His reaction to the none-too-subtle, condescending put-down of his perceptiveness and background in the description of the invitation to hunt, thinly disguised as an appreciation of a clumsy and insensitive effort to please, by a bear-like man, must have been equally furious.

Things didn't improve when Manchester moved on to describe the hunt. First, he suggested that shooting itself was not difficult. Anyone using the proper technique could hit a bullseye; "changing a tire," in his opinion, "requires more skill." Killing something, however, changed the nature of shooting. You must confront the prey in your sights. In Kennedy's case, "he looked into the face of the life he was about to take." Then Manchester continued: "He had committed himself; he couldn't flinch. He fired and quickly turned back to the car." But the act could not be so rapidly dismissed from his mind. "He could not," wrote Manchester, "rid himself of the recollection. The memory of the creature's death had been haunting, and afterward he had relived it with his wife, *vider l' abcès*, to heal the inner scar."

Johnson didn't bother commenting on Manchester's dropping a French tag into the sentence to prove his and JFK's erudition, then translating it for the benefit of the poor folks like LBJ and his friends who didn't know the language. What upset him was this: whether you wrote in French or English or Texan, this narrative did not accurately portray the reality of the hunt. When he read it in late 1966, he exploded to an adviser, "Forcing that poor man to go hunting? Hell, he not only killed *one* deer. He insisted on killing a *second*!"

The search for the second took two hours, a fact by itself that gave the lie to the report in the book about Kennedy's desire to end the hunt as soon as possible. So did this: after he had killed his second deer of the morning, the president-elect, according to Johnson, wanted to keep on hunting! "By God, he insisted on killing one for Torby [Macdonald]." To gratify his wishes, Johnson remembered, "We just worked so hard." After three hours of fruitless driving, "I finally gave up. I said, 'Mr. President, we just can't do it.'"

As for the haunting vision in the scope, LBJ scoffed at that. "Poor little deer—he saw it in his eye and he just could not shoot it? Well, hell, he wasn't within 250 yards from it." As for Kennedy's quickly turning away after his shot was concerned, that was equally far from what really happened. "He shot it and he jumped up and down and hoorahed and put it right on the fender of the car so he could kill another one." At this point, Johnson made sure the people listening to him in the Oval Office learned about the usual practice on ranches in the Hill Country. "Most of them," he noted, "have got a rule—they will not let you kill but one." This was the case on the LBJ Ranch as well. "But he was the president . . . and we wanted him to have whatever he wanted."

★ ★ ★

Which story is true? In one sense, they are difficult to reconcile. Upon hearing them, a friend of mine immediately pointed out that I couldn't compromise and credit Kennedy with one and a half deer killed that morning. She is certainly right. It's equally impossible to resolve conclusively how far the deer was from Kennedy. I'm sure it wasn't 250 yards away. When I was driven over the same pastures, I never passed a landscape where it was possible to see a deer at that distance from the road. The terrain rolls and dips, the fields are sprinkled with brush and trees, and there are no bare skylines within the range of a deer rifle. The furthest I saw a whitetail from the car was probably a little over one hundred yards, and that was regarded by me as a distinctly problematic shot to attempt. Finally, because of the land's nature and the deer's habits, the range where the rifles were sighted-in on the LBJ Ranch would not have been longer than one hundred yards. Seeing a deer further away and expending a bullet trying to hit it meant guessing where the shot would go, rather than precisely aiming.

Such an attempt would waste ammunition most of the time. It might also spoil the rest of the day's hunting. One reason why LBJ stuck to the customary one-buck-per-hunter rule was because other deer became much more wary after they heard a shot fired. (For this reason, I'm sure he wasn't surprised at all that it took two more hours for Kennedy to kill a second buck. It took time for the deer to quiet down and leave cover to graze. Killing a third would be very difficult. Multiple shots would drive whitetails into the brush and might keep them there until dark.) To guard against spoiling the outing for JFK, he would have advised against a long-distance shot first thing in the morning.

For these reasons, I believe the president-elect killed the first deer at a significantly closer distance than the one Johnson remembered. But I'm also sure it was not point-blank range. LBJ may have been exaggerating for effect, but he had no need to tell an outright lie in a private conversation. Besides, Kennedy's eagerness to kill another and then still continue hunting was more than enough by itself to erase the image of a haunted man painted in *The Death of a President*. For that matter, Manchester's version inadvertently but unmistakably suggests that the deer was not exceptionally close to Kennedy. In his words, JFK had killed his trophy buck with "a magnificent shot." Evidently, Manchester forgot as he praised it that he'd also said changing a tire was more difficult than shooting accurately.

In any event, what Lyndon Johnson saw at the time, and what Jack Kennedy told Jackie later, could very easily have been different. I'm pretty sure JFK would not be the first or only husband to have a great time with the boys, but afterward tell his wife it really wasn't that much fun. I'll bet, too, that this would not have been the first time he edited his experiences for her. Politicians tend to be masters at giving different people the messages they want to hear. Describing a deer hunt to someone more likely to be sympathetic to Bambi than the hunter is not the occasion to talk about how excited you were and how disappointing it was you couldn't shoot more game.

★ ★ ★

We must keep this in mind as we assess the final part of Manchester's narrative: the presentation of the mounted head. In *The Death of a President*, Johnson "lugged" the trophy over to the White House and urged the president to put it on the wall in the Oval Office. Kennedy was "inwardly appalled." He gave orders that it should be put away and forgotten. But Johnson persisted, calling about the trophy, asking when it would be hung, and "eventually... like any other gift that has been repeatedly declined, [it] became an issue between them." Once more, Kennedy yielded on what really was "a very small" point, "a half-forgotten fico." He had "the specimen... hung, not in the Oval Office, but in the nearby Fish Room." It was a favor—"how great a favor only the First Lady knew"—and Johnson was pleased. Kennedy, however, still remembered the incident as "distasteful." He dealt with it, according to Manchester, by incorporating it into a version of one of his favorite pastimes, making lists of whatever struck him at any given moment as the three most overrated things in the world. When he thought of this entire episode, he would tell friends, "'The three most overrated things in the world are the state of Texas, the FBI, and hunting trophies.'"

After reading this, Lyndon Johnson wasn't interested in making lists, or pointing out that it conveyed the insult that mere ficos (a word of Italian derivation, chosen to display the erudition of the author and his cultured readers, and to avoid repeating "very small" twice in one sentence) for Jack Kennedy were matters of consuming import to him. Instead, he seized upon Manchester's description of him early in the book as "virtually impotent in his own state" and used it to argue how preposterous the thrust of these remarks were.

Kennedy, Johnson began to an adviser, "wasn't competent to be president if he—"; then, breaking off that phrasing, he started over on this same thought: "I think it is the greatest desecration of his memory that an 'impotent' vice president could force this strong man to do a goddamned thing." Moreover, he never pressed Kennedy to hang the head anywhere. "My calling him up and making him put a deer head in his outer room and he didn't want to? I never called him in my life on it."

Then LBJ recalled that Kennedy had also placed a mounted sailfish on a wall in the Fish Room. "He had his fish up there that he caught on his honeymoon. He put his deer head up there." Warming to the task of refuting Manchester, Johnson sarcastically observed, "But even if we had made the *tragic* mistake of forcing this *poor man* to put up a deer head here along with his fish—I do not know who forced him to put up the fish in the Fish Room that he caught on his honeymoon, but *I* damned sure didn't force him to put up anything." His final words on the subject were these: "It is just a manufactured lie."

Once more, it's impossible to determine which account is true—or more accurately perhaps, which one is closer to the truth. Only Jack Kennedy could describe his own motives, and he would tailor them to suit who was listening. Certainly he could have made witty self-deprecating jokes about having one of the three most objectionable things in the world hung up, and also feel that it nicely complemented a leaping sailfish, stuffed with its mouth open for eternity and suspended on the Fish Room wall for the remainder of his term in office. The two reactions are not mutually exclusive. LBJ's views are clearer.

Johnson unintentionally revealed some things about himself in this critique of Manchester. He sure did know *that* the deer head was hung. He knew *where* it was hung. He knew *what else* was displayed on the walls of the Fish Room. And he sure wanted to make certain that the people who were listening to him fulminate against this "manufactured lie" damned well knew he did *not* force Kennedy to hang it up.

The impression that remains after reading the transcripts of his conversations in December 1966 and January 1967 is that he *did* want Jack Kennedy to be proud of this trophy. Whether he actually pressed the president to put it on a White House wall or not, it *was* important to him that the deer's head be there, where he and others could see it and know from where it came.

These feelings were so strong that he just had to believe the version in *The Death of a President* was a lie deliberately concocted by Manchester and the Kennedy family to do him political damage. To conclude otherwise, to accept that he and the trophy from the ranch were the inspiration of condescending jokes about Texas and hunting deer, was insupportable to him. Writing these things was another example of how self-ordained sophisticates either cruelly laughed at, or gravely bewailed, the inferior recreations, inadequate culture, and flawed morality of more backward citizens from the provinces. It shouldn't hurt. You should do what Mama always advised and consider the source. You should move on to other, more important things.

LBJ tried to do this. His final words on the subject were healthy and wise. The best thing he and those working with him could do "is try to refrain from getting into an argument or a fight or a knockdown, and go on and do our job every day, as best we can."

★ ★ ★

Following his own advice on the Manchester affair was difficult for Lyndon Johnson. To his credit, he did not involve himself in a public debate over *The Death of a President*. Nevertheless, the sting of these words must have lingered for a long time. Reading them did hurt. It was important to him that others admire the ranch and appreciate his hospitality. Hunting deer was a necessary part of ranching in the Hill Country. In his mind, he had turned this necessity into an interesting and attractive pastime for men who visited him at the LBJ Ranch. Criticizing hunting was denigrating the ranch and attacking him in ways that he believed were unjustified and vicious.

Conveniently repressed in this defense was his effort to punish and humiliate Robert Kennedy. Also left unsaid was his practice of demanding that if you got in the boat—and a Lincoln Continental of that vintage certainly boasted boat-like size and handling!—with him to go hunting, you'd better do it well. Poor shooting would get you put out of the boat, to go home with questions about your manhood echoing in your ears.

CHAPTER 9

Blind Trust

Most Americans of my generation can remember where they were and what they were doing when they heard the news on Friday, November 22, 1963. I'm no exception.

As I walked across the Stanford Quad toward my 11:00 Biology lecture, I noticed clusters of two and three faculty members talking. As I passed by, I heard snatches of conversations. Individual words caught my attention: "Kennedy," "president," "shot," "wounded." I didn't hear "Texas" or "Dallas," but I didn't have to. I knew the president was in Texas, and I thought he was scheduled to pass through Dallas that morning.

Because of Big D's reputation for rabidly right-wing politics, and because of the attack on Adlai Stevenson a month earlier by angry demonstrators at a speech he was giving there on the United Nations, newspapers in the Bay Area had given more extensive coverage to this presidential trip than most. The local media had quoted approvingly Stevenson's remarks to an angry woman who had just hit him with a placard, "I believe in the forgiveness of sin and the redemption of ignorance." Unsurprisingly, commentators also took care to clobber my hometown for its beliefs and behavior. I hadn't been unhappy at the treatment of Dallas. A principle reason why I chose to come to Stanford was its distance—geographically, intellectually, and culturally—from where I lived. In conversations with California friends, I defended myself, not the city, and posed as a refugee from a land of intolerance.

By the time I reached class, the buzz before the lecture was much louder than usual, as late arrivals came in with more news. The last one to enter before the lecture began reported that there had been a machine gun attack, and scores of people were dead, including the governor of Texas and other officials. For sure Kennedy had been killed; maybe Johnson too. I've marveled since then at the professor's calm, focused discussion of plant genetics to the excited students in front of him. I also remember he thoughtfully repeated that lecture's main points on the following Monday, after remarking we probably had our minds elsewhere last Friday.

When I met my roommates for lunch, they had heard the latest news from Dallas. The president was dead. The governor, whose name they had forgotten—he was John Connally, I told them—was wounded. Lyndon Johnson was all right and was now president of the United States. Two thoughts suddenly flashed into my mind: I'd shaken hands with a president, and my father was his attorney and adviser. These realizations faded as quickly as they dawned. My friends and I were much more interested in speculating on who was responsible for the assassination. Right-wing nuts, I predicted. One of my friends guessed the Ku Klux Klan was behind it and wanted to know how active the Klan had been in Dallas. Not very, I answered, not near as much as the John Birch Society, or the National Indignation Committee, or the people who wanted to impeach Earl Warren.

Quickly, conspiracy theories began to take shape. No wonder many Americans still can't believe that a loner and communist sympathizer—in Dallas, of all places!—acting for his own reasons and on his own impulses, killed John Kennedy all by himself.

No one at Stanford who talked to me that weekend or later blamed Kennedy's death on Dallas or on what was called by some pundits the atmosphere of hate there. Nuts are everywhere, a professor of medieval history said to me during a party at his house; you can't hold any city responsible for them. Of all the people I talked with, the ones who were most critical of Dallas were my friends *from* there, the guys who left Texas to go to college in other states. In letters between us, we exchanged judgments much more cutting than anything I heard in California. One of my old pals wrote if JFK had to be assassinated, he was glad it was in Dallas, because the city deserved whatever bad happened to it. He also advised me to do what he was doing and say I was from Houston.

When I phoned my mother on the night of the twenty-second, she wanted to be reassured that I wasn't being put in awkward or unhappy situations because of the accident of my permanent residence. Once she learned I hadn't been, she crisply advised me to talk as little as I possibly could about where I was from and what I thought about it. There was no sense in inviting trouble, she said, and no honor in joining in any chorus of criticism.

Mother laid special stress on the latter point, because she had patiently (if unsympathetically) listened to my frequent railing against the pretensions, philosophy, and politics of Dallas and lengthy listings of the bigotry, intolerance, Babbittry, and philistinism to be found there. (If Mother thought of Dallasites as philistines, she did so only because they were continually being smited by the jawbones of asses, in which number she probably included her son.) Aside from her fondness for living where she did, my mother did not believe in blaming the many for the sins of one. To her, sin was not collective. To think otherwise was itself an invitation to immorality, because it gave a plausible excuse for sinners looking to justify their behavior. "Everybody does it" was not a valid defense in the Court of Mother.

Of course, my mother intended her instructions would have two practical applications. I shouldn't explain away Lee Harvey Oswald as merely a product of Dallas. I should resist any temptation to prove my bona fides as a sophisticated Stanford student by joining in what could become a popular game—bashing the city and state. After she had done her maternal duty, Mother proceeded to tell me what she and Dad had been doing when they heard the news of Kennedy's death.

My parents had been separated for four years. They only occasionally spoke. When they did, the subjects of their conversations centered around their children and the maintenance of our house. For some reason, they decided to mix business with lunch on November 22. Dad came out to 6131 Lupton, and they were at the table eating when they heard the news. According to Mother, my father's immediate reaction was, "Well, I guess Dallas will never get that new Federal Building now." I'm not sure whether he meant this as a joke, as a way of using humor to distance himself from the shocking news; or whether he really expected his city would be blamed and punished for the murder of John Kennedy, and as a result would get no favors even from the Texan now in the White House.

Not long thereafter, the phone rang. It was Dad's secretary. Unable to find him anywhere else, she had finally tried Mother's number out of sheer desperation. There was a message that could not wait. Soon after Kennedy's death had been announced, Lyndon Johnson had tried to get in touch with him. Without question, the president would expect him to return the call. She had no idea why he had to talk with Dad. She only knew that he wanted to speak to him, and no doubt as soon as possible.

My father guessed the call had something to do with the Texas Broadcasting Corporation. The Johnsons simply could not continue to run it while they lived at 1600 Pennsylvania Avenue. Dad assumed LBJ must have moved immediately to start the process of establishing a blind trust, and wanted his legal advice on how to do this with a minimum of fuss and maximum of protection for the family. To him, this was reassuring. In the immediate aftermath of a shocking tragedy, one which, as Dad subsequently recalled, "set everybody back," the new president was swiftly and surely responding to personal and political necessities.

I couldn't wait to tell my roommates that Lyndon Johnson had tried to contact my father before Air Force One left for Washington. The news fascinated them, and we spent some time talking about why LBJ did this and what it might mean for the Bullion family. Obviously, I was proud that the new president would reach out so quickly for Dad's help, and I wanted people to know about his and my connection to the White House. Equally obviously, I was basking in the reflected glory of having met the president of the United States. I'd done more than just shake his hand, too; he'd given me a pen and a knife and said he hoped to see me again. My friends were impressed and about as eager as I to hear more about what my father's work for LBJ would be.

Notice two assumptions. It was terrific to know a president. Nothing but interesting and good things would come from that acquaintance. Second, these were our thoughts because we respected the office. That feeling was extended to whoever was currently serving, in this case suddenly and tragically, Lyndon Johnson. We didn't question that LBJ was worthy of every American's respect and support. We trusted him to do his best to deal with the challenges facing the country at home and abroad.

We didn't foresee that in eighteen months, we'd be wondering what in the hell was going on in Vietnam. By Graduation Day in June 1966, more pointed questions were being asked LBJ, such as how many kids did he kill that day. People had started counting the evasions, half-truths, and outright deceptions that widened what we were calling the credibility gap. In 1963 attitudes toward the American presidency in particular and national politicians in general were on the verge of a rapid and, thus far, irreversible metamorphosis from trust to cynicism, from respect to contempt, and from obedience to resistance. Many would later say that these changes began on November 22, 1963.

What strikes me even more as I look back is the largely unquestioned assumption that knowing a president couldn't be anything but good. Nowadays, no one with a lick of sense would go near a president or a candidate for that office without a good attorney to keep track of the laws you might be breaking. Nearly forty years ago, it was different. What bad could possibly result from such an association?

My mother, I must say, was the one person who could envision circumstances where knowing a president might be dangerous and harmful. She did not base this perception on a general principle, like the Psalmist's injunction to "put not thy trust in princes." Her caution was inspired by her personal knowledge of the risks attendant on a connection with this particular president. Though she wished LBJ well, she was wary of what the future might hold.

As far as I was concerned, that we knew LBJ and LBJ knew us was great. Only good things and interesting stories could come from this. And good things did happen to the Bullions. We got our share of interesting stories, too. None of us would say, though, that my father's association with LBJ was an unmixed blessing.

★ ★ ★

President Johnson did not want to talk to Dad on November 22 about arranging for a blind trust. He wanted to ask whether he should be sworn in as president immediately, or whether he should wait until he returned to Washington. The counsel he had received from others, including Robert Kennedy and Walter Jenkins, had been inconclusive. RFK was struggling to come to terms with his brother's shocking death; Jenkins was trying to get his mind around the numbing fact he was now one of the principal advisers of the president of the United States. Neither gave unambiguous advice. All accounts indicate that Johnson himself was strongly leaning toward taking the oath immediately. Still, he held back.

LBJ must have felt he needed the thoughts of a close associate who would unquestionably have his interests and no one else's at heart on this awful day. The new president also wanted to know the exact wording of his oath of office—the very sort of information he would expect a fine attorney to be able to find out immediately. Where better to seek that information than from a lawyer whose accuracy he had long appreciated?

As things turned out, Dad was of no help, because no one could find him fast enough to suit LBJ. Instead, Johnson turned to Irving Goldberg. My father's old friend urged him to take the oath as soon as possible, assured him that any judicial officer could swear him in, and

LBJ with Lady Bird, Sarah Hughes, and other witnesses immediately
before taking the oath of office on Air Force One, November 22, 1963.
LBJ Library. Photo by Cecil Stoughton.

suggested he select Judge Sarah T. Hughes, recently appointed to the
federal bench after LBJ had vigorously lobbied for her within the Kennedy administration and with former colleagues in the Senate.

By virtue of the accident of having lunch with Mother, my father
played no part in the decisions made in Dallas and Washington while
Air Force One remained on the ground. Thus he fortuitously was not
swept into the later controversies over who said what to LBJ that afternoon, and who deserved blame or—alternatively—earned praise for
the decision to take the oath of office before the flight back to the
nation's capital.

Within hours Dad was making the same journey. On November 24
he was in Washington meeting with the president, Lady Bird, Abe
Fortas, Carol Agger, A.W. Moursund, and Don Thomas. He had already
anticipated the purpose of this gathering. LBJ wanted to distance himself and his family from the direction and operation of their property
and investments as rapidly and publicly as possible.

★ ★ ★

My father's recollections about this meeting are sketchy. He remembers clearly the basic decisions that were made, and these I describe below. He also recalls that he and Don Thomas drafted the legal documents afterwards and along with LBJ played the major parts in the discussion. Interestingly, he has no memory of Fortas and Agger's presence. That may indicate they were mostly silent, since the discussion focused on matters much more familiar to Dad, Thomas, and Moursund.

It may also reveal how traumatic the assassination had been for my father. For him, as for many of his fellow citizens, many of the events of that weekend became a blur. When I asked how the Johnsons appeared on this occasion, he told me again that JFK's killing "set everybody back" and said he could only remember that everyone was subdued and thoughtful. Indeed, he does not even recall being with Mother when news of the assassination flashed onto the radio. "I was in Shreveport," he once told me, "when LBJ tried to reach me." In fact, he had been in that Louisiana city on November 21. Johnson had evidently tried to call him that day and been told by his secretary that he would return on Friday the twenty-second and could be easily reached then. Later, Dad telescoped the two days together. For a good portion of that weekend in November, he must have been operating on automatic pilot.

Still, my father's instincts and intelligence served him well. Along with the others at the Washington meeting, he quickly determined that the most appropriate way to protect the Johnsons politically and personally was the creation of a blind trust. The trustees would have overall management of the Texas Broadcasting Corporation and any other property. They were also empowered to make investments using capital generated by the entities under their oversight. They were charged to make decisions in the best interests of the Johnson family; acting negligently or illegally would make them liable to civil and criminal proceedings. Finally, the trustees were responsible for guaranteeing that the Johnsons had no involvement in either the day-to-day running of Texas Broadcasting and its wholly owned subsidiaries or any discussion and decision on investment strategies. In sum, the blind trust was intended to insure that Lyndon Johnson would not use the immense power of the presidency to feather his own nest. It also was meant to reassure the public and the politicians that he *could not* do this.

With the help of Lyndon, Lady Bird, and their other advisers, Dad completed the creation of the blind trust with impressive speed.

Lady Bird Johnson, November 30, 1963.
LBJ Library. Photo by Yoichi R. Okamoto.

November 24 was a Sunday, so the documents could not be filed in court immediately. First thing Monday morning the process began.

Before those papers were filed, the Johnsons, Thomas, Moursund, and my father made an important decision. They agreed that the trustees would make no controversial investments. Controversial meant two things. First: no highly speculative, economically risky investments. Understandably, the president didn't want to place this power in anyone else's hands, no matter how much he had confidence in the trustees. Second: no *politically* controversial investments. The advisers agreed that the trustees had to stay away from anything with even the most remote impact on the family's holdings in radio and television stations. Above all else, nothing could be done that might conceivably be interpreted as further improving the competitive position of KTBC. This decision was painful indeed for Johnson. The television station was the cash cow whose milk nourished everything else. Given recent technological advances in communications and the prospect of more to come, plus the virtual certainty that the days of its monopoly in the Austin market were numbered, KTBC's profits might decline and its competitive position in the future weaken before LBJ left the White House. Nevertheless, he agreed that this decision had to be made immediately and adhered to religiously.

The trustees could, however, make noncontroversial investments. These Johnson and the three advisers defined as buying rural land. If the trustees found acreage at a good price along the Pedernales River or elsewhere in the Hill Country, they were to take full advantage of those opportunities. LBJ was quite specific about which tracts were most attractive to him. Some were already for sale. Others were in the possession of owners who probably would respond favorably to fair offers. Finally, the trustees should target certain areas for investment. Johnson was fully conversant with the plans of the Lower Colorado River Authority to build more dams and create more lakes in Central Texas. Since he loved his house in the country by the Pedernales so much, he believed that others might want homes away from cities and towns and around water. If this happened, and if the trustees bought the right property, he could anticipate that these investments in land might be very profitable indeed.

And so they were. "The Johnson family made a mint off these investments in rural land," Dad recently told me. They became more lucrative than KTBC which, as the president predicted, faced competition from other television stations by the late 1960s. After LBJ's death in 1973, the appreciation of the value of his land in the Hill Country and the successful development of weekend homes on portions of it created a new and more bountiful cash cow for the Johnsons. The decision the president and my father made in late November 1963 proved to be a highly lucrative one. It provided the launching pad for the family's current fortune, which has been estimated recently at being worth approximately 150 million dollars.

"Was LBJ lucky, or was he farsighted?" I asked Dad. He smiled and shook his head. Then he referred to our own experiences in speculating on land. "Sure, nobody's making more of it," he said, repeating a bit of wisdom we'd used to justify a variety of purchases. "At the same time, when you want to hang on to it, potential buyers are as thick as

LBJ and Waddy Bullion in the Oval Office, November 29, 1963.
LBJ Library. Photo by Yoichi R. Okamoto.

ticks in the summer, and when you want to sell, you can't find anybody willing to come close to your asking price. And," he reminded me, "there's always what's going on around your land and what's happening to it." He began counting off disasters on his fingers. "There's drought; there's flood; there's fire; there's environmental regulations; there's restrictions on water usage; and," here he paused so I could chime in with him, "there's motocross!" My sisters' and my decision to part with the Sam Bass place was inspired by a neighbor's creation of tracks and paths for motorcycle racing. We glumly estimated it cost us between $500 and $1000 an acre when we sold the ranch. Insofar as my question was concerned, I could see the conclusion my father was pointing me toward. LBJ was at least as fortunate as he was prescient; i.e., he was both lucky and good.

I'd qualify this conclusion somewhat. My father is being modest, because he was one of the two men the Johnsons wanted to serve as trustees. Thus he was intimately involved in the negotiations for the land that the family later profited from so heavily.

The other trustee was A.W. Moursund, the Hill Country rancher and neighbor of the Johnsons who had been present when Robert Kennedy went deer hunting. LBJ lauded Moursund as being the equal of his

mother and his wife in intelligence and loyalty, high praise indeed from
him. Without question, this man would do whatever he could to serve
the best interests of the Johnsons. LBJ also trusted Moursund's knowledge of the rural real estate market in Central Texas. Probably he
would have chosen A.W. in any event because of their long association
and his assessment of Moursund's commitment to the Johnsons. He
was well aware of Moursund's feelings for him. As A.W. remembered
long after LBJ's death, "The president needed a friend. I liked him,"
Moursund continued, "and he liked me." But I suspect this was less
important to Johnson than their mutual successes in real estate investments. The choice of Moursund signaled the directions Lyndon
Johnson wanted future investments under the blind trust to take. Add
to A.W. my father, who had proven his loyalty and intelligence as an
adviser on taxes and as a deviser of the Texas Broadcasting Corporation strategy, and Lyndon and Lady Bird could rest assured their affairs
were in the best hands possible.

LBJ and A.W. Moursund, December 25, 1963.
LBJ Library. Photo by Yoichi R. Okamoto.

★ ★ ★

The creation of the blind trust was news. Recent Senate and Justice Department investigations of influence-peddling by Bobby Baker,

the Secretary to the Senate during LBJ's tenure as Majority Leader, had whetted the press's curiosity about the increase of the Johnson family's wealth during the 1950s. Announcement of the identity of the trustees renewed that interest and gave reporters new people to quiz about Lyndon's and Lady Bird Johnson's property and investments. As early as November 27, 1963, Larry Winship, the editor of the *Boston Globe*, was in Johnson City, investigating LBJ's business interests. Jesse Kellam, whom the trustees had appointed as their business manager, reported to the president that he was friendly when he visited with Moursund. In turn, the two trustees were trying to be as helpful as they could be to Winship.

If A.W. and my father hoped that journalistic interest in this subject would evaporate after one series of sympathetic in-depth stories, they were disappointed. In April 1964 they received a long wire from the *Wall Street Journal* asking what Walter Jenkins called "pretty pointed" questions. These were directed to Dad and Moursund because LBJ had told reporters he had nothing to hide: the trustees were the people to ask; he had nothing to do with running the businesses now. Clearly the *Journal* wasn't convinced that either statement was true. The editors wanted to know if Dad and Moursund were considering selling the businesses, since Johnson had said they could if they decided that was wise. The *Journal* also wanted the gross revenue and the net income of the family's holdings since Johnson had been elected vice president, and the amount of dividends paid to Lady Bird and their two daughters since my father and Don Thomas set up the trust. Finally, the paper wanted to know "what matters were discussed during a conversation between Johnson and trustee Moursund" during LBJ's visit to Texas in March, and what matters the president had talked about with Kellam "in his repeated sessions with the Johnsons in the White House and in Texas."

Jenkins characterized this request as "a nasty wire. It says that failure to answer these questions would also be newsworthy too. I mean," he concluded, "kind of bribery."

More accurately, LBJ termed it "a little blackmail." He was furious, insisting to Jenkins that he had not discussed anything about the business with Moursund, Kellam, or Dad. What concerned him—and understandably so—was the possibility that public pressure created by investigations such as this one resulting in unfriendly articles would compel sale of the properties, especially KTBC. Johnson wanted to hang on to everything because he was convinced his family would suffer in both the short and long run from a forced divestiture at this time.

Keeping KTBC would protect his family. He emphasized again and again that the station and other properties were the trustees' businesses, not his. He protested he didn't know "what they've done that caused this madness to descend...[and] this attack to be made." Finally, he insisted that accusations against his family were unjust, because they misrepresented the real situation. As he angrily told Bill Moyers, Bird and the girls not only weren't profiting from improper governmental assistance; they actually were losing money. Since the trust had been established, he claimed, they were making less than before.

Whether LBJ really expected to have no say in the trustees' decisions is open to question. Perhaps his sliding back and forth between using "we" and "they" when he referred to my father and Moursund is indicative of just how hands-off he planned to be if they confronted major decisions about the properties covered by the trust. Notice the pronoun he used (and I've emphasized) when he mentioned a hypothetical sale of property in his talk with Jenkins: "*We* can give 'em the public records and say that *we'd* be glad to consider any offer. *We've* had none." Johnson was far too careful to talk this way in public, where it would be awkward to explain away his choice of words by claiming he was merely pretending he was one of the trustees, and embarrassing to reveal his opposition to selling except for the most favorable terms. Without question, Dad and Moursund understood his thoughts on this subject. They knew it would have to be one hell of an offer for them to consider it at all. It's difficult for me to imagine that LBJ would not have insisted on being informed about any such deal, and on making his opinions known, almost certainly via Jesse Kellam, to the trustees. In the present situation, it was the job of my father and his fellow trustee to oversee the businesses and to supply inquiring reporters with as little information as possible, and that derived chiefly from the articles of agreement on the trust and the public records attached to it. LBJ left dealing with the reporters' bosses to that skilled practitioner of law and politics in Washington, Abe Fortas.

Fortas's April 30, 1964 report on his conference with the Washington bureau of the *Wall Street Journal* reveals how Dad and Moursund dealt with the press on these issues. He explained to the *Journal*'s men that "these were Texans and that they didn't feel that when they were running a business that they ought to be subjected to any kind of

LBJ and Abe Fortas, November 30, 1963.
LBJ Library. Photo by Yoichi R. Okamoto.

badgering that other people running a business were immune from."
Having set forth the issue of fairness, the trustees went on the attack,
by calling into question the motivation behind the *Journal*'s investigation. "Their position," said Fortas, "was that this was all politics and
from the Republican National Committee." When the bureau chief protested that this wasn't so, he bluntly replied, "Of course it's political."

Fortas spoke for my father as well as himself. When Dad was
approached by reporters in the future, he used the tactics described by
Tom Collins of *Newsday*, who complained to George Reedy that "he had
a very brief conference with Waddy Bullion" about the operation of the
ranch and KTBC, but "wasn't able to get any satisfaction." The less
said, the better. That was my father's rule when dealing with reporters.
If they wanted to pursue specific points, they'd have to take them up
with political advisers like Walter Jenkins, or with Washington lawyers,
principally Abe Fortas. Inevitably, this delayed stories. Invariably, it
produced only familiar stuff for the reporters, who got to hear all over
again that their investigations were politically inspired, and to listen
once more to an implied or explicit accusation that they were serving
the cause of the president's opponents within the Republican Party and
outside it as well.

What the reporters did not hear was the slightest suggestion they were asking the wrong questions and looking in the wrong places. For all the reportage about KTBC, the significance of the Texas Broadcasting Corporation's ownership of ranches and other investments as well as the communications companies went essentially unexamined and fundamentally misunderstood. When it looked like the newspapers might stumble onto this in late April 1964, Abe Fortas became concerned. "If you've got to get into all the rest of the property that Texas Broadcasting [Corporation] owns to correct inflated estimates of its profitability," he warned LBJ, it would be better to ignore the error. To make a full disclosure, he thought, "would be a mistake." Confident he and the trustees could avoid talking about all of the corporation's assets, Johnson brushed aside Fortas's fears. The reporters would be satisfied with a limited, selective account of the trustees' sale of stock in a television station outside Austin and "a bunch of cattle" from ranches in the Hill Country. The president proved to be right. Because investigations centered on KTBC and the possibly improper use of his political influence on its behalf, no one detailed the interlocking relationship of everything Texas Broadcasting owned. Dad had helped create and implement a plan that effectively removed LBJ's ranch and other real estate purchases from politically damaging scrutiny.

In much the same way, the press limited its own inquiry into the blind trust. Convinced that LBJ had pressured the FCC into giving KTBC a monopoly of the Austin market, certain he was continuing to pull strings in its favor, reporters concentrated on the television station. LBJ, Dad, and the other advisers on the blind trust had anticipated this and guarded against it already. The management of KTBC was cautious and careful. Nothing would be done that would raise the slightest whiff of political scandal. The press could dig and dig to its heart's content; nothing new would be found, because nothing new was going on. Meanwhile, at the behest of LBJ the trustees were aggressively and intelligently buying land in Central Texas. That these purchases might be guided by prior knowledge of plans by governmental agencies for the future development of the area's lakes and rivers evidently didn't occur to many journalists. Not only were they focusing on KTBC, but they also had conditioned themselves to believe that Lyndon Johnson's ranches were a sideshow, an uneconomic expression of his ego rather than the means to wealth in the years ahead.

The truth was the Johnsons and their advisers were shrewder than those who assumed they'd figured LBJ out. Unaware of the blinders they had fastened on their own eyes, those people were illustrating the truth of a bit of philosophy Charles Schultz put in Charlie Brown's mouth during the sixties: "We're never so dumb as when we think we're smart."

Of course, to be fair, I should point out that the nation's journalists were not the only ones in 1964 whose blind trust in their abilities to understand the present and to predict the future misled them. I certainly was one, as I blithely assumed nothing but good could come from knowing the man in the White House. There were others in the same boat, too. Numbered among them was the president of the United States.

CHAPTER 10

Scandals

Fencing with reporters over the operation of the trust took less of my father's time after mid-1964. By June of that year, the media's focus shifted to the Republican Party and Barry Goldwater. Afterwards their attention turned to the presidential campaign. Inquiries into the magnitude and sources of the Johnson family's wealth, and its management by Dad and A.W. Moursund, gave way to more immediately important stories. Because no one regarded Waddy Bullion as part of LBJ's political team, interest in him, which had never been great, waned.

That changed dramatically in late October, with the arrest of Walter Jenkins for public indecency in a men's room at the downtown Washington YMCA. Revelations about this first in the Washington press, then subsequently in the national media, set in motion events that nearly swept my father into the scandal. He emerged from the crisis unscathed. Indeed, he was even unaware of the full dimensions of what was going on around and about him until much later. Still, the aftermath of Walter's political and personal crisis serves as a reminder of what could happen to those who worked in the boat for LBJ. They could become totally vulnerable without warning, their weaknesses and mistakes stripped naked and exposed to full view.

The news about Walter Jenkins astonished my father. To Dad, it could only be explained by a combination of sheer exhaustion from the pace of work at the White House and the impact of several drinks on an empty stomach at a cocktail party before the encounter at the Y. Like Lady Bird Johnson, who eloquently expressed her love for Jenkins and

Walter Jenkins,
December 1, 1963.
*LBJ Library. Photo by
Yoichi R. Okamoto.*

her sympathy for his family, my father regarded this as an aberration, one which had no bearing on their friendship.

In contrast to his wife, LBJ did not publicly recall the many years of dedicated service Walter had given him. Nor did he send the Jenkins family heartfelt wishes for a happy resolution of their difficulties. Mostly he was silent. When Walter resigned from the White House staff, he acknowledged it with a terse, businesslike letter. Without question, this cold response was dictated in part by Johnson's sense of the political realities of a presidential campaign. I remember seeing a bumper sticker in San Francisco that read "Johnson for King; Jenkins for Queen." LBJ didn't want to add any fuel to those fires by expressing sympathy for Walter Jenkins in public.

Walter and his family understood why the president was publicly silent. What hurt them more was the absence of sufficient private reassurances from him that the friendship of the two men would endure. That wound still ached after LBJ's death in 1973. How much it did a friend of mine discovered by accident sometime in the mid-seventies.

★ ★ ★

My friend was finishing his doctorate in anthropology at the University of Texas when he met Walter Jenkins. To relieve the pressure of meeting graduate school deadlines for the completion of his dissertation, he played bridge. He was quite good at it, so good that he was invited to join other serious amateurs in regular weekly rubbers. Walter already played with this group. He loved bridge for the same reason my friend did, as a stimulating and challenging, yet relaxing and refreshing leisure pursuit. Mutual acquaintances thought they would enjoy being partners. They did.

The third or fourth time they played together, my friend suddenly realized his partner had the same name as the man who had served on Lyndon Johnson's staff at the White House. Without thinking, he asked, "Are you *the* Walter Jenkins? The one who worked with LBJ?" Silence abruptly settled over the table. Walter glared at my friend over the cards fanned in his hand. After a long moment, he coldly snapped,

"Yes." For the rest of the evening's play, he said nothing beyond terse bids when it was his turn. Nor did he say anything other than "two clubs" or "three spades" during the next three weeks of bridge.

My friend was appalled by what he had blurted out. Afraid that Jenkins believed that he had wanted to know if he was playing cards with a notorious pervert, he could think of no way of apologizing without making matters worse. One night one of Walter's daughters sat in at another table. When the players broke for drinks and snacks, my friend asked if he could speak privately with her. They went out into the hall, and he urgently told her he was terribly sorry and had meant no insult or harm by his question. "I'll pass that along to Daddy," she replied, "because I'm sure he'll appreciate it." Then she went on, "In the future, never mention those days to him. He doesn't want to think about them ever again." Then, after a pause, she concluded by saying, "Please don't mention Lyndon Johnson to him in conversation. Or to me either."

Instantly, my friend agreed. Because he is a courteous man, he would have respected the Jenkinses' wishes in any event. But, as he later told me, Walter's frigid stare from across the table and his daughter's intense reaction to the name of the former president would have made him afraid to cross them even had he been an utterly unmannered person. And, despite the apology made and accepted, Jenkins never lapsed into cheerful, casual card-table banter with my friend again. Uncomfortable, he stopped playing bridge with Walter.

Whenever Dad recalls what happened to Walter Jenkins, he just shakes his head. "That was bad," he once told me. He's never gone beyond those three words. He doesn't need to. What was bad about Walter's fate was certainly not any homosexual tendencies he might have had, and not even his arrest and public disgrace. Having to resign from the White House staff probably added years to his life. Friends found him work in public relations in Austin. Within a few months, Jesse Kellam hired him to do some consulting for KTBC. What was bad was the absence of immediate private and meaningful words of comfort and hope extended from his captain after he was tossed overboard.

"If ever a man loved another man," my father has said to me, "Walter Jenkins loved LBJ." I thought I knew what he meant, but I figured I should ask anyway. "You're not talking about erotic love, are you?" Dad reacted instantly. "God, no!" Then he added, "I'm not talking about neurotic love, either." After smiling briefly at the unintentional euphony of erotic and neurotic, he went on to explain.

Certainly part of Walter's love was emotionally based. He liked Lyndon Johnson personally, he enjoyed being with him during rare leisure moments and on the ranch, and his loyalty to him was strong and unwavering. But, Dad emphasized, Walter's love was also intellectual and rational, born of his mind as well as his heart. His reason convinced him that LBJ could and would change the world for the better. Such a man deserved the full support of like-minded people. Having reached these conclusions, Walter Jenkins decided to serve Lyndon Johnson. "He *decided*," Dad stressed. Walter was not carried away on the crest of emotion. His feelings did not render him powerless. He willed his love for LBJ. Then he accepted the consequences of that decision for his personal life and his professional career.

In return, Walter got put in the boat. Johnson valued his intelligence, loyalty, and utter commitment to the boat's captain and the voyage's purpose. That did not mean, however, that he ranked his appreciation and affection for Walter Jenkins as equal to his own self-love and his personal goals. Walter had to earn his place on the crew every day. If he failed, he had to go, without any hesitation or much remorse on LBJ's part.

Why would Walter Jenkins or anyone else expect any comforting or hopeful words from Lyndon Johnson? He hadn't pulled his weight to the end. Therefore he had to get out and walk home. By himself.

My father wrote a private, personal note of support to Walter. Unlike Lady Bird, he made no public statement. Nor did any reporter ask for his reaction or inquire into his relationship with Walter Jenkins. That their friendship continued after October 1964 seemed to be nobody's business but their own. But other people were interested in finding out more about the nature of their friendship. One of them was Lyndon Johnson.

Some years later, Mother told me that the FBI had conducted a secret investigation of my father during 1964 that was related to Jenkins's arrest. What prompted this, she said, was a report from a source LBJ regarded as reliable that a prominent newspaper was on the verge of publishing a story naming Dad and Walter as lovers and claiming they were part of an extensive homosexual "ring" at the White House. The president wanted to know the truth about this accusation as soon as possible. He turned to the agency officially responsible for investigating possible threats to national security, and unofficially habituated to catering to his appetite for reports on the private foibles of prominent people in Washington: J. Edgar Hoover's FBI. Agents from the Bureau were to check out as quickly and as quietly as possible the merits of this story. If it was accurate, LBJ intended to cut his ties with my father rapidly, decisively, and permanently. If it was false, his plan was to compel the paper's editors to spike the story immediately.

The president insisted that this investigation be a carefully guarded secret. He did this for a mixture of reasons. One surely was to avoid needlessly embarrassing Dad and members of the White House staff. That he was responsible for a currently active inquiry could be portrayed by his political enemies and the newspaper as his belief that this rumor might well be true. If he were perfectly confident in their heterosexuality, why have an investigation at all? That word had gotten out about the ongoing FBI investigation might lead to suspicions that he himself had been responsible for leaking it, in order to warn his attorney and his advisers to cover up evidence. Embarrassment for his friends and himself would equal serious embarrassment for his presidency. LBJ succeeded in impressing on the FBI agents the need to be quiet, discreet, closemouthed, and secretive themselves and to demand that those they interviewed kept this to themselves as well.

Mother remarked sardonically that the FBI ultimately was fully convinced Dad was heterosexual. Then she laughed as she said, "If the newspaper had printed that story, your father might have retired. He wouldn't have to practice law any longer; all of us could live quite comfortably off the proceeds from the libel judgment."

"You're surely right," I replied, "I'm just sorry I won't inherit any riches from that paper."

Dad never learned about this investigation. When I asked him about it as I was writing this book, he was astounded. The minute I described what Mother had said, he protested, "I had one of the highest security clearances in the country. There was no need for any investigation; I'd already been cleared." Gently, I pointed out that his clearance dated from his service as Admiral King's aide during the Second World War, and these questions about his sexual preferences and his friendship with Walter Jenkins arose as a result of events twenty years after his service in the Navy. This observation did not register in his consciousness. "I knew the date of D-Day," he reminded me. "I knew more than all of those generals and admirals who rushed into print with their memoirs. All of them boasted about how many secrets they knew, and I knew things they couldn't even have imagined." Suddenly I realized what he was saying without his explicitly telling me his secrets. My father was on the very short list of people who knew about ULTRA and MAGIC. He was aware the Allies had broken the most secret German and Japanese codes. He must have regularly abstracted material from our enemies' communications for the admiral.

As I digested this part of Dad's history, I realized something else. He did not complain, for he has never been one to anguish out loud about things he cannot change, but I could read his mind from his transfixed expression. He had served his country loyally and well, keeping some of her most closely held secrets to himself for years, never betraying them by any word he spoke or risking them by his behavior. That record did not count for anything in the fall of 1964.

My father was used to having his professional expertise questioned by clients reluctant to accept it when they wanted to do as they pleased. He was accustomed to having his legal arguments tested and challenged by judges and opposing attorneys. Courtrooms, after all, proceed on an adversarial basis, even when lawyers are straining to reach settlements. But nothing in his past experience prepared him for becoming aware of a wide ranging official investigation that culminated in a detailed report on his private life.

All of us have done or said things we wish we hadn't. Some of these may be illegal, some immoral, some just foolish, embarrassing reminders that we're human. We all would prefer that our venial and mortal sins of omission and commission remain secret. Dad is no different. And he had to feel that, given LBJ's intense interest in gossip and his penchant for studying raw FBI files, the president must have pored over the entire report. As for me, I'm sure Lyndon Johnson did just that. Why I'm so certain will become clear in due time.

For years my father has been a zealous defender of the right to privacy. He has always conceded that you won't find an explicit statement of this right in the Constitution. Still, he argues, it is nonetheless essential in modern America, where the government claims the power and has vast resources to gather, file, and use for various purposes all sorts of information about citizens. Learning about the FBI investigation of himself confirmed his opinion.

★ ★ ★

Hearing about it from me did not affect Dad's opinion of LBJ in retrospect. He continues to respect his former client and still thinks of him as a friend, while retaining the reservations I've already described about what he primly calls Johnson's "methodology" on occasions. No doubt this would have been one of those times when he looked askance at those methods, so if he had learned about the investigation at the time, a lot would have depended on how LBJ explained his decision. I believe Johnson would have done this well. He could argue that he needed to protect his presidency by establishing the truth as quickly as possible. He could point out that he had kept the investigation a secret. No scandal would be attached to Dad's name because he used the results of the FBI inquiry to squelch reports and speculation in the press. Besides, he and J. Edgar Hoover's boys had proven that Dad was a real man, a true stud—it's very easy for me to imagine Lyndon Johnson saying that with a smile and a wink.

The thrust of remarks such as these would be aimed at persuading Dad that the president had acted as his protector in this crisis. My father could draw the appropriate conclusion: he was obligated to Lyndon Johnson for his swift and decisive steps to resolve and conclude this affair. For him to break off the relationship because of this would be petty, unfair, and ungrateful. It might also be harmful to his future business. Arguments like these would, I am convinced, have kept Dad pulling on the boat's oars whenever the president asked him to help out. I doubt LBJ would have worried much about the possibility of losing his counsel as trustee.

Still, Johnson did not want to have to make these points to my father. There was no reason to risk upsetting Dad for no purpose other than informing him about an unpleasant truth after the fact and after he had been pronounced fit to be around the president. From LBJ's standpoint, it was best to keep him in the dark. Ironically, the president could not have accomplished this without the assistance of my mother. I'm certain she was furious at him. A man she detested had put her in the morally dubious position of withholding shocking and significant information from her husband when, unknown to him, his reputation and perhaps his family's reputation as well were at stake. She must have felt Lyndon Johnson had finally succeeded in corrupting her too.

★ ★ ★

LBJ did have to inform the editors of the prominent paper who were mulling over whether to publish a story on Waddy and Walter about the results of the FBI investigation. Why was he unconcerned about the possibility they might decide to print a piece about it? Had he been asked this question then, surely he would have responded with an incredulous look and the obvious truth: these findings of the FBI would not have been news.

Few people in Washington would have cared one way or another whether a Dallas lawyer was a homosexual and had one, or fifty, lovers. What interested them was whether one of LBJ's attorneys, just like one of his political fixers, was homosexual. Should that link be established, then it was news. It also afforded an opportunity to charge the president at least with poor judgment in choosing the people who advised him on important public and private matters.

Because the FBI had established Dad was heterosexual, he and the president did not need to worry about publication of either his secrets or the clandestine inquiry into them. During the sixties, how heterosexual men in public life conducted themselves was not news. Gossip about their adventures spiced private conversation, and these tales were regarded by many as proof of their manhood. In the case of politicians, sleeping with women other than their wives was evidence of their potency and prowess. Reporting of these liaisons, however, was virtually nonexistent. Yes, British politicians got in trouble over sex parties in the early sixties, and the American media reported the Profumo-Keeler affair and its consequences. But this was because issues of British national security were involved when the Minister of Defense shared a mistress with a Soviet diplomat. Ordinarily, the papers, radio, and TV winked at less-dangerous arrangements, regarding them in the spirit of boys-will-be-boys. Whatever the FBI might have uncovered about my father's heterosexual adventures, they would be of no interest to those who decided which news would be fit to print.

Though Dad's private life did not make him vulnerable, his professional advice to Lyndon Johnson had done so in the recent past and would continue to do so in the years ahead. Once again, his basic problem was his connection to LBJ. He knew the details of the Johnsons' family estate. Presumably he knew where the bodies were buried in it as well. He was legally responsible, along with A.W. Moursund, for administering that estate while LBJ was president. By the terms of the blind trust, he and Moursund made all the business decisions affecting the family's interests and properties without consulting any of the Johnsons. Was this merely a legal fiction, or was it actual reality? These sorts of questions—the details of the estate, how it was amassed, what role political influence had played in its creation, the role of Lyndon Johnson's official positions in this process, the extent of government favors, and whether LBJ was keeping his hands off the management of the property—had been news right after he became president. They could easily become so again when he ran for a full term of office. If they did, the media would be looking for scandals, because that was what caused people to buy papers and switch stations. The possibility always existed that this hunger would inspire more pointed and informed questions than the ones Dad had fended off during the first months of the blind trust.

Political considerations did not explain most journalists' interest in these topics, but their disinterest did not prevent their work from having political consequences. Some, of course, welcomed the chance to make partisan hay while the investigative sun shone on LBJ. The president had determined enemies. Some wrote for newspapers; others served in Congress. Both groups had political objectives; each wanted to clip LBJ's wings. Injuring or ruining Dad's reputation and career along the way didn't concern them in the slightest. They probably would have felt he deserved it, simply because he did the president's business. Dad needed to be careful. He had important legal responsibilities, ones he had to meet to the best of his abilities. At times, the attention of the media, the Republican Party, and Kennedy loyalists would focus on him. He would be watched by LBJ's enemies. They would be ready to inflate mistakes into serious scandals. So the president's foes became his own.

CHAPTER 11

Friends

LBJ's enemies, and what they could do to those in his boat, were not my father's only concerns. In politics, as in life generally, one's friends are capable of doing as much damage as one's foes. "God protect me against my friends; I'll handle the others myself," is a wry motto based on painful experience. It was unquestionably flattering, and certainly profitable, that the photographs of the president and Dad hung in his office at Thompson, Knight were inscribed "To J. Waddy Bullion from his friend, Lyndon B. Johnson." Still, he had to be extremely careful when dealing with this particular friend.

When the spirit moved him, Lyndon Johnson enjoyed rewarding those who were serving him faithfully and well. As president, he had a vested interest in bringing intelligent, highly capable individuals into positions of responsibility and power, especially those who would remember their maker and acknowledge that their first allegiance was to LBJ. For my father, he had two possible offices in mind. His first choice was Commissioner of the Internal Revenue Service.

Johnson was eager to put his principal adviser on taxes at the head of the IRS. He was confident Dad would do a splendid job. I believe contemplating my father's satisfaction at running the agency where he began his professional career pleased LBJ as well. Finally, the president knew—and he was hardly alone in this perception and desire— that it never hurts to be on a first-name basis with somebody at the IRS. If that somebody happens to be the agency's boss, so much the better.

Dad was proud to be the president's first choice to replace Mortimer Caplan, JFK's appointee, when he resigned. Nevertheless, my father refused to take the position. He informed LBJ that he had two children to educate, so he couldn't afford to give up the income he was earning as a senior partner at Thompson, Knight for the more modest wages of a commissioner of the IRS. The president did not quarrel with that. He could appreciate, he said, the price of learning at Stanford. "Who would you suggest for Commissioner?" he immediately asked. My father thought a moment, then nominated Sheldon Cohen. LBJ nodded. Soon afterwards, the White House announced Cohen's name would be placed before the Senate. Commissioner Cohen probably never knew that he was second choice.

Why didn't LBJ work harder to convince my father to take the position? This intrigues me, because it reveals that the president was not absolutely determined that he become Commissioner. When Johnson felt that way, it was, as Carol Agger remarked, "work" to say no. LBJ was fully capable of pathetically claiming, as he did in early 1965 when Abe Fortas turned down appointment as Attorney General, that "not even his dog would do anything for him." Since he didn't haul out Little Beagle Johnson to help persuade my father, it's fair to assume he was just as pleased that Dad would stay in the boat as his personal adviser. If Waddy wanted to be Commissioner, great. That he didn't—well, that was great too. LBJ couldn't lose either way. In fact, he may have calculated how he gained from Dad's refusal. From now on, Sheldon Cohen would be giving free advice too.

The expense of educating Ann and me was not the only reason my father said no to being Commissioner. As he pointed out to Mother, the position required Senate approval, and it demanded frequent appearances before Congressional committees. He would be under oath on these occasions and would have to testify on whatever subjects crossed the minds of senators and members of Congress.

Of greatest concern to my father were the reactions of senators and congressmen unfriendly to the oil industry. Several of the people's representatives wanted to reduce the current oil-depletion allowance, and thus raise the revenues collected by the government, especially from large companies such as Humble, Mobil, Gulf, and Texaco. Dad had represented all of those corporations at IRS administrative hearings and before state and federal courts. He also served as counsel for most of the major independent oil companies. Moreover, he had formulated, in collaboration with A.H. Meadows, an independent oil and gas operator, a brilliantly conceived, precisely executed method of trans-

LBJ applying the treatment to his friend Abe Fortas.
LBJ Library. Photo by Yoichi R. Okamoto.

ferring properties, known colloquially at the IRS, in the courts, and to the industry as the "ABC Transaction." It had saved oilmen millions of dollars. The Revenuers had tried for years to concoct administrative rulings or to win court judgments that would reduce ABC's impact on tax collections, with little success. Finally, they admitted defeat. Unable to win the game, they changed the rules by persuading Congress to legislate specifically against the transaction.

Given my father's remarkable record as an attorney for small and large oil companies, it required no genius to guess that his nomination

LBJ and Waddy Bullion in the Rose Garden, May 19, 1966.
LBJ Library. Photo by Yoichi R. Okamoto.

as Commissioner of the Internal Revenue Service would have aroused intense opposition from those senators and congressmen. Enough to defeat him? Probably not. Enough to embarrass him, both during confirmation hearings and subsequent congressional hearings, with pointed questions? Enough to inspire frequent efforts to trap him into unwise answers? Absolutely.

Besides the opponents of the oil industry, Dad knew that others on Capitol Hill inevitably would not be friendly to Johnson or his administration. They could be counted upon to ask questions and expect answers about the ranches, the banks, the television and radio stations, and the operation of the trust. KTBC would attract the most attention, but there was always the possibility that questions might drift into probing other investments of the Texas Broadcasting Corporation. Like Abe Fortas, Dad did not want to disclose any more about these than he had to.

My father could also expect that congressmen would ask him how he planned to handle the Johnsons' personal income tax returns while he was in office. At that time, the commissioner met with the president and the first lady every April 15. They signed their return in his presence; he read and approved it, then sealed it in a confidential file. Clearly Dad couldn't execute that duty, but who would, and under what circumstances? In the process of discussing this, he might have to reveal what he did for the Johnsons. While he did not prepare their returns, he had recommended strategies that enabled them to reduce their payments. What were those strategies? And Dad might have to go even further than this under questioning. He might have to reveal that he had been present when an IRS agent raised questions about details of the contractual relationship between Texas Broadcasting and the renters of the house on the LBJ Ranch.

Soon after LBJ became president, the regional IRS office in Austin did a thorough inspection of Texas Broadcasting's returns. What triggered this informal audit was never clear to Dad. Nor was he worried about defending the returns. He was confident they complied with the letter of the law. He was equally sure there would be no political repercussions from the audit. No one at the regional office could doubt what Lyndon Johnson's reaction would be should anything regarding this inquiry be leaked to the press. Besides, the IRS kept all internal examinations confidential, unless they ultimately required administrative hearings or litigation. (These were the days before anonymous Revenuers slipped Richard Nixon's returns to the national media.) And his confidence was fully justified, except on one point. In the investigating agents' opinion, the rent Lyndon and Lady Bird Johnson paid for the use of the ranch house was far enough below market value that it could not be regarded as a legitimate business arrangement. To gain that status, the Johnsons would have to pay more.

Pegging the rent for the ranch house to the rates for a room for two at the best hotel in Fredericksburg had been LBJ's idea. He remained as convinced of the justice of using this method to establish comparable market value as ever. When he requested that the regional office send John Barr, the chief investigating agent, to the ranch to discuss this with him and Dad, he took charge of the preparations for the meeting himself. Armed with graphs and charts, secure in the rectitude of his assessment of market value, the president of the United States awaited Barr's arrival. "I'll handle this, Waddy," he told my father. Dad let him.

Added to his other disadvantages, John Barr was both short and slender. LBJ invited him to sit on a couch in the office, then plopped down right beside him, "so I can go over these figures with you." Of course, he did this so he could loom over Barr as well and easily move a finger from the figures to a position fairly close to the eyes of the beholder. After going through his papers slowly and thoroughly, the president triumphantly concluded, "Look, this rent for the ranch isn't at all out of line with what it would take for Bird and me to get a room in Fredericksburg and live there when we're in Texas." He straightened the documents, crossed his arms, and peered expectantly at Barr.

The man from the IRS came armed with facts and figures as well. They didn't include data on hotel rooms in Central Texas, however. To judge from the surprised look on Barr's face, no one in Austin had anticipated how creative LBJ had been in choosing a method to calculate market value. In any event, the agent had come prepared to suggest the present rent seemed "only a little low." "How low is that?" demanded the president. "Not much," was the reply. The IRS would agree to "a slight adjustment upwards." The two haggled briefly over the exact sum. Finally, the president said, "Fine. Work it out with Waddy." He shook hands, then herded the two of them out of the office so he could get on with the people's business. In the hall, my father and Barr rapidly reached agreement on what Dad recalls as a small increase in the rent.

This story has an interesting denouement. The president had been impressed by John Barr during their encounter. So had my father, whose initially favorable impression was reinforced by their dealings in the days afterwards. Not much time passed before Lyndon Johnson somehow signaled to Barr that the Texas Broadcasting Corporation certainly could use the services of a fine accountant like him. In turn, Barr left the IRS, set up shop as a CPA in Austin, and began working on the personal income taxes of the Johnsons and the corporate taxes for the blind trust's trustees. Dad and John Barr became close professional associates. Rarely did a week pass without the two of them talking on the telephone about the Johnsons' taxes.

★ ★ ★

Later during his term as president, LBJ asked my father if he would like to be a judge on the Tax Court of Appeals. On most tax litigation, this is the highest court in the land. The Supreme Court rarely hears appeals from this bench, except in cases that have broad constitutional and political implications. Appointment to it is the highest honor a tax lawyer could aspire to if he or she has any ambitions to be a judge. And it does more than just cap a distinguished career; it gives the appointed attorneys the chance to decide the direction of statute and administrative tax law for years to come. Like all presidents, LBJ was keenly aware that the men and women he elevated to the federal bench would be among his most enduring legacies. Had my father agreed to accept this appointment, he would have spent at least the next two decades interpreting the tax codes. That he would have an important effect on them was Lyndon Johnson's expectation.

Dad has never compared to me the attractiveness of serving on this court with being the Commissioner of the IRS. I believe it was much less tempting. The money still wasn't good enough. He hadn't finished educating his children. Furthermore, he had begun buying land north of Dallas in Cooke County. He planned to start cattle ranching in addition to practicing law. Making money at the law was a lot surer bet than at raising and selling cattle. If my father wanted to do the latter, he had to keep on doing the former. A federal judge's salary wouldn't allow him to invest in land and cows, or build a house he could go to on weekends.

Another drawback was this: a federal judge could not practice law or remain on familiar terms with old colleagues and adversaries. To Dad, a judge's life had to be lonely. The only people one could socialize with were other judges. That prospect didn't appeal to a man as gregarious and as happy with the day-to-day exchanges between attorneys as my father is.

Because Dad had painted such an unappetizing portrait of the impact of the job on those who did it, I was surprised when I learned Irving Goldberg accepted appointment to the federal bench. Perhaps Dad was as well. I never saw Goldberg when he wasn't in an infectiously cheerful mood, or when he didn't seem unfeignedly interested in what I was doing or thinking. I never watched him in court, but I can't imagine his being overly impressed with himself or impatient and short with others. He had a wonderful gift for making people feel at ease. He was also a fine attorney in the opinion of my father and other peers. Remembering Judge Goldberg's adjustment to his position, I can't help believing my father would have found his life outside the courtroom less lonely and more interesting than he feared. But he wouldn't have had the W² Ranch, or the ranch house he calls The Barn. For those reasons, as well as the financial help he could give Ann and me, he never regretted his decision.

I don't know how much LBJ pressed him to accept. Again, the president accepted his refusal. It did not affect his status as adviser to Johnson and his family. Nor did it have any impact on the social relationship of the two men. The president continued to invite Dad to the ranch and to put him up at the main house instead of the cottages reserved for visitors who were there strictly on business.

What would have occurred if Dad had agreed to sit on the Tax Court of Appeals and moved to Washington? When I ponder this, I always think of Abe Fortas's years on the Supreme Court. Much presidential arm-twisting went into convincing him to accept nomination to the nation's highest court. Fortas finally gave in, and Johnson gained a justice who, he assumed, would defend Great Society programs and the cause of civil liberties on the Supreme Court for years. The two men also agreed that Fortas would continue to advise the president on a wide variety of issues in foreign and domestic policy, and be his personal confidant as well.

Within a year, the line between judge and adviser became blurred further. At least once, Fortas discussed a case pending before the Court with LBJ. He also boasted to his brother justices about lobbying the president on matters that concerned them. Such indiscreet acts and talk won him powerful enemies. They had their revenge first when Johnson unsuccessfully tried to elevate his friend to Chief Justice after Earl Warren announced his plans to retire in 1968, and again when controversy erupted over the size of the stipend and the source of the funding for a seminar he taught at American University during the summer of 1968. Scandal mixed with partisan politics forced Johnson to withdraw his nomination for Chief Justice and compelled Fortas ultimately to resign from the Court. But well before these events, LBJ's staff privately questioned the propriety and wisdom of Fortas's omnipresence at the White House, to the point that one secretary wondered if his frank remarks on proposed crime legislation should be destroyed rather than preserved for the presidential library.

If Dad had decided to become an appellate judge, would he have had similar experiences? Would he have suffered a like fate? Such questions are, of course, unanswerable. I still ask them seriously. My father and Lyndon Johnson never spent as much time together as the president did with Fortas. Nor did LBJ, to the best of my knowledge, ever seek my father's opinion on policy details, either on the war in Southeast Asia or Great Society programs. I must qualify this, however, by noting once more that my father and LBJ weren't often in the same town.

Had Dad lived in Washington, I can easily visualize impromptu invitations to stop by the Oval Office, to have a drink at the end of the day, or to share a meal in the family's quarters. Johnson could trust in Dad's complete discretion and his loyalty to the family's interests. At these times, the president could—and, I am convinced, *would*—have dropped into casual conversation questions about KTBC, or the cattle market, or the best tax strategies. In a relaxed atmosphere, it would be difficult and perhaps even ill-mannered for my father not to respond with his opinions and advice.

Even more dangerously, substantive issues of public policy could—*would*, I'm sure—be broached in such a setting. How should the codes be amended? How could the government collect more revenue from the laws presently on the books? What were likely sources for additional revenues? How could new taxes be imposed with a minimum of hindrance to the growth of the economy? These are important questions, ones deserving thoughtful answers. When a president of the United States asks for your opinions on them, anyone with my father's patriotism would feel duty-bound to answer. After a few times of doing this, a judge could suddenly look up and discover that he or she was enmeshed in a relationship similar to Abe Fortas's with the president. That judge could be right on the line, or have already crossed the boundary, separating the judicial from the executive branches of government. Moreover, having given advice and opinion in the past means it is harder to demur in the present or future, especially when asked by a longtime client who happens to be president. Dad had always been careful to preserve what he believed was a necessary distance between him and LBJ, by refusing to accept pay for his counsel. That distance would have become harder to maintain. Imagining Johnson maneuvering him into an awkward and troubling position—that's not hard for me at all.

I did have trouble at first picturing Dad in Fortas's role as all-purpose adviser on policy. Unlike Abe, who my father believed had an appreciation of his own talents that some might call arrogance, he would not have hesitated to say that any opinion he might offer was uninformed. After thinking more about this possibility, though, I'm less sure that such a response would have prevented the president from bringing up those questions and expecting answers.

For instance, while he was president, LBJ fell into the habit of talking with my father about two issues that confronted him daily. One was civil rights for African Americans. Johnson freely confessed to Dad that supporting this cause was the politically expedient thing for a Democratic president to do. Blacks had loyally supported his party since the New Deal. The more black voters, the more Democratic voters, he observed to my father. As for the impact of this on white voters in the South, it would be, he predicted, adverse for the Democratic Party. But those voters had already been tempted into casting their ballots for Dwight Eisenhower in national elections and for John Tower in Texas. Johnson believed that after the next few years, the Solid South would be no more. To the extent that white Southerners could be reconciled to civil rights, and LBJ felt they ultimately would be, it was fortunate indeed that a white, southern, Democratic president was lending his considerable support to that cause. In fact, Dad recalls LBJ saying that it was easier for a Southerner in the White House to fight for civil rights than it was for a Northerner. JFK, he argued, always had to struggle with the perception that he didn't understand the special circumstances in the South and wouldn't have to live with the consequences of change. Not so Lyndon Johnson of Stonewall, Texas. Dad was properly impressed by this analysis of the situation by a master politician.

Most of all, though, my father was struck by LBJ's conviction that doing all he could to attain the civil rights movement's goals was the right thing for him to do. "After listening to him talk about the injustices and indignities blacks suffered," Dad said to me, "I never questioned that the president firmly believed in the justice of their cause and truly wanted to help every way he could." He then mused, "Maybe he thought I was the typical Southern white. Maybe he believed if he convinced me, he could persuade others." If such were the case, then Lyndon Johnson had cause for optimism. Dad began the sixties as at best a neutral on civil rights. Before LBJ left the White House, he had been converted.

The other issue was Vietnam. Increasingly, when LBJ mentioned this subject to Dad, he portrayed himself as the victim of circumstances beyond his control. "Jack Kennedy passed this on to me; I had almost no freedom of action" was a frequent plaint as the two men relaxed over drinks. Just as others concluded, my father believed Johnson wished he could wave a magic wand and have Southeast Asia disappear. The sorcery went the other way. "That war, that war," LBJ once burst out to Dad, "has an insatiable appetite for men and material." He couldn't feed it enough, nor could it be put on a diet. All my father could do was shake his head in silent sympathy.

In neither case did Lyndon Johnson ask for any advice from my father. On civil rights and on Vietnam, what he wanted was understanding, sympathy, and support. Dad gave that to him gladly. Would he have done more if LBJ had asked him for advice? Would LBJ have ever considered doing this had he been more available for consultation? Perhaps the following vignette offers clues to what might have happened.

During the summer of 1972 Johnson suddenly asked Dad, who was at the ranch on business, to edit a statement of support for George McGovern he planned soon to release to the press. It was not Dad's usual assignment from LBJ. Nor was it one he found congenial. He confessed to Johnson that he disagreed with McGovern's position on many issues and planned as a result to vote for Nixon. That revelation, my father discovered, did not disqualify him from being editor of the press release. The coolness of the former president's endorsement accurately reflected views the two shared about the Democratic Party's nominee. If Dad had been readily available during the White House years, I believe he would have received several such assignments.

I also believe he would have executed them. Under these circumstances, if my father asked for more information on the topic under consideration, I'm sure the president would have provided it. Going from there to thrusting material on Dad before any request had been made would have been a short step indeed.

★ ★ ★

During his last years in office, LBJ was a beleaguered man. He had always been highly suspicious of others' motives and designs. As opposition to his presidency took on an unprecedented ferocity, his habitual obsessions about what people around him were up to expanded in scope and intensity. They troubled him when he was awake; they tortured his dreams when he slept. Among the most compelling passages in the conversations he had with Doris Kearns Goodwin after he left office are his accounts of personal versions of the classic anxiety dream he had at the White House. An especially haunting one featured Johnson lying helpless, while Joseph Califano, his principal adviser on domestic affairs, and others divided up his programs among themselves and laid plans to use his power for their own purposes. Another searing nightly image was that "whore of a war" demanding more and more of his attention and taking greater and greater sums of his money, while his true love, the Great Society, languished neglected and poor. Those who advised him about Vietnam had their own reasons—some altruistic but some selfish—for wanting to feed and clothe that whore at the expense of his true love.

LBJ with Harry Macpherson, Joseph Califano, Marvin Watson,
Waddy Bullion, and Bill Moyers, May 19, 1966.
LBJ Library. Photo by Yoichi R. Okamoto.

That Johnson would reach out to those he believed he could trust as he struggled with real and perceived opponents within and without his administration is both human and understandable. Thus Abe Fortas's role and influence grew by leaps and bounds. LBJ didn't have many people close enough to him to share his burdens and relieve his fears. That he would have wanted to lean on Waddy Bullion as well, had Dad been available to be summoned to the White House on a moment's notice, is very plausible to me.

What would have been the results? Since it didn't happen, I can't be certain. I do believe, however, that Dad would have found himself in a dangerous situation. To a large extent, I base this on my own experiences when I was chair of my department. To be sure, comparing the demands on me between 1991-1996 with the pressures on LBJ during 1963-1969 is measuring Lilliput against Brobdingnab. It is instructive nonetheless.

While I was chair, I depended on advice and sympathy from my closest friends, particularly former chairs and especially the department's administrative assistant, Nancy Taube. She and I had worked so long and well together that I thought of us as a hybrid "Taubullion" in running the department. For her and the XCs (my name for my predecessors) to be effective, I had to provide them with the necessary information in as neutral a fashion as possible and let them know I would accept criticism as well as advice. That's easier said than done.

I also learned that I had to take full responsibility for all decisions. I couldn't hide behind my friends. And, to the extent I could, I had to protect them from criticism. That was very difficult. Finally, I tried to avoid praising them, after my compliments were turned back as accusations against them, particularly in the form of comments from others that they had too much influence in areas where they had little, or no, business. Despite my best efforts, my friends were subject to whispered innuendo and open criticism. Nothing happened during my five years as chair that I'm sorrier about than what I inadvertently and carelessly did to the people I liked best and leaned on most.

Narratives of Johnson's presidency seem to portray that more often than not, he was utterly oblivious to the risks someone like Abe Fortas ran by advising him. When he did consider them, he blamed their existence on forces outside of the relationship, specifically on his enemies, rather than including himself among those responsible. Recall his comment that he inherited Vietnam from Jack Kennedy. That's a perfect example of his tendency to do this.

I've also found little indication that LBJ grasped how skewed information he passed along to them could be. Therefore he didn't understand how limited the usefulness of their reactions to it was. Now recall that Lyndon Johnson didn't want any comments from Dad about alternative approaches to the civil rights movement. He wanted my father to sign on to the way he was steering the boat through those troubled waters.

Finally, I've seen no hint that he realized either how difficult it was to say no to him, or how unreceptive he was to advice that was hard on him. I do know he could be quick to blame others for mistakes he and they made together. He could be equally quick to cast off staffers and advisers to appease criticism from others. Look at his treatment of Walter Jenkins; remember the clandestine investigation of my father.

Everybody knew and knows that Lyndon Johnson was a very difficult man to work with. He was also an extremely dangerous man to be close to, or to try to be friends with. My father was absolutely right to keep his distance from him during the 1940s and 1950s. He was equally shrewd when he turned down appointments as Commissioner of Internal Revenue and as a judge on the Tax Court. Whatever his specific reasons, whether they were personal, professional, or ethical, or a mixture of these, Dad was very wise to stay safely apart from him while he was president.

It's heartbreaking to write down these thoughts. Lyndon Johnson was blessed with a keen intelligence; remarkable energy; a compelling and noble vision of how to make his country a better place to live in; the determination and expertise to find practical ways of realizing parts of that dream; and the personality and character that attracted and attached bright, dedicated men and women to him and his cause.

He was also severely flawed, and at no area more so than his failures at real friendship. LBJ worsened the difficult problems facing him as president because he couldn't find it within himself to be a true friend. "We're pals!" shouted Froggy the Gremlin. "And pals stick together!" "To have a friend," advised my mother, echoing her mother and countless others, "you have to be a friend."

Reciprocal respect and affection on the basis of equality are at the heart of friendship; they form its vital center. At this season of his life and career, Lyndon Johnson would not, could not, concede equality with himself in the most personal sense to anyone. The world was composed of himself and inferiors. Thus his idea of reciprocity was favors, gifts, and *noblesse oblige* from on high, with deference, loyalty, and service from below. The concept of consistent, considerate decency as the guiding principle of relationships between people was utterly foreign to him. How he treated a person depended on the circumstances, needs, and imperatives of the moment. Allowing an abiding respect and affection to dictate the terms of behavior and to inspire complete trust and confidence were signs of weakness, not strength. These axioms helped raise him to power. They also helped make his and others' lives sheer hell at times.

As captains often do, LBJ relied on a combination of manipulative tricks and outright intimidation to extract work out of the lower ranks. Essentially and fundamentally, his power was the power of uncertainty and of fear. He made sure no one ever really knew where she or he stood with the president or what he was up to. All you could be certain of were these realities: you always had reason to be apprehensive and often had cause to be afraid. His was an unbalanced vessel; you could lose your footing when you least expected the waves or winds to shift.

These tactics worked for LBJ. The power of fear to call forth prodigies of effort and production from men and women cannot be denied. That it added to the burdens and increased the wear and tear of those weathering the storm aboard the boat didn't concern him, even when it drove some away and contributed to personal tragedies in others' lives, most notably Walter Jenkins's. Results were what he was after, and he was sure this was the best and probably the only way to get them.

Was LBJ right? What's more effective in the boat, the power of fear or the power of love?

Most of us know all too well what fear is. When I think about love, I can't help remembering a saying I once read. I believe the wit who formulated it was the great epigrammist La Rochefoucald, but I'm not sure. According to this definition, "Love is an agreement between two people to overestimate each other." This statement is literally true. We *do* overestimate the friends we love. When they return our friendship, they overestimate us. The dynamic force that pervades true friendship is a mutual desire to live up to each other's high expectations. Each is inspired to become better and to do more, because that is the way to please the beloved friend and to honor the relationship. These efforts become labors of love. They are borne more easily than the burdens of fear. And their fruits are far greater.

A more eloquent testimony than mine to love's power may be found in one of Paul's letters to the church at Corinth. He introduced the subject by writing, "now I will show you the best way of all," then going on to list the trials love could endure and the wonders it could accomplish. "In a word," he concluded, "there are three things that last forever: faith, hope, and love; but the greatest of them all is love." Therefore we should "put love first."

Of course, that's more difficult to do than to quote. I don't want to be understood as saying that true friendships are easy to achieve and maintain. They're not. This is not merely because of flaws in all human nature, but also because creating these friendships depends on some things beyond our complete control. We have to cross paths with others who have the potential to be our true friends. Then we have to recognize that potential. Then we have to risk rejection, disappointment, and even betrayal by offering our own friendship in return. That's risking a great deal. Lyndon Johnson was hardly the only person in the world who wouldn't take that gamble. In fact, I would bet he was among the vast majority. His unwillingness to be a friend certainly did not brand him either as abnormal or as a monster.

Still, that doesn't excuse LBJ's failure. All of us need friends. And he more than most, because of his personality, position, and power. He couldn't plead that he never met people worthy to be his friends. I'm convinced that they, like my father, wanted to be counted among his friends. It was Lyndon Johnson's own choice, freely made for a number of motives, not to offer friendship in return.

Lyndon Johnson did, however, hand out favors that proved how beneficial it was to get and stay on his good side. In the spring of 1965, my father decided I should be gainfully employed during my summers, ideally at a job with wages high enough to help with Stanford's tuition and with expectations demanding and enjoyable enough to pique my interest. These can be difficult criteria to meet in a summer job, but not if you can have the help of the president of the United States. A word with him, a follow-up letter to one of his Special Assistants, and presto! federal employees were calling with suggestions.

My nonexistent typing skills disqualified me from positions in our nation's capital. The assumption that I could swing an ax, dig with a shovel, and hike through the mountains landed me a position as a Fire Control Aide in Yosemite. Dad humorously predicted that I'd wish I could type before the summer passed. In fact, by season's end, I loved the park and the job. I had a great time with the guys I worked with. I also earned and saved enough money to completely pay the tuition for my final year at Stanford. The intangibles of firefighting, especially the knowledge I could do a physically strenuous and often dangerous job reasonably well, meant a lot to a young man who, like the boy he had been, looked for ways to test and demonstrate his manhood. By every standard, it was a wonderful way to spend my summer. On that, my father and I were in agreement. We also agreed that we owed that experience to Lyndon Johnson. It was a gift we both deeply appreciated.

In late 1965, another testimonial of LBJ's feelings for Dad occurred. I was home for the holidays, enjoying the company of my Dallas friends, and wondering what I'd made in my courses and how I'd scored on the Law School Admission Test. Right before Christmas, I learned that I'd done well on the LSAT. These scores, plus my academic record at Stanford, made me confident I'd be admitted to the Harvard Law School. When I reminded Dad how he frequently thanked God he never went to Harvard, "because then I'd think I was smart," he laughed and said he didn't doubt I was smarter than he was already, and three years in Cambridge wouldn't affect that. Then, on December 26, a Sunday, he called me at home. "I've just talked with President Johnson," he said. "He wants me to come down to the ranch on Wednesday. He invited you, too. He wants you to go deer hunting with him."

"What did you say?" I asked.

My father replied, "I said 'yes,' of course."

PART II

At the Ranch

Mark my teaching, O my people,
      listen to the words I am to speak.
I will tell you a story with meaning,
      I will expound the riddle of things past,
Things that we have heard and know,
      and our fathers have repeated to us.

          —Psalm 78: 1-3

CHAPTER 12

"This is my ranch..."

How often does the mind react to unexpected, extraordinary news by grasping at the familiar and mundane? My first reaction to LBJ's invitation to go deer hunting was to remember I'd promised a friend I'd take her to a cocktail party on Wednesday night.

Fortunately, I didn't blurt this out. Dad surely would have reminded me that you didn't turn down this president's invitations unless you were in the hospital near death.

Instead of mentioning my date, I proceeded—rather impressively, I thought at the time—to quizzing my father about details. Where would we hunt? How would we hunt? What about a rifle? Did I need a hunting license? What should I wear?

Dad had all the answers. What most surprised me were his instructions on how to dress. I should wear something suitable for having dinner with the president, Mrs. Johnson, and whoever else might be their guests. If we were lucky, Bill Moyers would be there. Bill was bright, able, young, easy to talk with, and interested in hearing what those outside Washington thought.

My father did caution me that there was no predicting how much time we'd spend with LBJ. Sometimes he spent hours talking with Dad after they'd finished their business; other times, the president would hurry through their meeting, shake hands, and almost push him out of the office. Chances were that we'd see a good bit of him. We'd be at the ranch, and he'd be as on vacation as he could ever manage. At the White House, where his staff jealously guarded every minute of his day and zealously tried to move him through the gauntlet of events and meetings, even LBJ had difficulty carving out more minutes to talk about anything other than the subject at hand. Now, warned Dad, things could speed up at the ranch, too, especially if something transpired as a result of the Christmas bombing pause in Vietnam. For that reason, I'd have to be in coat and tie the whole visit. The president wouldn't pause to let anyone change clothes. You had to go when he went, do when he did, hunt when he could, and eat and drink when he was hungry and thirsty. Everything revolved around him. Satisfied he had prepared me both for packing and for the unique world of President Johnson's residence, my father said goodbye.

My mother seemed pleased. She asked what I would need, and once we settled that, she said she thought I'd have an interesting time and a good one. Left unsaid was her new grievance against him, one she shared with growing numbers of her fellow citizens. On Election Day in 1964, Mother wrote me that she had just voted for Lyndon Johnson so her son wouldn't have to be a soldier. Barry Goldwater's impending defeat delighted her because she was sure he'd have us in a war and me in uniform in no time. Now there was a war, and her son might be drafted if it lasted long enough—and it showed no signs of ending anytime soon. Mother had mentioned these grim concerns earlier during this Christmas season. I was glad she didn't repeat them again.

★ ★ ★

Maybe I should have been worried about the hunting part of the trip to the LBJ Ranch, since at that time I'd never shot at a deer. But I felt no tension whatsoever, at least at that moment.

For one thing, I felt certain that the president would see to it that the weapon I'd use was in perfect condition. The rifle would be ready to go, all sighted-in for the appropriate range.

Second, I was absolutely confident I had mastered the mechanics of shooting. Not just, or even mostly, because of Big John's instruction. I'd learned much more by taking a PE course in marksmanship at Stanford. Typically, only ROTC students took the course, and they principally because it was required. I took it because I already knew how to shoot—or so I thought—and because it fit my schedule better than other PE courses.

The class met once a week for a couple of hours on Friday afternoons. The instructor, a sergeant in the army, was one of the best

John Bullion, Fall 1965.
Bullion Family Collection.

teachers I had in college. He was a model of patience, and a master at quietly encouraging students. We fired .22 rifles at targets about 25 yards away in an indoor range. By the time the quarter was over, all of us had become proficient at firing from the standing, sitting, kneeling, and prone positions. We knew how to adjust slings to the right tension, and how to wrap them around the arm we used to support the barrel to improve the stability of the weapon. And we learned how to sight in a scope, by firing shots until they clustered on the target then adjusting the knobs on the scope so many clicks up or down, so many clicks to the right or to the left, and firing more clusters until we tore the center out of the bullseye with our shots. This accomplished, you just *knew* if you had a stable rest, if you were sound in your posture, if you breathed in, then let it out, and if you squeezed rather than jerked the trigger, ten times out of ten you'd be in the black with your shot.

At that moment, you'd fall into a rhythm of shooting, not thinking about the shot anymore, but following routine and hitting the bullseye. After going to class, after studying in the library, after finishing an exam or turning in a paper, retiring to the range and shooting well was the most relaxing thing in the world. I looked forward to it every week, and I was sorry when time came to take out the ear plugs, clean the rifle, and put it back in the rack. That I did well enough to earn an A in the class was icing on the cake.

So I had no doubts about the rifle or my shooting ability. That reassured me sufficiently to keep me from fretting about my inexperience at deer hunting. Equally calming was the theoretical knowledge I had about it, thanks to Big John. He and I had once spent a frigid November afternoon in a blind when I was twelve. We'd seen nothing but doe, so I didn't fire my rifle. During our long and fruitless wait, he'd taken the opportunity to remind me of lessons he'd taught me earlier. As I thought about going to the LBJ Ranch, I reviewed my grandfather's instructions.

Aim just behind the shoulder blade and keep your sight on the deer after the shot. If I missed, no matter how fast it fled toward cover, almost always there'd be time for a second attempt. I should stay calm and lead it by about six feet. If I hit the deer, keep the rifle on it, because whitetails would play possum when slightly wounded and had been known to spring up and race away. For the same reason, I should approach a deer on the ground very cautiously; they were powerful, dangerous animals with sharp hooves and antlers. Finally, I had to track down all wounded deer, no matter how thick the brush, how cold the weather, or how long it took. "You don't let a hurt creature suffer," preached Big John, "you finish them off quickly and cleanly." When I recalled all this, I felt fully prepared to kill a trophy buck with LBJ watching me.

The only imponderable was, could I control my excitement over hunting with President Johnson, keep in mind my mechanics, and calmly go through the rituals of aiming, squeezing, and being surprised when the rifle fired? I was so sure I could that I stopped thinking about the hunt.

That Wednesday morning, our plane was late. Lyndon Johnson was not famous for his patience, and we were now two hours behind schedule. This was not a good start for the day. Once we were in our seats, Dad turned to me, smiled, and remarked there was nothing else we could do about the situation. With the discipline of the veteran business traveler, he hauled some documents out of his briefcase and calmly began to read. His ability to shrug off major and minor inconveniences and make productive use of his time impressed me. Since then, I've tried to imitate him, with varying degrees of success. This was one of my more successful efforts, chiefly because I had no business to conduct and bore no blame for the delay.

During the flight, as the attendants offered a variety of drinks, Dad remembered news he had picked up about LBJ. Someone had told him the president had decided not to have any alcohol over Christmas. "If he doesn't take a drink," Dad said, "I don't." He quickly added that I needn't be bound strictly by that rule. "If you're offered liquor, you can have it if you want it. Nobody will think anything about it if you have one. Don't have more than one." I promised I'd take his advice. It seemed like the right thing to say and to do.

This added tension to anticipation. Obviously, the whole trip was a novel experience for me. I hadn't been on the LBJ Ranch; I'd spent no more than two or three minutes total in my life with The Man; I'd never met Mrs. Johnson; and I had no idea what hunting with the president of the United States would be like. Dad's no drinking rule added elements of the unusual to the unknown.

Business and social gatherings were rarely dry in the fifties and sixties. Almost all people were like Dad: they enjoyed the camaraderie of drinking and found alcohol to be both relaxing and stimulating. And, along with many others, my father did not believe that it was an impediment to successful business negotiations. This was, after all, the era of the multiple martini lunch and the extended cocktail hour beginning promptly at five and lasting as long as people stayed upright. A client of his had gone so far as to have a watch made with twelve 5s on its face, so it was always time for a drink! In contrast, Dad periodically decided not to drink for a month or two. During the sixties, he welcomed opportunities to prove to himself and to show others he could take it or leave it alone. In these boozeless spells, he'd frequently be the only person in a room without a highball in hand. In fact, he once showed me an unposed photograph taken during a meeting in San Francisco when this was literally the case.

So my father's decision to abstain from alcohol at the ranch wasn't completely out of the ordinary. What was astonishing was the prospect of a dry social event that wasn't Baptists at Wednesday night prayer meeting. I didn't think LBJ and his guests would be the same as a gathering of those faithful to read scripture and petition the Lord, then sip lemonade and munch cookies afterwards. This group's sobriety would be vivid, unmistakable proof not of the power of God, but of Lyndon Johnson's ability to impose the terms of any contacts with him on others. That was the sort of power I'd have to keep in mind while in his company.

Jesse Kellam met us at the Austin airport. Dad hadn't been able to get in touch with him before we finally got on the plane, so he'd waited nearly two hours. It hadn't affected his temper. Breaking into a grin, he asked how we liked traveling on Braniff. He was glad to see Dad and pleased to meet me. After he shook hands with me, he swung back toward my father and said, "Waddy, let's postpone our talk until we get out to the ranch. We don't want to hurry through our business, and we don't want to make the president wait, either."

We carried our bags out to a KTBC station wagon he'd left outside the main door and tossed them in the back. I noticed no one had ticketed the car though Kellam had left it in a no parking zone. When Dad remarked if he'd done that in Dallas, his car would have been hauled away five minutes after he left, his friend replied, "TV stations have more privileges than citizens, and you oughta know that better than most, Waddy." He started the car and pointed it toward downtown and Austin's one and only television station.

As Kellam drove, he and Dad smiled and laughed with the ease of long and profitable acquaintance. They made a point of telling me how

Jesse Kellam greets LBJ, March 16, 1968.
LBJ Library. Photo by Robert Knudsen.

much Austin had grown since they first lived there during the thirties, when they were younger and certain they'd change the world and make money doing it. More to join in the conversation than anything else, I asked Kellam what he'd done before he came to Austin to work for LBJ at the National Youth Administration. "John, I coached football and taught school." "Why'd you quit?" I asked. His smile disappeared and his tone hardened. "I was fired." He didn't elaborate, and I didn't inquire further.

This reminded me that Kellam and my father belonged to a club that I'd never be a member of: the survivors of the Depression era. And they'd not only survived, but made good. Since I was with them in the flesh, I saw them in natural color. I thought at the time, though, that photographs of Jesse and Waddy ought always to be in black and white. That was the way my generation experienced the years of our fathers' youth, through black print on white pages and in the bleak grainy pictures in textbooks and on film. Perhaps it was the way they remembered their own past: the black years of unemployment and depression, and the hard work and good fortune that brought them out of darkness into light. More prosaically, black-and-white photography would heighten the set of their jaws, contrasting the tension there with the smiles on their lips. It would deepen the wrinkles in their foreheads, creating a counterpoint to the eyes gazing mildly at the camera.

This is a formidable man, I thought as I looked at Kellam. As I did so, I realized Dad was too, even to people who weren't his children.

Don't think this is an *ex post facto* reconstruction on my part. I thought that way then, always trying to transmute sensory impressions into self-consciously literary language. For most of my family, something hadn't really happened, no matter what you saw, felt, heard, or did, until you told it to someone else. I took this another step further. To experience things fully, I had to write them. So I was forever mentally composing in the midst of living. Not everything found its way onto paper; in fact, comparatively few events did. That was because I had to fit them into letters to friends and, particularly, to a woman I was desperately trying to please. This led me to choose scenes for their intrinsic interest to my intended audience, and to sketch them mentally in writing as they unfolded in life.

Why was this casual conversation so intriguing to me? All of my contemporaries, whether they confessed to it or not (and most didn't), were fascinated by the hard times of depression and war. We claimed to be sick of hearing about them, and sometimes after lengthy discourses from parents on the value of a dollar and the price of freedom, we were. Even so, to see these two veterans of both conflicts, to hear grim words about being fired without any explanation of why—this was the raw stuff of a great vignette! Whether Kellam and my father would appreciate being archetypes I'd describe and analyze in hopes of romance was another matter. They didn't know this, and I didn't intend to tell them.

KTBC didn't fascinate me nearly as much as the two men in the car with me. Kellam's office was a purely functional place. Nothing much was on the walls, and the furniture consisted of only an institutional desk, a swivel chair, and a couple of straight-backed chairs for visitors. What impressed me most was the first speaker phone I'd ever seen in action.

Perhaps just to show it off, Kellam returned a call to Walter Jenkins, punched the speaker button, and he, Dad, and Walter exchanged greetings. They mentioned that we were going out to the ranch later that afternoon, and he wished them a good time and me good hunting. Had I left Washington under a cloud, I'd never want to show my face again. Exhausted and distraught as he had been, surely Jenkins had moments when he felt that way. Buoyed up by his family's love and heartened by public statements of friendship from Lady Bird Johnson and Jesse Kellam, he had recovered enough to become a partner in an Austin public relations firm. From the conversation, I gathered that he was doing some work for KTBC, and everyone was pleased with the results. Public relations was probably a convenient euphemism for lobbying state legislators, Congressmen, and federal bureaucrats to delay the inevitable day when the FCC granted licenses permitting the operation of other television stations in Austin.

After the three joked idly for a few minutes about which shows KTBC's management should choose to broadcast from the offerings of the three major networks, Kellam glanced at his watch and told Walter it was time for us to go. He hung up, then opened a closet door and pulled out his own grip, a suitcase he kept packed for those nights he was called to Gillespie County. "You're always ready, aren't you," Dad said. "Waddy," he answered, "I've found it's best to be prepared." They laughed. Kellam instructed his secretary to call the Air Force and tell them to get the chopper ready, because we were on the way. After a fifteen-minute drive, we arrived at Bergstrom Air Force Base.

The guards at the gate knew the KTBC station wagon as well as the civilian airport's police officers did. The security check consisted of asking how Mr. Kellam was doing; no passes were proffered or requested. He said he'd vouch for the two fellas with him, and that made us okay too. He parked by a hangar, and a couple of airmen hustled over and moved our bags to the biggest helicopter I'd ever seen. The main rotors, I guessed, were twice as long as the ones on the Bell helicopters I rode on in Yosemite; the tail rotor looked at least fifteen feet long. One of the marines who flew this beast saw me mentally measuring them as I studied the copter, and he recognized the questioning look anyone who worked around helicopters took before doing anything else: where are the blades, how long are they, and are they moving. Probably he also noticed that I was reflexively starting to hunch over as we approached the machine, though there was hardly any need for that. "Ever flown in one this big, sir?" he asked. "Only in three-seat Bells," I answered, "the ones with the Plexiglass cockpits without any doors." The marine promised this would be different.

Which it was. The main cabin was living-room size. Gold carpet covered the deck; wood paneling was on the bulkheads. The presidential seal hung from what I could only think of as a wall. There were portholes cut in its side, but not of a size designed to encourage sight-seeing during flights. In fact, benches with cushioned seats and backs had been bolted into the walls. Once you buckled your seat belt, you had to face the center of the cabin. Only by twisting awkwardly could anyone look out.

There was a reason for this arrangement. At the absolute center of the cabin sat a large gold chair that resembled a very comfortable recliner. It was placed on a round platform that obviously could turn at the push of one of the buttons on the chair's arms. Next to the chair was a stand with a telephone on it. Not an ordinary phone, either. The receiver and transmitter rested on a base with a number of buttons, so many that the whole contraption reminded me of a miniature switch-board. I had no trouble guessing who sat in that chair. Nor did I wonder why all the other seating faced him. If Lyndon Johnson was riding on that helicopter, nobody would want or dare to look out the portholes. Dad, Kellam, and I settled ourselves in a space that could have seated fifteen more riders, and we sat facing the empty chair.

Almost no sensation of flight could be felt in the cabin. The engines whined as they reached take-off power, but there was none of the deafening whup-whup-whup the Bell made as it struggled in Yosemite's high elevations. Once we got to cruising altitude, their sound became almost like the "white noise" a television that is not receiving a signal emits. It wasn't noticeable unless you listened specifically for it. The rise off the runway was more akin to an elevator that very smoothly and slowly levitates than to the rattling, jerking Bell on take off. The flight was completely stable and—since we couldn't easily look out the portholes—gave no hint of how far we were above the ground.

Not much like flying to a fire, I mused. I was in a room that was magically moving from one place to another. Then I wondered if the president ever compared this helicopter to the tiny one he flew during the 1948 Senatorial campaign. I decided he probably didn't. Lyndon Johnson had been oblivious to the dangers of helicopter travel as he desperately ran against Coke Stevenson. Exhausted, he had slept through many shaky landings. Awake, he had urged the pilot to fly later and later into the dusk, maneuver through storms, and even risk setting down on a filling station's roof. He focused on his political problems, not on his means of transportation. The trip might be rough or smooth, dangerous or a stroll in the park. He didn't care or notice; what counted was how fast he would arrive where he wanted to be.

LBJ's helicopter on the roof in Rosenberg, Texas, July 1948.
LBJ Library. Photo by unknown.

By car, the trip from Austin to the LBJ Ranch took nearly two hours. The presidential helicopter, by flying over the Hill Country rather than traveling on roads winding through it, cut that time by more than half.

★ ★ ★

The Johnsons' house surprised me. I had expected to see a distinctive structure, constructed out of Hill Country limestone, and similar to the Frank Lloyd Wright prairie homes. In fact, the home the Johnsons had built in the early fifties closely resembled the ranch houses I had visited in West Texas during the same decade. The two-story frame house was painted a brilliant white. The trim and the shingled roof were a soft green.

A white picket fence enclosed a lawn of St. Augustine grass. If ranchers decided to spruce up the area in front of their houses, they planted what they called "Augustine." A transplant to the region, it cost considerably more than bermuda grass, required a great deal of care, and needed huge amounts of water. It also was much more fragile than indigenous varieties; Augustine lawns were fenced to prevent human traffic as well as animals grazing. But it was lush, soft, cool, and a beautiful green. Best of all for families with children, like the Johnsons, it

LBJ Ranch House, December 29, 1966.
LBJ Library. Photo by Kevin Smith.

was chigger-resistant. West Texans were fond of saying that having Augustine proved a man was rich enough to pour money into his yard. Having a big yard, as the Johnsons did, sent that message loud and clear.

Several mature live oaks spread their shade widely over the lawn and the house. This was typical as well. Many ranch houses in the Hill Country pre-dated electricity; central air conditioning for private homes hadn't been dreamed of when they were built. This house had electricity. It boasted central air too. Still, to be an authentic ranch house, it had to be surrounded by live oaks. Mature trees were essential to keeping homes reasonably cool during long, hot summers and lengthy, warm falls. Clearly, the site for this house had been selected because of the trees. I could tell that even before I learned the story of how and why LBJ got his hands on the Martin ranch.

The windows were large, but, again, not unusually so for that country. The house's second story was the most unique feature I could see. Second stories were comparatively rare. Like the live oaks in their yards, West Texas ranch houses tended to spread out rather than grow up. The Johnson's house was both wide and tall and considerably bigger than most I'd seen. Still, that was a difference in size rather than design. Because of our direction of approach, I didn't see the flagstone patio and swimming pool in back. Nor did I notice a garage that could shelter several cars and pickups a short distance away. I did see and appreciate the house's most striking feature: the broad porch across its front. Even in late December, there were still comfortable-looking wooden chairs on it with colorful cushions tied to them.

This was a house of comfort rather than luxury, a place a rancher wouldn't be afraid to enter with muddy boots. It was meant to impress the neighbors, no question about that. But most of what would fuel their envy or inspire their awe was the unmistakable signal that this home was *better* than theirs, not *different*. Better as the headquarters of a working ranch, not different like what West Texans called "show places," flashy without being functional.

There was no sign of any security. The Secret Service *had* to be there somewhere, but they sure weren't visible. No one stopped us from getting out of an Air Force van, going up the walk, crossing the porch, and knocking on the door. Lady Bird Johnson opened it for us.

I'd never met Mrs. Johnson before, so as we were shaking hands I was running through a mental inventory. Did she look like her pictures? Did she sound the same as she did on television? The answer to the first question was a qualified "yes." I could have picked her out in a crowded room with no trouble, though she was more slender than she looked in photographs and on the 6:30 news.

The second would be answered "no." As she spoke with us, Lady Bird had much more of an East Texas accent than I expected. East Texans sound more Southern than West Texans, and she fit that mold perfectly. Her "I"s were close to the deep South's "Ah's"; her pronunciation of words was soft and almost slurred; and her sentences ended in rising inflections, sounding almost like questions.

It wasn't until later that I understood why she sounded different. She was in her own home, greeting two old friends and the son of one of them. She was not on stage in the White House, talking to dignitaries and the press. Just as I had perfected for Stanford a California accent, from which I studiously excluded Texas words, sounds, rhythms, and sayings, and carefully added "n"s to length and strength, she had a formal, official diction and cadence she used outside the state and on public occasions. With far greater cause than I had, she knew our regional accents and vocabularies could make us figures of fun and brand us as slow-witted, uncultured provincials. At home, among friends, she could relax the discipline she imposed on her own speech.

There were other signs that Mrs. Johnson was in her favorite place in the world. My mother had two or three plain dresses she called her "uniforms," which she wore in the house. The skirt and blouse Lady Bird Johnson wore looked like those uniforms: comfortable, loose-fitting, softened by numerous washings, and unpretentiously belted at the waist. Her shoes were like Mother's "sensible" shoes—flats, carefully polished, but clearly not new. She wore hose, which, to judge again from Mother's habits of dress, was customary "house dress" for winter. I recognized light make up and freshly applied lipstick, the sort of cosmetics my mother would put on in the morning if she knew people might drop by. Mrs. Johnson's appearance, as well as the tone of her words, signaled a casual, friendly visit. She was at home, and she was happy we were there sharing it with her and her family.

Mrs. Johnson's handshake was firm and business-like: she reached out, grasped my hand, applied a steady pressure, then released it without going through the ritual of two or three pumps of hand and arm. While doing this, she looked me squarely in the eyes.

It quickly became apparent Lady Bird Johnson understood how to put young people who were meeting her at ease—or, more precisely, she knew how to avoid making them uncomfortable. There were no references to holding me as a baby, or how much I'd grown, or to how much I looked like Waddy, or any of the pat phrases adults fall back on when they're not quite certain how to react to friends' children. Instead, she smiled widely, said she was pleased to meet me, and was glad I was here. She hoped I'd enjoy my visit.

Then Mrs. Johnson asked if I had ever spent much time in the Hill Country. When I said no, she said I was seeing it in a season when growing things were fallow. "It's still lovely," she said, "but you must try to drive through it in the spring, when the grass is green and the bluebonnets and Indian paintbrushes are blooming. It's God's place then." The best she could do between now and then, she went on, was showing me some of the Salinas paintings of bluebonnets on their walls. She promised to do that before we left. Turning to my father, she said, "You should buy some of his work, Waddy." He laughed and told her, "I should have bought some before you and the president started collecting them. Now he's become famous and too expensive." "You're sure right about that," she said with a smile. "They're higher than a cat's back, aren't they? But John can still look, can't he?" Dad agreed that I could, and he planned to himself.

Without being effusive, Lady Bird Johnson welcomed us warmly. Without flaunting her talents, she had communicated her intelligence and sensitivity. From her lips, what might ordinarily be the cliches of greeting—"I'm happy you are here"—were clearly expressions of genuine pleasure and interest. Most impressive, she projected how much she was at peace with herself. She knew the price and the value of Porfirio Salinas's Hill Country landscapes. She had been sure that they were magnificent art before others proclaimed they were. She was pleased they had appreciated financially, because she still appreciated them aesthetically.

I'm sure Lady Bird didn't regard herself as perfect. The way she adapted her accent to fit her perceptions of the occasion and the attitudes of the audience revealed she had no illusions either about the world she lived in or the necessity of often appearing before it as someone different than she actually was. Some might say that in itself was a sign of weakness and deception; I'd call it a venial sin at worst, and certainly a useful defense in this vale of tears. She could do this without yielding to feelings of inferiority, because she was sure of herself and her own worth. And because she was so at ease with being Lady Bird Johnson, she had acquired the knack of making others feel at ease as well.

Although I was more comfortable around Mrs. Johnson than I expected to be, this did not inspire me to talk much. My responses were brief and, I hope, appropriately grateful for our reception and the invitation to her ranch. Of course, not much by way of answers was required of me. She had learned that people meeting her for the first time could be at a loss for words, and she phrased her questions so they would not require lengthy comments. For instance, although she later asked me what I thought of Stanford and how I liked the West Coast, she saved that for a time when I would feel more natural talking with her. For a young person somewhat unnerved by where he was and to whom he was talking, asking whether I'd been to the Hill Country before was perfect. "Yes" or "no" would suffice, and then she would pick up the conversational ball again. Her greeting to Kellam and Dad was the much more open-ended "how are you doing?"

Interestingly, the two men responded to her in different ways. The Kellams and the Johnsons had been linked together for years by politics, business, and Austin society. He was Jesse to her; she was Bird to him. Rather than shaking hands, they hugged, and Kellam kissed her cheek.

In contrast, Dad and Mrs. Johnson shook hands. He was Waddy to her, and it was obvious she was personally fond of him. I knew he liked her a great deal as a person and highly respected her talents in business. Although he had never discussed the details of the family's enterprises with me, he did emphasize that, contrary to the stories in the papers, the LBJ who had the dominant voice in the day-to-day running of KTBC before November 1963 was Lady Bird, not Lyndon Baines. As much as Dad prized her graciousness, he admired her intelligence equally, if not more. Despite this, she was not Bird to him. I believe he said, "Hello, Lady Bird," when we first arrived, but I don't recall his addressing her by name afterwards. She was always "you," never Mrs. Johnson or Bird.

Perhaps this was a mark of respect for her status as the First Lady. She would have objected if he had called her that or Mrs. Johnson; still, he couldn't bring himself to be conversationally familiar. After all, though he had known LBJ for a quarter of a century in 1965, he punctiliously referred to him as the President, or President Johnson, even in private, and whatever the company. (Incidentally, Jesse Kellam, who had known Lyndon Johnson much longer and more intimately, did the same.)

But I also think Dad's infrequent use of first names when he spoke with Mrs. Johnson was another example of how he tried to maintain a certain distance from her and her husband. That was not merely, or principally, due to his recognition that his association with them did not date back to NYA days in Austin in the mid-thirties, and did not include long months and years of political campaigning, as was the case with Jesse Kellam. It was more the result of a desire to avoid some of the dangers of forming too close an attachment with or becoming too dependent on the good will of Lyndon Johnson.

No one could miss LBJ's presence in the living room. At one end was a large, overstuffed recliner. It was remarkably like the one in the helicopter's cabin, except its occupant would have to swivel it around on its base using his own power. Couches and chairs were clustered around the recliner's sides and in front of it. The head rest glistened with the residue of hair oil. I didn't need to be told who sat in this chair. The presidential seal on it confirmed my guess.

A dusky, plum colored carpet covered the floor. It was not new. The color had begun to fade from sunlight, traffic, vacuuming, and cleaning. The couches and chairs had been chosen for comfort, not fashion. Although the fabric covering them was not worn, it was not new, either. At least a couple of the coffee tables bore the tell-tale scars of wet glasses set upon the wood. These lingering drink rings, more than anything else, gave the room a lived-in look.

Not lived-in, I hasten to add, in the way Bullion rooms were lived in: There were no papers lying around, no magazines, no open books, and no television console. It was obviously dusted and vacuumed frequently. But the living room was not at all pretentious. Seeing it without knowing who resided there, I wouldn't have guessed it belonged to the president of the United States. It was a place where people visited after supper on a working ranch. Nothing in it, even the Salinas bluebonnet paintings decorating one of the walls, would distract attention from the people who gathered there. The fact that whoever cleaned in here was neglecting to wipe off where LBJ's head touched his chair heightened the sense I had of the ordinariness of the room. It was a pleasant, comfortable place to sit and talk and, in our case, to wait.

We didn't wait long. A door opened, and Lyndon Johnson, smiling broadly, walked into the room. We all rose quickly and held out our hands. We were Jesse, Waddy, and John; he was Mr. President to Kellam and Dad, and President Johnson to me. His handshake hadn't changed since Brady seven years earlier; what grip there was, I supplied. I thanked him for his invitation. He replied that he was glad I was there, because he wanted to go hunting. "We'll take the helicopter over to the West Ranch," he announced. "The boys will meet us there with the car and the gun." With no more than that, we were on our way. LBJ pivoted suddenly and strode out the door he entered and down a hall. Confident we'd be following in his wake, he didn't look back. "Better get going," Mrs. Johnson advised. "I'll see to your bags." Dad thanked her, Jesse Kellam chuckled, and I stood stockstill, waiting for them to lead the way. Then we three hurried down the hall.

An Air Force van had brought us from the landing strip to the house. The trip back was made in a white Lincoln Continental. The driver, I told myself, had to be a Secret Service agent. LBJ didn't introduce us. In fact, he didn't say anything other than "helicopter." The agent nodded and slipped the big car into Drive. The engine purred powerfully, unlike my '63 Ford Fairlane's, and the ride was comfortable and smooth. That was owing not only to the Continental's suspension and the driver's care to avoid jerks of the wheel and sudden stops, but to the wide and deep back seat, which easily accommodated Dad,

THE WHITE HOUSE
PRESIDENT LYNDON B. JOHNSON
DAILY DIARY
The President began his day at (Place)   White House → LBJ Ranch, Texas   Date December 29, 1965   Day WEDNESDAY

Entry No.	Time In	Out	Telephone Lo	LD	Activity (include visited by)	Expenditure Code
	2:29			f	Under Secy. Geo. Ball - Washington, D. C.	
	2:45				LUNCH W/ Mrs. Johnson , Joe Califano, Mr. and Mrs. George Brown, Mr. and Mrs. Gus Wortham, Mr. and Mrs. Jim Elkins, Jake Jacobsen, Mr. J. C. Kellam, Judge Moursund, and MF	
	3:19			f	Luci -- Austin, Texas	
	3:27				Left the ranch house to take the Browns, Worthams, and Elkins to their plane on s. end	
	3:41			f	Joe Laitin - Austin, Texas of runway	
	3:45	4:15			Working his desk w/ MF -- mail that had come in on this morning's courier	
	4:12			t	Bill Moyers - Austin, Texas	
4:44					Departed the LBJ Ranch in helicopter w/ Mr. Watty Buillon and son John and Judge Moursund to go to the West Ranch arriving at 4:55	
	6:30				Left the West Ranch and returned to the LBJ Ranch	
	6:49				At the ranch house and went to his office went to work desk w/ mf and jj	
	7:30 pm				DINNER w/ Mrs. Johnson Mrs. Earle Deaths and son, Tre; Mrs. Kathy Teague, Mr. J. C. Kellam, Jake Jacobsen, J. W. Buillon and son, John, and MF	
	8:30			f	Director Chas. Schultze - Washington, D. C.	
	9:00				Retired for the evening.	
	8:15			f	Lynda Bird - Evanston, Wyo.	
	9:39			t	Bill Moyers - Austin, Texas (Driskill Club)	

SEE TRAVEL RECORD FOR TRAVEL ACTIVITY   Page No. 2

Daily Diary, December 29, 1965.
LBJ Library. Photo by LBJ Library.

Kellam, and me. Everyone seemed to take the car and its performance for granted. I tried to act as though I were equally accustomed to luxury.

Apparently forewarned, the marines had the helicopter fired up and ready to go. Our driver eased the Continental in next to it, so close that the president had to take only two steps to be at the gangway. We followed him on board and remained standing until he settled down into the chair at the center of the cabin. Then the three of us sat down on the benches that faced him and strapped ourselves in. A marine closed the hatch with a clunk that I could hear above the engine's whine. "Ready to go, Sir," he said. LBJ glanced at him and nodded. Almost immediately, we were airborne.

During the brief flight, the president swung back and forth in his chair, as regularly and rhythmically as a slow, powerful metronome. Perhaps out of habit, he'd slipped on a pair of reading glasses when he sat down. He removed them as he swiveled, holding them by the stems in one huge hand as he looked at us. Some people—me, for instance— would appear nearsighted or vulnerable in such a pose. Not LBJ. He obviously saw us clearly, and appeared to be weighing our talents and skills as he watched. His eyes fixed intently on each of us in turn as he moved. All of the talking was done by him. Mostly he commented on the unusual warmth of the days recently, predicted this would make for good hunting, and noted that we'd have a little over an hour for me to find and kill a fine buck. "Late afternoon's the best time, John," he lectured to me. "They're hungry and ready to start feeding." It was on the tip of my tongue to say, "I know; my grandfather taught me that." Instead, I said, "Yes, Mr. President." As his chair moved toward Dad, I sighed in relief. At that moment, while I was exhaling softly, I realized for the first time how curious this hunting party looked.

LBJ was dressed for hunting. He had on a khaki shirt, probably an upscale version of a Dickie's work shirt, and the tough khaki twill pants that many ranchers wore when driving, checking gates and fences, and working stock. Because it was getting toward late afternoon and cooling down, he had slipped into a tan windbreaker with the seal of the presidency on its right side. The contrast between the president and me could hardly have been greater. I had on a black Neiman-Marcus suit, white shirt, and a dark tie. I wore black loafers; the president had on roughout boots. Before we went outside, he had grabbed a narrow-brimmed Stetson off a peg. I was hatless. My father, who was wearing a dark suit, dark tie, white shirt, wingtips, *and* a black homburg, was the only one who was dressed more inappropriately than I for the expedition. He wasn't going to hunt, though, so I put him into a special category. I was willing to bet that I was the only person in the state ever to go deer hunting in a Neiman-Marcus suit. Probably I still hold that record.

With only the slightest of bumps, the helicopter landed. As we followed the president out, I saw we had landed in a flat meadow next to a gravel road. Less than twenty yards away, four men stood by a white Lincoln Continental and a government-green, though unmarked, pickup. They wore slacks and boots, what appeared to be polo shirts, and windbreakers. On the left side of their belts were compact walkie-talkies, the kind that operated on transistors. I'd seen only a couple of these in Yosemite. Much to our disappointment, they didn't work as well in the mountains as the bulky battery-operated army surplus radios from the fifties. Obviously, either reception was better in the Hill Country, or this was a model superior to the one the Park Service was experimenting with. On the right side of their belts were pistols, either .32 or .38 caliber. Dark-tinted sunglasses hid their eyes, even though the afternoon sun was low and only occasionally broke through

LBJ leaving the helicopter, April 11, 1966.
LBJ Library. Photo by Frank Wolfe.

the clouds. They stiffened slightly as we walked toward them. Their heads swung from the president to us and then back again. He spoke to them in light tones, asking if they were ready to go hunting. They smiled and said "Yes, Mr. President." "Well, here's the hunter," he said, pointing to me. One of the agents reached into the pickup's cab and pulled out a scabbard. He unzipped it, and I had my first look at the rifle I'd be shooting.

I knew very little about deer rifles, but one glance was enough to tell me this was not a 30.06 Winchester, that favorite game-hunting weapon of many West Texas ranchers. It didn't have the distinctive lever underneath the trigger. This meant I wouldn't need to manually eject a cartridge shell from the chamber and move another round into it before I shot again. I could fire, then release the trigger, and the rifle would automatically expel the shell and insert another bullet in the firing chamber. This would let me shoot as many bullets as there were in the clip in a brief period of time, without taking my eye away from the scope and lowering the stock from my shoulder. That knowledge comforted me. I was confident I could get off the two shots Big John said I would have at any deer reasonably within range. Awareness that I'd be compelled to work a lever or throw a bolt on an unfamiliar weapon would have shriveled that confidence considerably.

I had enough sense not to mention this to the agent. If I pretended to an expertise more extensive than I in fact possessed, he might omit instructions about any idiosyncrasies peculiar to this type of weapon. As it turned out, he supplied me with nothing like that. He stated what I already knew, and he told me that I would start off with one bullet in the chamber and four more in the clip. What concerned him most was showing me where the safety was, and how to tell at a glance whether it was on or off. After we went through that ritual, I put the safety on, and he inserted the clip. It caught with an audible click. "You're ready to go," he said, smiling. "Good luck."

I imagine he was wishing the same for himself and the other agents. A kid, barely twenty-one and looking even younger, dressed in Sunday-go-to-meeting clothes, was going to be riding around with President Johnson armed with a loaded deer rifle. In all likelihood, he'd be sitting behind the man they were sworn to protect. They'd be hoping he'd know to keep the safety on, and wouldn't get buck fever so bad he would accidentally fire before the barrel got clear of the car. Because they'd run a check on me sometime during the last two days, they could be positive I didn't intend any harm to the president. But had I been trained to handle a rifle properly? Would I be made careless by excitement when I saw a deer? They could predict with perfect certainty that if anything went wrong, their asses would be in the proverbial slings. That was part of the risk of protecting LBJ.

No one told me the rifle's caliber. I just knew it was a well-used Remington. It was a good weight, not too heavy, yet not so light that the slightest pressure or twitch would jerk it off-target. The stock was slightly worn from the cheeks that had been laid against it; the wood holding the barrel bore the imprint of the palms that had gripped it; the blueing on the barrel was slightly faded. However inexperienced I might be, the rifle was a seasoned veteran of deer hunts. The scope looked much newer; there were no scratches on its exterior. I had noticed as the agent loaded the rifle that the bullets were hollow points. If I hit a deer, they would expand on impact, shattering bone if they struck it, and maximizing the trauma of a wound in the flesh. I could be confident in the tools of the trade I'd been given.

Evidently I *was* confident. Either that, or I was too excited and apprehensive to notice what I had not done: I had never fired my weapon. I didn't know if it was properly sighted-in. And I hadn't dry fired it, so I had no idea of the pressure necessary to pull the trigger. I could hardly have been less prepared to shoot anything. At the time, that realization never occurred to me.

Thinking back on it, though, I'm not sure what I could or would have done if I had been aware of these things. Nobody suggested I squeeze the trigger; no one took me to a range to check the scope. The president apparently took for granted that my weapon and I were ready. He was eager to get on the road. The Secret Servicemen, I suppose, hoped I was ready; they knew what the rifle could do.

It turned out we'd be a party of seven. Five of us would go in the Lincoln Continental. An agent would drive. LBJ would ride "shotgun." Kellam, Dad, and I would be in the back; Jesse behind the driver, my father sitting on the hump, and I on the right side. As I'd just noticed, Continentals were huge cars, so the three of us would have lots of room. Still, these were not the best conditions for carrying a rifle and being ready to shoot. How would I get in the car with it? Where would I hold it once we were in? These may seem like trivial questions; I can testify they were not. Added to them was the further question: how would I slip out of the car smoothly and quietly, then ready the rifle, find the target, sight it in, and shoot? Obviously, there would be no rehearsal for this, either.

The Lincoln Continental, April 11, 1966.
LBJ Library. Photo by Yoichi R. Okamoto.

Then the president resolved all these issues. "John," he said, "we'll leave all the windows down. You keep the gun's barrel out your window. That way, you can shoot without leaving the car." I slid into the seat; an agent handed me the rifle and then carefully shut the door. I checked the safety once more. It was on. I was ready to go.

First Dad, then Kellam, got in from the other side. The president settled into his seat and nodded to our driver. He started the car, picked up the microphone for the two-way radio in the Continental, and quietly said, "I've got Volunteer." Someone acknowledged "10-4," and we were on our way to hunt deer. Two agents followed behind in the pickup.

"We'll start in the north pastures," LBJ told the driver, who said "Yes, Mr. President," and began winding his way down back roads to get there. At one point, we crossed a paved drive. For the most part, though, these were graveled roads, barely wide enough for the Continental.

Sound rather than sight kept me informed about the roads. My eyes were fixed on the back of LBJ's head, which filled my entire vision. The thought of riding in a car with the president of the United States had mesmerized me so completely that I saw no more than green and brown blurs out of the corner of my eye. If asked at that moment, I could not have begun to describe the pastures we drove by. My hearing was much keener because I was straining to hear every word LBJ said. The last thing I wanted to do was mis-hear or completely miss a command, request, or observation from the huge head not a yard in front of me. The crunch of the Continental's tires over gravel and the ping of small rocks as they were flipped against the oil pan sounded loud. So loud, in fact, that the hiss and sigh of the tires as the car slid across the paved road surprised me.

This spell was broken whenever we came to a gate. One of the agents in the pickup would leap out and open it, then close and lock it right after the two vehicles got through. When Big John and I roadhunted, it'd been my job to open and close gates. For some reason, I'd never been able to do either fast or smooth enough to suit him. A typical mistake of mine was not noticing which way a gate opened. Another was fumbling with the wire or chain holding it closed. "I forget, you're not a country boy," Big John would say, sighing impatiently. "A country boy could do it in a second." He must have offered that as an explanation to avoid bringing up the true causes: mechanical maladroitness, made worse by inattention, caused me to forget how to work even familiar gates. So I was grateful someone else was doing it, and doing it well, for city or country fellows. LBJ's fingers drummed on the dash while we were stopped at gates. The sound told me he would be both more impatient of delays and less forgiving of mistakes or clumsiness than my grandfather.

Whenever we were moving, the president was a relaxed passenger who obviously delighted in pointing out the sights of his country. Since none of these remarks was addressed directly to me, I continued to listen rather than look. Thank God LBJ was oblivious to my inability to focus on the land for very long or with any comprehension. "Look at the grass, Waddy. It's been a good year." "This fall, I had the pasture brushed. You can see how it's cleared off and easier to keep track of stock in." Other details of ranch planning flowed smoothly from him. Let it get a little dryer, and the next windless day, the hands would burn these brush piles. That rye could be cut within six weeks, maybe sooner. Some of it could be sold, because the range looked so good for the spring. What about next year? Should we buy more cattle to fatten for fall sales? For a time, what to do in Vietnam or where to go with Great Society programs were the furthest things from the president's mind. Ranch matters completely occupied his attention. Around Dad and Kellam, he did not have to maintain the fiction that the operation of his businesses did not concern him or was totally out of his hands.

When we reached the north pastures, talk about ranching abruptly ceased. With an effort, I wrenched my eyes away from LBJ and looked out the window. What I saw first were the fences enclosing meadows on this ranch. They were higher than they were on other ranches I had visited. The significance of that was lost on me then. Another gate was opened by the agent, and we were on a dirt road.

The car made a softer sound on dirt. It felt as if it were gliding rather than rolling. The road followed the contours of the land, rising abruptly ten or twenty yards, gradually falling back to the original level, and then repeating the process. The grass by the road and in the pastures was a couple of feet tall; its brown and yellow colors revealed it had entered a dormant season. If the land had been brushed, the process was not complete. In addition to motts of live oaks with grey limbs and dull green leaves, mesquite thickets dominated the ridge lines running parallel to the road between seventy-five and one hundred yards away. I couldn't see their distinctive fringe-like leaves, the seed pods that looked like dried green beans dangling from twigs, or the sharp thorns on their branches, but the gnarled and twisted trunks were unmistakable. My first real glimpse of the Hill Country didn't impress me. Compared to the spectacular scenery of Yosemite, it wasn't much.

I kept that thought to myself. LBJ remarked, "It's beautiful, isn't it?" and then told me to get ready. We'd see deer soon, he predicted.

★ ★ ★

It was a little after five, and the browns and yellows, greys and greens of the landscape were beginning to deepen. Because there was very little sunshine, shadows were not a problem for me, but as the temperatures began to cool, a haze settled around trees and in hollows. Its color startled me. In Yosemite, ground fog and haze had been a wispy, dirty white. Less experienced firefighters were prone to mistake it for smoke. You had to trust your nose, not your eyes; you smelled fire more often than not before you could be sure you were seeing it. In the Hill Country, the haze was a striking, lovely shade of blue that verged on deep violet. It tinted everything that was further away from us than twenty yards. Struck by the abrupt change in color, I wasn't searching the fields for whitetails. I wasn't even aware of individual trees or rocks or brush. I was caught up in the gestalt of everything in front of me, the landscape palette of browns and greens blending into a dramatic purple.

"Deer!" whispered LBJ suddenly and urgently. "There they are." "Where?" I blurted out, startled. "Right there. Can't you see them?" he asked. I followed along the sight his finger made. "I see them," Dad said. But I couldn't. There was only a purple haze where the president was pointing. "It's just doe and yearlings," he said with disgust. Oh, God, there was more than one! I couldn't see a herd under these conditions! You can't shoot what you can't see. My father, sensing my agitation from the tensing of my posture, tried to help: "Right by the trees, John."

Probably that last whisper reached a doe. Suddenly, her tail flashed white, and they moved, not with alarm, but with a deliberate stride, over a low ridge and out of sight. Their coats looked to me like a mixture of deep blue and brown; as a result, they were perfectly camouflaged by the vegetation and the haze. I couldn't get over it. These were purple deer leaving the pasture, tan coats absorbing the haze, making its color their own. The children's verse sprang into my mind: "I've never seen a purple cow/I never hope to see one/ But I can tell you anyhow/I'd rather see than be one." It didn't comfort me. These deer *were* purple; they *were* there; and *I wasn't* seeing them. My vision, that recurrent problem that sank me into prolonged batting slumps and exasperated Big John when we hunted, couldn't pick the

Deer on the ranch, July 2, 1966.
LBJ Library. Photo by Frank Wolfe.

deer out of the background. I'd be utterly dependent on my guide for the rest of the day's hunting.

The deer weren't cooperating any more than my eyes. They weren't particularly wary; the approach of the Lincoln and the pickup spooked very few. President Johnson hunted the West Ranch infrequently, so the animals were unconcerned about dangers presented by the vehicles that drove around them. But they weren't interested in foraging closer to the road. They remained in the middle distance, where LBJ always saw them first, and where I continued to have trouble. The deer he spotted were invariably doe and yearlings. No trophy bucks appeared on the scene.

This combination of things, I'm sure, frustrated LBJ. Here he had set it up for the son of a friend to hunt on a ranch where the deer should feel perfectly safe and therefore be oblivious to any danger, and it just wasn't working out. If he could have willed a mighty buck with a huge spread to come up, he would have done it. The deer were impervious to his silent commands. The hunter was more receptive to his urgent requests to look, and look again, but with only limited success. My mood wasn't improving, either, because his impatience with my inability to see the deer was becoming more pronounced in his voice. As time passed, he continually commanded me to look here and see there. As the haze deepened, that became harder and harder for me to do.

We came to a more open field. Across it, at a distance I estimated was around one hundred yards, five or six deer were cropping at the yellowed remnants of a stand of tall grass. They still looked bluish purple to me, but the contrast between their color and the grass's yellow allowed me to see them clearly. To the president's disappointment, there were no bucks. The biggest, a mature doe, looked almost buck-size. LBJ exhaled deeply, then pursed his lips. We waited expectantly for a pronouncement that was obviously on its way. "Go ahead and take a shot at her," he ordered. "It'll let you try out the rifle."

I lowered the barrel as slowly and smoothly as I could, bringing the stock up toward my shoulder. Safety, off. The click, easily audible in the quiet car. Left arm on to the window, barrel into palm, grip firm but not tight. Right eye to the scope, left closed but lid relaxed. I could see as well as feel the preparations for shooting I had learned at Stanford mechanically, automatically slide into place. The magnification of the scope was less than I'd expected; the range hadn't closed as much as I'd hoped. The doe still looked purple, as the cross hairs of the sight moved over her. She raised her head, then lowered it to graze again, turning slightly toward me as she did so. An excellent chance: her left side was toward me, and her left shoulder was barely visible, flexed under her hide. Breathe in; breathe out. The sight was wavering on her, because the car door was uncomfortable on my elbow, and I didn't have enough room to extend my hips further back on the seat. Short breath in, slowly out. The sight still moved, but it was moving vertically up the doe's front shoulder, not horizontally along her side. Breathe in, then out. Cross hairs a tad low, but the rifle would move up, squeeze, squeeze, slow, WHAM!

As it was supposed to, the shot surprised me. I had no sense of any recoil; without thinking, I'd snugged the stock perfectly into my shoulder. There was no jerk. The scope stayed right on the doe, and I could see her legs fly up into the air and her body slam backward and onto the ground. Hold the sight, I reminded myself, but the rifle was already moving as if by its own power, finding the doe on the ground and centering her belly in the cross hairs. "Good shot! Fine shot!" LBJ was saying. Kellam said it was a pretty one, and I could hear my dad murmuring praise. "Get on the phone and get the boys over here," ordered the president to the driver, who called back to the ranch and asked for some hands to come over and get the carcass. The deer didn't stir at all. I breathed in, raised the barrel, and clicked the safety on.

The Secret Service agents in the pickup obviously hadn't studied with my grandfather about seemingly dead deer playing possum. One stayed with the truck and the president; the other loped over to look at the doe. Just as Big John would have, I noted disapprovingly that he didn't approach cautiously. Too close, I thought, too close to her hooves. He studied the doe briefly, then walked back to the Lincoln wearing a smile on his face. The president smiled and asked him, "What does it look like?" "A lot of good meat on that deer, Mr. President. It was a clean heart shot." "Would you like it?" LBJ asked. "We'd sure appreciate it, Mr. President." "All right," he said. "You guys get the doe over to Fredericksburg, and the meat's yours."

The two Secret Servicemen would have high-fived each other, had we known how to do that back then. I'm sure they were also elated because it appeared I could handle a rifle safely. Both of them thanked me for good shooting. I smiled and said they were welcome. "You ought to thank him," LBJ scolded them with mock anger. "A clean shot on a tender doe, rather than a tough, stringy buck!" They grinned and repeated their thanks. "Now," ordered LBJ, "let's go look for that buck, since these boys are happy." By that time, the truck with the ranch hands pulled off the road and bounced toward the doe. The agents returned to the pickup, our driver started the Lincoln, and we were hunting again.

★ ★ ★

The section of the West property we wound through next was much more open. The terrain still gently rolled up and down, but the mesquite was not as thick at the ridgetops, and grass grew only in isolated clumps. The dominant vegetation was prickly pear cactus; numerous limestone rocks jutted up through the soil. This part of the ranch had eroded over the years, because less prairie grass held the soil. Branching off from rises in the land were arroyos, cut in the land by years and years of sudden, heavy thunderstorms. They also served as a reminder to someone who had struggled through Physical and Historical Geology that the Balcones Fault, which traversed the Hill Country, had been geologically active long ago. The president pointed out the change in the topography as we traveled and wondered aloud how grazing on it could be improved. I noticed that there was much less haze here. Browns and yellows of the sparse grass, the dusty green of the cactus, and the white of caliche dust and the limestone predominated. The environment was so different that it was difficult to believe we'd traveled no more than two or three miles. As we rounded a curve, deer grazed at bunches of grass about twenty-five yards from the road.

Ranch vista, June 5, 1966.
LBJ Library. Photo by Yoichi R. Okamoto.

No trophy bucks stood among them. The doe were not as large as the one I'd just shot. But there was one mature spike buck with two slender antlers protruding from his head. He was big. Despite his size, had it been earlier in the day, I bet we would have driven on. I also bet the deer would have fled, because heads shot up as the car approached, and some of them began nervously twisting around, assessing the potential danger while checking for routes of escape. Light was dimming fast, even though the sun was peeking through the clouds. The onset of dusk must have given them a false sense of security. "Stop the car," LBJ commanded, as we slowly moved even with the deer. "Shoot that spike," he told me.

I could see him clearly. He had edged even closer to the car and showed no more interest in grazing. He must be curious, I thought to myself, as I eased the rifle barrel down and brought the stock up to a firing position. Safety, off. The button made its snick as it disengaged, and the sound seemed louder than before because of the alertness of the deer. I checked the safety again. Nothing would be more amateurish or humiliating than squeezing a trigger that was locked. The rifle was ready. Elbow on the window, grip firm on the barrel, stock pulled against the shoulder, eye to scope. The magnification brought him closer, but once more, I was surprised how little it enlarged the target.

Deer on the ranch, July 7, 1966.
LBJ Library. Photo by Kevin Smith.

Cross hairs on his side, breathe in, then out, relax. He moved two or three quick steps. Follow him, cross hairs moving, breathe in, out, left shoulder, sight a little low, relax. *He's off!* From a standing start into a bound, legs reaching out. I never heard or saw what caused this sudden flight. It could have been anything or nothing. He was moving.

And so was the rifle, as if it had a will of its own, as if I'd seen, rather than sensed, the strong muscles gather for flight, swinging, leading, a body's length ahead, squeeze, WHAM! The spike cartwheeled into the air and landed in a heap and a puff of dust. Hold the sight, hold the—*Jesus!* He's up again! Another bound up and away, rifle moving, one length, squeeze, WHAM! Down again, knocked off his feet, hold the sight, *up again!* Quick, swift, rifle not moving, because I sensed that I could not swing it any further without hitting the window post between the two doors, the deer running down an arroyo, gone from sight.

The president pointed out his window to where it had disappeared; my father, concerned that I might try another shot, said quickly, "Watch your finger, Mr. President"; and I, aware I'd had my two shots at a running deer, raised the barrel and moved the safety to the on position. "You hit it," exclaimed LBJ. "Twice," he added. Then he turned and looked at me. "You've got to go after it." I nodded, then said, "I'll do it." We both knew the rule.

I got out of the back seat awkwardly, swinging the door open while holding the rifle up and pointed away from the president and turning my legs outward. Then I retracted the rifle out through the window space, taking care again not to point it at anyone, most particularly LBJ. This procedure left me feeling clumsy and, therefore, self-conscious. Here I was, in my suit and tie, wearing black loafers with slick leather soles, about to go down an arroyo looking for a wounded animal. The spike might run for miles, I glumly thought. He could be gathering himself to come out of a cul-de-sac at top speed. Hurting and panicked, he wouldn't hesitate to run right over me if I got in his way.

I wasn't very sure-footed with the most appropriate footwear on; indeed, I was notorious among the firefighters in Yosemite for slipping and falling. Picking my way over rocks and scrambling up and down slopes while carrying a loaded weapon with its safety off would not have appealed to me with my Red Wing hiking boots on. In dress shoes, every step would be an adventure. Last and far from least on my mental inventory of hazards were rattlesnakes. It had been a mild day. Rocks and ledges would have heated up, and the snakes might have decided this was a good time to warm themselves before winter closed in again.

On the plus side, I wouldn't be following the deer by myself. LBJ told the two agents in the pickup to go with me. The three of us moved toward the mouth of the arroyo. We stopped momentarily where the buck had fallen the second time. "You hit him, all right," the other one said, gesturing at the blood smeared on a clump of grass. "How good, though?" I thought aloud, and we all shook our heads at once. "He's bleeding," the first agent said, pointing at drops on the ground and rocks leading down. They weren't big drops by any means; they looked like red spots sprinkled ever so often. We didn't say anything else. The Secret Servicemen drew their pistols, and in the still I could hear the snick, snick as they pressed their safeties off. I took mine off, hearing the click but still checking to make sure. Without speaking, one agent moved ten feet to my left and about five feet behind me; the other stationed himself the same distance from me on the right. As I'd been taught by my grandfather, I pointed the rifle low and away, to my left, with the stock held higher and close to my right hip. That way I could swing the weapon smoothly—in theory, at least—and the stock would rest against my hip if I had to fire in a hurry. There'd be no aiming if the deer ran at me; I wouldn't have time.

Experienced hunters will have noted that what we were doing was dangerous. Three of us were carrying loaded weapons, ready to shoot, over unfamiliar terrain. We'd spaced ourselves out, lessening the danger that an accidental discharge from one weapon would hit another person. What we hadn't done was determine who would call shots in the event quick firing was necessary, or divide the 180 degrees in front of us into arcs of individual responsibility. I didn't even think of this until later, probably because at the time I had no experience working my way through a field with other hunters. I don't know what the agents' excuse was.

Of course, they had been intensively trained to react and fire quickly and to exercise strict firing discipline when shooting. And they'd put me at the point, which made it less likely I'd accidentally shoot one of them in a moment's excitement. Of the three of us, I was the most at risk of being hit by a bullet. Factor in their training and discipline, and the chance of that happening weren't very great. Understand that their immediate assignment had been changed by LBJ, the man they were duty-bound to defend, into protecting *me*, and the odds in favor of my safety got higher still. Obviously, I wouldn't want to be shot, but the thought has crossed my mind that I wouldn't want to be the Secret Serviceman who accidentally wounded or failed to protect Waddy Bullion's son, either.

All of these thoughts are *ex post facto*. Had they occurred to me then, they would have been quickly rendered moot. About ten yards from the mouth of the gully, the deer lay dead.

The three of us looked at him briefly, then moved up beside his body. The Secret Servicemen holstered their guns; I moved my safety back on. The two wounds were within three inches of each other and exactly in a horizontal line. The one closest to the deer's shoulder was no more than two inches behind it. I'd led the buck about half a foot too little. "That's fine shooting," one of the agents said to me. "It sure is," agreed the other. All I could say was, "Thank you." I felt both happy and dog-tired. All three of us were relieved we weren't still walking and looking for drops of blood. We turned away and returned to the car.

President Johnson, Dad, and Jesse Kellam were talking as we emerged from the arroyo. LBJ had swung his frame around so he could look directly at the two in the back seat and was gesturing widely with his right hand. Long practiced at evading presidential gestures, the agent was leaning to his left. Everyone was smiling at whatever Johnson was saying.

On hearing us approach, he turned around and asked what we had found. I briefly reported that the deer had died pretty close to where we last saw him. "Did you hit him twice?" the president demanded. I said I did and described where the shots had gone. He nodded, glanced at the Secret Servicemen, and then spoke. "A fine doe and a tender spike. They're gonna want you hunting every day, John. I suppose you boys want this venison too." They said they did and mentioned it was sure fun watching me hunt and sharing in the meat. He told them they could have the spike, and to take it to Fredericksburg for processing along with the other. "Call the ranch and get the boys over here," he ordered the driver.

When the agent back there acknowledged the message, he passed along the news that Victoria wanted to know what Volunteer was doing, and when he would be back at the house. The president took the microphone from the agent and said, "Tell Bird we'll head that way in about ten minutes." Then he observed to all of us that it would soon be too dark to hunt, and the deer would be skittish after the shots anyway. The two agents returned to their pickup. Another truck drove up, and they directed it toward the arroyo, no doubt laying claim as they did so to the carcass once it had been bled and gutted.

Shifting around in his seat, turning to his right so he was looking directly at me, Lyndon Johnson said, "John, I believe you're the best shot on this ranch. I was just telling your dad that, and I wanted to tell you too."

"Thank you, Mr. President," I stammered. "It's a very good rifle." Quickly my father interjected, "John *is* a good shot." Perhaps he was afraid LBJ would take my comment as contradicting or rejecting his praise; perhaps he wanted to be sure I received full credit for my marksmanship. "He sure is," the president said, as he smiled.

I kept the rifle out the window as we headed back, but as the president predicted, we saw no more deer and light dimmed with the rapidity typical for late December. The agent drove faster, choosing paved roads once we left the West Ranch. It was full dark by the time we returned to the house. I handed the weapon back to one of the two agents in the pickup, and he carefully ejected the bullet in the chamber and removed the clip. Observing this, LBJ walked over and promised me we'd hunt again tomorrow. "We'll try to get you a buck with a good rack you can put on the wall now that you've fed a couple of families and their friends." I said that would be wonderful, but no matter what, I had

The Pedernales at sunset, December 12, 1965.
LBJ Library. Photo by Yoichi R. Okamoto.

had a great time today. "So did I," he said, as the four of us approached the house.

LBJ turned to my father and asked to talk with him in preparation for their business the next morning. They were making arrangements for that meeting when Mrs. Johnson appeared. "Did you have a good time?" she asked. I said I did and gave her a brief sketch of the hunt: two deer killed, no trophy head. She was obviously pleased, then she smiled and asked if I needed to wash the rifle's oil off my hands. I recognized a discreet and welcome suggestion when I heard one and gratefully asked her where the closest bathroom was. I excused myself with a sense of relief. Dad announced he was going up to our room for a while before dinner.

When I came out of the bathroom, I intruded on a touching scene. The two Johnsons were standing in the hall close together. Lady Bird reached up and laid her left hand on his cheek. Then she asked, "How are you feeling, darling?" Sounding for all the world like a small boy who craved his mother's touch and her sympathy, he said plaintively, "I'm better, but I still don't feel perfect." She leaned into him and stroked his cheek. I coughed to reveal my presence.

Neither of them was perturbed. Mrs. Johnson gracefully circled her husband's arm with her hands and explained, "Lyndon has been suffering from a cold for over a week." He sighed. "I take Contac and I get sleepy. I don't take it, and I have a sore throat and a headache." I told him I had the same reaction, except I couldn't stay awake after the Contac began to take effect. On that homey note, I went up the stairs.

Boy, you're stepping in tall cotton, I said to myself, when you're swapping complaints about cold medicines with the president of the United States. I was deeply pleased by the casualness of the exchange and the mundane nature of the subject. At that moment—even more than when he praised me as the best shot on the ranch—I could feel how seductive it was to be on familiar terms with a very powerful person.

I was also struck by the open affection that Lady Bird Johnson had for her husband and the equally open dependence LBJ had on his wife's love. Skeptics such as my mother would say that she was babying him, and of course, like any man, he was delighting in her attention and wanted even more. Some might say she was putting herself in a mother's place, treating him as a favorite son rather than an ailing husband. The president's expression, his tone of voice, and his words themselves conjured up that metaphor in my mind. He just didn't sound like the same Lyndon Johnson I'd hunted deer with that afternoon. He sounded small, not large; bewildered, not confident; in pain, not vigorous. More than a sore throat or a headache was plaguing him at that moment.

I knew he had ordered a bombing pause over North Vietnam, in the hopes of creating an environment for negotiations. What I wasn't aware of was the tense struggle taking place within the administration over whether to propose new Great Society programs to Congress during 1966. LBJ wasn't meeting only with Dad the next day; Joseph Califano was at the ranch to talk over various drafts of the State of the Union address. Nothing must have seemed settled to him, in foreign or domestic affairs, and the protest over the war, so puzzling and infuriating, was growing in what had been once the most reliable constituencies for the Democratic Party.

What a comfort his wife must be. A passage from Scripture flashed through my mind then, from Psalms I believed. After we returned to Dallas, I found the verses in Psalm 131. Verse 1 reads "Lord, my heart is not haughty, nor my eyes lofty. Neither do I concern myself with great matters, nor with things too profound for me." It is the second verse that I had thought of on the stairs at the LBJ Ranch: "Surely I have calmed and quieted my soul, like a weaned child with his mother; like a weaned child is my soul within me." Of course, he usually *did* concern himself with great matters, and he surely was thought haughty by many. But at that moment and no doubt at others, when he had to calm and quiet his soul, Lady Bird's loving presence made it possible, however fleetingly, for him to do just that.

Much later, I wondered why he wouldn't permit others to get close enough to offer the same solace. I also pondered whether Lyndon Johnson sought only succor and pardon from love. Did he realize he could gain strength and renewal from it as well?

This vision of a vulnerable LBJ sticks more in my memory now than it did on that particular day, because of what happened after I left the Johnsons downstairs. In the bedroom Dad and I were sharing, as we worked out who would sleep in which twin bed I suddenly remembered I'd never contacted my friend to tell her that I couldn't take her to the party tonight. A phone sat on a small table between the beds. Could I use it? Dad's answer revealed to me how even in the smallest things, he was scrupulous about not indebting himself to the Johnsons. The phones in the bedrooms were for guests' convenience, he said; still, I should make the call collect. And, since it would be collect, the call should be to Mother, who would accept it without question and be glad to pay the charges. She could call my date and give her my regrets.

My father's instructions didn't really surprise me. I remembered how in 1963 "Light Bulb Johnson" had very publicly insisted on saving money by turning out lights at the White House. And Dad had also told me that the Johnsons, like many of his wealthy clients, paid very close attention to small costs, especially when they themselves didn't incur them. Dad didn't want the number of one of his son's friends showing up on either the government's or the family's phone bill for December. It wouldn't escape notice, and it might invite sarcasm from the president about playboy sons. My father didn't need that extra charge in his own dealings with LBJ.

I'm certain he didn't want me to jeopardize my present high standing with the Johnsons, either. Although it would have been fun to have a White House operator announcing a call for my friend and creating excitement at her house, that would be a prideful vaunting of self-importance I could easily forego.

Before I dialed Mother's number, I looked out our window. It was the first time I'd seen what lay behind the house. There was a long garage, with places for more vehicles than I could quickly count. Next to it was a small corral with steel fenceposts and railings. Beyond that was a fenced-in field, planted in either winter wheat or rye. From the front of the house, you could see pretty motts of live oaks and the green Pedernales River backed up behind a concrete dam that doubled as a low-water crossing for cars and trucks. The landscape in back looked more like the flat farm land around Dallas. This vista inspired me to match the Hill Country against the Sierra Nevada once more, this time aloud.

"I know the president loves this area," I remarked to Dad, "but it's really not very impressive compared with Yosemite."

"John, I wouldn't say that over the phone if I were you."

Startled, I turned away from the window. He wasn't smiling, and I knew it was no joke. I assured him I wouldn't, and I got through the call to Mother without saying anything about the day beyond describing the successful hunt and making sure she knew that I was enjoying the visit, the Johnsons, and the scenery. To my own ears, these sounded like pious banalities, but I wanted to put Dad at ease and cover us both should anyone else be listening in. I also wanted to avoid a quarrel with my father.

Years later, I instantly recalled this conversation when I picked up *Taking Charge*, Michael Beschloss's edited version of Johnson's White House tapes during the first year of his presidency. Did Dad know for certain at that time that some presidential conversations were being recorded? The answer is no. He would have objected, had he been aware it was going on, to any taping of LBJ's consultations with him.

Did my father suspect that the president would check into conversations his guests had on the telephone, either by listening to tapes or by reading transcripts prepared from them? Obviously, he did.

Dad was aware how much the president coveted all sorts of information about the people he dealt with, and how eager he was to use what he collected to his advantage in relationships with them. Part of this was the desire to dominate, to bend others to his will. Part of it was a compulsion to be ready to defend himself against the schemes he assumed those around him were always plotting. Life had become a series of contests for him well before he ran for office, not only as a result of his personality, but because of politics as well. Now that he had reached the pinnacle of power after winning the competition that mattered most, he was deeply suspicious others would take advantage of any weakness and every moment of inattention to seize by force or finagle by stealth parts of his power.

To me, it was inconceivable the president would care enough to want to know what a twenty-one-year-old university student said in a call to his mother. To my father, this was naivete born of inexperience and ignorance. Everything interested LBJ; he listened and watched constantly for bits of information he might wield against others. He might, for example, tease my father goodnaturedly about my scenic comparison. More likely, he would retain it in his memory and be ready to call it forth if he ever thought doing so would be helpful in dealing with Dad or, perhaps, me in the years ahead.

That evening in our bedroom, I was still basking in the glow of seeing the Johnsons in a tender moment and having a spontaneous, casual conversation with them. My father, on the other hand, was aware that you should never relax your guard and speak or act carelessly around Lyndon Johnson.

★ ★ ★

I didn't have to wait long to learn this lesson for myself. Ironically, it was as the result of Dad's efforts to joke with the president, not two hours after he had warned me to watch what I said.

There was an informal gathering in the living room for cocktails before supper. A handful of people had been ferried to the ranch from Austin for drinks and food. None of them was a politician or a public official; all were known to the Johnsons socially. Mrs. Johnson graciously handled the introductions; their names slipped out of my mind as quickly as I'm sure mine did out of theirs. She also made sure I met Jake Jacobsen, one of the president's assistants, who had been included in the gathering. Because I automatically assumed he was important, I made a point of repeating his name aloud as I said, "It's nice to meet you." That way, I told myself, I'll be able to recall which prominent people were there, besides the two Johnsons. As things turned out, I didn't need any memory tricks. LBJ made Jake unforgettable.

The party seemed relaxed and casual. Mrs. Johnson still wore the same skirt and blouse she was wearing when we arrived; the president had not changed from his hunting outfit. Both were talking cheerfully about such relative inconsequentials as the weather, New Year's plans, and the sad football season the Texas Longhorns had suffered. I did notice Jake Jacobsen kept an eye cocked on LBJ and hovered near enough to hear everything he said. That, however, didn't set him apart from anyone else. After all, this was the president of the United States sipping Sprite and asking about bowl games ten feet away from me. Aside from his office, Johnson's size and his aura of confidence and command made him a natural center of attention. But even these considerations did not detract much from the relaxed environment. When

LBJ and Jake Jacobsen, December 5, 1965.
LBJ Library. Photo by Donald Stoderl.

LBJ wondered which teams were playing in the Sugar Bowl, he wasn't upset that no one could tell him. I knew the answer, but I paused too long in deference to others, and the conversation moved on before I could blurt out, "Missouri and Florida." I hadn't been intimidated; I was just too slow. In fact, I felt pretty comfortable in LBJ's living room after my successful hunt. So comfortable that I ordered a scotch, and thereby became the only person drinking alcohol in the group around the president.

Right after I missed my chance on the Sugar Bowl, one of those abrupt and total silences that invariably punctuate every social gathering occurred. Thus everyone heard what my father said as he and a woman he had been talking with moved closer to LBJ. Pointing at my scotch, he chuckled and commented, "John told me he'd never burn his draft card. He needs it to prove he's twenty-one and can legally buy a drink."

My heart sank. I had in fact said those very words to Dad a week or so earlier. He had been much amused, which seemed to me another sign that he really didn't know his son well. This was self-deprecatory humor designed to help me live with something I did not find funny in the slightest. Because I was so baby-faced, I was always carded. In

California, these were invariably protracted and, therefore, extremely embarrassing experiences. Texas driver's licenses did not have pictures on them during the sixties, and the men and women who waited on me demanded to see my Selective Service card as well. To my delight, the steward serving beverages in the Johnsons' living room had not hesitated a moment before mixing me a scotch and soda. Now, just as I was feeling so adult and sophisticated, Dad had called attention to how young I looked.

I was beginning to drape a smile on my mouth when I noticed the silence had deepened. No one but Dad was smiling, much less laughing. President Johnson had drawn himself up to his full height and was scowling down at my father. Others in the immediate circle were either frozen still or instinctively shrinking away. Without intending to, Dad had brought the protest against the war in Vietnam right into the living room at the LBJ Ranch. Lyndon Johnson clearly didn't like that. He didn't want to be reminded of this opposition to him and his administration; that was one thing. Another thing was this: his compressed lips and squinting eyes revealed that he did not think anyone should joke about burned draft cards or any young American's patriotic duty to his country. He didn't say a word; he didn't have to. Clearly, he was furious with Dad right there and then.[1] It was equally apparent to me that when he thought further about what my father had said, he'd be unhappy with the original author of the joke.

Dad's response to LBJ's unmistakable anger was a masterpiece of courage and courtesy. He looked directly back at the president, smiled slightly, and shrugged, as if to say, "Well, what can you expect?" A long moment passed. Johnson's features relaxed. He cleared his throat loudly. Then he reached out to shake hands with the woman who'd been talking with Dad. A moment later, they were smiling and talking about people they both knew in Austin.

---

1   LBJ may have been particularly angry that evening about domestic protest against the war. The night before, he had spent three hours listening to Robert McNamara argue in favor of extending the bombing pause. The Secretary of Defense had stressed the necessity of convincing an increasingly restive and concerned public that the government was willing to do anything reasonable to gain a negotiated settlement. The president reluctantly agreed. As Robert Dallek observes, mostly he agreed to counteract communist propaganda. He expected nothing would result from the pause in bombing. This failure, he hoped, would incline the nation to support further escalation of the war later in 1966. Had my father been aware of this painful and difficult decision, one LBJ resented having to make, he would not have joked about my draft card.

Soon afterwards, Mrs. Johnson announced, "Zephyr says supper's ready and we should eat it right now." We filed into the dining room, eager to sample Mrs. Wright's famous Southern cooking and to leave behind the momentary tension in the living room. As I left, I noticed for the first time a needle-pointed pillow on one of the couches. It had a brief and appropriate message on it: "This is my ranch and I do as I damn please." Nobody there would have questioned that sentiment.

Like the rest of the house, the dining room was neither spectacular nor unusual. A long buffet rested against one wall, a table and plain wooden chairs seated a dozen people. The furniture was simply designed and sturdily built by careful craftsmen. It had been in the family for a number of years, or was collected from ranch sales. It recalled the heavy yet graceful oak pieces my Lewis grandparents had hauled from their ranch into Menard.

The one difference between the Johnsons' dining room and Grandma's was the presence of a telephone bolted to the underside of the table at the host's place. I didn't inspect it closely, and LBJ didn't talk on it while we ate. I assume it was some sort of radio-telephone, because I saw no wires, and it was shaped like the trim-line phones of a later vintage, not like the clunky rotary-dial machines of that day.

To people taught by the Cuban missile crisis and the movie *Dr. Strangelove* to be aware of the possibility of grave national emergencies, the phone seemed a sensible precaution. Seeing it reminded me that I had not noticed any military officer carrying the fabled black box full of missile codes that would launch an immediate response in case of a Russian attack. What would have happened if war had broken out while we were hunting on the West Ranch? Would we have had to lead-foot it back to the house? Evidently LBJ thought the risk of nuclear attack was minimal, and that was good enough for me.

LBJ was served first, not just before anyone else, but before any other food was brought from the kitchen. This protocol was probably the same for any president. This particular one added to it a ceremony all his own: his contests with his weight and with his cook. LBJ struggled with both in front of us that night.

Concerned about the strain additional pounds would place on his heart, Johnson's physicians had put him on a diet. To insure he would observe it, Zephyr Wright measured his portions in the kitchen before she put his plate in front of him. "Is that *all*, Zephyr?" he lamented when she put it in front of him. "I've been hunting all afternoon and working all morning. You're going to starve me." "That's it, Mr. President," she said smiling, "and no second helpings." He rolled his eyes and said he guessed he'd have to be satisfied, because she was the boss over his food. It was clearly a sparring ritual they'd staged before for guests. We reacted as I'm sure they expected we would: with smiles at the sight of someone firmly laying down the law to an atypically (though bogusly) docile Lyndon Johnson. He took a bite of pot roast, pronounced it very good, and asked once more for a larger helping. She refused again and went back to the kitchen. Stewards served the rest of us, and we started eating.

Mother always began our evening meals with prayer, thanking God for His bounty and promising we'd be mindful of our blessings. No such petition to the Almighty occurred at the LBJ Ranch. The agnosticism I'd cultivated in an effort to appear sophisticated while in California caused me to conclude it made a lot more sense to thank Zephyr Wright than some problematic deity. Perhaps Lyndon Johnson felt the same, and assumed this crowd did too. Whenever Billy Graham or other religious leaders broke bread with him, I'm confident they were asked to say the blessing. Absent anyone overtly connected with organized religion, there evidently was no reason to pray aloud.

Everyone was dividing his or her attention between eating and paying close attention to whatever the president said or did. Of course, he dominated conversation. Much of his talk was about commonplace things—the beauty of the day, the good shape the range was in, the end of one year and the coming of another, the weather here and on the East Coast. Occasionally, thoughts about what he needed to have done around the ranch would occur to him. At those times, he would suddenly focus on Jake Jacobsen and order him to remember to call somebody about something. There was nothing casual about these commands. This was not the relaxed LBJ of twenty minutes ago, the one who didn't insist on knowing about the Sugar Bowl. His words were clipped and blunt; his tone was harsh and preemptory; his expectation of instant obedience unforgiving and unmistakable. Jacobsen visibly snapped to attention and dutifully replied, "Yes, Mr. President!"

Jacobsen had prematurely white hair; unlike me, he was one of those people who are born looking older than they are. He appeared to be older than LBJ, in fact. And when I say he snapped to attention, I'm

LBJ preparing to give orders to Jake Jacobsen, December 24, 1965.
LBJ Library. Photo by Frank Wolfe.

not exaggerating. One moment he would be somewhat slumped at his place, engaged in eating; the next, his shoulders would be drawn back straight, his head held high, his chin thrust out, his eyes trained on the president, and his voice perfectly subservient in tone. I'd never seen one adult react in that way to another adult's commands. At that moment, I understood what working for Lyndon Johnson could be like.

The next minute, I understood it even better. LBJ began to praise Jacobsen for his commitment to religion and to improving the conditions of worship in Gillespie County.

"Tell them about your kneelers," he directed.

Jacobsen remarked that he had seen the poor state of the kneelers in the small Catholic church in Stonewall one Sunday while he was there with the president. They were in such bad shape that he'd ordered new ones.

"And paid for them with his own money!" interrupted LBJ. "For a Jewish fella, you're the best Catholic in the county."

No one around the table had any illusions about either who had first complained about the kneelers or who had inspired Jake Jacobsen to do something about them.

"When those people kneel, they'll be thankful to you," continued the president, his grin encouraging others to smile. "For a long time," he added, "until they wear out. Then they'll look around for you again."

The best Jewish Catholic in the Hill Country gamely smiled too. "I'll always be glad to help them out," he promised.

"*I'm* sure *you* will," the president replied. Jacobsen surely would continue to be that parish's benefactor for as long as Lyndon Johnson wanted him to play that role.[2]

Soon afterwards, I had an opportunity to witness LBJ's impact on the minds of his people. Someone dropped the topic of newspapers into the conversation. If my memory serves, it had something to do with an incorrect announcement in the society pages.

The mere mention of the press called forth a vehement snort from the president.

"I wouldn't believe a Goddamn thing I read in a newspaper."

If my fellow guests were like me, they were wondering whether to nod and smile.

"Most of them don't care about the truth."

What next?

"Not only that, a bunch of the reporters are communists."

What?!

"Take the *New York Times*, there's nothing but communists there."

I could feel my eyes widening. The *Times* was revered at Stanford; to the extent the university's secular society could be said to feel religious about anything, it worshipped the newspaper that plumed itself for delivering all the news fit to print. And now the president of the United States was charging its reporters with being communists!

Then, as abruptly as he had taken up the cudgels against the nation's most famous newspaper, LBJ stopped whacking it in favor of violating his diet. Taking his spoon, he reached over and began transferring potatoes from the plate of the woman next to him to his own. From there, they moved rapidly to his mouth. It was almost time for dessert, and Mrs. Wright would soon be back on patrol.

---

2   No doubt Jacobsen was thankful that LBJ did not go on to recount their meeting with Pope Paul VI two months earlier. At the president's request, Jake genuflected and kissed the pontiff's ring. Johnson also made certain that a White House photographer captured the moment for posterity. Probably he wanted proof that his aide was the best Jewish Catholic in the world, not just Gillespie County. It was a good thing for Jacobsen that St. Peter's Basilica in Rome wasn't as needy as St. Francis Xavier in Stonewall.

LBJ, Jake Jacobsen, and Pope Paul VI, October 4, 1965.
LBJ Library. Photo by Yoichi R. Okamoto.

I glanced around the table. Most of the guests wore studiously neu-tral expressions. Mrs. Johnson's eyes were fixed on the door leading toward the kitchen. My father looked the most natural; he was calmly cutting the last bit of roast. And Jake Jacobsen had already assumed the position: alert and attentive, ready for the inevitable. It came between bites of potato.

"Am I right about the press, Jake?"

"Yes, Mr. President."

★ ★ ★

Mrs. Wright had prepared rice pudding, apparently a presidential favorite, because he pointed out how cruel it was to be denied it. No one took him seriously. We'd seen how he'd bent the rules on potatoes and expected another proof of his power would be in the pudding. As soon as Mrs. Wright left, LBJ's neighbor edged her bowl closer to him. He nodded, drew it over to him, and polished off her helping. It inspired him to pursue a new topic, with Dad as foil this time.

"John here shot two deer," LBJ noted, "and those deer are mine. Waddy, I ought to be able to deduct them on this year's taxes. They're business losses. How much do you think they're worth? Deduct that off the company's return."

Once more, I almost smiled at the wrong moment, so sure was I that this was a joke. But, spoon poised in hand, no hint of humor in his expression, LBJ was eyeing Dad expectantly. My father glanced up from his pudding.

"I wouldn't do that if I were you," he said in an even voice. Then his eyes dropped again to his dessert, and he took another bite.

What would the president say to this? Probably to everyone's surprise, the answer was nothing. LBJ said not a word and made no movement other than dipping his spoon down and returning to the rapid consumption of his guest's pudding. I didn't doubt he had instantaneously accepted Dad's advice. The contrast between Jake and Waddy could hardly have been greater. It could only be surpassed by the difference in the way Lyndon Johnson treated the two men.

Dad had an advantage Jake and the rest of us didn't. He knew LBJ was not serious about deducting the deer I'd shot. "The president never discussed personal, family, or corporate business in front of outsiders," he later told me. "In particular," Dad added, "he never, ever seriously talked about taxes except in small, confidential meetings where he had the protection of the attorney-client privilege." No matter how he seemed to us when he brought up writing the doe and the spike off on the Texas Broadcasting Corporation's return for 1965, that he mentioned it in front of a table of strangers signaled Dad that he did not intend to do this. My father's laconic, matter-of-fact response, delivered in between bites of pudding, communicated to the president that he wasn't going to strike this lure and be reeled into prolonged talk on this subject.

That was part of Dad's message to the president. Another part was this: LBJ should not continue to dangle this bait, because some sitting around the table might think he really was considering claiming this deduction. After reaching this incorrect conclusion, they might spread the word around. That could embarrass the president and tarnish his reputation; it might also renew partisan and journalistic interest in the blind trust and the legal owner of the ranch. The "that" in "I wouldn't do that if I were you" referred not just to the proposed deduction, but to the consequences of his making public "orders" like this to a supposedly independent trustee, then dangerously dragging out talk on the "company's," not "the ranch's," return. No fool, Lyndon Johnson shut up.

But not before I was convinced he meant what he said. My guess is most of the others at dinner that night believed it, too. What saved the situation, and possibly prevented gossip about Johnson and his deductions, was the appearance that the president's trusty adviser had stopped this scheme in its tracks. It became to the president's guests merely a passing incident, not worth notice or recounting.

But deducting the deer is a story worth telling, because it raises the interesting question of what caused Johnson to bring it up in the first place. What moved him, I think, was a determination to let people know that on the LBJ Ranch even the wild animals were possessions. Those whitetails were his.

I have no doubt LBJ believed this. Indeed, I shouldn't have been taken off guard—though I was—by his comment, "those deer are mine." That afternoon, the president had given the two carcasses to the Secret Service agents without asking my permission. The hunting licenses Big John and I had gotten before we shivered in the blind that November day informed us that a wild animal's remains were the property of the hunter who killed it, and it explained how we could protect those rights by—in the case of deer—attaching an official tag to the antlers. And my grandfather had often warned me that if I accidentally shot a cow, sheep, or goat, I'd owe a rancher money, because killing an animal someone owned would not transfer property rights to it to me. In the excitement of this afternoon's hunt, I hadn't noticed that the president was not acting as though he believed the dead deer were mine. Rather, he was handing over the venison in full confidence it was his to give away.

★ ★ ★

After dinner, we returned to the living room. LBJ didn't let anyone settle down into chairs. He simply announced that he was going to bed.

Then, as if suddenly remembering his manners, he said that he'd enjoyed the evening and the company. Kissing women's cheeks, shaking men's hands, murmuring goodbyes to each guest, he moved toward the door. He looked and sounded like a tired man as he did this, but it seemed like a tiredness resulting from a long afternoon outside, and from physical weariness, the sort that ends in a deep, dreamless night's sleep. It was the reverse of exhausted despair from struggling with unbearable burdens, the kind that leaves you hopelessly tossing and turning in the wee hours. It was as though the whole world was the LBJ Ranch. He'd do as he damn pleased. After he and I shook hands, and I had thanked him again for the day, he smiled and promised, "Tomorrow we'll get that buck." I knew if Lyndon Johnson had anything to do about it, we would.

CHAPTER 13

"…and I do as I damn please"

My next day at the ranch began early. Dad and I have always waked up around dawn. He claims it results from having to milk cows before daybreak when he was young; in my case, it has to be genetic. On this morning, he had an incentive to get going as quickly as he could. There was no telling when the president might summon him to the ranch office or the master bedroom. Those who served LBJ were well-advised to be dressed, fed, and in motion on short notice at any hour; The Man himself felt perfectly comfortable lounging in bed in his pajamas, conducting business soon after awakening.

This caused my father less grief than it did many. He was a morning person. Moreover, he had steeled himself never to appear surprised or uncomfortable, no matter how the president reacted or what he said; and he disciplined himself to speak in a matter-of-fact tone, with respect but without any tinge of subservience. If Johnson wanted to talk taxes in pajamas, fine. If he wanted to discuss deducting dead deer while having dessert, Dad could do that, too, without missing a bite while nixing the idea. The trick was to keep your head and be prepared.

While Dad showered and shaved, I stared out the window at the dawn. Sound carries a long way in the early morning quiet of the country. I could hear the low, mournful coos of doves and the slightly shriller mimicking of them by mockingbirds even over the shower's noise. I looked for the blue-violet haze that had been at the West Ranch. There was none. Dawn moved rapidly from gray to full light. There were some clouds, but it looked as though it would be a sunnier day than yesterday. Just two days left in 1965. Just one more day at the ranch, plus a few more hours tomorrow morning.

What would this day bring? You couldn't tell how much time you'd have with LBJ. Anything could come up demanding his attention. Although the phone under the table hadn't rung yesterday, who could guess what would happen this morning or this afternoon. How much hunting could we do, if any? Part of me hoped we wouldn't go out again, because now I'd be competing against my own performance of the previous day. The best hunter on the ranch felt some qualms that morning. I brushed them aside. After all, I'd shot well, and I had perfect confidence in the rifle. If I could just see the deer clearly, I should be okay. See them, sight them, and let the mechanics of shooting take over.

Dad has always said some of his best ideas came to him while he was shaving. I asked if he'd been inspired this morning; he said he had not. I was certain I wouldn't be. At that time, I used an electric razor. That Remington Rand shaver was fast. By the time I'd be trying to think great thoughts, the process was over. Dad used a Gillette razor that he'd had since the late 1920s. It definitely was not a safety razor. Gillette Blue Blades snapped on to the top of the handle; there was no sheath to protect one's face from sudden laceration. He *had* to be thinking when he shaved. The wonder was he could concentrate on anything besides the danger to lips, nose, cheeks, throat, and even ear lobes. He didn't casually stroke his face with this tool. He paused between every movement, and great thoughts must have occurred in these interstices of shaving. What I did on this morning was look around the bathroom while my safer and duller razor whirred and trimmed.

Right here around me was one major difference between this house and the ranch houses I'd been in before. There were far more bathrooms in the Johnson's home; in fact, there was apparently one per guest bedroom on the second floor. Most of the ranch houses in Menard County had one, period. For it to be indoors and have hot and cold running water were sufficient causes for boasting. Insofar as quantity was concerned, this was luxury indeed.

In terms of aesthetic quality, though, there was nothing luxurious about the house's facilities. Our bathroom was purely utilitarian; no fancy tile. The tub's size could accurately be called cramped; the shower head, faucets, and handles were unadorned chrome; the sink was small and freestanding; the toilet was plain white and operational; and the mirror was tiny. The only splash of color was the deep blue of the towels and the shower curtain. Its dimensions, amenities, and decor closely resembled the bathroom my three roommates and I shared in our apartment in Palo Alto. This one was much cleaner.

I was fascinated by the difference between how LBJ projected his own power, prestige, and authority and the way he and his family arranged and decorated the house in which they lived. If Johnson's personality suited the imperial presidency, his ranch house was pure down home. "This seems just like a plain ranch, except for the bathrooms and the telephones," I said. "It's really not as luxurious as I expected." Dad pointed out that I hadn't been on the patio or in the swimming pool, two other features of life on this ranch that weren't standard equipment. As for the rest, he said, that was just the way they liked it: unpretentious; familiar; a place they'd be at ease in, as unlike life in Washington as possible.

"What about cars?" I teased him. "A Lincoln isn't your typical hunting vehicle." He conceded it wasn't, but it provided plenty of space for a big man and was powerful as well. "The president likes large cars he can stretch himself in, and why not? Nobody who can avoid it wants to be uncomfortable."

Then my father went on to say that he believed LBJ needed this ranch. It was a place where he could be close to nature and away from cities. The formalities and proprieties of Washington didn't exist here. He didn't have to dress for dinner. He didn't have to invite anyone to eat with him because protocol demanded it. And when he stepped away from his desk, he was free to call for the car or the helicopter, and in ten minutes he could be deep in the Hill Country looking at the land, studying his cattle, inspecting fences, and in the right season hunting his deer. The ranch was his refuge; here he recharged his energy. It was the place, Dad was convinced, where he could be himself.

Dad paused and watched as I nodded agreement. Encouraged by my understanding that even presidents needed to be offstage at times, he used this opening to emphasize another point. "John, this is a place where he can say what he feels or thinks at that moment. He doesn't have to worry about what others might think, or how they might work it around to fit their own purposes." Then he looked straight at me and spoke firmly but quietly. "That's why you shouldn't repeat some of the things you hear around the table."

Things? Deducting deer? Burning draft cards? The *New York Times*? Grabbing others' potatoes and pudding?

"I'm referring to what he said about the *New York Times*," my father said.

As I opened my mouth, he raised his hand, forestalling one of our frequent but futile debates about the nature of truth. "I know, I know," he began in a weary tone of voice, "all the reporters at that paper aren't communists. The president doesn't believe that himself. But he gets frustrated. You can understand why. He's afraid some of the news encourages the communists in Vietnam. If you're helping them, then you might as well be one. That's what he thinks. When he's angry and among friends in his own house, he sees them as communists."

My mind, never as quick as Dad's, was still trying to devise a rebuttal, when he concluded by saying that talking about these angry remarks would harm LBJ and help his enemies. "They would seize on this as proof he was truly dictatorial and would be happy to suppress or intimidate the press anyway he could. And that really isn't true about him. He'd never actually do that."

Realizing he had strayed into another area of controversy between us, the distinction between appearances and realities, and the hypocrisy—from my perspective—of insisting on maintaining appearances, my father again tried to stop me before I started.

"I know what you believe. But for lots of folks, appearances *do* count, and bad ones can hurt people. Nobody should have what he says in anger at his own dinner table while talking to guests held against him and given more weight than it deserves in judging his real policies. That happens, even though it shouldn't. It could happen with this thing about the *Times*. Please keep it to yourself."

I nodded and promised I would. My father smiled and said, "Good." I kept my pledge until after LBJ's death. Once that statute of limitations passed, I used it to buttress examples my students read in their textbooks about his nearly paranoiac reactions to domestic dissent against the war. Those accounts have persuaded me what I had witnessed was a peek at the real Lyndon Johnson. In 1965 knowledge of his attitudes was not widespread, principally because he was still relatively careful about when and where he expressed them. Later he was less guarded. But his beliefs had been formed before he stopped being so discreet. Contrary to what Dad said then, LBJ *did* believe some *New York Times* reporters were communists.

At that time, though, my father saw no reason to buy that at all. To him, newspapers were thoroughly capitalistic enterprises that had to sell their product in order to survive. Allowing communists to dictate a paper's handling of the news didn't strike him as a good way to do business. He wasn't fond of the *Times*. To him, it was too dull, especially when compared to his favorite paper, the *New York Herald Tribune*. For some reason, dullness seemed to be prevailing over wit and style. He regretted that, and not only because of his personal preferences in newspapers. Dad was convinced that on one matter LBJ was right:

reporting in the *Times* was encouraging our enemies abroad to continue fighting.

Whatever weakened the president's credibility, my father was certain, would have the same effect. Talking about reporters as communists would transform them into potential martyrs and raise questions about LBJ's judgment and motives. Some of this was implicit in Dad's argument that morning; some of it was all-too-familiar territory we'd fought over before. (We'd do much more of that in the years just ahead.) But his best-chosen argument, the one that convinced me then and there I should keep quiet, didn't have anything to do with the press, policies, or perceptions. In our own house, opinions served up around our dinner table were supposed to be kept private whenever it appeared that discussing them with others might be embarrassing or hurtful. Dad was appealing successfully to one of the understandings I grew up with.

I'm sure he felt it was useless to try reason or reality with me. To Dad, my generation had no sense that doing and saying things had consequences in the real world. In that arena, people could, and would, take umbrage at acts and words they believed were directed against them and then attempt to repay those who had said and done those things. It wouldn't help much to cry "First Amendment rights" if LBJ decided you were his enemy. He wasn't an abstraction; he wasn't a metaphor for potency. He was a ruthless man who loved exercising power and who was ever ready to demonstrate his willingness to use every means to achieve his ends. Crossing him would be extraordinarily unwise.

None of this could my father say to me in December 1965. Neither fear nor common sense would have stopped me from disputing hotly this argument. I would have denied that such pragmatic considerations should govern my actions. Probably I would have given in, at least for that morning, but only after a long and emotionally charged exchange of views that would have left us both worn down at the beginning of a long day. Because he knew his son so well—much better than his son gave him credit for—my father shrewdly chose to stress what I'd been taught about conversations at home. Dad's diplomacy enabled us to go downstairs to breakfast reasonably happy with each other and prepared to enjoy the day at the LBJ Ranch.

★ ★ ★

A wide selection of food and drinks were on the buffet in the dining room. We filled our plates, sat down, and ate alone. We were finishing up when a marine orderly came in and told Dad the president and Mr. Kellam were ready to see him.

As my father rose and reached for his briefcase, I looked at him expectantly. He could guess why. Dad glanced at his watch and guessed that he and the president would have to talk at least until 9:30. He suggested I walk around outside until then. If I were needed before that time, there was no shortage of people to come get me. "Be sure to stay in sight of the house," he reminded, "so we can find you if we have to." A walk sounded like a good idea to me.

I saw nobody as I went through the house. The front door was unlocked. No one was in the yard. Once more, I was struck by the absence of guards. I unlatched the wooden gate and stepped through it. Then I carefully closed it behind me, making sure it would stay shut. The last thing I wanted to do was carelessly give some cattle a free pass to the president's St. Augustine. I strolled through some young live oaks toward the fenced-off family cemetery. Beyond the graves lay the route to the Pedernales River. With nothing better to do, I went toward it. If all else failed, I could always skip stones off the river's surface, a tried-and-true method of passing time in the country.

Front gate to the LBJ Ranch House, December 5, 1965.
LBJ Library. Photo by Robert Knudsen.

★ ★ ★

In its natural state, the Pedernales was a typical Hill Country river. In drought years, it shrank to the size of a creek, exposing its banks and the stones on its bottom that centuries of flowing water had worn smooth. In better years, it was a lovely, slowly flowing stream, tumbling over and around limestone rocks as the land sloped, gathering in deep pools perfect for swimming. But when thunderstorms struck and settled in for a day or two, the Pedernales, just like the Colorado, the Concho, the Llano, the San Saba, and the Medina, was a killer. Banks that seemed high would be completely submerged in a matter of hours. Barely moving currents became rip-roaring torrents almost in a flash of lightning. Low-water crossings—those bridges and dams that often had two or three inches of water gently flowing over them—that were usually perfectly safe for car, trucks, animals, and humans could become death traps in minutes as floods from upstream rushed toward and over them.

Every low-water crossing I saw as a young man had a flood gauge next to it. Timbers were sunk in holes dug by the rivers, cemented there, and painted a luminescent white, with black numerals that marked how high water was above the crossing. Some went as high as fifteen feet in the air. Ideally, headlights would catch the flood gauges in their glare, and motorists could tell in an instant how high the water was.

Practically every spring and summer there was fresh evidence that this wasn't enough to keep some from being swept away and drowned. "Never try to go over a low-water crossing with water running over it above the one-foot level," was preached to me by both grandfathers. "Get away from the river when you see that"; so went their second commandment. I heard the same rules from other ranchers. By the late fifties, you could hear these warnings repeated on the radio during bad weather. No matter—impatience, stupidity, foolhardiness, and inattention regularly took their toll on humans and livestock.

There was no flood gauge at the Johnsons' low-water crossing over the Pedernales. By itself, that informed me the river had been tamed along this stretch. It was placid and green and looked deep and almost still behind the dam. Two or three inches of water flowed gently over the top, slid down an abutment six or seven feet, spilled across a flat concrete roadway wide enough for a car or truck, and went on downstream. Above the dam, water reached the top of the bank; below it, I could see a four or five foot high bank of eroded soil. What people saw

The Lincoln Continental at a low-water crossing,
with water at the one-foot level, May 29, 1965.
LBJ Library. Photo by Yoichi R. Okamoto.

LBJ and Lady Bird Johnson on the dam, December 1959.
LBJ Library. Photo by Frank Muto.

from the front of LBJ's house was the Pedernales above the dam. They had a vista of a tranquil, green, twenty to twenty-five yard wide river, with low banks free of debris. A few live oaks and mesquites grew along its edge. Nothing completely obstructed views of the water.

Taming the Pedernales in front of the Johnson ranch house had not been the work of the Lower Colorado River Authority. Instead, the Johnsons had paid for the dam. Their intention, as Dad observed, was not so much flood control as scenery management. The river simply was prettier full, and Lyndon Johnson saw no reason to be satisfied with nature's work on his ranch if he could improve upon it. And, since it was his ranch—well, you already know what he'd do.

The tricky part, my father had mentioned to me earlier, was not rights over the land the Pedernales flowed through in front of the house. LBJ owned both sides of the river. But the Pedernales itself belonged to the public and had been placed by the legislature under the administrative control of the LCRA. No one could dam a river in Texas without surveys of usage, studies of water flows, and estimates of the impact on the public and on property holders above and below the proposed construction. Dad never commented on how hard or easy it had been to persuade the LCRA to let LBJ build a dam at this ford. Either that fell under client business not to be discussed, or he trusted I was intelligent enough to figure out that a person named Lyndon Johnson just might have an easier time with the agency charged with regulating the use of and access to Texas's rivers than you or I would.

LBJ sure had less trouble with the bureaucrats in Austin than many of his neighbors. With a smile, Dad admitted that the Johnson dam was not popular. Those above it believed that it backed up a volume of water sufficient to put them at greater risk of destructive flooding. Those below had the opposite complaint. The dam was restricting the flow of water to them too much, and thus potentially posed a grave danger to their stock whenever there was a drought. My father wasn't sympathetic to either point of view. "Farmers and ranchers are always complaining about something," he said with a laugh. "It's never wet or dry enough; it's always too hot or too cold; crops are too sparse or too plentiful; the price of stock is too high (if you're buying), but too low (if you're selling)," he went on, thereby dismissing the subject.

I doubt LBJ was very sympathetic, either. To him, more control over the river must have appeared obviously better. Anyway, he wanted a pretty river flowing by his house, so he could brag about the view to company and enjoy it himself. What he wanted, he generally got. In the process of building better scenery, I suspect he began to think of the Pedernales as he thought of the deer of the ranch: they were his deer; it was his river. The only difference that I could distinguish between what I had killed yesterday and what I was looking at presently was this: without Dad's approval, he wouldn't deduct the animals; but with Dad's help, the Texas Broadcasting Corporation would absorb the expenses of his improvements to the Pedernales.

At that moment, what the dam signified most to me was the removal of good skipping stones from my reach. No stones were visible above the dam. Below it, I'd have to step down into muddy reeds to pick up the few that were there. Dressed again for a semi-formal occasion rather than for hunting rocks or deer, in a sports coat, tie, slacks, and loafers, I didn't dare do this. Besides, I had another errand on my mind at that moment.

Guests on the banks of the Pedernales, perhaps
looking for stones to skip, December 5, 1965.
LBJ Library. Photo by Robert Knudsen.

I went to find a likely bush or tree, remembering as I surveyed the scene a story I'd read in *Time* magazine. During the search for outdoor privacy, I translated it into a less sanitized but, to me at least, more accurate form.

LBJ loved to drive around his ranch at high speeds while sipping from a paper cup filled with beer. He also loved to take reporters from outside Texas with him, not only to show them the scenery as he toured the Hill Country, but to observe how they reacted to the combination of high speed on winding dirt roads with a mild beer buzz. When the inevitable occurred, and bladders had to be emptied, he would stop the car, leap out, stride into the brush, unzip his pants, and noisily urinate, all the while inviting others to join him. Few of the new initiates to rural rides did, which gave Johnson the chance to watch gleefully as their discomfort visibly increased while he bounced the car through potholes and over cattle guards. One time, a reporter from the east, who had been warned about the presence of rattlesnakes in bar ditches and under mesquite trees, asked LBJ, who was merrily pissing and talking over his shoulder to the others, "What if a snake is there? Aren't you worried?" Turning back to his company, and grinning as he shook himself dry and rearranged his pants, Johnson answered, "Naw. It's too tough."

I laughed at the memory. But even as I did, I reminded myself the reporter's concerns were not baseless. Snakes really do hang out under trees near water. Their prey tend to focus on drinking, and ignore the possibility that death may be coiled nearby. Imagine, I mused, the reaction of a rattler suddenly roused from a torpid, sated-with-food slumber by being pissed on, or unexpectedly routed from his hidey-hole by a stream of urine. I wouldn't want to confront that snake with nothing but my dick in my hands. Unlike LBJ, I had no illusions about how tough it was. So I looked carefully for snakes as I wandered through the live oaks.

Five or six years after this, I happened to be talking with a very eminent historian who taught at Yale, when the subject of public lavatories in Europe came up. He had nothing but praise for the *pissoirs* on Paris streets, and he condemned their absence at the great formal gardens at Versailles. His wife and he had been shepherding their four kids around those gardens, when the coffee at breakfast, the passage of time, and the spraying of fountains had a familiar effect on everybody. The nearest restrooms were back in the chateau, nearly a half mile away; given typical French treatment of foreign tourists, they were probably closed for the morning anyway. "I sent the boys behind a couple of ornamental trees," he said, "and I stood guard while the women went in back of some hedges." I told him that I'd once had a similar problem, and recounted my adventures in finding an appropriate tree on the LBJ Ranch.

LBJ and a dead rattlesnake, April 10, 1966.
LBJ Library. Photo by unknown.

My friend just stared at me. Then, chuckling, he shook his head and asked how I could possibly compare the *lèse majesté* of soiling the Sun King's gardens with emptying my bladder on one of LBJ's live oaks. I replied that this made for an interesting comparison, Louis XIV with Lyndon Johnson, and observed that it would be worthy of a historian of his skills. He wasn't interested in pursuing the matter. Just as well, because he might have passed on to asking why I felt any hesitancy at all about relieving myself outside on a ranch, and that would have taken some time explaining.

In the context of my visit to LBJ's ranch, my cautiousness, though without question extreme, was more understandable. Dad had just warned me not to repeat the conversation of the night before about the *New York Times*. He'd expressed concern about my saying anything critical about the Hill Country over the telephone. I'd seen with my own eyes how quickly the president reacted to my father's retelling of my reason for preserving my draft card intact. I'd witnessed how LBJ belittled Jake Jacobsen and helped himself to a guest's potatoes and pudding. I'd sensed his impatience with my inability to pick out deer in the violet-blue haze of the West Ranch meadows. There was no sure way for me to predict how he might respond to anything I or anyone else might say or do.

To be perfectly honest, what I feared most was some sort of presidential commentary on my masculinity. The moral of the story of LBJ urinating in the brush with no fear of rattlesnakes was obvious to me: his was tough; others' were not. The time I had spent with him yesterday had reinforced a conviction I'd already gleaned from reading and hearing about him: that Lyndon Johnson could turn the most mundane exchange into a matter of—as a friend of mine aptly describes such contests—my dick is bigger than yours. For many reasons, that was the sort of competition I wanted to avoid.

More generally, I didn't want to expose myself to teasing, questioning, or criticism, in part for Dad's sake, but mostly for my own. Protecting yourself completely against these misfortunes is tough enough under any circumstances. It's especially nerve-wracking when you can't be certain of a person's reactions to even the most casual or trivial words or acts. I'm sure that Lyndon Johnson understood this effect he had on others. I'm positive he welcomed this condition, relished it, and took advantage of it whenever he chose.

My father was habituated by many years to this climate. I had neither the experience, nor the confidence, nor the useful (to LBJ) knowledge and skills Dad possessed. I had no feeling for what was right or wrong conduct on the ranch. I knew the consequences of being wrong could be humiliating personally. Whatever a mistake might be, I didn't want to make one. More precisely, I didn't want to be seen making a mistake.

So far, visiting President Johnson had been fun. It certainly was interesting, indeed fascinating. But I was by now well aware the ranch was not the place to expect a low key, restful vacation from the troubles of the world. Guests might forget their problems there, but my strong impression was they did so because they had new ones that demanded all their attention.

I felt uneasy and edgy being out by the Pedernales alone. If asked at the time, I would have sworn I could take care of myself. The truth, however, was I wanted my father around while in this place. Not only could I look to him for cues, I could also be confident that he'd help me out if it became necessary. To be sure, this was the same man I'd frequently complained about in Dallas and Palo Alto to my mother and my friends. Our conversation in the bedroom this morning made clear he hadn't changed overnight. He still held the same opinions I disliked elsewhere. Here, though, I depended on him and trusted in him.

Aside from this unexpected admission to myself of Dad's abiding love for me and concern for my own well-being, I was discovering another unfamiliar feeling: pride in my father. The president listened to what he said and followed his advice. Even more impressive, Dad didn't spring to attention at a glance from LBJ, lick his boots, or kiss his ass. Compared to others I'd seen here, he was a real man by any definition of that word. Certainly he fit the West Texas understanding of what a man was: he did a full day's work for the boss; labored long and well at the job, above and beyond the call of duty; respected The Man; yet did it all without brownnosing or crawfishing. Through it all, too, he kept his sense of humor and his perspective on himself and others. For really the first time, I'd seen my father interacting with adults who were not relatives by blood or marriage. At that moment, I could understand why his clients and peers respected and liked him so much. I did myself, for many of the same reasons. So it was great to rejoin him in the living room and settle down together reading some newspapers and skimming through a couple of somewhat dated magazines.

Nearly an hour passed. Dad and I had about exhausted the available reading material when the president walked in. Dressed in khaki like yesterday's, he was obviously prepared for an expedition. We stood up quickly. He smiled at me as he said hello, adding that he was ready to show me more of the Hill Country. "We'll hunt late this afternoon," he explained. "Right now, let's go riding." He turned to Dad. "Waddy," he said, "I want to look at some of the accounts in the bank at Johnson City. We'll stop in there, too." That said, he beckoned to us, and we followed him down the hall.

My stomach rumbled as we walked toward the Continental. It was after eleven, and I had expected lunch would be the next item on the agenda. LBJ had other plans. So I focused on willing my hunger away and silencing my belly completely. To my surprise, they obeyed. Perhaps they were as concerned about the president's possible reaction to human weaknesses as I was.

As we were getting into the Continental, the president announced to us and the agents, "We'll look in at the Boyhood Home while we're in town." He swiveled around in the seat and looked at me. "Have you ever seen it, John?" I replied I hadn't, but would like to. "It's interesting," LBJ told me. Then he turned to Dad. "Waddy, I want you to notice what they've done with it. Tell me what you think. I'm counting on you, because John here doesn't know what it's like to cook on a wood stove and have to heat all your water there too."

I sure as hell do, I thought. I had cooked on one all summer, thanks to economy measures in Yosemite. I had more recent experience than LBJ or Dad did with splitting the wood, feeding the fire box, adjusting the damper, waiting for the stove to heat up enough to cook at anything but a glacial pace, and then suffering from the warmth in the kitchen as it slowly cooled off. I also knew, as they probably did not, that it takes water longer to boil at high altitudes than it does in the Hill Country. I'd be inspecting it with an expert's eye. I'd also, I knew, be keeping that expertise to myself.

As I was recalling cooking at Crane Flat, the agent started the Continental. "Heath Ranch," LBJ commanded tersely. "Yes, Sir," our driver answered. He pointed the big car down the road, accelerating smoothly while telling the unseen listener on the radio about Volunteer's whereabouts and destination.

For the next couple of hours, we drove slowly around and through ranches in the Hill Country. First, we went to the Heath Ranch. Then we inspected what LBJ called "the Lewis property." Since I already knew that family was no kin of mine, I didn't ask which Lewis originally owned it. The tour was nothing like a Sunday drive in the country. Sure, the president said he wanted us to see the natural beauty of the Hill Country, and he happily pointed out vistas of rolling hills, live oaks, and mesquite. But his main attention was elsewhere. How were the fences holding up? Was the barbed wire taut or sagging? Were the cedar fence posts erect or tilted? What about the stock? Were the cattle getting enough feed? Were any bulls limping and unable to support their own weight when they reared to service a cow? Did any of the herd need worming? Had any been wounded by the wire or in the brush? And, of course, the perennial question, the most crucial to a profitable ranch: how was the grass?

Lyndon Johnson did not need to ask these questions explicitly for me to understand what he was doing and thinking. What he commented on as we were driving made it obvious. He was just like other ranchers I knew. His eyes moved constantly over the landscape, looking for signs of trouble ahead with fences, cattle, and the range itself. As he did this, he was also checking for indications that his hands were not doing their jobs. No one who rode around a ranch with LBJ, sitting behind him as the car systematically went up and down the roads that crisscrossed each pasture, could ever doubt again how serious he was about ranching. He didn't play at it. He worked at it.

And I caught the spirit from him. Once I realized that he was gauging the countryside from an occupational perspective, I found myself doing the same. My viewpoint was not a rancher's, though. I scanned the hills and motts, the grass and thickets, as if I had to fight a fire there. What was it like to fight a hardwood fire? If the blaze got going, it'd be hot and fast. Cutting hardwood was exactly that: *hard*. Axe blades and chain saw teeth would dull more quickly than they would on pine. Human minds and bodies would lose their sharp edges sooner, too. So while LBJ surveyed the productive possibilities and pitfalls of his land, I looked for the best and easiest places to slash fire lines and confine flames.

Now I knew I was playacting, thinking about hypothetical possibilities, unlike the president. He was making real assessments, weighing real decisions, judging real human beings. As for me, I was conscious that hunting deer in a coat and tie was plenty strange. The mere thought of fighting a range fire dressed that way made me smile. Still, there were similarities between our reactions that caused me to suddenly appreciate what his ranches meant to him. We both were confident of our expertise, he in ranching, I as a firefighter. Both of us believed we could control the environment. Cattle could safely and profitably graze in this meadow; a brush fire could be stopped in its tracks on ridges, where shovels could clear a wide line from one rocky outcropping to another, the sparse brush and stunted trees cut and removed quickly with axes and saws, and the prairie grass on the slope below ignited as a back fire. Neither of us felt omnipotent. Mother Nature could defeat our best-laid plans. Even LBJ had no defense against prolonged drought or sudden floods. No firefighter could control any fire when the fuel was dry and the wind was high. These circumstances were beyond control for ranchers and firemen. Things could be done to mitigate them, but these efforts wouldn't stave off a real licking. And nobody could blame anybody for that outcome.

There it was. On the ranch, LBJ knew where problems might arise. The solutions to those problems were straightforward and obvious. He had the intelligence and the power to deal satisfactorily and swiftly with the usual difficulties. Abnormal, extreme conditions were another matter. But the impossibility of dominating them was recognized by everyone. Compare all this with that whore of a war, domestic protest, and the unmistakable signs of a backlash benefiting a resurgent Republican Party. No wonder coming to the ranch relaxed him. No wonder he needed these trips to the Hill Country. Here he could be what he wanted to be—the LBJ of lore and legend—and not what he was—a politician in (to borrow firefighters' language) deep, deep smoke. Suddenly I understood all that. Ironically, I could feel what he was feeling because while I thought about ways to deal with fires on these ranches I forgot I still had to hunt deer with Lyndon Johnson.

That memory abruptly returned as other Secret Service agents driving a convoy of cars met us at the Lewis ranch house for the trip to Johnson City. Going to town clearly demanded a greater degree of planning and precaution than driving over to the West, Heath, and Lewis ranches. The presence of the agents and their cars also revealed that LBJ was less cavalier about being protected than his behavior yesterday had led me to believe. This was not a spur-of-the-moment trip to town. Perhaps as a result of his conference with Dad, he had decided to inspect the bank's books. At that point, he let others know what his plans were, and he instructed them to make the appropriate arrangements.

To get to U.S. Highway 290 to Johnson City, we took Texas Ranch Road 1. In tribute to the state's most distinguished living citizen, the legislature had changed the number of the paved road that went by LBJ's ranches. No one commented on this as we swung onto it; I noticed only because Dad had mentioned to me why it had that number. This seemed to amuse him in the same way the siting of the Johnson dam on the Pedernales tickled him.

Did the legislators expect this would endear them to the president? If they did, they must have been disappointed. My father never heard anyone, including the president, refer to RR1 by its official name and number. That was for tourists. To those who lived in Gillespie County, it was simply the state road. They were accustomed to calling it that, and no one in Austin could change that habit. To them, it was enough that where I was staying was now known as the LBJ Ranch, not the old Martin place.

When we left the state road for U.S. Highway 290, cars driven by the agents slid into positions ahead and behind the Lincoln. Our driver's head moved slowly and systematically, checking the side mirrors, the rearview mirror, and the view through the windshield with robotic regularity. There wasn't much traffic. No one in cars traveling the other direction stared or pointed. The locals in their pickups probably recognized the convoy and the Lincoln Continental, but they saw Johnson and other VIPs frequently enough to take little notice of their

A presidential convoy, April 11, 1965.
LBJ Library. Photo by Yoichi R. Okamoto.

comings and goings. The travelers who were just passing through the area toward Fredericksburg whipped by too swiftly to grasp the significance of the line of cars going east toward Johnson City. They didn't expect to see The Man, and thus didn't look for him. I figured the agents were aware of these reactions and used them to justify taking the risks attendant on sudden presidential dashes around the area.

Once we were in town, we left 290 and went down back streets to the bank's rear door. All of the passengers jumped out of the car. One Secret Serviceman opened the door into the building and went in first. Another held the door for the president and his guests. Our driver kept the car running. We looked like we were about to stick the place up.

LBJ strode in, proceeded directly to a table near the cashiers' stations, and began flipping through ledgers someone had already placed there for him. That someone had also left a large magnifying glass, and the president used it to study two or three pages of figures. I could see around his shoulder and was surprised to notice that all of the numbers had been entered by hand. Mostly they were in black ink, with only occasional splashes of red. The book itself was leather bound and huge, measuring at least four feet by five feet and at least six inches deep. No one spoke while LBJ's glass moved up and down the columns toward the bottom line. No officers of the bank were visible to me, and only

LBJ at the Johnson City bank, April 15, 1965.
LBJ Library. Photo by Yoichi R. Okamoto.

one middle-aged woman was working as a cashier. She barely looked up when Johnson burst into the room.

As he hunched over the figures, nearly bent double as he peered intently at them, an old rancher came in. Without taking his Stetson off his white hair, and expending no more than a glance at Johnson, he went straight to the cashier, touched his hat in a gesture of respect, and began writing a check. One of the Secret Service agents moved in front of the president, watching with fingers lightly gripping the pistol's butt while the bank's one customer tilted his hat back on his head, tugged at the belt that struggled to contain his sagging pouch of a stomach, and signed his name. The cashier opened her till without speaking, counted out the correct number of bills, and handed them over silently. Another pull at his britches and a slight but courteous tip of the Stetson as he pulled it down on his head, and the rancher turned and walked out the door. The agent stepped back.

With a tiny movement of his hand, Johnson motioned my father to join him. He pointed at some numbers. Dad examined them for a moment or two. Finally, he nodded. LBJ put down the magnifying glass, closed the ledger, and walked toward the back door. He and my father exchanged brief murmured words—"See what I meant?" and, "Yes, you were right." Otherwise, nothing was said during the ten to fifteen minutes we spent in the bank.

Neither man's face betrayed either pleasure or anger; neither looked surprised or satisfied. The president's speech, gestures, and expressions were as economical as the agent's movements. In the literary terminology of today, it was a minimalist episode. To me, it was a striking, even bizarre one, because the Lyndon Johnson I had observed over the past day was anything but silent and restrained. That he was this way in the bank, and that he clearly had insisted on the books being left for his inspection without the presence or assistance of anyone did not, in my opinion, bode well for the bank's officers. His silence was ominous and threatening, perhaps even more so than his furious frustration with opponents of the war in Vietnam and his ferocious glare when Dad repeated my joke. I got back in the car in a somber mood. The relaxed happiness I'd felt in the country was utterly gone. Once more I was mirroring what I believed were the president's thoughts and emotions. He seemed pensive and edgy. Only my father and Jesse Kellam, who once more was riding with us, maintained a demeanor of calm and cheerful expectation for what else the day might bring.

Like others around Lyndon Johnson, I had swiftly become extremely sensitive to his moods. Like them, too, I was very concerned about accurately predicting his probable reactions in the immediate future on the basis of how he appeared to be feeling at the present moment. These were unsettling, not to say unnerving, sensations. It gave me a taste of what his secretaries, his staff, the Secret Service, and his advisers endured constantly.

Apparently, my father wasn't worrying about any imminent explosion. Nor was Kellam. The two of them, though, knew what had been going on at the bank. They could interpret the president's unusual behavior on the basis of that knowledge. Right before me, I could see the tremendous advantage insiders had in serving this president. Their positions might not be secure, and they were still defenseless against sudden demands and fiery tantrums. They had the comfort, however, of knowing—as much as anyone could expect to know—what LBJ was wrestling with. Outsiders could only guess.

In retrospect, my guess is that the Texas Broadcasting Corporation had invested in the bank we went to that day. It may even have had a controlling interest. LBJ clearly wanted to check on the books at the end of the calendar year. To avoid confirming suspicions that he was not a passive onlooker while Dad and A.W. Moursund managed the family's businesses, he made this fast, essentially surreptitious visit to Johnson City. Our route via back streets, our entrance by the way of the private door, and his uncharacteristically unobtrusive, even furtive behavior while in the bank were designed to avoid drawing attention to his presence there. The absence of the bank's officers, plus the lack of any comment from him about this, smack of what later American politicians would call "preserving deniability" for them and him. How they planned to account for the books laid out on a table, with a magnifying glass conveniently close at hand, is unknown to me, but surely they could have found an explanation in the unlikely event they were interrogated about these preparations. I thought of all this later as I replayed the scene in my mind, and my conclusions were reinforced when I read the misleading entry in the president's Daily Diary for December 30, 1965. On the day itself, when I got back in the Lincoln I was focused instead on the visit to Lyndon Johnson's boyhood home.

The house where the Johnson family had lived during the 1910s and 1920s had been taken over by the National Park Service after LBJ became president. He had already arranged for the care and preservation of the house, fence, and yard before 1963. Afterwards, the Park Service applied more paint, made some minor repairs, and collected some pieces of period furniture. I can't remember whether it was open for public tours by December 1965. Certainly that day it was closed to everyone but a very select few.

The boyhood home under the administration of the National Park Service.
Bullion Family Collection.

As we pulled up, a ranger was waiting for us by the white picket fence's gate. No mind reading was necessary to figure out what he was thinking. If anything was wrong or went awry, he'd sure as hell hear about it, if not right on the spot, then soon thereafter. Moreover, if bad things happened, his career might be cooked.

My summer spent in the Sierra Nevada had taught me how rangers referred to historic sites, monuments, and battlegrounds back east. These were "cannonball parks." Working at them wasn't deemed nearly as interesting or challenging as rangering at the great western parks: Yosemite, Grand Canyon, Glacier, Olympic, Rocky Mountain, and Yellowstone. Despite this, serving at cannonball parks was very important to a person's career. This was where the Park Service's hierarchy tested the administrative, managerial, and public relations skills of the most promising young rangers. Do well, and you were on the way up.

One look at the young man waiting by the gate at the Boyhood Home as we pulled up at the curb, and I knew he was wondering whether he was on the way out.

As the ranger smiled, said, "Good afternoon, Mr. President," and swung open the gate, I felt another pang of sympathy for him. Ranger culture was intensely macho. Once, the Assistant Fire Control Officer was talking with me about being the fire boss on a two-man fire crew. During the height of lightning season, established fire crews were broken up, and each veteran firefighter was sent out with a permanent or seasonal ranger. "You're the boss, John," he reminded me, "you know what you're doing, and they don't." I observed that it was hard for a twenty-year-old to give orders to men twice my age. What should I do? What should I say? He didn't think twice. "You *do* everything better than anyone else on the crew. You *say*, 'Follow my ass.'"

This wasn't entirely helpful. At twenty, I weighed around 120 pounds. Many rangers were much stronger than I; most could do at least some things better. And how did I establish my authority by demanding someone follow me, when my own sense of direction in the woods was so faulty that I had to continuously ask if I were going the right way? I had to lean exclusively on what my friend said first. I did have much more experience than almost all of the rangers in fire control and suppression. I also had the knack of explaining why we had to do things in such a way as to make the men who worked with me believe they were part of an effective, tough team. The role of hardnosed commander fit neither my abilities nor my style. I led by persuasion, not example.

The ranger for the Boyhood Home had none of these options. How could you claim to know more about growing up in Johnson City in the century's early decades than LBJ? How could you pretend to a greater expertise about the furniture or the house or the town? There was no point in contemplating being macho with the president of the United States. "Follow my ass" wouldn't be what a ranger said at the Boyhood Home. "I'll kiss your ass" was a much more useful administrative philosophy for Johnson City.

If this ranger wasn't resigned to this by now, if he didn't make the right adjustments, if he wasn't lucky in guessing the correct answer to a variety of questions, then he was in for a rough ride indeed. This afternoon, he worked for Lyndon Johnson, not the National Park Service. That cannot have been a comforting thought as the president walked through the gate, up the steps onto the porch, and into the house he had lived in long ago.

The ranger also had the discomfort of not knowing exactly what to do with the gate after some Secret Service agents and LBJ went through. Did he continue to hold it for Kellam, Dad, and me? Or did he hustle to catch up with the president?

Those who have never dealt with these dilemmas may scoff at them. It does seem trivial, but not knowing just how important the others were—though certainly less important than LBJ—must have heightened the ranger's tension. Clearly the Secret Service wasn't going to help. A few of the agents were busy scanning the street; others were eyeing closely a family that happened to be taking pictures of the house when we arrived. I could hear the father excitedly whispering to his young and obviously bored son, "Look! Do you know who that is? Look! Look right now." Meanwhile, Mama was trying to advance the film as quickly as she could, while maneuvering to get a clear shot at LBJ amidst the agents who were barricading themselves between him and the people at the fence. As this was going on, I reached the gate and with a sympathetic smile told the ranger I'd see the others in. A grateful "thanks" later, he was hurrying toward the house.

We three followed on behind. "Poly-ticks," I thought, recalling a sign in the main fire station in Yosemite Valley, "equals many bloodsuckers." It reflected one of the realities of employment in the Park Service.

Because the NPS hired so many seasonal personnel, it was a glistening sugarplum of patronage for politicians. I had no qualifications whatsoever to be a firefighter. Not only did I lack any experience in the woods, I was woefully out of shape at summer's beginning and so inept at driving a stick-shift pickup that I failed the driving test for my federal operator's license the first time I took it. Given a chance, my bosses would either have rejected my application to become a Fire Guard or fired me at the end of the first week. But the one who got me the job meant they didn't have those options. It's to my supervisors' credit that they trained and inspired me and other political appointees—of which there were several—into becoming very good firefighters and, according to them, "damned good" fire crews. To succeed as an administrator in the Park Service, you simply had to resign yourself to dealing with many bloodsuckers every summer.

As I went into the house, I played with the insight that the Boyhood Home ranger was getting a real education in the power of polyticks—or should I call it mono-tick? If he survived this, he should be ready for any challenge that the public, the politicians, the Park Service, or old Ma Nature could throw at him.

The White House President Lyndon B. Johnson - Daily Diary The President began his day at (Place)				White House -- LBJ Ranch, Texas	Date December 30, 1965 Day THURSDAY
Entry No.	Time		Telephone f or t	Activity (include visited by)	Expenditure Code
	In	Out	Lo	LD	
	9:44		f	Bill Moyers - Austin, Texas	
	10:01		f	Under Secy. Geo. Ball - Washington, D. C.	
	10:44		t	Marie Fehmer	
	11:30			The President, w/ Mrs. Johnson, Mr. Kellam, Mr. J. W. (Waddy) Bullion, and his son, John -- departed the LBJ Ranch house...	
	11:51			Riding around the Heath Ranch	
	12:29			On the Lewis Ranch property	
	12:52			To the Lewis Ranch house	
	1:32		t	Col. Cross - main ranch	
	1:11			Departed the Lewis Ranch house and drove w/ the same group to Johnson City, Texas	
	1:22			Looking at the new apartments at the Bank in Johnson City (Mrs. J. left at this point at the apartments and went to the beauty shop in Johnson City/Stonewall)	
	1:32		t	Col. Cross - main ranch	
	1:56			To the Boyhood home w/ Mr. Kellam, Mr. Bullion and John Bullion	
SEE TRAVEL RECORD FOR TRAVEL ACTIVITY					Page No

Daily Diary, December 30, 1965.
LBJ Library. Photo by LBJ Library.

My memory of the ranger's plight is clear; my recollection of the Boyhood Home itself is far less so. This was the first time I'd ever been in a restored historic house. None of them, with the exception of

Monticello and, possibly, Andrew Jackson's The Hermitage, have interested me much. LBJ's Boyhood Home, which was my first, remains the worst. Perhaps it's different now that thirty-five years have passed, but when I was there, the place looked positively new. Sure, it boasted period wallpaper, some of the Johnsons' furniture and more from ranches around the area, and a couple of woodburning stoves, one for heat, the other for cooking. Unfortunately, all of them had been spruced up way too much. You'd never guess by looking at the place that Aunt Frank had spent a few years here during the fifties, thanks to selling her ranch and its attractive mott of live oaks to her nephew.

Most jarring to me was how clean the Boyhood Home was. "Antiseptic" described it. In my grandparents' homes, no matter how hard both Grandmommy and Grandma worked, fine, dry, white caliche dust settled everywhere. Keeping that out of a home when streets were dirt and gravel would have been impossible. My grandmothers didn't succeed, and their streets (though not the driveways) were paved. There was no trace of the outside world here.

None of the wallpaper had faded. There wasn't any of the clutter—books, newspapers, shoes, bootjacks, bonnets, hats—that I associated with family life in small Texas towns. No tang of mesquite smoke scented the kitchen. When I touched the cook stove, I could be confident no soot would come off on my fingers. Moreover, when I ran my eye up the stove pipe, I didn't see any damper. If the ranger had tried to light a fire in this stove, either it wouldn't have started or it couldn't have stayed lit. I could not believe Lyndon Johnson could look at all of this and be reminded of what his life had been like in this place.

Perhaps that's why the president appeared more dutiful than enthusiastic as he ushered us through the parlor, the dining room, the kitchen, and his old bedroom. As a guide, he was uninspired. He directed my attention to the stove, pointing out the oven where his mother baked biscuits each morning. I half expected some panegyric on Mama's baking; there was none.

"My brother Sam and I slept together in a bed like this in this room," he observed to me in the bedroom. I knew I should ask a question, but the only one I could think of was how long had he and his family lived there. He wasn't sure, but it was at least ten years, and I should pick up some of the literature on the house when we left.

Dad looked at the high ceilings and the big windows in the parlor, the December sun streaming through them. With a wry expression, he shook his head and asked how we lived before air conditioning. LBJ laughed, then assured him that it was air conditioned now. "I'm glad," answered Dad, "otherwise it'll be hard on summer visitors."

This prompted the president to wonder how many visitors the Boyhood Home would draw. "How many stop by to look now?" he suddenly asked the ranger. "A steady twenty to twenty-five a day this fall. Fewer around Christmas," was the swift answer. Apparently this response satisfied LBJ. After guessing that there'd be more in late spring and summer as the schools let out, he walked toward the door. One Secret Serviceman preceded him outside; another held the door for him and for Kellam, my father, and me.

No one waited by the fence. What happened to that family? Did the agents politely chase them off, or did they just get tired and leave? Did Mama get the picture she wanted, or would they have to be content with memories of LBJ's sudden appearance and snapshots of serious men in twill britches, pullover shirts, windbreakers, sunglasses, and pistols holstered on their belts?

I realized that the president, who was famous in the newspapers and newsmagazines for loving to press the voters' flesh, had shown no sign of interest in the family by the fence. Why? Were there security considerations?

None of the agents had appeared terribly concerned as they moved protectively around LBJ. To be sure, they were probably trained to do nothing to leave a bad impression about their service's attitude toward ordinary citizens unless they anticipated or saw danger. Still, in my opinion there wasn't anything that hinted these people wanted to harm the president. They were even whispering, as if they didn't want to intrude on his thoughts, and no one addressed him directly.

If I were president, these were the very sort of folks I'd go over to and shake hands with. If I had a stash of souvenirs, I'd give them some, just like LBJ had given me the ballpoint pen and the knife in Brady. I wasn't president, and the man who was didn't waste more than a glance on the family. No smiles, no waves, no nothing. Having seen him insist on Jake Jacobsen's displaying his subserviency in public, I wasn't surprised I didn't witness any thanks to the ranger who had opened the gate and the house for us. But brushing off voters who were obviously thrilled to see him was very unexpected from LBJ. Saying a few words to them wouldn't have taken five minutes. We had no urgent business in the Boyhood Home that justified behavior that bordered on rudeness.

Reflecting back on it, I wonder if I had seen one of the first signs that domestic protest was beginning to take a toll on Lyndon Johnson.

Had he become wary about approaching his fellow Americans except under the most controlled of circumstances? Did he feel apprehensive about what average, middle-class citizens might say to him?

If so, it betrays an already rapidly eroding confidence in his own political instinct and judgments. From the outside, LBJ was a very impressive figure. A bundle of contradictions, unquestionably, but through them all the most powerful presence in any room he entered or any conversation he took part in. What if on the inside he felt much less powerful and confident than he appeared? The discrepancy between his assessment of himself and the opinions others held of him had to be painful, had to be the reverse of assuring. As self-doubts bloomed within him, the desire to dominate those closest to him, to lash out at them, to criticize sometimes and ignore other times, must have been a powerful, irresistible, nearly primal impulse.

Maybe this helps explain what happened to me later that afternoon.

From the Boyhood Home we went down more residential streets until we reached the outskirts of Johnson City, then headed west on 290. After about fifteen minutes, the driver turned off the highway. We spent another quarter of an hour going down dirt ranch roads before pulling over at a gate. An agent from a following pickup hustled out and opened it. The Lincoln and the pickup passed through, while the rest of the convoy went on toward the LBJ Ranch. The president turned to me and said we were on the Scharnhorst, one of his favorite places in the world.

He didn't say why as we methodically worked our way through its pastures. What placed it high in his affections wasn't immediately apparent. The scenery looked about the same as the other ranches, and the cattle populating it were equally sleek and healthy. Years afterwards, I learned this was the ranch where he hunted deer himself. Probably that explains his affection for the Scharnhorst: it was his private preserve. Most of the time, it was reserved for Clarence and the rest of his breed herd. There they could safely get on with the business of producing bigger, stronger deer that would become prime sources of meat and antlers. Shots fired in these pastures would interrupt the process and might even persuade Clarence to swear off tobacco. And, when the breeding stock needed to be culled, this was strictly posted range. Only one person was allowed to hunt there—the owner of the

Clarence comes for tobacco during deer season, something he would not have
done had there been hunting on the Scharnhorst, December 28, 1967.
LBJ Library. Photo by Michael Geissinger.

Scharnhorst. LBJ's silence on these points that day was probably the
result of one of two considerations. Either he didn't want to wound the
feelings of Waddy's son by denying him hunting rights, or (more likely)
he didn't want to bother with any explanations.

It was apparent to me that when we entered the Scharnhorst, the
president's focus had shifted back to ranching, and his mood had corre-
spondingly lightened once more. In contrast, I did not revert to
constructing imaginary firefighting scenarios on this tour. A glimpse at
my watch told me it was nearly three o'clock. Hunting time had to
come soon. My shooting would be tested once more. Apprehensions
about my vision came rushing back. My nervousness was further
heightened by hunger and its effects. It had been hours since breakfast.
Not only did I feel empty, but my hands were slightly trembling from
too much coffee and not enough food. Could I see the target? Could I
stay steady enough to hold the sight while I squeezed the trigger?

The car went over the crest of a hill and followed the road around a
bend. There ahead was the gate we'd entered. As an agent trotted up to
open it, LBJ said, "That's plenty of sightseeing for today. Let's go home
and have lunch. Then we'll go hunting." The Lincoln pulled on to the
paved road, and the agent hit the accelerator. We left the trailing pickup
behind. I watched in the side mirror as its passenger struggled to lock
the gate. Then it vanished from my sight.

★ ★ ★

Lunch was informal, a catch-as-catch-can meal. The president disappeared into his office, so Dad and I helped ourselves to the meat, bread, pickles, lettuce, tomatoes, potato salad, and iced tea set out on the buffet in the dining room. Mrs. Johnson joined us soon after we began eating. Her daughter Lynda had called that morning. She hadn't gotten from Wyoming to Denver until well after midnight and, according to her mother, was "mad as hops" at the delays she'd endured. Dad asked how she was. "Other than tired," he added.

Daily Diary, December 30, 1965.
LBJ Library. Photo by LBJ Library.

Mrs. Johnson thought she was doing well. She had met an interesting young man, much to her mother's obvious pleasure, and this one "might definitely be in the picture." Dad didn't ask for, nor did she volunteer, any more information. That her daughter had met an attractive man and seemed happy meant a lot to her. Because it did, her listeners were also pleased. Dad and I smiled and nodded, and both of us thought, "Great."

I appreciated Lady Bird's tact almost as much as I did her graceful expressions of personal happiness. Many of the ranch women I knew would have followed an accounting of their daughters' romantic interests with broad hints and not-so-subtle questions about my own situation. She did not come close to bringing up that subject. Perhaps she had heard about the arguments Dad and I had over "suitable" women; more likely, she knew better than to steer conversations into uncharted and potentially rough familial waters. About this time, the president charged into the room with a couple of his secretaries, and the atmosphere around the table heightened dramatically.

For whatever reason, LBJ was pleased. He didn't volunteer why, and nobody asked. The food set before him was gone in a flash. Then he looked at Dad and me. He smiled and said, "Let's go hunting."

When we got outside, a Secret Service agent brought the president a rifle. It was new, so new that a price tag was still dangling from the trigger guard. "I thought somebody who shot so well deserved a rifle of his own," the president said. "This is yours, John, from me to you." With that, he handed it to me.

Nearly stunned speechless, I could barely mumble, "Thank you," and "You really shouldn't have, Mr. President, yesterday's rifle was fine." Grinning broadly and gesturing widely, he waved off my comments. "You're welcome," he said, "I hope you'll enjoy hunting with it." "I'm sure I will," I stammered back. As the president turned to instruct his driver on the route he wanted take to the Heath Ranch, I stared dumbfounded at my new weapon.

My father came up beside me, and we looked at it together. The first thing he did was pull out his pocketknife and cut off the price tag. As a result, I've never been sure whether it cost $129 or $229. "President Johnson sent a Secret Service agent to Fredericksburg the first thing this morning with instructions to buy it," Dad whispered in my ear. "We'll have a plaque made for its stock, saying that LBJ gave it to you on this date." "I can't believe it," I muttered back, "God, it's beautiful." Dad grinned. "It ain't cheap, either. He spent some money on this."

By tossing this in, my father reminded me of two things that to my mind distinguished him from me: he always knew the bottom line, and he invariably emphasized how important the cost of things was. The president obviously did the same. I couldn't believe anyone smart enough to choose a fine weapon for a gift wouldn't be sufficiently bright to remove the price tag. LBJ must have instructed the agent who purchased it for him to keep it on. Certainly, the president had a chance to remove it before he handed the rifle to me. That he hadn't was a sign to me of the high value he put on his association with my dad and—could it be?—me, too. I confess that the traits that I found so irritating in my father had no such effect on me when the president of the United States exhibited the very same characteristics. Far from being angry or feeling superior to crass market measurements, I was flattered and excited. What did this mean for my future? I tucked that thought away and examined the rifle closely for the first time.

It was a beauty—in fact, still is. A .270 caliber Winchester with a pristinely dark barrel and a lovely deep brown stock, it was semiauto-matic and held a clip with five shells. An agent came up with a clip, and we went through the process of checking the safety and loading it together. Then he unloaded the rifle, slid it into a new scabbard—which evidently was also mine—and put it in the trunk of the car he was rid-ing in. As I thanked him for his help, he remarked on what a pretty weapon it was. "It'll be a good one," he predicted. "You'll like it even better than the one you shot with yesterday." Then another agent smiled encouragingly at me. Both wished me luck. They probably hoped to be dividing up some more venison in the near future.

As for me, I'd be hunting antlers, not meat. Would we see any bucks worth shooting? More to the point, would *I* see the buck in time for a good shot? A sudden twist of apprehension knotted my stomach. I couldn't banish that thought from my consciousness. It stayed there, breeding unnerving doubts and anxious reassurances.

Don't worry. It's much brighter than yesterday. You'll probably be hunting earlier in the afternoon. The haze was only in some parts of the West Ranch, not everywhere. Yes, yes, yes, I fretted in interior monologue, but what if...? My confidence in my vision, never strong, began to wobble and waver. I wished I'd had a chance to look through the scope. It was bigger than the other rifle's; was it therefore more powerful? It certainly was newer. With these thoughts, I calmed myself somewhat.

It never occurred to me to be concerned about my rifle.

Perhaps that's not surprising. After all, I'd shot very well with an unfamiliar weapon the day before. Had Big John and the sergeant at Stanford been there, they would have shaken their heads. In the excite-ment of being with the president, in my astonishment and pleasure at his generous and unexpected gift, as I focused on the one difficulty I had yesterday, I made the sort of careless, amateurish mistake no one would expect the best shot on the ranch to make.

★ ★ ★

During the drive to the Heath Ranch, my rifle remained where the Secret Serviceman had stowed it for the trip, in the Lincoln's trunk. After we got there, the car stopped at LBJ's command. "Get your gun, John," he said. The agent who had just done the honors at the pasture's gate already had it out. He and I checked the safety two or three times. He loaded it. I went back to the car, climbed in, and rolled down the window. He handed the rifle to me. I rested the barrel on the window frame, checked the safety again, then said I was ready. The driver put the Lincoln in gear, and it cruised on down the road at about fifteen miles per hour.

It remained a lovely afternoon: clear, warm, without much breeze. The sort of day that Big John said encouraged deer to leave the windbreak and shelter of thickets and go foraging. Best of all, no haze. I was sure I'd have no trouble seeing the deer, if any were to be seen. I did caution myself they would be more alert than the day before, since it was earlier than the time they usually settled into serious feeding, and the craving to fill their bellies wouldn't be distracting them. They also would have no difficulty picking up movement on such a bright day.

In my mind, Big John started talking to me now. You aren't hunting feeding animals, he was saying. You're going to be aiming at big bucks that are eager to fight, then enjoy victory's rewards. They won't be peacefully cropping grass and leaves; they'll be restive, on edge, pawing the ground. "One shot," Big John advised. "One shot, and make it quick."

Not *too* quick, I reminded myself. It had to be a good, clean opportunity to kill, and I had to go through the proper procedures of breathing in and out, centering the sight, and squeezing the trigger with a firm but gentle pressure. Hunters who failed to do all of this had bad cases of buck fever. They were too eager to bag a trophy, and thus too excited to shoot straight. I didn't want to miss. I also didn't want to be picking my way down another arroyo, this time tracking a large whitetail who ached from a gunshot wound and was pumped full of adrenaline- and testosterone-fueled desperation. Patience. Make haste slowly.

The car turned into another gate and another pasture. Now we were going south. Shadows were coming toward me, dark fingers reaching out beneath bright rays of light. The sun was not so low that it presented problems for seeing and shooting, but it would pose difficulties if we kept on this course much longer. I squinted, more out of anticipation than necessity.

"Deer!" LBJ suddenly whispered, pointing into a rolling meadow. I sighted along his finger and saw them. "There's a good buck among 'em! Look, he's right there," he whispered again. The urgency in his voice stoked my own excitement. Again scanning along the imaginary line between his finger and the cluster of three or four deer, I could see him perfectly. The largest one in the herd. I couldn't count antlers. "Do you see him?" the president said in a slightly louder and more peremptory tone. "Yeah," I said.

Deer on the ranch, July 7, 1966.
LBJ Library. Photo by Kevin Smith.

Damn! The buck had heard us. Head up, neck craning, prancing nervously in place like an athlete loosening muscles and rising on his toes before a sprint. The driver had stopped the car. I squirmed in my seat, sensing rather than feeling Dad lean away from me. Barrel down, stock up, safety off, eye to scope, finger to trigger. The buck's head was still up, but he obviously hadn't decided what we were or whether we posed a threat. Would I have to try a shot at his neck? He was directly facing the car. Right then, he swung toward a doe, head still up—was he looking for an escape path? Left shoulder is there; in the sight; in the cross hairs; breath in; breath out; scope bobs down; scope moves up; squeeze, WHAM!

Missed! Didn't hold the sight, find him, find him . . . gone.

"You missed," the president said. It sounded like an accusation. "I didn't see," I began, my voice squeaking because I hadn't breathed in yet. "Didn't see? He was right *there*," he snapped. "I pointed at him.

Why didn't you see him? He wasn't forty yards away." Then he continued, "You must have been way off. I didn't even see where the bullet went."

What I'd been trying to say, before the air in my lungs gave out and he interrupted me, was that I didn't see where the shot went. There'd been no puff of dust, and nothing had showed up in the scope. Meanwhile, the president was demanding to know if anyone saw the bullet ricochet off the ground. No one had. They'd been watching the deer, thinking, I'm sure, on the basis of yesterday's success that I would hit him when I shot. "Well, let's get going," commanded LBJ. I put the safety on and raised the barrel.

An intimidating, icy silence filled the car. That quiet was only broken by LBJ's directing the driver to hurry on to another part of this ranch, so we could find some more deer for me to *try* (the president's emphasis) to shoot.

What went wrong? As I reviewed the shot, I concluded I must have jerked the trigger. I didn't think I had, but that was the sort of mistake that moved the barrel and caused misses. Be more careful next time, I lectured myself. Squeeeeze slow; light pressure from start to finish.

The other part of my self-admonishment focused on holding the sight after the shot. Without question, I hadn't done that. And this was the sort of mistake that most often resulted from pulling, not squeezing the trigger. So I must have yanked on it. I didn't think I'd had buck fever, but I must have.

Reaching this conclusion did not calm me down. I cycled back over my reasoning several times, a little more frantically with each repetition. My mental state was the opposite of relaxed, yet this was what I'd have to be. When—if—I shot again.

Bucks had been in short supply the previous afternoon, to the president's dismay. Today, it seemed as if he could summon them up at will. One gate later, one pasture over, and there was "another big 'un," as LBJ called him. Unlike the buck I'd just missed, this one was grazing placidly. He was further away than the last one, say between sixty and seventy yards. Still, it was not a hard shot.

"Shoot him," the president ordered. Barrel down; stock good and tight against my shoulder; eye to scope; perfect. I could see him clearly, and I laid the cross hairs right on his shoulder, then moved it slightly further back. He raised his head, and I tensed. As he was lowering it, I remembered the safety. I pushed it off, and the click was loud in the silent car. Now everyone knew I'd nearly messed up the sequence, a realization that accelerated my heartbeat.

"Calm down, look away, ease your finger off the trigger," was what Big John would say. "Start over, John, that buck's not going to run off." But I didn't feel I could do that. LBJ would ask me what in the hell was going on, and I wasn't about to tell him I needed a moment to relax.

Sight in again. There's the shoulder. That's where the heart should be. Lord, let me kill this deer. Breathe in. Let me kill him. Breathe out. Come on, now. Cross hairs at the bottom of the transit, about to move up. Relax your left hand! Gentle, gentle pressure, squeeze, squeeze, WHAM!

Missed! He's gone, long gone.

"What in the hell happened?" LBJ demanded. "You can't hit anything. Where in the hell did that shot go? It was nowhere close. What's wrong with you? Did anybody see that shot?"

No one had, so the president got on the radio and asked the agents trailing us in the pickup. There was a brief crackle of static, and I used it to cover up the click of the safety going back on. A disembodied voice came over the speaker, "I saw the dust fly pretty wide to the right and low, Mr. President. It wasn't very close."

"Did you hear that, John?"

"Yes, Mr. President," I said.

"Well, aim straight, boy. I want you to shoot a buck with the gun I got you. I'm starting to think I wasted my money. You can't hit anything today. It's not the gun; that's brand new. It's the best. It's you. Settle down."

I didn't respond; no answer was expected from me.

"It's gonna be dark soon," LBJ observed, "let's get going and find something you can maybe hit."

"Maybe hit" was the best way to put it. The agent in the pickup had solved the puzzle for me: far wide to the right and low, not close to the deer—*this rifle wasn't sighted-in!*

The scope targeted one thing, but the rifle was in fact aimed elsewhere. And not a close elsewhere, either. In the surprise and pleasure of getting the rifle from LBJ, I hadn't thought of this. Where was my head? The rifle couldn't have been fired before; for God's sake, it still had the price tag on it! Ergo, Brains, it couldn't have been readied for hunting!

I tried to soothe my pride by telling myself that I'd just assumed this had already been done. Everything at the LBJ Ranch was done ahead of time. All of the president's wishes were fulfilled; if they couldn't be anticipated, they were done posthaste. Why wouldn't I assume the rifle had been sighted-in this morning, perhaps in Fredericksburg, perhaps on the ranch? Truth to tell, though, whether the rifle was ready to hunt had never crossed my mind.

You flatass forgot about sighting the rifle in, I lectured myself. Then I drew the proper conclusion and expressed it in language I never used except while firefighting: "You've fucked up big time."

★ ★ ★

So, why didn't I say, "Look, I believe this rifle hasn't been sighted-in yet. That's why I'm missing so badly. Why don't we stop and I'll fire a few rounds at a tree and try to adjust it?" No such words came out of my mouth.

For starters, saying them would be contradicting the president, who had just pronounced my weapon to be in perfect condition. It would sound like a pathetic attempt at an excuse, and he would doubtless treat it as such. The simple fact was that I wasn't willing to stand up to LBJ.

I also lacked confidence in my ability to sight-in my rifle. I'd only done that at a range, under controlled conditions, where I knew the distance, was close enough to the target to group shots on it, and could determine the number of turns to give the screws on the scope by counting how many rings up and down, right and left the group was from hitting the bullseye. Sighting-in a rifle in the field was something that even competition shooters had trouble doing, because you had to create on the spot all the elements of precision measurement that were already present in a range. If I suggested trying to sight-in the weapon, the odds were I couldn't do it. That would make me the object of presidential impatience and the target of LBJ's sarcasm and scorn.

The next moments I spent thanking the Lord I'd kept my mouth shut. LBJ would immediately label any thought of trying to sight-in my rifle on the spot as monumentally stupid. Firing several shots would finish hunting for the day, he'd point out. The deer would bury themselves in the brush until darkness fell. Indeed, the president might even belittle my plan as a weakling's attempt to avoid further tests of his marksmanship and manhood.

I was screwed. I didn't dare say anything, and I couldn't do anything. All I had left to fall back on was this: the rifle was firing low and wide right. I desperately tried to comprehend what that meant for a minute or two, until finally I mastered my panic enough to figure out I'd have to aim high and wide left. How high? How far? I had no idea, because I hadn't seen where any of the shots I'd missed hit the ground. I'd have to fire by guess and by God.

The best luck would be to see no more deer. The afternoon was slipping away. It was already 5:30, and we couldn't hunt much past 6:00. Maybe the two shots I'd already fired had driven all the bucks on this ranch into deep thickets. Fervently, I willed them to do just that. Go to cover. Stay there for a couple of hours. Forget that you belong to the president. I was even ready to pray to the God whose existence I claimed I doubted. But before I could petition the Lord, I could tell the answer would be "no." The president was taking matters into his own hands.

Unfortunately for me, LBJ had thoughts similar to mine about what the deer on this ranch might do. Shifting in his seat, he ordered the driver to go to a different one. "There," he announced, "John's luck might change." To my ears, his tone indicated he didn't think this was too damned likely. The agents obeyed. The Lincoln and the pickup turned around, and we went back toward the gate we'd just entered.

LBJ and Jesse Kellam started a conversation. My father participated infrequently; I, not at all. To me, they might as well have been speaking in a foreign language. It sounded like English, but I couldn't follow any of the dialogue. All of my attention was focused on my own difficulties. The tension was awful. I had no control over what would happen next. Either the president wouldn't find another buck, or I'd have to take a shot without aiming. I decided to leave everything in the hands of Fate, or God, or Diana, the Roman goddess of the hunt. That didn't comfort me.

Many times, when people struggle with problems beyond their ability to resolve, a calm settles over them when they finally give up trying and honestly admit to themselves that they are powerless. When I've lectured on American Puritanism, I've even speculated that what Puritans described as the movement of God's grace in their souls was the physiological and psychological relaxation that follows close behind acceptance of a total helplessness either to resist life's temptations and wickednesses or to change the course of events. On those occasions, one can experience what the Book of Common Prayer calls "the peace that passeth all understanding."

I guess I wasn't sufficiently resigned. I felt none of this deep calm, or for that matter, any degree of calm at all. For this situation, my grandmothers would have counseled prayer. Mother would have too, after admonishing me to stand up to Lyndon Johnson. Pop would have tried out a familiar, open approach: "Now Lyndon, don't you know..." As for Dad, he'd tell me to do my job the best I could. I'd get the same advice, with several "fucks" and "fuckings" tossed in for good measure, from rangers and firefighters at Yosemite. Big John would have raged against the predicament. "God dammit; God dammit to hell." His had been the dominant voice in my head while I hunted. It continued to be so. God dammit! What the hell am I going to do?

We weren't very far into the meadow where the president had promised we'd find deer when I was saying to myself, "Just my fuckin' luck, there they are again."

We all scanned the herd for bucks. I couldn't see any; LBJ thought he'd caught a glimpse of one moving among the trees. He signaled the driver to move the car slowly along the dirt road. For a bit, there was only the low purr of the Continental's engine and the soft murmurs its tires made passing along the rutted track through the meadow.

"There! In the trees!" the president triumphantly pointed. I could make out a flicker of movement; I heard my father draw in his breath.

Deer on the ranch, July 5, 1968.
LBJ Library. Photo by Yoichi R. Okamoto.

"Move the car closer," urged LBJ. "Not too fast, not too fast." The path swung toward the thicket where the buck had vanished. I listened to the scrape of the tough, coarse prairie grass against the car. We rounded a gradual bend, came up and over a rise, and there he was, silhouetted against a mesquite mott the ridge over from us.

The president signaled with his hand for the agent to stop the car. We watched as the buck paused, looked, lowered his head to nibble some grass, moved on a few feet, and then repeated the process. The driver, on Johnson's gesture, inched the car forward again. The buck paid no attention.

LBJ and I saw why at the same moment. He was drifting slowly but deliberately away from the car toward a swale thick with prickly pear, ocotillo, and the low, thorny brush popularly known as catsclaw. In less than a minute, he'd be out of sight if he kept on in this direction at the same pace. He was much closer to cover—no more than ten or fifteen yards—than he was to us, at least one hundred yards across the field.

This would be a tough shot, not merely because of the distance and the buck's movement, but also because it would have to be made quickly. The rhythm of firing would have to be sped up, and this increased the likelihood of a miss. If I missed, that was that. Two leaps and he'd be in deep cover; there'd be no time to lead him properly. Furthermore, if I hit him but didn't drop him on the spot, tracking, finding, and finishing off a wounded animal in that dip in the terrain would be pure hell. No question about it, this was a very problematic shot. With a properly sighted-in rifle, it was an iffy proposition. Without one, you'd just waste ammunition unless God dropped everything else and guided the bullet.

All this had already zipped through my mind when I heard the president whisper, "There. You've got a shot, but hurry!"

I have no idea whether LBJ appreciated how difficult this shot was. That didn't matter to me then, and there's no way of telling now. I obeyed instantly. Click! Safety off as the barrel came down, stock to shoulder, left hand firm but not clenched, eye to scope, finger inside trigger guard. I found the buck in the false focus of the scoped sight. High and to the left, I repeated, high and to the left. Cross hairs on shoulder, now move and raise the barrel. Cross hairs on the horizon, a piece of antler still in view, move a little more, high and left. Breathe in and out, relax, firm pressure, hold the sight, squeeeze, WHAM!

The deer suddenly filled the sights. For an instant, I thought I'd hit him and the bullet had lifted him up into the air. Then I saw him land and bound away toward the brush. I couldn't tell where the shot went, because when I fired the buck wasn't in the sights.

To this day, I believe I came pretty close, that his gorgeous, powerful spring straight up was the result of the whine and wind of a round passing just behind him. If that was the case, I didn't allow quite enough in my inexact and rushed calculations for how far the sights were off. That wasn't a failure of skill, though. If I'd killed the buck, it would have been—literally—blind luck.

The president snorted his disgust, sounding much like deer do when they signal each other. He made sure I knew that another excellent chance had been wasted, that I'd had prime shots at three of the finest bucks on his ranches, that we might as well quit for the day, because it was getting late and I wasn't getting any better. I sat and took it silently.

In terms of actual time elapsed, I'm sure he didn't critique my hunting abilities for very long. It just seemed like for-nearly-ever. At some point in the midst of it, I remembered to click the safety on. That done, I raised the rifle barrel, pointed it straight up and out the window, and sank back into the seat. The hunt was over. LBJ told the driver to head back toward the house. I'd never felt as tired in my life. I wasn't angry; I wasn't resentful; I didn't curse my luck; in fact, I didn't curse at all. The best shot on the ranch, now known as the worst shot on the ranch, was simply worn out.

Another lengthy, frigid silence settled in. Let this trip pass quickly, was my heartfelt wish; let me take a shower, have a drink, eat dinner, go to bed, and head for home tomorrow. That's all I asked. Okay, I also hoped I wouldn't hear anymore about my shooting, but I wasn't going to bet on that.

To my relief, a muted conversation sprang up. I must have been somewhat calmer than before, since I could comprehend that it was about cattle breeds and the prospects for the beef market during the next year. The president solicited my father's opinion, because "I've heard you've thought about ranching here lately." Dad confessed he had and further admitted to a preference for white-faced Herefords. LBJ had been thinking about a cross-breed, a mixture of Brahma and Angus that had been dubbed Brangus in the cattle business. Nobody seemed to have very firm or very enthusiastic opinions on any of this. Thank God the subject had changed from venison to beef.

As the car swung back on the main graveled county road, the president noticed a familiar pickup coming towards us. "Stop the car," he commanded, "I want to talk to these boys for a minute." The agent obviously recognized the vehicle and its passengers as belonging to the ranch, because he flashed the Lincoln's lights and pulled over.

LBJ got out and walked toward the truck, which had stopped on the other side of the road. Two cowboys stepped out to meet him. The agents in their pickup drew up close behind us. They left their truck and stationed themselves on our side. One faced one way down the road. The other went to the back of the truck and stared down the other direction. Dust hung in the air, drifting in the slight breeze, translucent in the lowering sun.

"Hell, let's get out and stretch our legs, too," said Jesse Kellam. We did, Dad sliding over to the other door, and I maneuvering my way out with my rifle. Kellam wandered off toward the president, probably because he suspected Dad and I would want to talk.

"The rifle isn't sighted-in, Dad," I said as softly as I could manage without appearing to whisper conspiratorially. "I can't hit anything with it. The scope is so far off that every shot is wide to the right and low." He asked, with equal softness, "Are you sure?"

I thought, "Fuck yes"; I said, "Absolutely." I hurried on. "The scope is new. The agent bought it straight out of a display case, and the guy in Fredericksburg put it on without making any adjustments." No comment from my father. "He didn't have time," I added, more to break the silence than to excuse the gunsmith. Dad said no more than, "I see." He looked right at me. "You're sure about this. It's not, what did you say, 'sighted-in,' and that makes it miss." Like the light bulb going on over a cartoon character's head, I suddenly understood. Dad hadn't ever hunted with a telescopic sight. He didn't even know what the term meant.

Glancing at the president, who was lecturing his cowpokes, I explained as quickly as I could.

Dad rubbed his lips and chin with his left index finger, a sign I recognized that he was thinking hard about something. "I see," he finally said, nodding. "I see what happened." I relaxed. Nothing was more important in the world to me at that moment than getting my father on my side. I didn't feel great when he nodded his understanding, but my spirits were no longer at rock bottom.

Were we in fact through hunting? I asked Dad, who said he'd go find out. As he walked across the road, I glanced at the driver, who stared back blankly, his eyes concealed by his sunglasses. I didn't bother speaking to him about what to do with the weapon; I knew he didn't know and wouldn't dare presume to hazard a guess. The radio squawked. Victoria was wondering when Volunteer would be back for dinner.

Lady Bird's call coincided with the end of LBJ's speech to his cowboys. They touched their hats and drove off, while the president remained standing in the road talking quietly with Jesse Kellam. Dad walked up, and the three men conversed for around five minutes. It wasn't an animated conversation. Although they looked into an adjacent pasture, the absence of any gestures toward it led me to speculate that wasn't what they were talking about.

No one went over to tell the president his wife was wondering when we'd be back. The agents, I suppose, kept alert for the possibility of an attack or other mishaps. They didn't see anything, and neither did I. The sun, which had been dipping toward the horizon, suddenly seemed to speed up on its path downward. Soon it would be dark.

Finally, Johnson shrugged and walked back to the car. Our driver told him about the call, and the president picked up the microphone and told home base we were headed in. Dad told me it was time to pack up the rifle. One of the agents from the pickup took it from me, checked the safety, and ejected the bullet in the chamber. Then he carried it to the truck and slid it into its scabbard. "I'll give it back to you at the house," he said to me, just as I was beginning to wonder if the president was taking his gift back. I thanked him, and he smiled and said, "You're welcome."

No venison for you guys tonight. Perhaps they were thinking the same thing. No trophy head, either, and I had no doubt that the president was thinking that. "Let's go home," he told us. "It's getting too dark to see much, and John hasn't done well when he could see. Might as well quit."

What was I supposed to say? A more gracious person would have said he enjoyed the day anyway and regretted not being able to kill a deer. A perfectly honest person would have pointed out the rifle wasn't sighted-in, so the hunt was doomed from the start. An angry person might have snapped, "Why the hell didn't you realize the damn thing wasn't sighted-in, if you're such a fine hunter yourself?" Someone wise in the ways of the world would have found another to blame: "Mr. President, the gunsmith screwed up and didn't sight-in this gun for me." A resigned soul simply would have muttered, "I'm sorry." I remained silent, partly because I was too numb to think of anything to say, but mostly because I feared any reaction would call down more scorn and sarcasm.

The drive back was made in near silence and in deepening dusk. As I peered out my window, I noticed that there still was none of the violet-blue haze I'd seen the day before. Was it only in certain locales? If so, which ones? Did the ranchers have a special name for it? Under different circumstances, I might have asked LBJ about this. After the day's disappointments, I didn't feel he'd welcome these questions.

We saw no deer on the return trip, a development for which I was duly thankful. Not that I would have fired another shot; my rifle, after all, was in the pickup trailing us. But sighting another trophy buck surely would have brought forth some sort of derisive remark from the front seat; of that, I was sure. By the time we reached the house, it was dark. The lights in the windows could be seen clearly as we turned up Ranch Road 1, spilling pale yellow over the porch.

★ ★ ★

When we circled behind to the garage, that soft pleasant glow disappeared. The building and the corral were lit up like an operating theater by arc lights on poles. It was so bright that it dimmed all colors on people's clothing and formed an arena where everything appeared to be in stark black and white. I was mesmerized by the lights' intensity.

As the agents walked toward the Lincoln, they moved like actors in a silent movie, their strides exaggerated and jerky. When I got out, I noticed my skin shone as though it had been bleached. LBJ's khaki shirt and britches were almost bone white; in his dark suit, my dad looked like black ink had been poured all over him.

I suppose these lights were for security reasons. If so, they had the reverse effect. Once you were in the ring of light, the darkness surrounding it was impenetrable. The light was too bright to see anything outside it. In contrast, those walking or standing inside the circle would be perfect targets. Attackers would have to oblige the defenders of the president and his home by coming into the light, something I didn't believe they would do, unless they were nuts.

No one asked my opinion about the usefulness of this circle of pure white for the protection of persons and property, but I'm confident Dad was having similar thoughts. Six years later, he decided against putting up any security lights on the W² Ranch. Their brightness, reasoned my father, merely located ranch houses for thieves and often advertised when people weren't at home. Admittedly, the president's ranch was not the typical case. Guards protected it all the time. As a result, these lights served to intimidate rather than invite. They certainly had that effect on me as I blinked in their glare and waited for the president to lead us inside.

LBJ walked over to a group of cowboys and spoke to one of the older ones. That cowboy nodded; another one went off toward a shed. I watched idly as he disappeared into it. Soon he came out, holding a metal wash basin about two feet in diameter. He held it up for the inspection of LBJ and the old cowboy. "That'll do," I heard one of them say. Then he carried it over to a fence post, where he propped it between the post and a rail. The tub balanced perfectly, resting there like a target.

At my side, Dad moved slightly. Out of the corner of my eye, I could see he was again stroking his face with his finger. An agent brought my rifle to the old cowboy. He took it, then snapped a fresh clip into the magazine.

The cowboy looked to his left and right, then straight ahead to the wash basin no more than fifteen yards away, across the parking area, in the light, with darkness behind it. For a moment he paused, the rifle resting comfortably in his arms, barrel pointed to the left, and stock at waist level. Breathe in, breathe out—this guy had a flair for the dramatic—then he swung the rifle smoothly and swiftly to his shoulder.

Even in that fierce stark glare, there was nothing jerky about this movement. It flowed with the grace of a practiced marksman. Another pause, just for an instant. Lord, I thought, the rifle is rock-steady, and he doesn't have a sling! I was watching him, not the target, and WHAM!

I saw the flash as the bullet zoomed on its way. The basin still rested on the fence. The old cowboy had missed.

My eyes went back toward him. He was still holding his sight. Breathe in, breathe out, WHAM! *Ping!*

The basin flipped up into the air. When it landed, it rolled toward the rest of us. The old man lowered the rifle, walked over to it, and inspected it as he came back. Then he held it up for LBJ to see. There was no bullet hole anywhere in the bowl; he had barely nicked the edge, and that had spun it off the post.

Johnson asked him loudly, "Well, why couldn't you hit it?" The cowboy replied in such a low voice I had to strain to hear him. "The sight's way off. It shoots to the right and low." My father had stopped rubbing his lips. LBJ took the wash basin and brought it over to me with a smile. "John, if he couldn't hit this tub square in the middle, nobody could shoot that rifle straight. I'm sorry I got on you so much today; it wasn't your fault you didn't get a good buck."

As usual in my conversations with the president, I wasn't sure what to say or how to respond. Since I didn't expect an apology, I was utterly unprepared. I managed to get out something to the effect that he shouldn't think twice about it; that I wasn't upset; that once I realized the sight was off, I tried to make adjustments, but wasn't skilled enough to do as well as this man did. So, two lies from me and one effort to shift the responsibility back to myself later, we dropped the subject. Dad said we'd get the rifle sighted-in, and I chimed in that it was a fine weapon. An agent unloaded it, retrieved its scabbard, and slid the rifle into it. He brought it over to me. Carrying my new rifle with its skewed telescopic sight, I followed LBJ, Dad, and Kellam into the house.

★ ★ ★

As we awaited the cocktail hour in our room, once more Dad remarked that we should have a plaque made for the stock. In addition, he called my attention to the fact that the president had bought me a cleaning kit for the rifle. "You'll need to clean it when you get home," he lectured. "You won't be going hunting again anytime soon, and you don't want to leave it dirty for a long period of time." I said I would, refraining from adding that it needed to be sighted-in too. My father has never had much patience for self-pity or sour grapes. Anyway, I was too whipped that evening to indulge myself in either.

" I don't know who'll be there tonight," my father said. "I still hope Bill Moyers will be, so you can meet him." "He's not like Jake Jacobsen, is he?" I asked with a grin, glad that we were on another subject. "Lord, no!" laughed Dad. "Bill's interesting to talk with, and he really likes young people."

This judgment inspired him to describe his last meeting with LBJ's right-hand man. It was in Washington, right after Moyers had been photographed twisting at an embassy party. "God, Bill, you looked great in the *Post*," Dad told him the next time he saw him at the White House. "Oh, Waddy, not you too!" groaned Moyers, who went on to say he'd heard about twisting from everyone, including the president, and he didn't want to talk about it anymore.

"I wonder what LBJ said. What do you think?" I asked my father. He was sure that Bill was reminded this wasn't the sort of thing young men from Marshall, Texas, who had once aspired to being Baptist ministers usually did.

I remembered the picture. Moyers looked awkward but enthusiastic. Most of all, he looked like he was having a great time. I described my reaction to Dad, who said those were his impressions too. In person, he noted, Moyers was usually more serious and stuck closer to his Baptist roots. "Does he seem to be having as much fun the rest of the time?" I teased. "Not openly," Dad conceded, "but he's still a wonderful guy."

I was certain Moyers was not enjoying himself as much at the White House as he was at the embassy party. No one can judge much from newspaper pictures, of course, but his happiness at the party seemed to have a frantic quality to it, as if he were saying, "I've got to have fun now, 'cause who knows when the next chance will come." When I mentioned this to Dad, he seized upon the chance to preach a little about the necessity of working hard at every job. I'd heard this paternal homily before. That it was true didn't make it any easier to sit through. If Moyers was going to be there, and I got to talk with him, I hoped he had either fresher things to say, or more interesting ways of saying them. Even more fervently, I hoped he'd be easy to talk with.

Daily Diary, December 30, 1965.
LBJ Library. Photo by LBJ Library.

★ ★ ★

As I've already said, Bill Moyers was not at the ranch during our visit. I subsequently discovered that Joseph Califano had been there, but President Johnson boarded him at one of the outlying guest houses

I'd seen as we drove to and from the LBJ Ranch. I learned later that the staff regarded an invitation to stay at the main house with the Johnsons as a badge of honor. For whatever reason, during our visit LBJ kept business and personal guests totally apart from those who had journeyed to the Hill Country to confer with him on the nation's domestic and foreign affairs.

Because of this preference, there was no one famous in the Johnsons' living room that night, besides the renters of the place themselves. A.W. Moursund, his wife, and her sister were there. So were two couples from Austin, the Maguires and the Butlers. Jack Maguire was president of the University of Texas Ex-Students Association; Roy Butler owned the Lincoln-Mercury dealership in Austin. Finally, the Johnsons had invited out Dr. Harry Ransom, the chancellor of the University of Texas. I flattered myself into thinking Ransom was there to talk to me about American higher education. As for Roy Butler, I had no trouble guessing that he'd been summoned to Gillespie County for professional as well as social reasons. From his tight grip on a glass of bourbon, it was evident he was thinking like I was. I forgot about Jack and Pat Maguire as soon as Mrs. Johnson introduced us. They did the same. Ten years later, I came to know both Maguires pretty well when my wife worked for them at the Institute of Texan Cultures in San Antonio. We didn't remember meeting earlier in Lyndon Johnson's house. I wouldn't know that now had I not recently read the guest list in the president's Daily Diary.

An awkward moment followed the flurry of introductions. We stared at each other without speaking, the men in dark business suits that duplicated Dad's, I in my hunting outfit of sports coat, tie, and slacks, and the women in conservative, semi-formal dresses with hemlines modestly at or below the knee. Lady Bird Johnson had on a similar dress. The company had caused her to change from her usual daytime attire. The real center of attention at the gathering, the president of the United States, had not yet appeared on the scene. He loomed large in people's minds, overshadowing even in his absence those who were physically present. When would he come? Which door would he enter through? Most important, what mood would he be in? With the exception of his wife, everyone found it hard to engage in any sustained conversation while remaining alert for his arrival.

Dad and I had just gotten drinks—orange juice for him, Fresca for me tonight—when Lady Bird Johnson beckoned me over to her. She wasn't smiling as I approached, and I noticed others were edging away from her.

God, what now? Then she smiled and asked about the day. I gave her a much-abbreviated version of the hunt, without including the problems with the sight because I didn't want to seem as though I was blaming anyone. I added that I enjoyed the drive and liked the tour of the Boyhood Home very much. She commiserated with me about my failure to kill a buck and said she was glad I was enjoying my visit anyway. She set her jaw for a moment, then relaxed a little and asked, "John, how is your mother?"

Mrs. Johnson was going to do the right thing, even if it meant asking about a woman who had never hidden her dislike for the Johnsons.

I thought hers was an admirable act. That she could not wholly conceal her true feelings about Mother actually made me like her more. Lady Bird, I concluded, was a true lady, reminiscent in her own way of my mother's mother. Grandma and she would not have shared the same sentiments about Mother, but they had a lot in common in their lives and their codes for dealing with whatever happened to them. I assured her Mother was fine. She replied briefly, "Good."

We chatted for a few moments about the colors of the Hill Country. I asked her about the violet haze in some places. She had no explanation for it, other than it appeared in fall and winter at the West Ranch. As we smiled and gestured, others began moving back toward us. They could tell from our expressions that the moment of privacy Mrs. Johnson had wanted with me was past.

Soon afterwards, LBJ came to the party. To my relief, and no doubt to others' as well, he entered smiling and laughing, ready to hug and kiss the women and shake hands with the male guests. He was by far the least formally dressed person in the room. He was tieless and wearing a light blue sportscoat over an even lighter blue button-down shirt. His slacks were periwinkle-blue flannel. A little too short for his long legs, they fully exposed wool socks that were another shade of light blue. The length of his britches also called attention to what looked for all the world like leather bedroom slippers on his feet. With no compelling reason to dress up for these particular guests, the president had made sure that he'd be perfectly comfortable. To people today, he would have been the height of business casual fashion. At that time, he appeared startlingly underdressed for cocktails and a sit-down dinner. No matter! None of us men reacted by loosening his tie and shrugging off his coat. Lyndon Johnson was the president of the United States. He could dress to suit himself, and to fit the motto on the pillow in his living room. We weren't. And we couldn't.

Other proofs of his power and position were readily apparent too. When LBJ swore off booze for the time being, he'd effectively put everyone but old friends on the wagon with him. That night, among the guests only Harry Ransom, with a solitary glass of wine, and Roy Butler, nervously trying to ration his bourbon intake so his drink would last till dinner, imbibed. The alcohol they consumed added no sparkle to the party. Running the country on one-calorie Fresca was new for Lyndon Johnson. It was plainly and simply a trying adjustment for those around him. Whatever Fresca's fuel provided for the president, the citrus drink didn't lend any pizzazz to this social hour.

In the absence of alcohol, smoking might have ignited a much-needed spark for the party. LBJ himself had been a heavy smoker before his heart attack in 1955. Not now, though. On doctors' orders, he'd quit instantly and totally, absolutely cold turkey. Everyone else did, too, when they came in contact with him. In particular, people on his staff felt obliged to stop smoking, if not completely, then at least around him. This led them to invent the office smoker's customary refuge in today's world: the furtive trip outside for a fast smoke by the door. A White House photographer managed to catch Jake Jacobsen, who needed all the help he could get, in the act. The result was a striking, artistic shot of a wary Jake through partially closed blinds. Whether LBJ ever saw the evidence of his aide's apostasy is unknown.

Jake Jacobsen blind-sided, December 19, 1966.
LBJ Library. Photo by Frank Wolfe.

I bet he did. I also bet Jake paid the price. On this evening, the Johnsons' guests were much more careful than Jacobsen. Long friendship let Jesse Kellam get away with puffing on a cigarette. No one else dared to. A woman who hauled out a pack of Pall Malls without thinking immediately dropped it on a chair unopened.

No liquor. No cigarettes. Unaided by relaxants or stimulants, we had to deal with LBJ all by ourselves. Fortunately for us, he was happy. If the others felt as I did, they were resolved to do their best to keep him in that frame of mind.

Without any instruction or command, we guests arranged ourselves into a line. It wasn't single file, men first, as it would have been at the White House. Couples stood side by side. So did Dad and Jesse Kellam. Still, I realized, we were trying to follow Washington protocol in Gillespie County. So was LBJ. Of course, I chided myself, he'd time his arrival to be after everyone was there and waiting. That's what presidents do; they come into rooms last on social occasions. Johnson had done that constantly while my father and I were in the house. Business was different. He was first into the helicopter, the Lincoln, the bank, and the Boyhood Home. Did that mean eating was business, too? I recalled he went to the table first and got his food before everyone else. God knows he took dinner seriously enough. As I was smiling inwardly at that thought, I saw that I'd been thinking rather than acting. I joined the line at its end, next to Harry Ransom.

Mrs. Johnson had told the chancellor I was a student at Stanford. This bit of information enabled him to break the conversational ice between us. "Stanford's a fine school," he observed quietly. "It certainly is," I said, "and I enjoy going there." Silence descended again. We peered at each other for a long moment. Ransom had an intelligent, cheerful look on his face and a quick, winning smile. His heavy horn-rimmed glasses gave him an academic appearance; the cut and fabric of his suit revealed he had done well in academe. For all his outward friendliness, he was eyeing me speculatively, as if trying to place who I was and figure out why I was there. Perhaps he was wondering, like I had, if he'd been brought from Austin to talk with me about higher education. If so, we didn't play our assigned parts well. To end the silence, we fell back on that common topic among strangers, the weather. It had been, we agreed, unseasonably pleasant. I contributed a few additional comments on Bay Area temperatures and rainfall in late autumn; he rhapsodized about business trips to a blessedly cool San Francisco in the summer.

We had ample time for matters meteorological, because the line had stalled. Right ahead of us, LBJ was quizzing Roy Butler about how well his cars were selling. His questions were terse and pointed; Butler's answers were much longer and involved not only sales figures and the virtues of owning a Lincoln, but the state of the local economy. (Without question, my descriptions of Palo Alto's climate were prosaic and banal because I was trying to give equal attention to Harry Ransom, LBJ, and Roy Butler.) I gathered from what Butler said that he'd sold the Johnsons the Continental we'd ridden in that afternoon. Forgetting about the need to conserve alcohol at this party, he was taking nervous, deep gulps of his bourbon as he talked. In no time, he drained his glass. Just as he did, the president turned toward Ransom and me. Butler eased to the side, no doubt relieved and happy at not hearing any complaints about the car.

LBJ's greeting to us was pleasant and perfunctory. Perhaps he would have said more, but one of his secretaries caught his eye at the beginning of our howdying and handshaking, and he excused himself to have a word with her in his office. Again, the group had lost its center. Before we could start milling aimlessly, Lady Bird Johnson recruited the women among us to look at pictures and talk about the holidays. Left to our own devices, the males took up the weather again, expanding the topic to include the condition of the land. All looked at Harry Ransom enviously, as he continued to nurse his wine.

Just as I asked Dad whether I could get a refill of Fresca, the president strode back into the room, a fresh glass of that beverage gripped in his huge hand. He walked over to us with what the singer John Prine would later call "an illegal smile" curling his lips.

"Waddy," he said, "you know about the guest houses we've got, don't you?" My father nodded. "Well, they're good places to get away from it all," the president pointed out, "especially when I'm in Washington and there's nobody here." Then he said, "Waddy, I want you to feel free to come down and use one whenever you want to. Call Jesse, and he'll get it ready."

With a glance at his right-hand man in Austin, LBJ confirmed this assignment. No more prompting was required for KTBC's boss to say, "Sure thing, Waddy. It doesn't need to be more than a few hours notice. You can come to Austin, and I'll get you out here."

After Kellam piped up, LBJ arched his eyebrows and smiled risquely once more. "Now, Waddy, I don't care who you bring with you down here. It can be anybody. That's up to you."

God! I thought, One Johnson is asking how my mother is, while the other furnishes my father with an open-house invitation to shack up. That, I concluded, concisely highlighted the differences between them.

To be sure, Dad and Mother had been separated for over five years, but even so, they were still legally married. I was shocked that LBJ would make such an invitation in front of me, their son. I'm not sure whether my surprise showed, or how closely he was observing me as Dad answered, "That's nice of you, Mr. President." There was no enthusiasm in his voice, and I could tell he had no intention of accepting the offer.

Apparently, that was equally clear to the president. "Well, keep it in mind. Anytime, when we're not here, it's yours." Soon after this exchange, Mrs. Johnson announced dinner, and LBJ led us into the dining room.

★ ★ ★

At the time, I had no idea about the FBI investigation. Dad didn't either. But I'm certain he received the message sent by LBJ's expression and words loud and clear. "I know something about you, Waddy," the eyebrows and lips were saying. "You may not know precisely what it is, or how I found out, but I do know it." This invitation to use the guest house was a reminder of the power of Lyndon Johnson.

In this case, the president intended to use his power with a rough-handed benevolence. "I don't care if you fool around," his tone of voice conveyed. "Hell, I'll make it easy for you." No doubt if Dad had seemed interested in his offer, he would have followed it up with a nudge from his elbow and a knowing wink from his eye. That message would have been, "We're real men, aren't we, enjoying one of the perks of our power and prowess."

This silent conversation between them never reached that point, because my father steered carefully between two rocks. Had he rejected the proposition, LBJ might have continued to hint with barely veiled words and suggestive body language that Dad had not always been so prudish. Of course, my father was fully aware that if he accepted this invitation, he'd be getting more than nudges, winks, and a presidential blessing for illicit adventures. He'd be adding to Lyndon

Johnson's mental file on him and placing himself within his client's control. His skillfully neutral answer gave LBJ no opening to apply either tactic. It also informed the president he would not play this game. Just as he did after demanding that the deer I shot be deducted, Johnson dropped the subject, at least for the time being.

As LBJ went toward the table, he must have been concluding again what a formidable opponent my father was whenever they crossed swords in the subtle, secret contests he set in motion. I agree. Thirty-five years later, I marvel at Dad's self-control and steely determination to remain his own man, even when surprised by Lyndon Johnson.

So many of us were eating that evening that the stewards set up a card table in a corner of the room for the overflow. Mrs. Johnson steered me toward it, saying that she'd decided "the young people" would eat at this table.

Two women in their mid-to-late twenties joined me there. One was named Marie Fehmer; the other, Vicky McCammon. Their slacks and sweaters, accessorized by their look of bone-deep weariness, defined them as secretaries. So, I subsequently discovered, did their attractiveness. LBJ insisted that secretaries at the White House not only be highly efficient and absolutely untiring, but good looking as well. Fehmer and McCammon met that standard. Both had lustrous brunette hair and round, pleasant faces with engaging smiles. Neither wore much make-up, and I didn't sniff any trace of perfume. The most striking thing about their appearance was how their posture and their eyes betrayed how tired they were. Privately, I hoped they didn't have to go back to work after dinner.

Talking with Marie and Vicky was a struggle. I could hardly ask how they liked working for the president of the United States while he was stationed not ten feet away. Also, I couldn't be certain if they'd been placed there to report on me. On reflection, the whole afternoon seemed like a battery of tests of my reactions and, of course, of me. How would I react to the ranches and to the Boyhood Home; how well would I shoot; how would I respond to the sarcasm and criticism I took from the president; were the rifle's sights really off; would I be as moralistic as my mother when LBJ offered a guest house to Dad? Perhaps the latest exam was this: how would I deal with being put with his secretaries at a card table during dinner while everyone else dined at the big table?

LBJ, Lady Bird Johnson, and from left to right, Ginny Thrift,
Vicky McCammon, and Marie Fehmer, April 11, 1966.
LBJ Library. Photo by Frank Wolfe.

If these were tests, what were they designed to determine? What were their ultimate purposes? How was I being judged? And, of course, the most interesting and significant question of all, how was I doing?

To be honest, I *did* want to impress Lyndon Johnson. I had been pleased to be called the best shot on the ranch. Even now, when I knew I didn't come close to the old cowboy who tested my rifle's sights and thus also knew the president was deliberately exaggerating when he praised my marksmanship, that memory was sweet. What impact had the day's events had on my standing with him?

Indeed, as I looked at my dinner companions while we ate, I guessed no small part of their weariness stemmed from the fact that everyone who worked for LBJ believed she or he was being observed, measured, weighed, and placed in the balance every day. So long as it remained important to pass muster on the latest of a series of unending examinations, he kept a hold on them. For as long as they wanted to stay in the boat, he could use their uncertainty about what grades they were making to extract more and more effort and production from them. It had been impossible for me to gather my courage and respond to his words of criticism by pointing out what was wrong with the rifle. It was proving equally impossible for me to claim to myself that I didn't care whether these were tests, or how they were graded, or what my score on them was, or if LBJ thought favorably of me. The simple, fundamental fact was, I did care.

Unsurprisingly, conversation at the card table wasn't particularly memorable. The magnetic field of Lyndon Johnson's personality and presence bent even the most trivial subjects toward a potential judgment on him. We sure tried to avoid that.

The only time we drifted close to a dangerous area was when I asked them about life in Washington. Relying on platitudes to hold up my end, I observed that working in the White House must be like living in a fish bowl. What you did one day was instantly visible, the stuff of that evening's televised news. And you could read about yourself or what you'd done in the next morning's newspaper. Marie and Vicky must have wondered whether I'd stray on to the subject of leaks to the press, a pet peeve of the president's. If they did, they were unprepared for my actual question, and this eventuated in a moment of candor. "Which papers," I asked, "do people at the White House like? Which do they read?"

After the briefest of pauses, Vicky McCammon answered, "They read the papers that agree with them. They're like most people that way." She seemed about to add more, then thought better of it.

I turned back to my food until I could come up with something else to say. Meanwhile, I was thinking that the odds weren't great that the *New York Times* was read front to back, or at all, by the president and his staff. LBJ might see abstracts of articles and hear others' opinions about *Times* reporters, columnists, and editorial writers, but he didn't read the paper for himself. I realized I had just had a glimpse of how isolated one could be at the White House if one avoided direct, personal contact with anything that questioned the administration's policies on the issues of the day. By no stretch of the imagination was 1600 Pennsylvania Avenue the LBJ Ranch. Still, it appeared that in both places the president tried to do as he damn pleased.

★ ★ ★

After dinner, we returned to the living room. A steward had set up a screen and a projector, and we watched a black-and-white documentary on the presidency. It was terrible. Toward the end, the narrator quoted Thomas Jefferson on the splendid misery of the office and prosed on about the superhuman demands it placed on the men who held it. The only redeeming thing about the evening's entertainment was the fact we were seeing the film with the current president of the United States.

We didn't wait long after The End to hear his opinion. "I didn't like that at all," LBJ said. Others chimed in with the same verdict. Then, even though we remained seated in a semicircle around his recliner, conversation groups began to splinter off. Without much ceremony, Johnson wandered in and out of the room. A.W. Moursund quietly told Dad and me that the president periodically checked the news ticker in his office and always watched the ten o'clock news there. Nothing must have happened that disturbed or concerned him, because he was always cheerful when he returned to his chair.

The day's events had worn me down. I was sufficiently aware of my surroundings to stifle yawns and to appear attentive. But I recall very little about what was said, other than LBJ's determination to celebrate the arrival of 1966 quietly. That seemed a good idea to Moursund, Butler, and the two Bullion boys, as he outlined his plans to us. I suppose we each had a different understanding of what constituted "quiet." We certainly had different ways of ringing out the old and bringing in the new. Listening to this with half an ear, I didn't notice a White House photographer working his way unobtrusively around the radius of the group. Thirty-five years would pass before I'd see the pictures of LBJ talking to the four of us about the advent of 1966.

LBJ, A.W. Moursund, Waddy Bullion, John Bullion,
and Roy Butler, December 30, 1965.
LBJ Library. Photo by Donald Stoderl.

LBJ at the party, the Bullion boys' heads in the foreground, December 30, 1965.
LBJ Library. Photo by Donald Stoderl.

The party broke up before eleven. LBJ announced he was tired and still fighting a cold, so he was going to bed. We chorused, "Good night, Mr. President."

No one lingered after his exit. Dad and I thanked Mrs. Johnson again, and I made a point of saying I'd enjoyed my company at dinner. She was pleased. Then we said goodbye to Jesse Kellam, who was heading back to Austin that evening. He said he hoped to see me again soon and wished me luck at Stanford next year. We walked with him into the hall, where he picked up his bag. Before he went through the door leading into the bright circle of light around the garage, there was a last round of handshakes.

Afterwards, Dad and I climbed up the stairs to our room. "Let's pack tonight," he suggested. "Our flight to Dallas is around noon, and the president will want to see us before then if he can manage it. We should be ready to leave before we go down to breakfast."

We set to work, both of us silent. The only conversation was brief. "What about the rifle? How will we carry it on the plane?" I asked. Dad didn't know, but he assumed Braniff would tell us before we took off. "*If* we take off," I joked. "Don't worry," my father said, "we'll get back to Dallas tomorrow."

CHAPTER 14

"The other stuff"

Probably because Dad had stayed up reading later than he usually did, I beat him out of bed and into the shower the next morning. When I finished dressing and tossing pajamas and dopp kit into my suitcase, he rewarded my early vigor by sending me for coffee. I crept softly down the stairs toward the dining room, wincing at each faint creak, marveling at how empty the house seemed and how quiet it was. A glance at my watch explained why: 6:30. Light was just beginning to spread outside, and coffee had not yet arrived in the dining room. I wasn't discouraged, because I could smell it somewhere. Made bolder by the fact this was, after all, my third day at the ranch, and by my craving for caffeine, I decided to look into the room beyond. I crossed over toward the swinging door separating the two rooms and had almost reached it, when it suddenly flew open.

There I was, startled and flinching, face-to-face with Pat Nugent. We stared at each other for a moment, long enough for me to see he was taller, broader, and better looking than I, and to notice his eyes, which I remember as being a light, light blue. He was dressed casually in a sweater and khakis, in contrast to my sports coat, tie, and slacks. Since he was carrying a cup of coffee, I knew it was available somewhere. I was too surprised by his sudden appearance to say good morning or ask where the coffeepot was. He didn't speak, either.

Nugent passed silently through the living room. Not married yet and already the heir to the manor, I thought uncharitably. At the next moment, I felt guilty about my touchiness. It can't be easy, I scolded myself, living up to the image of the perpetually smiling, always attentive boyfriend pictured in the papers. Perhaps he was enjoying a few peaceful moments by himself and didn't want to break the spell by speaking with a stranger who'd nearly run smack into him.

A carafe of coffee was in the next room, and the kitchen staff had put out cups and saucers. I filled two of the cups to the top and balanced them on saucers. Then I gingerly pushed the door open and walked briskly and confidently to the stairs. As I mounted them, I started to giggle. What if I spilled coffee? Should I try to mop it up with my hand-kerchief, or hope no one noticed the incriminating stain until I was far away? There I was, body swaying, knees bent, steps as precise as if I were on the high wire defying death, all in an attempt to avoid losing a drop so I could avoid making a decision. At last! the top of the stairs, down the hall, into the room. I set Dad's cup on the chest of drawers as carefully as if I was—as my family was fond of saying—Mama putting Little Precious down with a kiss. Mission accomplished.

How could anyone function around the Johnsons for very long? I mused to myself. I quickly amended my thought to, how could anyone go through day after day working for LBJ? Lady Bird Johnson, I was positive, was thoughtful and empathetic; she'd forgive or overlook minor mistakes or misjudgments. You could feel and behave naturally around her once you got used to being in the presence of a famous person. I was certain she would have told me not to worry about spilling coffee. As for the president, I couldn't imagine anyone being relaxed around him. He was too moody; too suspicious; too whimsical; too domineering; too mean; he was—let's face it—too much of a bully toward anyone who wouldn't stand up to him. And he came in contact with damn few of those people. Coffee sloshed over the side of a cup might be shrugged off, or it might call forth a barrage of presidential sarcasm or wrath. I didn't want to risk it.

Now, if I'd voiced these thoughts to my father that morning, surely he would have dismissed them, saying I was making too much out of a petty thing. I kept my reflections to myself. Abruptly, my mood dark-ened. I wanted to release all my pent up feelings. Then, as I was on the brink of working myself up into what both my parents called "a state," I cooled off. Airing my feelings to Dad would not win me much sympathy. He might agree it was hard to get used to being around presidents, but he'd add that I'd need to learn to deal with the whims and the demands of other people if I were going to live in this world. It wasn't what I wanted to hear right then, even though I was ready to concede its wisdom.

Instead, I speculated on how Pat Nugent dealt with his situation. Very carefully, I wagered. Perhaps he'd already devised his strategy. Move through the house purposefully; speak as little as possible; act like you belong. That sounded good to me. The only suggestion I'd make to him would be this: if you're placed near LBJ at a table, be ready to sacrifice potatoes, pudding, and anything else the president might take a hankering for. It would also be a good idea to sight-in his rifle and shoot straight. Had the prospective son-in-law been hunting yet with Luci's dad? If so, what had he gone through during the quest—or should I say, test?—for a trophy buck he could hang on the wall?

LBJ, Luci Johnson, and Pat Nugent, December 24, 1965.
LBJ Library. Photo by Frank Wolfe.

My father broke into my reveries. He suggested we gather our baggage up, go downstairs, and eat. "What about the coffee cups?" I asked Dad. "We can leave them here," he said. "Someone will have to clean the room anyway."

We ate alone. Like breakfast the day before, this was a quiet meal. Both of us were hungry, and our minds were on departure. "How will we get back to Austin?" I asked. "By helicopter?" Dad said we probably would. I began talking about the differences between this helicopter and the ones I'd ridden in Yosemite. My father grinned and interjected, "There's nothing like traveling on the president's aircraft, is there?"

He also observed that President Johnson didn't have to worry about getting to airports on time or about Braniff's trademark tardiness. He went when he wanted to. That was an impressive perquisite of power.

This reminded Dad about the man responsible for safely delivering LBJ wherever he wanted to go. He asked if I'd met Colonel Cross, the pilot of Air Force One, yet. I couldn't remember out of the jumble of faces and names. "Jim Cross is a good man and an interesting fellow," my father continued. "The president trusts him and likes him." I supposed it was a good thing to trust someone who flew you all over the world at a moment's notice, and Dad said he certainly agreed with that.

As we finished up breakfast, a marine corporal entered the room. "Mr. Bullion," he announced, "the president would like to see you and John." Then he added, "Right now," with a slight but unmistakable emphasis on the words. We picked up our gear and followed him.

"You can leave your bags here in the hall, sir," the marine said. We set my rifle and our luggage down. He led us down the hall to a closed door. He knocked once, then opened it when LBJ answered, "Come in."

★ ★ ★

My two days with Lyndon Johnson had convinced me of the truth of one thing I'd heard about him: he loved surprising people. I hope my expression gratified him. Dad and I weren't entering into an office. This was the president's bedroom.

It was huge: as large as normal folks' living rooms. It was plain: a polished wood floor with small woven area rugs scattered about, walls paneled with blond pine lumber. It was furnished eclectically and functionally: bureaus, a large chest of drawers, a sturdy bedside table holding a telephone with multiple extensions on it, and, off in the corner, one of LBJ's famous television sets, equipped with three screens so he could watch the three major networks simultaneously. Shoved against one of the paneled walls was an extra long full bed, with an exquisite dark, high headboard made, I think, of walnut.

The president was propped against the headboard, his legs extending far down the bed. He was holding one large hand over the telephone's mouth and, as he beckoned us in, said in what passed for a *sotto voce* comment from him, "I've got Dean Rusk on the phone, but we'll be through in just a minute." Then he returned to his work, which was assuring the Secretary of State that he thought the foreign relations of the United States were in capable hands. "Thanks again, Mr.

Secretary," he purred into the phone, while winking at the two of us. Once he broke the connection, he grinned and announced, "We've sent Goldberg to talk to the Pope about the bombing halt." While he and Dad shared a laugh over the thought of a Jewish fellow going to speak with the Roman Catholic pontiff, I smiled timidly as I worked out that the Goldberg going to Rome was Arthur, the Ambassador to the United Nations, and not Irving, the Dallas lawyer I knew and liked.

I should be forgiven for my confusion. My attention was hopelessly divided between what the president was saying, and what he looked like dressed in white boxer shorts and nothing else, on top of the bedcovers. When he was covered in khakis, anybody could tell he was a big man. Seeing him nearly nude, I realized that "big" did not begin to describe him.

Lyndon Johnson was giant-size. He had huge bones, and he was carrying too much weight even for his expansive frame. But the overall impression was one of size, power, and force, not soft flabby fatness. His gut, though pooched out, looked rock hard, the result of hearty eating after heavy work, not the souvenir of hours idled away drinking beer. And when he motioned me closer to shake hands, I saw how thickly muscled his forearms were.

That handshake was the only one I ever had from LBJ that was firm and solid. I don't believe this was coincidence. Both the image and the reality he was consciously projecting in his bedroom were ones of powerful maleness, of a potency that went beyond the political and economic. As he shook hands with Dad, I inched around so I could see clearly the large half moon-shaped scar on his side from his gall bladder surgery. When the president had pulled up his coat and shirt to display it at a press conference, the photographs published on newspaper front pages made him look awkward, injured, and unwell. In the flesh, the surgical incision looked more like a wound suffered during some terrible battle that he had fought and won against great odds. It was a mark of triumph, not a sign of weakness.

I could sense LBJ was fully aware he had this effect on those who actually saw him and the scar. It's not that he flaunted his body to people in close quarters with him when he was either naked or nearly so. He knew he didn't have to flex, or pose, or show off to achieve what he wanted. However much it might photograph poorly—especially when others chose the pictures they showed to the public with the intent of exposing Johnsonian crudeness for all to see—in the flesh his body supremely amplified his brute masculine strength and determination.

It was a powerful weapon in his quest for domination over men, women, and events, and he wielded it with confidence, pride, and skill.

While I was standing there, in that large room that suddenly seemed filled by the one who slept in it, the president called to his orderly, "Bring those pictures of me over, and a pen." The corporal gathered them up off the bureau, carried the pictures to the bedside table, and uncapped the pen. LBJ picked up the first one, a close-up photograph of his face, and confidently scribbled across the base: "To John Bullion." He paused for a moment or two to think about what to write next, and finally settled on: "With Affection, Lyndon B. Johnson." Then he dated the inscription, "Xmas 1965." He handed it to me and while I was thanking him, proceeded to put the same inscription on five other photographs of him. At first glance, my favorite was one taken of him on the porch at the ranch house, speaking to an unseen audience, with an American flag at his side.

That finished, he directed his orderly to get "some of the other stuff." It turned out this consisted of a medal on a stand commemorating his inauguration in January 1965, a bust of his head about eight inches high, a small pocketknife with his signature embossed on it, some cufflinks with the presidential seal on them, and buttons for a blazer, also with the presidential seal. This largesse stunned me.

I was not, however, so overwhelmed that I couldn't come up with an appropriate half-fib, half-truth by way of thanks. I told the president that he had given me a pen and a knife in Brady when he was a senator, and I'd kept them for years. Today's gifts would add to my collection of Johnson memorabilia, and I thanked him for that. This seemed to please him. "But you need something more useful to you right now than this, John," he added. "You boys can't work all the time at school. You need to watch a little TV to have some fun and keep up on things."

Flabbergasted, I conjured up a mental image of a set like his with three screens in our apartment in Palo Alto. This picture was so real to me that I began to wonder how I would carry it back to Dallas, then transport it to California. "I'll get you one," the president declared, and swung his thick legs down to the floor to make good on his promise.

Watching him rise out of bed was also a revelation. Lyndon Johnson could move powerfully, quickly, and gracefully when he chose to. When I remember this, I can understand his fury when William Manchester described him *lumbering* around Air Force One right after John Kennedy's assassination. He knew he was big; indeed, he regularly used his height and bulk to achieve advantages over people. But LBJ must have associated lumbering with moving clumsily or comically, and he was certain that when he walked he was neither clumsy nor comical.

He was right about that. Not only did he swing around speedily, but he raised right out of bed with no visible effort from his legs and no push from his hands. One moment he was propped up in bed watching the marine hand over "the other stuff"; the next, he was on his feet.

The president's orderly had witnessed this impressive spring before, because he had already turned smoothly to a clothes rack where a khaki shirt and pants were hung. Shirt first, the marine holding it as LBJ slid his arms into it. While LBJ fastened its buttons, the orderly grabbed the britches and handed them over just as he finished with his shirt.

"Did you press these?" Johnson demanded. "The last time, my pants weren't ironed too well, and one of the cuffs needed hemming," he reminded the young man.

"They're like you like them, sir," the corporal answered.

"Well, I'm glad of that, 'cause last time you didn't have your mind on *my* business. You were thinking about *your* business down in Austin, chasing around and getting laid."

LBJ wore a grim look. To my amazement, the marine smiled as he handed over a pair of white socks. LBJ sat down on the edge of his bed and began pulling the socks on. While the corporal reached for a pair of boots, he was listening to his commander-in-chief talk about how he knew damn well what young guys thought about all of the time and wanted to do as much as they could manage it, but that occasionally they had to do their jobs, which generally didn't involve doing it with every woman in sight. Unfazed, still smiling, the orderly gave the president one boot and then the other at precisely the right moment. He stepped back as the president rose, once more without pushing with his hands and arms. Then he admired his own work, as LBJ inspected the creases. To me, they looked like you could give yourself the proverbial shave with them, they stood out so sharply from the rest of the fabric. Johnson nodded his approval, and the marine kept smiling.

At first, I'd been embarrassed to be present during these dressing up and dressing down exchanges, but then I recognized the whole scene from Yosemite days. God knows firefighters weren't marines, but the two groups experienced one common reality: every now and then, you have to take shit from the boss.

Sometimes The Man isn't even angry; he simply wants to show you he's not dumb and can't be fooled. Maybe he hears an internal alarm, telling him he should chew ass to stay in practice, if for no other

reason. If a boss really started putting on a show, and you could sufficiently detach yourself from a colorfully profane description of your
own errors and shortcomings, you could find yourself objectively judging expressions, language, cleverness in discovering and orchestrating
variations on the firefighters' favorite word, and overall performance. I
especially treasured the memory of a classic from our Fire Control
Officer, who explained the differences between effing, effing up, and
effing off, then stressed he was in favor of none of these while we were
fighting effing fires. His tongue-lashing was so wonderfully delivered
and beautifully detailed that he lost no points for his highly unusual (for
Yosemite) refusal to do more than abbreviate the ineffable word.

Compared to the FCO's effort, Johnson's was much less witty but
considerably more frightening. The corporal did not reply to the president as one of us did to the ranger, by expressing mock horror that our
mistakes had been so awful they'd turned him against fucking. Wisely,
he remained silent. He'd heard all this before, and he'd mastered doing
what was required of him while it was going on. Moreover, he'd also
become adept at distancing himself from what was being said about
him. Nothing he heard perturbed him, especially since the president
might just be going through the motions for the sake of impressing his
guests. Each in his own way—this young man in his early twenties and
my father in his early fifties—handled dealing with LBJ with greater
ease and self-possession than anyone else on the staff. They certainly
did better than I did, or any other guest.

★ ★ ★

Dressed in acceptable style and satisfied that he had reminded his
orderly to keep his attention on the president's pressing business, LBJ
led me over to what appeared to be the door to a closet. In fact, it was a
small room, originally intended for storage of whatever didn't fit in the
bedroom. At that moment, it looked like a mini-warehouse for
eight-inch portable RCA televisions.

There were easily twenty of them in boxes stacked against one
wall and extending six feet out onto the floor. Five more of the TVs sat
as if displayed on top of those boxes. Pointing to the unboxed televisions, the president told me to pick one out and take it with me. As I
said thank you and assured him that my roommates and I would enjoy
it, I wondered whether to acknowledge his comment about "watching a
little TV." Was it a joke? Figuring it was safer to say nothing more than
thanks, I stuck to standard expressions of gratitude.

I could tell I was repeating things I'd already said, but what new could be added after being showered with a handful of autographed pictures, an assortment of souvenirs and memorabilia that advertised my connection to this president, and a portable television? I almost told him he was being too generous, but the thought flashed across my mind that he might take the TV back if he believed I'd questioned his decision. I confined myself to praising his generosity and emphasizing my gratitude. He smiled and said I was welcome.

I'd told a couple of what Mark Twain memorably called "stretchers." The sheer volume and value of Lyndon Johnson's gifts, starting with the rifle and winding up with the television, were parodies of generosity. One of these would have been a nice reminder of my visit to the ranch. The numbers I received were overkill; they were simply too much. They called to mind not gracious giving, but Jesus' parable about rich men at the temple ostentatiously clanking money into the pot while the poor widow was humbly pitching in her mite. They meant to reap their rewards on earth, right in the here and now. So, obviously, did Lyndon Johnson. Whether he'd pay later, as Jesus implied the rich men would, remained to be seen.

Moreover, it was clear that I wasn't the only one to get souvenirs out of this treasure trove. That stuff was warehoused there to be given away to whomever it suited his fancy and in whatever amounts he deemed appropriate. To be sure, he could have chosen to have done nothing for me that morning. That, however, would have been atypical. As Dad later observed, LBJ delighted in "really reaming people out, then turning around and being extraordinarily magnanimous." He'd experienced this himself; the last morning of 1965, I did too. No doubt my father and others who benefited from this magnanimity reached the same conclusion I did. Such gifts were only partly inspired by a desire to ease the sting of uncomfortable moments. Probably they were mostly designed to display unforgettably what LBJ could do *for* as well as *to* those who crossed his path. Having decided to give me lots of "the other stuff," he drew them with a flourish out of what obviously was an inventory of hundreds of photographs, countless pens, knives, cuff links, buttons, busts, and medals. I'm sure he didn't hand out these things promiscuously to whoever entered his home, but they were all there ready for plucking from his stash whenever he felt like it. He made certain I was aware of that fact. That I had been shown how many televisions he had in his storeroom was no accident, either. He could have ordered the corporal to go get me one. He meant to show me both how powerful he was—how many of us stockpiled TVs to give away?—

and how generous he could be to those he felt affection for. He meant to inspire awe. Those who received under these circumstances were supposed to be more impressed by the giver than the gifts.

Contemplating this plenitude reminded me of a couple of immediate problems and a future one as well. Maybe I didn't have to worry about moving a three-screened TV, but I still had an awful lot of other stuff. How was I going to get all these gifts to Dallas, let alone California? For that matter, how would Dad and I get them out of Lyndon Johnson's house?

I shouldn't have worried. We were dealing with LBJ. He took care of details like that. He had people at his beck and call who would help us. Without his saying anything, the orderly hauled out a large, sturdy paper bag with handles from Scarborough's, the most exclusive department store in Austin. As the president and I were coming out of the storeroom, he was already wrapping up everything in tissue paper, then placing each item carefully in the bag. Practice had made him perfect at this.

As far as the rifle was concerned, the president had a solution for it too. "Waddy," he said, turning toward my father, "you could have some trouble with Braniff about carrying John's rifle on the plane. Jim Cross is flying up to Dallas this morning to get some watches for me from Linz Jewelers. You and John can catch a ride with him on the little jet."

"Are you sure that's no trouble, Mr. President?" asked Dad. "We've got our tickets on Braniff, and we can check the gun."

"Hell, no," LBJ snapped back, "it's no problem. Like I told you, Jim's got to go up there anyway. I want those watches by New Year's Eve, so I can hand 'em out then. Look, this way you can save your money and walk on the plane with the rifle."

Dad said he was grateful for this thoughtfulness, and LBJ thanked him for coming down, helping out with business, and going hunting. He held out his hand to me, said he enjoyed our time together, and—just as he'd told me years before in Brady—hoped we'd be seeing more of each other in the future. I praised his hospitality, told him I appreciated very much the amount of time he'd spent with me, said I hoped to see him and Mrs. Johnson again, and wished him good luck with the nation's business. He smiled and said he guessed he'd better get to work on that. I thought, you've already started. You're shaking hands like a politician campaigning again.

He and Dad shook hands briefly. "It's always a pleasure to see you, Waddy. You're the best." "The pleasure is mine, Mr. President. Thank you for having John and me." LBJ stepped away as if to leave, and we simultaneously reached for the Scarborough's bag so we could follow him out. At that moment, he turned back toward us and reminded Dad, "I'll see you soon, Waddy. And don't forget: the guest house is yours if you want it." Then, after the final flourishing of his power during our visit, he left.

★ ★ ★

As we walked toward our luggage and my rifle, I looked around, hoping to see Lady Bird Johnson. The most comfortable moments I'd spent during the last forty-eight hours had been in her company, and I wanted to thank her personally. I also had an ulterior motive. One of the pictures the president had autographed was of the two of them, standing facing the camera, with arms linked. It would mean a lot to me to have her sign that portrait. I asked Dad if she'd be there to say good-bye. He didn't know for sure but doubted it. She'd be busy preparing for the next round of guests and for New Year's Eve.

"What you should do, John," my father advised, "is write to them when you get back to school. Say, 'I'm back at Stanford, and would like to thank you both for your hospitality.' That would be a good thing for you to do."

Dad didn't elaborate beyond these words. He didn't say why I should mention Stanford, and I didn't ask. But I could tell how proud he was his son was at that place and doing well at his studies. Perhaps he thought that wasn't bad for someone whose father had worked his way through Howard Payne as a soda jerk and whose grandfather had been a busted stock farmer from Concho County. Whatever his thoughts on that score, clearly he believed my connection with Stanford would be an important point in my favor with the Johnsons.

Mrs. Johnson didn't appear while we were gathering up our stuff. When we looked out, we saw an Air Force car. The driver came to the door. He verified our identities, loaded our things, and drove us over to the hangar by the landing strip. There he deposited us by a small air-craft with jet engines on its wings. It was painted pure white, with touches of red and blue. Rather than any insignia or number, the two sides of its fuselage simply read, United States of America. While it wasn't Air Force One, it certainly was Air Force Something, part of the presidential fleet of planes. A couple of enlisted men stowed our luggage in a storage compartment. I kept the rifle and the Scarborough's bag with me.

The aircraft didn't have the standard rows of seats. Instead, four padded chairs were placed in a square, with nearly ten feet between them. Like the chair in the president's helicopter, they could swivel around in a complete circle or be locked into place by depressing a handle. A footrest popped into place when passengers pressed a button and pushed back. Ashtrays were built into the arms; a serving tray could be raised from one side and locked into place for drinks or food. In the rear, there was a small refrigerator and a built-in cabinet with a sink on top. Opposite this tiny galley area was a jump seat that unfolded from the wall for a steward, should any be along on a trip to serve passengers. At the very end of the compartment was a restroom.

Our traveling companion was already there. The colonel was in a chair, sipping a Fresca and talking with an airman. I'd noticed him in passing my first day at the ranch. He'd been wearing his uniform, and I'd assumed he commanded the military stationed there. Today he was in a dark blue suit, white shirt, and blue tie, as befitted his errand to a Dallas jeweler. He had an expressive face, a poised manner, and thinning black hair slicked down with hair oil. Heavy dandruff powdered his coat. Its profusion suggested he clawed at his scalp in private. However cool and collected Jim Cross appeared, beneath the surface he must have been as tense as could be. Working for Lyndon Johnson could do that to a man. Was he required to go to Dallas? Was that part of his duties? Could this possibly be misinterpreted by, say, the *New York Times*, as a misuse of government personnel?

I know Colonel Cross wanted to preserve secrecy about his identity and his mission. After he greeted us with "Nice to see you again, Mr. Bullion, pleasure to meet you, John," his features tightened when my father said we looked forward to flying with the pilot of Air Force One. "I'm not flying today," he quickly said. "For once, I'll be a passenger."

I asked how long he'd be in Dallas. Would he be returning this afternoon, or staying the night? The colonel did not know how to answer this. For a moment, there was an uneasy silence. Dad dispelled it by saying, "Don't worry, Jim. We know what you're doing. The president told us."

Cross exhaled and sank back in his chair. "I'll come back late this afternoon. The watches are ready, and all I have to do is go there, pick them up, and come back to Love Field."

LBJ and Colonel James Cross, February 1, 1966.
LBJ Library. Photo by Yoichi R. Okamoto.

Dad offered him a ride downtown to the jewelers, if that would help save time. The colonel politely declined, saying a car would be waiting for him. All the arrangements clearly had been made for getting him in and out of Dallas as quickly and unobtrusively as possible. Acknowledging this without referring to it directly, my dad commented, "We're sure lucky to catch a ride with you." "I'm glad for the company," replied Cross.

The pilot and copilot came up the ladder and entered the cabin. Both smiled at Dad and me, then brightened considerably when they saw Jim Cross. Without pulling rank or being condescending, he quizzed both of them about how they liked flying this plane, which I recall they referred to as a Queen Air. He listened closely as they praised its reliability, speed, responsiveness to controls, and steadiness in turbulence. (I listened too, though out of concern for personal safety, not from professional curiosity.) They were happy with the plane, and the colonel seemed satisfied enough to allay my concern

LBJ and the Queen Air, December 21, 1966.
LBJ Library. Photo by Frank Wolfe.

that the three were hardly likely to discuss an aircraft's flaws in design and weaknesses in performance in front of human cargo they had to believe were VIPs. Playfully, one of them invited him to take the controls during the flight. He hesitated long enough to reveal he was tempted. Then he smiled, thanked them, and said he didn't want to spoil his busman's holiday.

They went on into the cockpit and left the door open. We watched them flip switches and read gauges. When take-off time approached, the copilot came back to see if Dad and I wanted anything and to make sure we were strapped in. "You can unfasten these once we level off," he told us, "and you can get another soda or go to the restroom. It should be a smooth flight. It'll take a little less than an hour. Do you have any questions?" We didn't, and he told us to come up to the cockpit and ask if we wanted anything during the trip.

With Cross, he went into a little more detail about atmospheric conditions and about predicted winds in the Dallas area. Then he asked, "What's it like to land One under windy conditions?"

The colonel told him that plane was both extraordinarily stable and extraordinarily heavy-feeling. He began gesturing, forming wings with his hands and simulating landing. "No matter what the wind is, you have to practically drop it on the ground. There's not much glide in it." As he said this, he let his hands fall suddenly straight to his lap. The other pilot whistled silently and shook his head. "Not that way with this one," he said. Then he glanced at Dad and me and added in a reassuring voice, "And not today. Conditions are very good all the way."

For the next hour, Dad and Jim Cross talked quietly about odds and ends, finally settling on good places for him to eat lunch in downtown Dallas. I skimmed the sports page of the *Austin American-Statesman* and stared out the windows. Pilots and plane did their jobs.

We parted company with the colonel at the private plane hangars. His car was already there. It was not the standard Government Issue green, and no agency name was stenciled on the side. He offered us a ride to our car, but my father told him not to bother, it wasn't very far away. Dad carried his suitcase and the Scarborough's bag; I toted the rifle and my grip. We loaded it all into the trunk of his Oldsmobile Cutlass, and he drove me home.

We didn't have too much to say during the twenty-minute drive. A few banalities about the last three days—it was a good time; it was interesting, etc., etc.

When we got to 6131 Lupton, Dad helped me carry LBJ's gifts in. He spoke briefly with Mother, then shook hands with me. "It was a good visit, Pal," he said. I answered, "It sure was. I enjoyed it." As we walked to the door, I thanked him. He smiled, replied he'd had fun too, and reminded me we'd get together on New Year's Day. "Not too early, I hope," I said as I smiled back. He drove away. I watched the Cutlass until Dad reached the end of our street and turned left onto Preston Road. The trip to the LBJ Ranch was now really over.

Mother listened to a capsule version of the visit with obvious interest. She didn't ask many questions, because she knew that in all likelihood she'd hear more details as they occurred to me during the next few days. I made sure to tell her that Lady Bird Johnson had asked how she was. Mother said, "That's nice of her," in the tone that she used when something really wasn't nice as far as she was concerned, but proprieties had to be observed. When I told her about the rifle's sights, she shook her head without speaking. No word criticizing Lyndon Johnson passed her lips that day. Nor did any of praise. Mostly, she wanted to be certain her son was all right. Once assured of that, and aware my energy was running down and my interest in discussing hunting with the president was flagging, she said, "We'll talk more later."

I'd spread the pictures and "the other stuff" LBJ had given me out on our dining room table for Mother's inspection. I left them there, all but the TV, which I carried to my bedroom, plugged in, and turned on to make sure it worked.

Back to the dining room for my other expensive gift from Lyndon Johnson. I removed it from its scabbard and cradled it in my arms. This gift, I knew all too well, didn't work right. I felt no urgency about fixing it. I did, however, want to clean it. I went through the rituals of attaching a soft rag to the ramrod and working it through the barrel into the chamber. When I finished, everything looked fine. I slid the rifle back in the scabbard and took it to my room.

My mind returned to the question I'd asked myself the night before. Had I been put through a test, or a series of tests, by Lyndon Johnson? Yes. I didn't know exactly what those tests were, or what they were designed to measure. I wasn't sure what the right answers were, or even if there *were* any right answers. But I had been tested. The more I rolled this thought around in my mind, the more certain I became.

What was my grade? In terms of the Stanford grading scale of A, B, C, D, and F, I had no idea. Graded on a pass-fail basis, I was certain I'd passed. Despite the undeniable reality that LBJ was as mysterious, unsettling, and unpredictable to me as he was to his staff, I couldn't believe I would have left the ranch with autographed portraits, television, and all "the other stuff" unless he approved of me. For that matter, the sheer quantity of these gifts perhaps indicated I'd done better than just pass. In fact, it seemed as though he was interested in impressing me with what he could do for me, almost as if he was trying to recruit me for something.

There was the rub. I didn't believe Lyndon Johnson did very many things purely out of affection for the person involved. There was, after all, a price tag on my rifle. I also didn't think I had done anything while I was on the ranch to make him regard me "with affection." He must have had some angle, some goal he was pursuing. Or, perhaps, he could see some possibility for the future, an option worth keeping open.

What were these possibilities? What did he have in mind? There was no way of telling. Whatever they were, nothing would come of them soon. I had two more quarters at Stanford and three years beyond that at law school. My mind began to turn toward tonight and next week, not four years away. Even so, I wondered briefly what it would be like working for Johnson.

Would I want to? I'd observed his demanding mannerisms. I'd personally endured sarcastic criticism from him that was out of all proportion to the significance of the events that inspired it. I'd witnessed his extraordinary suspiciousness of those who crossed him by questioning his motives and policies, at the *New York Times* and, no doubt, elsewhere. I'd seen the impact of his personality on his staff. I'd also seen the curious and troubling moodiness that seized him at times. On the flip side, I'd gotten a lot of gifts. And, when he'd been satisfied that he had been wrongfully critical of my shooting and equally off-base in questioning my analysis of the problem, he had apologized to me. That "I'm sorry" meant something to me, and the more so because I was sure he didn't say these two words as often as he should.

Unquestionably, people who worked for Lyndon Johnson wrestled with great issues and did important things. "Yeah," an inner voice mocked, "they hold gates open and sneak off to Dallas to pick up watches." That very moment, I also realized the agent who ran LBJ's personal errand in Fredericksburg had doubtlessly already caught hell from his angry boss because he hadn't arranged to have my rifle sighted-in. Well, I didn't have to think anymore on the subject or do anything about it in the near future. I put speculation aside, much like I'd set the rifle on my desk after cleaning it. After all, this was New Year's Eve. Parties lay just ahead. So did celebrating with my friends. It was time to think about things other than deer hunting on the LBJ Ranch and people more pleasant than the president of the United States.

PART III

By the River

By the rivers of Babylon we sat down and wept
    when we remembered Zion.
There on the willow-trees
    we hung up our harps,
For there those who carried us off
    demanded music and singing,
And our captors called on us to be merry:
    "Sing us one of the songs of Zion."
How could we sing the Lord's song
    in a foreign land?

If I forget you, O Jerusalem,
    let my right hand wither away;
Let my tongue cleave to the roof of my mouth
    if I do not remember you,
If I do not set Jerusalem
    above my highest joy.
Remember, O Lord, against the people of Edom
    the day of Jerusalem's fall,
When they said, "Down with it, down with it,
    down to its very foundations!"
O Babylon, Babylon the destroyer
    happy the man who repays you
For all that you did to us.
    Happy is he who shall seize your children
And dash them against the rock.

                    —Psalm 137

CHAPTER 15

Jokes

I never saw Lyndon Johnson in the flesh again. Of course, I could hardly miss him on TV as long as he was president. More often than not, I watched him on the television he gave me. Every day I glanced at one of the pictures he inscribed. Between 1965 and 1970, it always hung on a wall wherever I lived, successively decorating an apartment in Palo Alto, a room in Cambridge, and a house in Austin. LBJ and I moved together from the Left Coast to the Right one, and then Deepintheheartof. I wound up in graduate school at the University of Texas in January 1967, so the real Lyndon Johnson and I were often less than a hundred miles apart. But he never invited me back to the ranch, and our lives did not intersect in Austin.

I wasn't surprised I didn't see him around town. Jesse Kellam was a much more accessible and visible person than LBJ during these years, and I only bumped into him once, at the Austin airport when we were both greeting visitors from out of town. And, aside from the different people we knew and the different neighborhoods of the city we circulated in, Lyndon Johnson was very reluctant to appear in public during the last years of his presidency. Demonstrations against the war had become familiar events in Austin, just like in other university towns. For the president to shake hands along Guadalupe Street, or even in the State Capitol, would be to invite certain protest and insult, and potential danger. His policies in Southeast Asia had cut him off from the city he had represented for over a decade in Congress and for two terms in the Senate.

Why no more invitations to the ranch? My own explanation at the time was self-exalting: Lyndon Johnson became less interested in me after I left Harvard Law School and took up the study of history at the University of Texas. His affection for me, his desire to see me again, were grounded in his hope or expectation that *I* would work for him. Once it was clear he wouldn't get legal advice *gratis* from two generations of Bullions, he saw no reason to cultivate yours truly. Obviously, this interpretation allowed me to plume myself on what I arrogantly believed was my commitment to higher ideals than black ink on the bottom line.

I have no way of knowing whether my interpretation of why I received no more invitations accurately depicts LBJ's thoughts, or partially accounts for them, or is utterly wrongheaded. Thirty years of water under the bridge has led me to conclude one thing I am certain is correct: he didn't think very often, if at all, on this subject. My explanation revealed a great deal about me (and not very flattering things at that!), without offering any reliable insight into LBJ's opinions. I do remember that Dad said he mentioned my change in careers to the president, who had no comment. Now that I am a father myself, I suspect he was thinking that there are some decisions parents just have to accept, because they sure can't change them.

My sister went to the ranch in December 1966, almost a year to the day after I did. Her visit was shorter than mine, and she spent much less time with the president. She also said it was far less exciting, a sentiment I agreed with after I heard about her day at the ranch. When I asked her about it as I was writing this book, she laughingly referred me to the article on it in the Hillcrest High School *Hurricane*. Just as mine did, her trip coincided with Dad's traveling there on Johnson family business.

Ann did not go hunting. Going out after trophy bucks was a purely masculine pursuit where LBJ was concerned. Years earlier, he had admonished Robert Kennedy that he had to learn to handle a gun "like a man"; I can't imagine his giving the same advice to a woman. Nor can I visualize LBJ critiquing my sister's shooting with the same harsh words he lashed me with. He probably wouldn't have had to be critical. She is an excellent shot, and she certainly knew about checking a rifle's sights before doing anything else because she'd heard enough about it from me.

Ann did go driving with him over the same roads I traveled. The president drove, with only my sister and father in the Lincoln Continental riding with him. There were Secret Service men in a car ahead of them and others in a car traveling behind. Their job, my sister noted to her amusement, was opening and closing gates.

During the drive, LBJ brought up Vietnam. He wanted to impress on Ann, a high school senior, how much it troubled him. She recalls quite distinctly his stressing how much he worried "every night about those boys in green fatigues." That she was the same age as many of those boys may have inspired his words. Also, LBJ may well have been one of those men who finds it easier to confess deep concerns to women. Sadly, they do this because they are convinced they must always appear tough before other males. I have no trouble believing this about Lyndon Johnson. After all, he felt more comfortable discussing the details of his childhood and the secrets of his nightmares with Doris Kearns Goodwin than with my father or any other man. The same thing happened within the Bullion family when LBJ discussed Vietnam. In private with my father, the war had an insatiable appetite for men and material. With Ann, that hunger did not crave abstractions. It wanted the flesh and blood of the boys next door.

I'm certain LBJ was being honest with her. I believe the deaths of young Americans in that terrible war did weigh heavily upon him. Yet I can't help wondering about how calculated his remarks were, and what other purposes he hoped to achieve by unburdening himself in this way. For my father and sister to mention his worries to others would present a more human side of the president. It could help reassure his fellow citizens that he understood their sacrifices, shared their fears for sons, husbands, brothers, and friends in green fatigues, and did not make his decisions lightly. Nevertheless, he would continue to follow the same policies, because he was convinced they were necessary for the country's best interests.

★ ★ ★

After she got back, Ann asked me whether anyone had had a drink while I was at the ranch. She remembered my comments about the general abstinence from alcohol and was curious to learn if she'd understood me correctly. I said that very few drank, and they, like I, limited themselves strictly to one. Everyone was drinking, she replied, during her visit. Since LBJ was no longer sticking to Fresca, his staff and guests could drink booze again at pre-dinner gatherings at the ranch. The results were about what you'd expect.

The get-togethers became more festive and relaxed. They were truly happier hours. They also became longer hours. My sister didn't think anyone at the LBJ Ranch got even close to intoxication, but during her visit people reacted to Zephyr Wright's call to dinner much more slowly.

I immediately interpreted the president's return to drinking as a sign that he was trying to deal with the pressures of increasing tension. I'm much less confident about that judgment now. Different people drink for different reasons. The same person may drink for different reasons at different times.

My own relationship with alcohol before I quit drinking for good in 1993 was complicated. "Texas medicine," particularly beer, always tasted great to me. In good times, it made life even more fun. During somber moments, I used alcohol to pick me up when I was down. Whenever I started drinking again after abstaining for any period of time, it usually was an effort to relieve stress and to "happy up." That's why I reached the conclusion about the president that I did. Ultimately, only he would know the reasons why he started taking a drink or two again, if in fact he ever understood for sure himself.

Learning how LBJ explained to himself the decision to have a few before dinner would be illuminating. I'd also like to hear how he announced it to others the first time he ordered a Scotch. However he served up that news, clearly those around him started bellying up to the bar at staff parties too. When he had abstained, they rode that wagon. Then, when he drank, they were back on the sauce.

Ann came home with a comparable number of autographed pictures and assorted examples of "the other stuff," though evidently the supply of portable televisions had been exhausted. Her visit ended with a hug and kiss from LBJ and the hope that he would see her again. As before, he knew that he would be seeing Dad again in the near future, either at the ranch or in Washington. Such was the case.

Dad continued to serve as trustee of the Johnsons' blind trust. Indeed, he may have been the only trustee in reality, because LBJ and A.W. Moursund for some reason became estranged during these years. The causes of their falling out were unknown to my father. Don Thomas told him the president and A.W. had "split the blanket." He didn't elaborate further, and Dad didn't inquire. The end of this close business and personal association took my father by surprise, as it did most people who knew the two men. It dismayed Lady Bird, who was very close to Moursund's wife. When Dad learned she felt compelled to break off all contacts with both Moursunds, he made a point of sympathizing with her.

The end of LBJ's friendship with A.W. may have been a casualty of the growing pressures on him. Without question, the seemingly endless war, the stagnation of Great Society programs, Republican gains in the 1966 elections, and the acceleration of domestic protest bore down hard on the president. Under the stress generated by these troubles, it would have been uncharacteristic for him, and perhaps for most human beings, had he not periodically taken his anger out on those closest to him. Frustration with his political life must have fueled impatience and misunderstanding in his business and personal relationships.

It's conceivable, too, that Moursund exacerbated these feelings. He was never comfortable with the media attention paid to the Johnsons' investments. Many years later, he complained that "reporters were always telling lies about our business dealings." To Moursund, this was more proof that "smaller people think tearing down someone builds them up." To Lyndon Johnson, press criticism was just par for the course. The reactions of his friend amused him when he was in a good mood and irritated him at other times. "Back in the fifties," remembered Moursund, "I was particularly mad at one story, and [LBJ] just laughed and said, 'A.W., don't you know if a chicken wants to get his head above the weeds, he's going to get rocks thrown at him?'" Then Moursund added, "I didn't get much more sympathy from him." Comparing a friend and business partner to a chicken stretching his neck up and peering with beady eyes over weeds is an unsympathetic remark, one not too far from contempt. And that was LBJ's response when he was at the height of his power in the Senate. When he was enduring savage attacks as president, any complaints from A.W. Moursund must have seemed like pathetic clucking from some rock-shy rooster who had no idea what real boulders were. In those circumstances, I can easily imagine comments so cruel and unforgivable from the president that they inspired angry exchanges and ruptured a long, close, and profitable friendship.

The same thing may well have nearly happened between my father and LBJ. Around this time Dad swore to me that he wouldn't charge Lyndon Johnson so long as he continued to be president, but once he left the White House, he'd be getting bills from Thompson, Knight. That my father would even consider abandoning the strategy that had insulated him for years against LBJ's need to command and to dictate reveals his dissatisfaction with the president's darkening moods and his own determination to do something about the situation. Billing him would certainly end what the two referred to as their friendship. Johnson might choose to replace it with a strictly business relationship. Or, if he regarded this decision as a personal betrayal, he would use it as a pretext to break all ties with my father. To me, the latter would have been the more likely reaction. I suspect it was Dad's assumption as well. Either way, my father would be freed from what appeared to be an

LBJ with A.W. Moursund; the cigarette in Moursund's hand reveals the special relationship he had at one time with the president, December 29, 1963.
LBJ Library. Photo by Yoichi R. Okamoto.

increasingly unpleasant arrangement. If it wound up with his being tossed off the boat, so be it.

None of this actually happened. Whatever tensions were building up in Dad's relationship with LBJ dissipated soon after he made his comment to me. There were no more vows to start sending him invoices as soon as he left the White House.

This change in mood probably had more to do with my father's outlook than the president's. In late 1967, after years of separation, Dad and Mother finally divorced. Soon after, my father remarried. His marriage to my stepmother was an immediate and enduring success. It was obvious to Ann and me that he was happier than we had ever seen him, and we quickly came to love Wilma ourselves.

LBJ approved of Dad's decision, too. After Dad and Wilma married, the Johnsons invited them to the ranch. Lady Bird was gracious as always. Just as she had made Ann and me feel easier, she did all she could to make my stepmother comfortable in an atmosphere that could be intimidating. The president was effusive in his welcome to them and enthusiastic in his assessment of Wilma to Dad. Unknown to them, he had also planned a practical joke to "test" their love.

Somehow LBJ had gotten his hands on an amphibious car. To the uninformed eye, it looked like a squat, broad, ugly, blue convertible. It had no ornaments identifying it as the product of any manufacturer, which enabled him to describe it to his guests as an experimental automobile, a prototype of future vehicles.

LBJ and Lady Bird Johnson in the amphibious car on land, April 11, 1965.
LBJ Library. Photo by Yoichi R. Okamoto.

Perhaps it was, if American automobile makers were anticipating a consumer demand for cars you could drive directly into water. In theory, this family convertible would serve equally well as a motorboat. In practice, it was a seriously underpowered motorboat, more akin on the water to a slow golf cart than something capable of pulling water skiers. On the water, it would have been swamped by the wake of cabin cruisers and speedboats, and it could have been easily outmaneuvered by a tacking sailboat. On the highway, it didn't have much get-up-and-go either. It could not have kept up with traffic in an era when American cars were fondly called "Detroit iron," big, heavy, powerful gas guzzlers that could accelerate rapidly. That this hybrid mess was never mass-produced should not astonish anyone. But for practical jokers, an amphibious car was a seductive product indeed.

When newly married couples came to the ranch, LBJ would take them for a test drive in this "experimental" car. Husband and wife were

LBJ and Lady Bird Johnson in the amphibious car on water, May 29, 1965.
LBJ Library. Photo by Yoichi R. Okamoto.

in the back seat; Johnson drove, and someone in on the joke rode in the front passenger seat. As they toured the countryside, the president would drop into the conversation his general dissatisfaction with the car. Not enough power—although that means we can get a good look at the country, it won't do for the road. The steering, it seems loose—but at this low speed, so what? The brakes aren't very tight—we'll have to ease into these turns. This was accompanied by presidential frowns and shaking of his head, and then he would again start pointing out wildflowers or deer or cattle. Before it was time to go back home, the passengers had become aware that there were problems with the car, but the president had adjusted to them.

Finally, LBJ reached the last leg of the journey toward the house. The route he had chosen approached it from the other side of the Pedernales, so he had to go over the low water dam. At this point, the Secret Service vehicle ahead of him would speed up, leaving plenty of room for his maneuvers. As he came toward the dam, LBJ would floor the accelerator, making the car go as fast as it could manage. At the same time, he would begin swinging it back and forth, cursing the unreliable steering. The final step was to suddenly yell that the brakes weren't working, just as he careened onto the low water crossing. With one hand, of course, he was surreptitiously pointing the car at the deep side of the dam. Then he drove it into the water, shouting that he couldn't control it and urging everyone to jump. The real test on this drive had begun.

For the joke to work perfectly, at least one person had to bail out. Ideally, it would be the wife, because then the husband had to decide whether he would plunge in after her. If he did, then Johnson would laugh and announce it was obvious that he really loved her, because he was prepared to risk his life to save hers. Should the husband jump first, the president would note that he clearly was more interested in preserving his own neck than his bride's. The wife, if she leaped in after her spouse, received the praise she had earned. If each one jumped out of the side of the car closest to them, LBJ's reactions varied according to how rapidly they sought each other out in the water. There would be some comment about looking out for one's own hide first, to be sure; whether he judged them to be truly in love depended on the speed with which they looked for one another and swam closer. After he'd delivered his judgment, soaked guests were hauled back into the car by the passenger in the front seat and taken on a brief water cruise up the Pedernales.

The amphibious car afloat, with LBJ at the wheel, and nervous-appearing passengers, April 15, 1965.
LBJ Library. Photo by Yoichi R. Okamoto.

What if no one responded to his commands? I suppose then there might be sardonic remarks from LBJ about people frozen in fear. I can't say, because I believe the trick always had the result he hoped for. What he could count on was the understandable and natural apprehension people felt at the prospect of being trapped in a car and drowning. As I've already said, this was a fear particularly acute among those who had grown up in places near low-water crossings. Parental warnings and local stories would immediately come flooding into their minds. Thus instinct and intellect would cause them to disregard their clothing and jump out of the car.

This exploiting of primal and acquired fears reveals how vicious the joke was. LBJ had designed it to activate those fears, and the nearer one's reactions approached unreasoning terror, the better. Moreover, it posed a test of marriage that could have profound implications for the future of the relationship.

Everyone wants to believe that in moments of physical danger the partner closest to him or her would react immediately to protect and to save. This doesn't always happen, because people do not confront actual emergencies every day, and the shock of such a crisis can immobilize as often as it energizes. Freezing up leaves both the unresponsive one and the one in trouble feeling awkward, angry, guilty, or a combination of those deep emotions. Without question, the feelings generated by an unrescued leap of faith would be intensified at the moment and cemented in their memories by the laughter and comments of the president of the United States.

I must add, too, that the fact that LBJ was president meant the hapless victims could not take a swing at him or pull him into the Pedernales in revenge. Nor, because of his office and his overbearing persona, were those in the water able to express their anger by chewing him out. This was not simply a cruel practical joke. It was perpetrated by someone who knew he was perfectly safe from physical and verbal reprisals. Playing this prank brought Lyndon Johnson perilously close to playing the role of schoolyard bully, pitilessly picking on those weaker than he.

★ ★ ★

If bully LBJ was, he was a foolish one. Not because he risked being sued or pilloried in the media. The 1960s were a less litigious age (who would dream of suing the president then, anyway?), and journalists regularly covered up the sins and foibles of the mighty (at least in the pre-Chappaquidick era). LBJ's foolishness was defined by this oversight: He assumed all of his guests could swim. That just wasn't so among rural Texans raised in the twenties and thirties. It was especially not the case for women of that era. They had grown up in a time when swimming holes were the province of boys, and in places where mixing scantily clad young people of different sexes was frowned upon. My mother never learned to swim and always felt uneasy around water. Wilma could dog paddle, but she was very uncomfortable in water and avoided swimming. For her, jumping into a river fully clothed was not escape. It was almost tantamount to certain death by drowning.

Traveling by automobile makes my stepmother nervous as well. Not when she's piloting the car: Wilma is an excellent driver under all kinds of conditions and on all types of roads. She becomes less than calm, however, when another person is at the wheel. For years, whenever I drove a car she was riding in, I could count on sudden intakes of breath and quick stamps of her foot whenever I was in traffic. While other passengers might hear LBJ's complaints about the steering and the brakes without attaching much significance to them, Wilma would regard them as important, pay close attention, and be alert for trouble ahead.

As a result, when the president began to weave the car toward the low-water crossing, Wilma was ready to move much more rapidly than he expected. As he slid onto the dam, with the front of the amphibious car headed toward the water, she vaulted over its side. As she hoped, she did not land in the water, but on the concrete dam. At this point, her plan broke down. She could not maintain her footing. The velocity of the car, the urgency of her leap, and the slickness of the dam from the water flowing over it caused her to wind up flat on her back. Her pelvic area absorbed the brunt of the impact. She was sore and bruised for months; the orthopedic specialist she went to told her she came very close to breaking her pelvis.

The president was very upset, as well he might be. Inflicting the physical discomforts attendant on a plunge into the Pedernales and the psychological embarrassment of exhibiting unwarranted fear and then enduring a critique of your actions while in that state was great fun for him. Actually injuring someone was not. He must not have even considered the possibility that his prank might be dangerous. To be fair, he wasn't the only one overlooking the risks. The Secret Service agents were participants in the joke. They must have believed it was safe. The knowledge they would be rescuing guests from the water if that proved necessary, and the certainty they would be sharing the blame if a death or serious injury occurred, did not convince them otherwise. Now they and the president were confronted by the reality of an injured woman, lying on the dam with two to three inches of water flowing under and around her, groaning in pain.

LBJ immediately apologized and kept on saying he was sorry as the agents helped Wilma to her feet and got her back into the car. He also reassured her that he didn't think the less of her for jumping early. Joe Califano, he told her, had also bailed out before the car entered the water. Apparently he expected the news that a man who was still in the boat and among his most trusted advisers had done the same thing would soothe any fear she might have about his reaction to her jump. This would let her know that he did not feel she suffered from an obvious lack of trust in his ability to handle an emergency situation. He was equally concerned about her physical condition. The president drove the short distance from the low-water crossing to the house in record time. There, he and the agents determined that she was only shaken and bruised.

My stepmother, who is among the most forgiving souls I have ever met, assured the Johnsons that she was all right. She wasn't angry, and I know she bears no grudges against Lyndon Johnson for either the injury or the months of careful walking and sitting that followed. Wilma told him it was an accident, and she regarded it as such.

Which, in the narrowest sense of the word "accident," it was. LBJ certainly didn't intend for her to nearly break her pelvis. But his intentions cannot mitigate the danger of such a prank and how terribly reckless he was in planning and executing it. This joke was a disaster waiting to happen. His experience with Califano should have taught him that. But instead of recognizing that it was pure luck that his principal domestic adviser wasn't injured by landing on the dam, he took this as proof that no physical harm could possibly happen to the victims of the joke. He surely also realized that a panicked lunge from the car before it went into the Pedernales gave him the perfect chance to make pointed and sarcastic comments about the leaper's courage and his or her faith in the president. If anything, this made the joke even more fun. When what should have been foreseen did in fact occur, Lyndon Johnson was very fortunate that the injury was not nearly so serious as it might have been.

When I say this, I have more in mind than Wilma's pelvis, painful though that was. Recently, I told the story of her and the amphibious car to a friend who is a clinical psychologist. He commiserated with me over her physical injuries, but what clearly concerned him more were the probable psychological impacts of LBJ's joke on its victims. He viewed the prank from the perspective of the current rules governing the use of deception on human participants in psychological experimentation. "This 'experiment,'" as he sardonically called it, "would never get past any committee charged with approving research designs that depend on the reactions of human subjects." Then he explained why. "The possibility of enduring trauma is too great."

Despite the psychological jeopardy LBJ placed both Bullions in and the bruises he inflicted on Wilma's backside, his obvious horror at her accident, his equally obvious contrition, and his unfeigned concern for her recovery assured that her fall at the low-water crossing would not affect the relationship between him and Dad. The president continued to consult him; my father kept on running the blind trust. Wilma became one of the Johnsons' favorites, not only for her many virtues but because she had proven to be such a good sport about the accident. The two slept over at the White House after state dinners and went back to the ranch a number of times.

They much preferred the ranch to the White House. Bunking in the Queen's Bedroom was, Dad complained, "very uncomfortable." The bed was too narrow and "too fancy for a country boy to sleep in." For her part, Wilma disliked being served breakfast in bed. That was too rich for her blood, and this feeling was heightened by the custom of serving guests very thin toast soaked in butter. I believe the two let their hosts know, in a courteous but unmistakable fashion, that they liked visiting with the Johnsons much more in the country. I don't doubt this improved their standing with Lyndon and Lady Bird, who had always loved the ranch and now felt besieged in the White House. Invitations to Gillespie County from them to the Bullions increased and were deeply appreciated by the recipients. At first, the president avoided driving Wilma over the dam. Later, when his memory of her accident faded, Wilma always smiled and never flinched as he sped across it.

I heard about Dad's meetings with LBJ during these years very infrequently. The late sixties and early seventies were not high points in inter-generational relations in the United States. My family was no exception. Vietnam never split us apart as starkly or as dramatically as it did the homes of some of my friends, but it certainly widened the gap between Dad and me. Because he agreed with the president's use of Munich in 1938 to justify involvement in Southeast Asia in 1968, Dad maintained a hawkish position. He was philosophical about the prospect that I might be drafted, telling me that if I had to serve, there were useful things to be learned in the military. Judging from his experience in the Navy, he did not think those would be lost years and didn't hesitate to say so. I suggested he might feel differently if I came home in a box, a riposte that should give you a fair idea of the quality of my exchanges with him.

Despite his philosophical differences with me about military service, my father was as relieved as I was when my physical at the Dallas induction center revealed that my vision was so poor that I should only serve in a national emergency. I got the much-envied 1-Y classification. In effect, that certified I would not be drafted. Vietnam was an undeclared war and therefore technically did not qualify as a national emergency. The fact that the situation in Southeast Asia certainly appeared to be an emergency didn't trouble Dad or me. Nor were we bothered that my vision could on one hand be sufficiently good for me to be (for a while) the best shot on the LBJ Ranch, and on the other be too poor for me to be in the army. Justly or not, I did not serve my country during the Vietnam war. This left me free to criticize at length Lyndon Johnson's policies around my father and elsewhere.

On one occasion, I thought about doing something more than sniping at the president within my family and joining in the fun of running him down with other graduate students. That day, I thought that I could embarrass him by writing a harshly critical account of hunting at the ranch.

I had become a fervent admirer of Eugene McCarthy and decided that if I described how LBJ made deer hunting easy, how he wanted to deduct the deer I shot, and how he slandered reporters at the *New York Times*, it would wound him in campaigns against Clean Gene. Leave out any mitigating impressions of Johnson, toss in an extended comparison à la William Manchester between the slaughter of deer and the murder of Vietnamese, and I'd have a piece that surely would persuade undecided voters to abandon him.

This fantasy even went so far as to include the best journal in which to publish it: the *New York Review of Books*, where savage David Levine caricatures would perfect it. I didn't wonder whether its editors would be interested in such a piece. I'm not sure why I thought the average voter in Democratic primaries read this magazine. Finally, why this treatment of deer hunting on the LBJ Ranch would influence people when they went to the polls remained unanalyzed by me. But what perfected the remoteness of this scheme from any contact with reality was my failure to commit one single word about the trip to the ranch to paper. Soon I didn't need to. Less than one week after I hatched my plan, the president announced he would not seek re-election. So much for literary fame and political influence!

That was just as well. I didn't have the confidence or the skills in 1968 to write a publishable essay on LBJ. If I had ever begun it, I would not have finished. I believe I sensed that at the time, whether I admitted it to myself or not. I was not disappointed by the lost opportunity, and thirty-one years went by before I thought again about describing our family's relationships with Lyndon Johnson in writing. There are many reasons for the passage of so many years. Perhaps the most telling is the fact that after he announced he was leaving office, the strong dislike I had had for his foreign policies faded into an absence of interest in the man and what he had attempted to achieve.

When Dad did say something to me about LBJ during the last year of his presidency and the four years of mostly unhappy retirement left to him, he usually emphasized how the former president seemed determined to do things that endangered his health and the sanity of those around him. My father told especially troubling stories about his behavior at the ranch.

When Johnson was back in the Hill Country, Dad thought he no longer even made a pretense of following a diet. He ate voraciously at meals. There was no need for him to dip into neighbors' plates and bowls; he demanded and received generous helpings of everything. When Lady Bird tried to restrict his intake and modify his choice of foods, he confided to Dad that it was easy to evade her vigilance. "I jump in the car, Waddy, drive to the store in Hye, buy five or six Snickers or Milky Ways, and eat 'em on the way home." Dad could only shake his head in response.

As this story indicates, LBJ still prowled the roads around and on his ranches. This was much to the dismay of his foreman and the cowboys. With little else to occupy him, he micromanaged his acres and livestock and the men who tended them. At one point, he went so far as to require the hands to write him memoranda at the end of their work day, discussing what they had done and outlining plans for tomorrow. His energetic assumption of the role of ranch boss was fueled not only by frustration and boredom, but also by the steady supply of candy from Hye. As he moved around his property, he would haul Snickers out and devour them in two or three bites. They had a predictable effect upon his weight. But most disturbing of all from Dad's viewpoint, LBJ confessed to him that he had begun buying packs of cigarettes at country stores and smoking them on the road. My father was stunned by this news and disturbed when LBJ proceeded to light up in front of him.

The Hye Country Store.
Bullion Family Collection.

This resumption of smoking convinced Dad that Lyndon Johnson no longer really cared about living. What had kept him interested in life after his heart attack had been first the possibility and then the reality of ultimate political power. To achieve this and to maintain it, he was more than willing to cut down on food, to abstain from alcohol for extended periods of time, to lay off of between-meal Milky Ways, and to stop smoking. Once he had renounced the presidency and had no chance of ever regaining it, the motives sustaining his self-discipline were forever gone.

Dad did not question whether LBJ knew the highly probable consequences of his indulgences. Indeed, to my father, these acts were consciously suicidal. Seeing a once supremely confident, nearly omnipotent man surrender to self-destructive habits was profoundly saddening. Given a choice, Dad preferred the old Lyndon Johnson, the one who had welcomed him and his family to the ranch, however he might have acted and whatever he might have done while we were there. That is why my father loved to repeat a story LBJ told him about how he put new pews in the Catholic church in Stonewall, and who got the credit for this good deed.

★ ★ ★

When he was president, LBJ became interested in Roman Catholicism. Initially, his curiosity was stimulated by Luci's conversion to the faith. After she became a Catholic, he attended Mass and prayed with priests often enough to give rise to rumors that he, too, was planning to convert. I doubt he ever seriously contemplated taking that step. To the extent he was religious at all, Lyndon Johnson was so steeped in the evangelical Protestantism of the Hill Country that had he been an atheist, he would have been a Southern Baptist atheist. I question whether he would have been comfortable with the Church's emphasis on works over grace. After all, the people LBJ grew up with scorned Methodists for believing (as the joke went) that all one had to do to get in Heaven was to bring a covered dish. Catholics were even worse. At least Methodists conceded God Himself had to approve the casserole or cobbler. Catholics believed priests shared the divine power to forgive sins and popes spoke eternal and unquestionable truths just like the Lord. I believe LBJ would have disapproved of the sacrament of Holy Penance. I don't wonder at all about what his opinion of papal infallibility would have been.

Far more comforting and useful to a man like LBJ were the doctrines of once saved, always saved and the priesthood of believers, which held that every person had an equal right to seek the meaning of Scripture for him or herself. Acknowledging the power of the Lord was one thing; bowing to the authority of popes and priests was something quite different. LBJ might have accepted God as his superior; it's far less likely he would have accorded the same status to His representatives on earth. Nevertheless, he had become intrigued by Catholicism and had come to know and like Father Thomas Schneider, the priest at St. Francis Xavier Church in Stonewall.

I've already noted that the president "persuaded" Jake Jacobsen to pay for new kneelers for that church. Johnson had taken special pleasure in bullying a Jew into donating furniture essential to worship in a Catholic parish; this demonstrated his absolute power over Jacobsen and proved he could command complete obedience from Jake. I also suspect the thought of devout Catholics worshipping on "Jewish" kneelers tickled his sense of humor. Now, however, it was apparent that the small parish had to replace the pews those kneelers were fastened to. There had been talk in church about a fundraising drive. Evidently, neither priest nor parishioners were optimistic about getting enough money. Their numbers were few; their treasure was small. LBJ decided he would donate the new pews.

Merely writing a check and giving it to Father Schneider would have been sufficient to accomplish that end. It would not have been spectacular enough, though. So the president bought the pews and had them shipped to his ranch. Once they were there, he alerted the Secret Service and his ranch hands to the rest of his plan. That it required them to put in extra hours without pay did not bother the president. He assumed they understood they were there to serve at all times and places and in ways he chose for them.

Some agents who were going off duty on Saturday afternoon were to invite Father Schneider to have a few beers with them in Fredericksburg. That he would accept was a foregone conclusion. A German himself by birth, Thomas Schneider had long since shown that

LBJ, Luci Nugent, and Father Thomas Schneider, October 12, 1968.
LBJ Library. Photo by Jack Kightlinger.

he possessed more than enough *gemütlichkeit* to fit right in with the deeply religious German Catholic beer drinkers who had founded and continued to run "Fritz Town." At the beer hall, the agents were to bait him into drinking pitcher after pitcher of beer and telling round after round of stories. Their assignment was straightforward: to get him drunk. After this, and as night began to fall, the most sober agent would offer to take him home.

By these means, LBJ intended to insure that Father Schneider would be gone from Stonewall for some hours, would return inebriated and after dark, and would not come to the church before the first Mass the following day. The president had observed that his habitual practice before the earliest Sunday Mass was to go straight into the sacristy through an outside door, vest in that room, and move through another door to the altar. He did not enter the church via the front doors and walk through the nave to get there. Thus his first sight of the new pews would be from the altar, in front of the parishioners already gathered for the service. What would be his reaction? LBJ could hardly wait.

Enticing the priest to Fredericksburg proved to be easy. This part of the president's scheme worked perfectly. So did the other. The dust from the agents' cars had hardly settled before cowboys drove up to the church with the pews. As always, the front doors were not locked. They rapidly removed the old pews, replaced them with the new, and attached Jake Jacobsen's kneelers. Well before dusk, they were finished. No sign of their presence remained when agent and priest returned to the rectory. Even had there been, darkness and drunkenness had rendered Father Schneider incapable of detecting or comprehending it. The agent went beyond the call of duty to LBJ; he tucked Thomas into bed. Then he reported to the president that everything was set up. Very pleased at how smoothly his plan had gone, LBJ gave orders that he and Lady Bird were to be awakened in plenty of time to make the first Mass.

The next morning, the two of them were there before anyone else. The Johnsons sat in the front pew, where they could clearly see and hear Father Schneider's initial reactions. Staff members stationed themselves at the front doors and warned entering parishioners to be as quiet as possible. LBJ did not want any premature exclamations of surprise, joy, or thankfulness to alert the priest while he vested that something unusual was happening in the church. There could be no excited buzz from the nave, only the near silence of the still sleepy faithful. This, too, was achieved. So when the priest emerged from the sacristy, looking to LBJ's delight the worse for wear, he was as totally surprised as the president could have wished.

I cannot do justice to the rest of the story. My father couldn't either, because, he confessed, he could only approximate how LBJ acted it out. I can't duplicate the gestures on the printed page, and I won't try to match Johnson's (and Dad's) mimicking of Schneider's German accent. Imagine them for yourselves.

Father Thomas immediately noticed the new pews as he looked around the nave at the congregation. Ordinarily, he would have proceeded to the center of the altar, genuflected, and lighted the candles. This Sunday, he stopped cold, with the torch in his hand. After taking a moment to gather his wits, he began to speak.

What a wonderful surprise this is. St. Francis Xavier desperately needed new pews but didn't have the money to buy them. Now, through the grace of God, a generous donor had accomplished this great work for this church. Who could that donor be?

St. Francis Xavier Church, Stonewall, Texas, November 3, 1968.
LBJ Library. Photo by Yoichi R. Okamoto.

Could it be our good friend, the president of the United States? He has honored us with his presence on many Sundays, and he has helped us in many ways. Despite his great responsibilities and duties, he has taken time to be with us and do for us. Could it be our friend President Johnson?

(Here switch your mental image from priest to president, who has cast his eyes down modestly and is beginning to smile, preparatory to acknowledging Father Thomas's eloquent thanks. But the best laid plans...)

No, it couldn't have been the president. He simply is too busy to have gone to the trouble to buy the pews and then install them.

(Back to the front pew: the real benefactor of the parish no longer has his eyes downcast—instead, they are staring at the priest and bulging out—nor is he smiling. I'm *not* going to get the credit!?)

It must have been Mrs. Johnson. She, too, has been a great friend of ours, not only in this church, but in her tireless efforts to beautify our country and protect the lovely wildflowers, whose colors are truly a blessing from God.

(*What*? Sidelong glance at Bird, who is staring at Father Thomas as well and also not smiling anymore. She looks nonplussed by this undeserved praise.)

No, it couldn't have been Mrs. Johnson, either. She's extremely busy, almost as busy as the president himself. She has her special causes, and she fulfills her duty to comfort and support her husband in his awesome responsibilities. There's just not enough time for her to have done this. Who could have given us these pews?

(A slight frown is now moving toward a near scowl. Could it be that Father is going to credit someone who isn't a Johnson? Does he think these are *Jewish* pews?)

It might have been Miss Lynda. She has a warm place in her heart for us, and she is a generous person. She's done countless acts of charity and kindness.

(Lynda? The president's arms cross; his face arranges itself into a resigned expression. I know who'll get the credit for this. Sure enough...)

But no, it couldn't have been Miss Lynda. She's too busy as well, at other good works. I know who bought our new pews and had them put in. It was Miss Luci. I thank her, we must all thank her, for this wonderful gift.

(Father Thomas turns to light the candles. The Mass begins. The president of the United States ponders the events of the morning thoughtfully and formulates a moral.)

"Waddy," he summed up the story for Dad, "they'll always give credit to one of their own." He said this in a tone that was half-amused and half-irritated. Then he joined in Dad's laughter at this history of the new pews for St. Francis Xavier in Stonewall and the person honored for such a wonderful gift.

The parents of St. Francis Xavier's benefactor leave church, November 3, 1968.
LBJ Library. Photo by Yoichi R. Okamoto.

The moral of this engaging story is significant for understanding the president's moods as he approached the end of his term in office and his public career. *Why* is best explained by beginning with the part the priest played on Sunday morning.

Notice the speed and shrewdness of Father Schneider's reactions. Almost instantaneously, he must have understood the dimensions and details of the plot to get him away from Stonewall on Saturday. By not describing how he was fooled, he denied the president the satisfaction of the victim's revealing the story to the parish. With equal rapidity, he figured out who gave the pews and arranged for their installation. No other member of the family could have paid for them without LBJ's approval. No one but the president could have commanded the Secret Service agents to take him to Fredericksburg. Nobody else could have commandeered the vehicles and labor necessary to remove the old seating, replace it with the new, and attach the kneelers. This was Johnson's work, without question.

Still, Father Schneider did not give him the credit. He might flatter LBJ by calling him a good friend and by reminding others about his many duties. This had the effect of publicly drawing the sting from the comment that the president simply could not have been responsible for this generous act, while privately taking a measure of revenge for Sunday morning's hangover. Moreover, stating that Luci was the parish's benefactor and thanking her was, from the priest's standpoint, only just. He believed that LBJ's interest in this parish had without question been sparked by her conversion to Roman Catholicism. Had the daughter not embraced the faith, the father would not have donated the new pews. In the strictest sense, she deserved the credit for them. As for the president, his joke cost him even honorable mention.

Father Thomas's performance was worthy of Dad or the marine orderly. In his own way, the priest had figured out—just as each of them did—tactics that would preserve a certain amount of independence from the gravitational pull of the most powerful man on the planet. To extend the astronomical metaphor, none of these three was a moon so caught in a circle around this great planet they were in danger of being pulled into it and consumed. They were their own planets, with their own orbits. They might come near to LBJ; they might stay close to him for extended passages of time. Ultimately, though, they could and would move away, following the path of their own destinies.

Was the president aware of what his own story revealed about the foil for his scheme? I'm sure he was. He did explain Schneider's response by implying it showed the bias of a Catholic priest in favor of another Catholic, an accounting that ignores the possibility of a joke's being played on him in return. But if he believed this, then he was remarkably obtuse in his judgment of those he dealt with personally. Lyndon Johnson was many things; obtuse about such matters, however, he was not. He had figured out Thomas's game, and he was determined not to acknowledge his friendly adversary's clever counterattack because its broader implications frightened him.

Then why did LBJ tell this story? For starters, he wanted to get the credit for the new pews. Dad and the others who listened to it knew the truth; the president had given the pews and seen to their installation. His plot's unanticipated end did not detract from his charity. Nor did he permit the public thanking of his Catholic daughter to distract his listeners from his munificence. Indeed, he used the occasion to draw a painful moral: they'll always give the credit to one of their own.

Johnson did not say *Catholics* always give the praise to their own; nor did he say priests or ministers or members of the same denominations always did this. Instead, he used the more sweeping and more indefinite pronoun "they." Those who are part of any group will invariably claim the glory for words and deeds for members of that group, which, of course, includes themselves.

In LBJ's formulation, the insight remains uncompleted. They'll give the credit to one of their own *rather than*—to whom? Anyone else? Everyone else? Perhaps these are good answers, but they too are incomplete. Insert instead "even when another truly deserves it."

That is what LBJ meant for his audience to understand from this moral. Those who have done good works, who should have earned the applause and gratitude of others, don't always get their just deserts. Even when the beneficiaries of these acts recognize how fortunate they are, they are prone to thank people other than the true giver when it suits their purposes or their group identities.

Now remember what my father said to me: LBJ stated the story's moral to him in tones that were half amused and half annoyed. The matter of who was thanked for the pews was an amusing story. LBJ told it that way, with appropriate accents and gestures. Those who heard it were meant to laugh. And he intended that they would laugh at the priest. His recounting of the session in the Fredericksburg *bier halle*, and his expert mimicking of Germanized English accomplished that. By doing that, he belittled the priest and drew attention away from how cleverly Father Thomas turned the tables on him. This explains his amusement at the story, an amusement reflected in his tone as he narrated it. The annoyance in his voice was the result of the moral.

As his days in office dwindled, the president surely feared that what he had done for his country would be at best underappreciated and at worse totally *un*appreciated. What he had achieved with the Great Society, for education, in support of civil rights for all Americans, would not win him praise. The merits of those advances would be given by others to people like themselves, not to some hick from the Hill Country. Blame for his failures and his frustrations—principally, Vietnam—would, of course, be his alone.

But it was not blame that troubled Lyndon Johnson most. To be sure, he didn't like that prospect. As often as he could he tried to shift it elsewhere; witness his comments to my father about inheriting Vietnam from JFK. The unfairness of being blamed for this by anyone, especially Bobby Kennedy, galled him terribly. But the burden of blame for things going awry must have been light compared to another fate. What he feared most was this: his real accomplishments would go unrecognized. It was the cruelest joke his enemies could play on him. What awful luck to be the helpless victim of such a colossal, cosmic prank.

This fear, I believe, tormented this proud and powerful man. For that reason, the story of who got the credit for those pews in that little church had a metaphorical significance for LBJ out of all proportion to its actual import. Father Schneider's assignment of the credit for the pews to Luci stood as an ominous symbol to him of what he feared would be his fate at the hands of his fellow citizens and history itself.

So LBJ acted out the story with mixed feelings. Telling it allowed him to make fun of his deep-rooted anxieties and to explain why perfect justice was not done. It also let him worry out loud about what might happen to him and his reputation, without revealing any weakness to others by discussing his fears in the broader contexts of the presidency and his entire career. Evidently he didn't expect any response beyond delighted laughter at his acting, sympathetic smiles at the tale's moral, and nodding agreement at its truth. All of those reactions my father gave him, plus another.

The pews, Dad confirmed, were deductible. They were charitable donations to a legally recognized religious institution. They would, therefore, reduce what LBJ would have to pay in personal income tax. Thus my father solaced Lyndon Johnson with the laughter of a sympathizer and the expert advice of a tax attorney. I'm confident he appreciated both.

LBJ, Lady Bird Johnson, and Waddy Bullion, March 7, 1967.
LBJ Library. Photo by Yoichi R. Okamoto.

CHAPTER 16

Gifts

For my father, the telephone conveyed the first proof that Lyndon Johnson really was no longer president. Calls from the White House or the ranch between November 1963 and January 1969 began with an operator saying, "Mr. Bullion, please hold for the president of the United States." Then Dad would sit, pressing the receiver to his ear, for as long as it took for LBJ to get around to him. The record for time spent holding, he informed me, was nearly forty minutes. The post-White House Johnson placed most of his own calls. My father doesn't remember ever waiting for LBJ to get on the line. Rather the reverse: now phone conversations began abruptly, "Waddy, this is Lyndon Johnson. I want to . . ."

The calls also came more frequently than before. Dad's partner in the cattle business told me he rarely sat down in the office at The Barn without listening in on one side of a conversation with the former president. "I'd look at my watch," he said with a laugh, "and time how long it was before Waddy would say 'Mr. President, you can't do that.'" When I reminded my father about his partner's observations, Dad smiled and said he wasn't stretching the truth very much.

Making his ranches profitable obsessed LBJ. The formidable energies that formerly had been focused on the nation's affairs now were poured into an attempt to bring the LBJ Ranch and other properties to the point where they could stand alone without KTBC's support. To achieve this, he sought every tax advantage he could think of. Many times, my father's job was to rein in this enthusiasm and direct it toward different strategies. Some were tax-related; some, purely agricultural; others had to do with the Texas Broadcasting Corporation as a whole. Johnson listened closely. Usually, he followed Dad's advice. And, by the next phone call, he'd have fresh ideas.

One of the best of these had to do with the future of his ranch house and the nearly sixty acres surrounding it. Dad arranged a transfer of title to this property from the Texas Broadcasting Corporation to LBJ. This done, Johnson deeded the house and land to the National Park Service, reserving a life estate for himself or Lady Bird, whoever survived the other. So long as one of them lived, they could stay on the ranch. Afterwards, these acres and the buildings on them would be the Park Service's, contingent on their being maintained as a working ranch. LBJ and Dad had an assessment made of the value of the bequest, and they calculated what a life estate was worth. The difference between the two sums was deducted as a charitable contribution on the Johnsons' personal income tax. And, as my father is quick to point out, the people of the United States one day will receive a carefully preserved replica of what the LBJ Ranch was like during the lifetime of the thirty-sixth president.

Another good idea had nothing to do with the ranch. Soon after he moved back to Texas, LBJ asked Dad to draft an indenture establishing a charitable foundation. Thus was born the Lyndon B. Johnson Foundation, a nonprofit organization funded by money from the Johnson family and from donations in LBJ's honor. Within a year, the foundation was dispensing grants to assist in social and educational reform programs. Later, it provided funds as well for the LBJ School of Public Affairs and the Johnson Library. That these memorialized the former president goes without saying. That they also expressed and advanced his commitment to education as *the* surest way of improving peoples' lives is equally true. In all of its activities, the foundation he named after himself was a source of great satisfaction to Lyndon Johnson and his adviser.

Dad firmly believed both Johnsons were deeply committed to charity. He's repeated to me many times that LBJ was determined to help society's less fortunate by providing the wherewithal, financial and otherwise, that would give them a good chance to succeed. In fact, Johnson enjoyed doing this very much. He never doubted it was the right thing to do, because he believed assistance from the outside, whether from the government or private charity, could help the poor reach their full potential, as individuals and as citizens. As my father is fond of observing, Lyndon Johnson remained a New Dealer to the end. He might no longer guide government policy, but he was ready to create and direct a foundation that would further this great enterprise. He intended it would be one of his enduring legacies.

Of course, the Johnson Foundation also provided a considerable tax break for LBJ and, especially, for his estate after his death. Neither he nor Dad was ignorant of that aspect of this decision. The deductions he could claim were without question one of the attractions of the foundation to him. "So what?" my father would say. This isn't cause for cynicism as far as he's concerned. Rather, we should applaud the wisdom of the Tax Code in encouraging the wealthy to spend some of their resources on churches, charities, and foundations. For many years now, Dad has seen first-hand how much foundations can accomplish. He still is a trustee in the Meadows Foundation, an enterprise he and A.H. Meadows set up years ago. The two progenitors of the ABC transaction together channeled a considerable percent of the profits from it into public libraries for small Texas towns, including an expansion in Eden named after my aunt. As far as my father is concerned, if Al Meadows or Lyndon Johnson could do well while doing good, so be it. That's no cause for doubting their commitment to their country and its people.

LBJ was also generous to Dad. Chief among his gifts to my father, in my opinion at least, was the house the Johnsons gave him. It was in Kingsland, a small Hill Country town near the confluence of two of the region's largest rivers, the Colorado and the Llano. But while my father regarded the foundation as an unalloyed good, he came to believe the lakehouse was at best a mixed blessing. Like many things in life, good intentions inspired it from start to finish. Experience has taught most of us, though, which road—or driveway—is surfaced with that paving.

Texas wanted to pay homage to the native son who had reached the nation's highest office. Ranch Road 1 was not enough. So as a man-made lake began to fill as the result of the latest efforts to harness the power and utilize the beauty of the Colorado and the Llano Rivers by damming them, Austin politicians decided to name it after the thirty-sixth president. Not content simply with the honor, the Johnsons wanted to profit from Lake LBJ as well.

The blind trust had earlier bought land on the outskirts of Kingsland. No doubt Dad and A.W. Moursund anticipated that its value would rise as the lake filled. As that happened, the Johnsons decided to enter into a partnership with other investors to develop a subdivision named Comanche Rancherias on this property. This was one of the first steps toward "the mint" the family would later earn from its invest-ments in land. As is often the case with first efforts, some mistakes were made.

Houses in the Comanche Rancherias were of identical design and construction. People who lived in Central Texas recognized them for what they were: H.B. Zachary pre-fabs. That San Antonio contractor had pioneered pouring concrete walls at a central location, then truck-ing them to subdivisions, where they were attached to concrete slabs that had water, electrical, and sewer connections already in place. Fit the walls on the slab, hook up the connections, slap on a wooden roof covered with composition shingles, and a house was ready to sell. Three days was plenty of time to transform a level patch of dirt into a typical Zachary home. All of the residential units at Comanche Rancherias were done within that period. Everyone who watched the process was reminded of a child putting together Lego blocks; the main differences were the adult builders moved faster and thought less. Soon there was evidence that supported these impressions.

Comanche Rancheria homes originally enclosed 960 square feet of living space, divided into a master bedroom with three-quarter bath, two tiny guest bedrooms, a full bath off the hall between all the bed-rooms, a living room, a dining area, and an all-electric kitchen. They also boasted central air, propane heat, a septic tank, and town water.

Although this sounds like a standard design for a small tract home, it wasn't. By itself, the master bedroom took up 400 square feet, over forty percent of the whole house. No doubt the builder wished that bed-room had been even larger, or, failing that, the closet-sized guest bedrooms had been slightly wider.

When the Johnsons and other investors in Comanche Rancherias sought permission from Kingsland's Planning and Zoning Commission to build, they agreed that no house in the development would be under 1,000 square feet. They did not discover until after the Lego blocks had been interlocked that the Zachary design provided homes forty square feet shy of that requirement. Rather than go through the delay and embarrassment of seeking official approval to change the restriction, the partners had the contractor add storage space to each home. An entryway was carved out of one of the exterior walls, and the extra room was attached. Its exterior was wood, not concrete, and it was impossible to look at it without thinking this was an afterthought. A window air conditioner confirmed that impression. The central air con-ditioning in the houses could not cool the additional one hundred square feet, so chugging, dripping room units extruded from their sides.

These houses were sited on large lots about fifty feet wide and 120 feet deep. Ours had a large mesquite tree in back, which shaded the rear of the house pretty well during the afternoon. In the front, the developers had also scattered some coastal Bermuda sprigs, in the hope that hardy grass would spread and create a lawn. Unfortunately, it barely held its own against weeds and the vicious stickers Texans call sand burrs, which have sharp spines and are virtually indestructible. Two young live oak trees rose out of the competing vegetation. We owed their presence to the former president of the United States. Appalled by the house's unadorned appearance from the street, LBJ insisted that his partners plant two saplings in the yard. They were far too slender to provide more than elongated, tiny shadows in early morning and late afternoon. Dad estimated that if the trees survived the high temperatures and low rainfall of Kingsland summers, they might provide a fair amount of shade in a half century or so. Still, he observed, it was nice that LBJ had thought of planting live oaks. In my judgment, the young trees fit in perfectly with the rest of the house and yard. Presently modest in looks, they had the potential for growing on you.

The principal attraction of owning a house that was neither aesthetically pleasing nor attractively landscaped was obvious: its close proximity to Lake LBJ and the dock that all homeowners in the subdivision were entitled to use. Certainly this was what delighted me about the Johnsons' gift. In 1970 I'd paid ninety dollars for a sailboat kit. When I finished assembling the parts, I had a training sailboat popularly known as a Snark. The hull was made out of styrofoam, so I'd invested extra money for fiberglass and super glue to protect it. My inexpert craftsmanship resulted in several splinters in my hands and forearms and a ten-foot boat that some friends described as a floating ice chest covered with crooked, buckled, and overlapping yellow stripes.

Whatever pain the fiberglass and insults caused me was more than bearable when balanced against the hours of unalloyed pleasure sailing gave me. Her name was *Clio*, after the muse of history. I loved her more than anything I'd ever owned. For me, being "in the boat" certainly did not mean working hard for that demanding taskmaster,

Lyndon Johnson. When I was in my boat, I was generally alone and decidedly not working, for myself or anyone else. Sailing was the place of refuge and refreshment for me that the ranch was for him.

The prospect of having *Clio* so close to a lake that I'd never again have to mess with tying her to the roof of my car and worrying she might fly off in the breeze during the hour's journey to good sailing waters was a vision of heaven. I was eager to move her from my dining room in Austin to the storage room in Kingsland, then revel in launching her after a one-minute trip. This was pure good fortune, no question about it!

I never changed my mind about my luck, even though Lake LBJ near the subdivision fell short of being an ideal place for fun on or in the water. The part of the lake Comanche Rancherias abutted looked like what it had been in a prior life: the Llano River. From one shore to another, it was barely a quarter of a mile. Keeping *Clio* on a tack for very long was impossible. Distances were so short that whenever I stayed there during the summer, I regularly swam across and back in the morning and evening. After a rain, I had to be careful doing this. Any increase in the water level floated cow patties off the banks and down toward the main body of the lake, so I quickly learned both to dodge them and to avoid getting water in my mouth. I never worried much about boat traffic, whether I was sailing or swimming. Only a few motorboats ventured up this inlet, and they usually went very slowly, looking for a place to swing around safely without reversing. Mine was not only the one sailboat on this part of the lake, but also the only boat many days. As far as I could tell, no one else swam in those waters.

The boat dock at Comanche Rancherias.
Bullion Family Collection.

It's obvious to me now that the developers and investors hoped to sell weekend places and retirement homes to middle- and working-class Texans. There was nothing opulent or luxurious about anything in Comanche Rancherias. There was nothing offensive about it, either. I loved the concrete block we called the lakehouse. As far as I was concerned, it was wonderful to go to Kingsland for a week or a weekend, to swim, sail, and work on my dissertation. Most people who visited there shared my feelings. My father was not one of them, for reasons I'll discuss soon. But both of us were grateful—in his case, at least initially—for the gift of one of the Zachary houses from the Johnsons.

Lyndon and Lady Bird Johnson gave away five of these homes. Indeed, they did more than that: they furnished them completely. I'm confident LBJ chose these furnishings. When he bought a house along the Pedernales from local ranchers named Reagan, he proudly informed Wilma that he decorated it himself "with no one's help." He even went to a Sears store, pored over the selection of drapes, and finally picked some out. Not content with telling her, he insisted on showing her as well. Off she and he went to the Reagan House, as LBJ called it. To Wilma's relief, they traveled by land in a conventional car; to her consternation, the trip was made at breakneck speed along gravel roads. Her final judgment was the drapes were "okay."

LBJ at the Reagan House, October 23, 1972.
LBJ Library. Photo by Frank Wolfe.

In my opinion, LBJ did better than okay with the lakehouse. Its features included a king-size bed, bunk beds, a trundle bed, a huge couch with a fold-out bed, dining table and six chairs, two overstuffed living room chairs that swiveled, a coffee table, end tables, chests of drawers, shag carpeting in the living room and halls, a stove, refrigerator, dishwasher, and disposal. After all this stuff had been moved into our house, LBJ impulsively decided that we should have a good rocking chair as well. Within two days, a handsome wooden rocker with comfortable cushions tied to its seat, back, and arms arrived from San Antonio.

Every appliance and piece of furniture was high quality. The living room couch from the lakehouse sits in my basement as I write and has withstood the wear of thirty years, two children, three dogs, two cats, and too many history department parties. The only questionable purchase was the carpet; sand burrs brought in from outside nestled in the shag and became so lethal and plentiful that everyone wore shoes in the house in self-defense.

Once I knew the names of the other four who got these furnished lakehouses. Now I only remember two of them: Don Thomas and the pastor of the First Christian Church in Washington, D.C., where the Johnsons worshipped when they were in the capital. I do recall who was not one of the two I've forgotten: Father Thomas Schneider. Perhaps he was excluded because the Johnsons assumed the Church would take care of him after he left Stonewall; perhaps LBJ was paying him back for a certain Sunday morning. Whatever the reason, he was not blessed in the same way his Protestant counterpart was.

To be sure, being generous to people close to them was not the Johnsons' sole reward. Subdivisions without residents are a harder sell than those with cars and boats in the driveways and traffic in and out of houses. The presence of people deters human vandalism and discourages the roaming of coyotes and rattlesnakes. Residents also have to bear the costs of utility bills, property taxes, and house insurance. They become responsible for hacking down the grass and weeds and fighting a losing battle against sand burrs. This transfer of obligations from developers to homeowners lowered the overhead on LBJ's investment.

All these were trade-offs I was more than willing to make. I stayed there frequently. I cut the yard—once at the gentle but firm request of Lady Bird, who saw my car in the driveway sometime in the mid-seventies, and stopped by to say hello and remind me of my duty. I played a crucial role in varmint reduction. During my first days there, I killed two rattlers, one in the driveway (I bravely drove over it), the other in the front yard (I broke its back with a rock, then chopped its head off with a shovel). Thereafter, I saw no more snakes. As for the utilities, taxes, and insurance, plus the cost of a telephone, those were Dad's business.

After three or four years of paying these bills, Dad grew tired of them. Wilma and he came to Kingsland no more often than once a summer. When there, they had no interest in swimming or sailing, the major reasons for having the house. Two events tipped the scales in their minds against the lakehouse even further.

Thieves broke into it one night, shattering a window in the master bedroom, tearing off its blinds, and stealing the pillows from the bed. This proved the vulnerability of the house and raised the price of insuring it. The burglars' curious choice of what to take did nothing to reassure my father about the safety of his family there.

Second, nearby neighbors complained to Dad about the people who stayed there. Not about me, they hastened to say, but about the strangers who came to Kingsland in my absence. My father quizzed me about this and discovered I was letting friends use the house and take *Clio* out for a sail. All they had to do was ask. If it was all right with me, they could drive straight out, because many people knew I hid the key under a picnic table beneath the backyard mesquite. This revelation touched off an angry exchange between us. Predictably, I cursed nosy neighbors, "who should mind their own Goddamn business"; understandably, my father raged against my friends "shacking up" in his house and his bed, using his water, and running his air conditioning.

In this dispute, the prerogatives of ownership and the preservation of morality at Comanche Rancherias won out over the right to privacy. Dad's short-term solution was instructing our watchful neighbor to collect the key from under the picnic table. Then he rented the lakehouse to a nephew of Wilma's who was studying for the ministry and needed a place for him and his family to live in Central Texas. Finally, he wound up selling it to the same man.

At the time, I was furious. Reflecting on it later from the perspective of a property owner who now pays city and county taxes and utilities bills and presently concerns himself with the impact of the general state of his neighborhood and the occasional visible eccentricities of his neighbors on the value of his home, I am much more sympathetic to the points of view of my father and those who lived near the lakehouse. I'm also keenly aware of something else, something I was oblivious to while I railed about our neighbors to Dad.

In December of 1965, Lyndon Johnson's offer of the use of a guest house on the ranch to my father, complete with assurances he could bring whomever he pleased there, presumably to shack up, had upset me. A decade later, I was making the same offer to people who I knew weren't married to each other. "Just let me know ahead of time, then go on. You know where the key is; be sure to put it back when you leave." I even had a hierarchy of guests: the best ones washed their sheets and towels and hung *Clio*'s sail out to dry before rolling it up. Extracting morals from others' deeds, words, and stories and then criticizing them is easy to do. Indeed, it can become *too* easy. Excavating morals from your own history and critiquing your own acts is more demanding. It can also be more painful.

Our lakehouse was the fruit of long-term, carefully considered planning by the Johnsons. In this case, their generosity was not the result of impulsive, spontaneous thoughts and acts. As such, it was an exception to the usual rule for dealings with LBJ. Restless in retirement, he was prone to making decisions suddenly and implementing them instantly. I've already given you one example. One moment, Wilma was talking with him about styles and colors of drapes. The next, she was in a Lincoln Continental tearing toward the Reagan House, with Lyndon Johnson driving and talking a mile a minute. What a good sport my stepmother was to get back into a car with him! And she did it more than once.

The most memorable of these impromptu trips was to a football game. The Bullions happened to be at the ranch on a November Saturday when Baylor was playing Texas in Austin. My Uncle Thomas was driving down from Taylor to the game, and for some reason Dad mentioned this to LBJ. Johnson's expression immediately brightened. "Waddy," he asked, "do you know who the finest administrator I've ever met is?" Resisting the temptation to say, "yourself?" my father replied he wouldn't even try to guess. Which son of a bitch could this be, he was certainly wondering. "Darrell Royal," said LBJ, "and I'll tell you why. He hasn't just won for a season or two. He has managed to sustain success for a long time at Texas." Then he added, "There's nothing harder to do than sustain success. I know that for a fact."

This thought didn't depress Johnson. Instead, it fired him up. They had time to see with their own eyes what Royal had achieved with the Longhorn football team. If they left the ranch right now, they could be in Memorial Stadium in time for the opening kickoff. He reached for the phone, called the chairman of the UT Board of Regents, and secured three seats on the fifty yard line. Then he swept Dad and Wilma into the Lincoln Continental. Off they went, over the state road to 290, and then on into Austin.

To quote Wilma, "He drove like a bat out of hell." The Secret Service had summoned up some highway patrolmen to serve as escorts, but that didn't comfort her any. Entering into the spirit of LBJ's dash to Austin, the officers seemed bent and determined to establish a new speed record from Johnson City to the main gate of the stadium. To my stepmother, the journey was a frightening blur.

A veteran of traffic jams around the Cotton Bowl and Texas Stadium, Dad was more impressed by the absence of any difficulties associated with parking once they got there. "Go to a football game with a former president," he advised me. "You'll have a clear path and a reserved space not too far from your seat. After the game, the cops will hold up all other traffic until you're on the road home."

The game itself was much more forgettable. Texas must have won, because the Horns almost always did then. Coach Royal sustained success one more Saturday. All Wilma remembers was how unseasonably warm it was, and how much she wished she wasn't wearing wool. My father still complains that he saw very little of the game, because fans stopped short in the aisles when they noticed LBJ and blocked his view. The bolder ones wanted to shake hands, and the former president did a brisk business in autographing programs for women and children. Johnson had a great time, far better than he would have had today in a modern stadium, where the athletic department surely would have stuck him in a luxury box. No one mentioned Vietnam. If his presence offended some people, they contented themselves with staying away from him.

With a few moments left and victory for the home team in the bag, the impromptu party from the LBJ Ranch left the stadium. Johnson had no interest in speaking with the greatest administrator he'd ever known on this occasion. He was ready to get back to Gillespie County. Returning was as speedy as going. Night was just falling as LBJ drove across the low-water bridge over the Pedernales. It was time for a drink or two, some talk about the day, and Zephyr Wright's dinner.

★ ★ ★

During the years between the finish of his political career and the end of his life, Lyndon Johnson gave generously of his time, his attention, and his money to the Bullion family. We were touched by this and grateful for his gifts, even when they caused trouble. And we all hoped this giving made him happy. That it is better to give than to receive is a piece of wisdom my family recognizes as almost always true.

I'm not sure Lyndon Johnson shared that sentiment. There continued to be a frenetic quality to his giving, and an attention to detail and quantity that verged on overkill. Yet there was also a fundamental difference between the spirit animating his gifts to me in December 1965 and the motives behind his later gifts to my family. I don't think of the lakehouse or the spur-of-the-moment trips around Central Texas as parodies of generosity, the way I do about "the other stuff." LBJ was self-satisfied about the gifts he lavished on me during my visit to his ranch. He'd achieved what he personally set out to do. But his pleasure in what he gave us and others after his retirement was predicated upon making the ranch and Comanche Rancherias profitable, or curing the ills of society with the limited resources of a foundation, or planting live oak saplings without expecting ever to feel their shade, or choosing just the right drapes, or sustaining success like Darrell Royal. These just couldn't be achieved to his enduring satisfaction, at least in the time left to him and in his present circumstances.

What I'm afraid happened to LBJ is this: far from being a source of happiness, his generosity proved to him once more how far he had fallen short. That's a species of bad luck that shouldn't be wished on anybody.

CHAPTER 17

Luck

I've frequently remarked how my family's association with Lyndon Johnson was a mixed blessing. Many times—perhaps even most times —it was a stroke of exceptionally good luck. It certainly did not hurt Dad's reputation as an attorney or Thompson, Knight's profits as a law firm that he was known to be one of LBJ's principal tax advisers. And my father's advice helped Senator and President Johnson a great deal, not just directly by improving his personal fortune, but indirectly by allowing him to turn more of his formidable energies and talents to governing our country and leading it in different and better directions. All of us, I am convinced, live in a finer nation at the beginning of this new century thanks to Lyndon Johnson. To the extent Dad assisted him in his mighty accomplishments, my father's presence in the boat was good luck for all of us.

There was a darker side, however. The luck of Lyndon Johnson was not always good. Toward the end, I believe he feared that fortune had inexplicably but irrevocably turned against him. I'll elaborate on that later on in this chapter. Right now, I'm going to tell you how LBJ's bad luck reached out and touched our lives.

During the five years Richard Nixon was president, the Internal Revenue Service audited my father's returns four times. One year this was a full, field audit, which employs numbers of agents sifting through every scrap of fiscal records a taxpayer has. Such audits are time-consuming, both for the IRS and the person under review. In these cases, time equals money. Expenses are considerable, both for the agency and for the individual or corporation under investigation. After six months of shuffling papers, the IRS found just one error: my father had over-paid his taxes by nearly thirty-three dollars. With commendable speed, a check was prepared and sent to him. The very next year, however, the Revenuers were back doing business at the same stand. Dad has always scrupulously refused to claim that these audits were politically motivated. He certainly would never claim they were calculated efforts to get LBJ's tax attorney in trouble first, then use the threat of fines or prosecution to coerce him into admissions about the administration of the Johnson family trust.

I have no evidence that my father is being too forgiving. Nevertheless, the well-known and fully documented threats by President Nixon and others in his administration to use the IRS to punish political enemies make me suspicious. So do the hints in a few histories of the period that the White House tried to get LBJ under its control, an attempt the former president fought off by threatening to make public something he had on his successor, probably the then still secret steps Nixon took to stall peace negotiations in Paris during late October 1968. Does this equal irrefutable proof that the IRS was conducting a political vendetta against Waddy Bullion during 1969-1974? The answer is "no." Still, because I'm a Missourian now, you'd have to show me unmistakable evidence demonstrating the audits were not inspired by desires for political revenge and power before I'd stop believing those were the motives behind them.

★ ★ ★

By the time Richard Nixon resigned, Lyndon Johnson had been dead for eighteen months. The natural death of one president and the political demise of another marked the end of any risks my father might run by representing LBJ. He continued to advise Mrs. Johnson, but the challenges and perils of being the tax attorney for a president of the United States were gone.

Very occasionally, Dad wondered aloud how LBJ would have reacted to succeeding events and ideas. "What would he have thought about Watergate?" my father asked once. Recently, we both chuckled over what LBJ would have said about modern politicians' determination to exclude fellatio from the list of sexual activities. Dad and I agreed we'd pay a considerable sum of money to hear these comments, not least because we doubted Lyndon Johnson would use Latinate, technical language. More seriously, last year my father quietly noted how furious LBJ would have been at charges he plotted the death of Martin Luther King Jr. "After all he did for civil rights, to be accused of that." Dad shook his head at the injustice of it. I thought this would have been Johnson's worst nightmare, the very horror he sought to exorcise by telling about the pews in the Stonewall church. Not only did this deny his greatest accomplishments as president. It maliciously and falsely accused him of being in league with the worst racists of his times. Thank God he was long dead.

Only once has Dad commented on the work he continued to do for the Johnson family to me. Again, it centered on LBJ's probable reaction to events. When Luci obtained a divorce after tense and protracted negotiations, Dad remarked that her father would have been beside himself at the amount of money Pat Nugent received in the final settlement. "It's lucky he's not here," he said, again shaking his head. As I heard this, I realized that—though acts of legislation, the ranches, KTBC, a radio station renamed KLBJ, the Johnson Foundation, and an impressive presidential library remained—both the broader and the more intimate worlds created, sustained, and ruled by the energy and power of Lyndon Johnson were gone forever.

Which was okay with me. The last time the worlds LBJ molded intersected with my life, it had nearly been disastrous.

Early in the summer of 1974, I applied for a one-year position as an instructor of history at Southwest Texas State University, the modern avatar of Johnson's alma mater. It was a grim time for me and for most other young academics. The job market for freshly minted Ph.D.s in history had contracted sharply, suddenly, and, it seemed, permanently. Hundreds of candidates applied for each opening in American history. My writing on my dissertation had stalled, in large part because I could see no reason to finish it. But I knew I had a real shot at the job at SWTSU. Many of the historians there had Ph.D.s from the University of Texas, and the department was in the habit of hiring promising doctoral candidates in the graduate program at Austin to teach at Southwest Texas for a year or two. Even more fortunately for me, the historian at UT who maintained the closest and most amicable ties with the colleagues at San Marcos was my mentor and dissertation director. He was pushing me hard for this position. He realized that I needed a job teaching to boost my morale and give me the impetus to finish my degree. It also would provide the practical experience that would make me more attractive to prospective employers in the future. He was optimistic. So was I. I shared this optimism with Dad when I spoke with him by phone right after I sent my application to the chair of the department at Southwest Texas.

Not long after my father hung up, Jesse Kellam happened to call him. With no urging from Dad, he decided to do what he could to help. He announced that he would call the chair and recommend me as a bright young man he had met and as the son of an old friend and important adviser of the Johnsons. Dad was inexperienced in the ways of academics and didn't tell him not to do that. He had no idea this was the worst thing Kellam could possibly have done.

To say professors do not appreciate direct intervention by political figures in personnel decisions at a university is to understate their usual reactions considerably. Not only does this call into question principles of academic freedom; it also has the potential to create dangerous precedents for future abuses. The chair felt obliged to report Kellam's call to his colleagues. Predictably, they were less than happy. Some observed there were plenty of other qualified candidates; at least one, according to report, was ready to reject me on principled grounds. Luckily for me, the meeting ground to a halt without any immediate decision.

By pure chance, I phoned Dad again that afternoon on another matter. As we were talking, he mentioned that Kellam promised to recommend me to the department. I was stunned. It is the only time in my life I have ever truly felt my blood run cold.

With an effort, I made myself dial the chair's number. When he came on the line, I hadn't rehearsed myself. I didn't know exactly what I'd say, but I sensed I had to risk the job to preserve any possibility of getting it. In rapid-fire succession I told him that I knew what had happened; that I had nothing to do with Kellam's call; that I was sorry for it; that I would perfectly understand if he and the faculty wanted nothing to do with me; and that I was willing to withdraw my application if doing so made rejecting me easier and safer for them. I closed by offering to withdraw it right then and there if he wished.

A pause followed, then a dry laugh. "I don't think people should be held responsible for what friends of their fathers do out of the goodness of their hearts," the chair said. "I don't see any reason for you to withdraw." A week later, he called to invite me down for an interview. It went well, and by the Fourth of July I had the job.

When I got the offer, I called my father with the good news. It was a joyous occasion. Our happiness was not diminished by our discussion of Kellam's role, which I brought up. Dad said he was glad he now knew more about how professors reacted to personal intercessions from the political realm. Then he observed that the UT Law School had finally decided against requiring any references for applicants in an effort to avoid the problem. He was much more gracious than I was. I didn't keep to myself my pleasure and pride at entering a profession that, I was convinced, resisted the open and crude applications of power and influence identified with LBJ and his cronies. Academe was a finer, more humane, more principled world. It would not be perfect; I was smart enough to figure that out ahead of time. But it would be better; of that, I was sure.

Dad was too kind to point out the similarities between the two worlds. He did not remind me that my dissertation director had played an important part in my getting the offer. Many of my new colleagues at San Marcos were friends of his, trusted his judgment, and were eager —once they had been reassured by my reaction to Jesse Kellam's phone call—to help out a student of his. My father refrained from observing that academics evidently had an "old boy" network, too, and from speculating that favors were exchanged in that marketplace of lofty ideas as briskly as they were in the political arenas of Austin and Washington. He expected, I suppose, that I'd learn that for myself. Certainly I didn't know it then. At that time, though I was aware I wasn't entering a perfect world, I was sure it was better than the one he and Kellam and LBJ inhabited, at least for me. As things turned out, I've learned that being a professor of history was better for me than other careers. I no longer believe, however, that academics are any more principled than people in other lines of work or walks of life. But that's another book!

★ ★ ★

When historians, journalists, and people who knew him try to sum up Lyndon Johnson, invariably they fall into a recitation of extremes. He was this, but he was also that. He was an elemental force; he was monumentally insecure. He was enormously hard working at all times; he was prey to periods of depressed inaction in certain crises. He was stunningly generous; he was incredibly mean-spirited. And so on, and so forth. Much of this ranging through thesis and antithesis overlooks the fact that the same could be said, to a lesser degree, of almost everybody. All men and women are mixtures of good and bad, rough and smooth.

Some of the people who lived, worked, and visited with LBJ loved him. Some despised him. I've known representative members of both groups. A remarkable woman married Lyndon Johnson, and I'm certain she loved him deeply and faithfully. Another remarkable woman, my mother, could not stand him. To her, he was an immoral bully; to say he was self-centered was, for Mother, belaboring the obvious.

Many other people had mixed reactions to Lyndon Johnson. My father was one. Impressed with his intelligence and his obvious talents, grateful for his gifts and favors, proud of their friendship, and yet determined to maintain a healthy independence and distance from him: that defines the boundaries of Dad's relationship with him over thirty-three years. I'm one of the ambivalent ones, too. During my visit to his ranch, Lyndon Johnson showered gifts upon me and graciously offered me the hospitality of his home. To be sure, his hospitality turned into hostility when I started to miss shots. I must concede he ultimately said he was sorry—publicly and gracefully—and apologized for doubting my skill as a marksman and my explanation of the problem with the rifle he gave me. That apology does not, however, cancel out the biting cruelty of his comments on my shooting that second day of hunting. Nor does it make up for the fact that he tested my analysis of the problem with the rifle before an audience. I can continue this litany: his barely masked contempt for Jake Jacobsen disturbed me; his treatment of the agents and his staff as mindless servants who opened and closed gates and drank or abstained at his command troubled me; his identification of dissenters with communists astonished and concerned me; and his appropriation of his neighbor's potatoes and pudding without permission or thanks forever defined bad manners for me. You'll notice these lists aren't equally long. My reactions to LBJ ranged between two extremes, attraction and repulsion. If you conclude from what I've just said that on the whole I'm closer to the repulsion end of the spectrum, you'd be right. If you also gather that LBJ fascinated me, and that my fascination stemmed both from what I liked and what I disliked about him, you're right once more.

But as I look back on my time at the ranch and the stories I've heard about other visits by members of my family, my thoughts return time and again to how lucky Lyndon Johnson was at crucial points in his life. I'm reminded of that because, now that I'm close to the age the president was in late 1965, I've learned that no one succeeds in any profession or calling purely on the basis of her or his own skill and intelligence. As I've just noted, take away two phone calls on a June afternoon in 1974, and my life in all probability would have been very different. The first of those calls, the one to my father, was pure good fortune. Without it, I never would have known about Jesse Kellam's intervention until it was too late. For that matter, had someone else been the chair of that department, the fate of my candidacy might have already been sealed. In LBJ's life, there were much more dramatic strokes of luck. Two stand out from all the rest.

The first happened in the South Pacific on June 9, 1942. When LBJ prepared to go along on a bombing mission from northern Australia against the Japanese base at Lae on New Guinea, he chose to fly in a B-26 named the *Wabash Cannonball*. During a delay before takeoff, he stepped off the plane to urinate. Another officer took his place and refused to give it back to Johnson, who then switched to the *Heckling Hare*. Enemy fighters attacked the squadron near its target. Despite losing its right engine and subsequently being mauled by Zeroes, the *Hare* managed to make its way back home. The *Cannonball* crashed into the Pacific. No one on board survived.

What saved Lyndon Johnson that day wasn't his intelligence, or his hard work, or his courage under fire, or his political skills. It was a delayed mission and a desperate need to piss. Without this, he wouldn't have become president. He would have been dead.

The other dramatic swing of fortune occurred in Dallas on November 22, 1963. Lyndon Johnson became president because John Kennedy was murdered that day. This, of course, was obvious to everyone. Less apparent, perhaps—or, maybe, just unremarked—is the answer to this question: how else could he have become president?

I cannot imagine the Kennedys supporting LBJ for the Democratic nomination in 1968. In fact, once the 1964 campaign was safely behind them, I believe Johnson's position as vice president and his reputation would have deteriorated even more rapidly than it did between 1961-1963. By 1968 few would remember and fewer would care about his Senate career in the 1950s. Robert Kennedy wouldn't forget his dislike and distrust of Johnson just because his brother won re-election. And LBJ would still confront the nearly insurmountable obstacle of being a "Southern" candidate. Moreover, this scenario presumes the Kennedy-Johnson ticket won in 1964. Had it lost, Johnson would have come in for a full share of the blame, especially since any victorious Republican would have carried several states in the South. It is hard to imagine a defeated party turning to the losing vice presidential candidate in a later election, unless it had to settle for a sacrificial lamb like Walter Mondale in 1984. On November 21, 1963, LBJ stood absolutely no chance of becoming president. His dream was dead.

Would there have been a Johnson presidency if LBJ hadn't needed to take a leak at Garbutt Field in June 1942 or if Lee Harvey Oswald hadn't shot straight at Dealey Plaza in November 1963? No.

Did Johnson know this? You bet he did.

LBJ and JFK in Austin, November 16, 1960.
LBJ Library. Photo by Art Kowert.

For the rest of his life, he wore the ribbon of the Silver Star Douglas MacArthur awarded him for going on one mission and being under fire. To give him his due, he was cool and courageous when the *Heckling Hare* was in dire straits. Still, there was no way he'd earned his country's third highest-ranking medal for valor. Unembarrassed by this fact, over the years he inflated his role in the South Pacific.

The grimmest part of Johnson's recounting of his wartime experiences was the fate of the *Wabash Cannonball* and its crew. We know about his narrow escape from death because he talked about it. We know that the officer who took his seat "just grinned" and told him to "find another plane" because LBJ described the scene so colorfully to his audiences. No intelligent, thoughtful person could tell such a story without being aware of the critical role luck plays in life. Lyndon Johnson was certainly intelligent and thoughtful. And, because he was LBJ, he could turn his brush with death into a harbinger of future destiny.

Johnson never discussed his deepest, most private reactions to John Kennedy's assassination. Was this evil deed a piece of good or bad luck for him? No question it was a traumatic event. In its immediate aftermath, the new president was so disturbed that he insisted that an aide stand watch by his bedside while he slept. What the nature and dimensions of that trauma were cannot be gauged. Perhaps LBJ didn't try to measure them himself; surely, no one else can plumb their depths. We can be certain that he had no illusions about Robert Kennedy's attitude toward him, and that he distrusted the loyalties of Kennedy appointees in the federal government and in the Democratic Party's hierarchy. The tapes of his conversations in the Oval Office leave no doubt that he felt these people would have preferred someone else as president and might turn against him in 1964 if he did not handle them carefully. Until he won election to the office himself, he was an accidental president, elevated by tragedy to a position many believed he never would have attained under any other circumstances. The political ramifications of this belief challenged his powers. They also served to remind him of the central part fortune played in human affairs and how it had shaped the destiny he yearned to fulfill.

I believe the man I hunted deer with in December 1965 was someone who was starting to be scared that luck had turned against him. The principal cause of his fear was Vietnam, although other problems contributed to it as well. More clearly than those other difficulties, though, the situation in Southeast Asia seemed to be slipping beyond his control.

An article published during those years on Johnson and the war so perfectly captured his frustration that I still recall the image, even though I have long since forgotten the author and the journal. The president was likened to the billiard shark in the song "Let the Punishment Fit the Crime" from Gilbert and Sullivan's *The Mikado*. "The billiard shark/Whom anyone catches" had a fate "extremely hard." "He's made to dwell/In a dungeon cell/On a spot that's always barred." There, he must play endless "extravagant matches...

> On a cloth untrue,
> With a twisted cue,
> And elliptical billiard balls!"

All his skill, all his experience did not count for much under these conditions. He could no longer call his shots and be sure that his stroke would deposit the proper ball in the right pocket. He might even inadvertently sink the eight ball and lose the game. No shot could be exactly calculated and precisely executed; no result predictable and secure. And this was only part of the punishment. Worst of all, he couldn't stop playing.

Whoever wrote this, the allusion was brilliantly chosen. It was also a vicious metaphor, for it portrays Lyndon Johnson, who wanted to do good for his country and change lives for the better, as a hustler, someone who tricks people into thinking he is not what he is and fleeces them of their money. A kinder choice would have compared him to a good shot who is handed a rifle with an inaccurate telescopic sight and told to kill a trophy buck.

I didn't visit Lyndon Johnson in Washington. Nor did I sit in on any meetings over Vietnam or the Great Society. Thus I never saw this frustration or this sense of ebbing fortune directly expressed. But I was with LBJ at his ranch, where he could do as he damn pleased. On the ranch, he could control people and events. There he could pretend that luck didn't matter and that hard work, an informed intelligence, and a determination to achieve would always prevail. So if I didn't shoot well with the rifle he had given me, that was my fault, not any failing of his or of those he sent to buy and bring it to me. The wages of failure, as I discovered, were sharp, pointed criticism and an unwillingness at first to believe that the weapon itself might be flawed.

LBJ's practical joke with the amphibious car and his elaborate preparation for surprising the priest with new pews also illustrate how compelled he felt to demonstrate he hadn't lost his power to control. The enjoyment a successful practical joker derives from his or her plot is based upon the ability to deceive others, to predict their reactions, and to manipulate the human and physical environment to get the desired effect. It is one of the cruelest forms of humor precisely because in the end the victims realize they have been played for fools. Whether they join in the laughter or not, the joke is on them. The architects of the deceptions earn their guffaws by proving themselves smarter than those who fall into the traps. In the case of Johnson's "experimental car," the newlyweds leaped into the trap and became literally all wet.

Yet many things that happened at the ranch revealed the president's inability to dictate the course of events even in the small corner of the world the Texas Broadcasting Corporation owned. Dad flatly and publicly advised him not to try to deduct the deer I shot, and thereby quietly and privately refused to play along with whatever game the president had in mind by making such a proposal. LBJ ended this sport immediately, without protesting. The marine orderly patiently and slyly bore up under his harangues. LBJ couldn't provoke a response. The priest paid him back, by crediting Luci for the new pews. Finding or putting people in awkward situations where their religious heritage might embarrass them had always amused LBJ: witness his delight at Bill Moyers twisting the night away, Jake Jacobsen genuflecting and buying kneelers on command, and Arthur Goldberg flying off to see the Pope. Father Schneider denied him that pleasure by giving credit to one of his own. And, although the president made a funny story out of the episode, it also clearly reminded him of the galling reality that many other people denied him any claim to the much good he had done. The old cowboy proved at the corral that no one had sighted-in my rifle. LBJ was certainly moved by this revelation to apologize to me; I also believe the overwhelming number of gifts he gave me afterwards were partially intended to offset his harsh criticism the day before.

More dramatically than these other episodes, Wilma's hard landing on the dam, the extent of her injuries, and the narrow margin by which she escaped a broken pelvis revealed Lyndon Johnson to himself as well as others, to be extremely careless of human limb and life. He was horrified and apologized profusely, then and later. As he did, he had to confront the truth that he had been incredibly negligent not to realize the potential for harm. He also had to notice that his planning had not allowed for the possibility of serious injury, and it definitely should have. After my stepmother's fall, there were no repetitions of the amphibious car prank. Wilma later heard that Lady Bird bluntly told the president "to put a stop" to that prank. Wisely, he obeyed her command. But even so, LBJ could not resist acting out the stories of couples who did spring "safely" into the Pedernales, carefully cutting my stepmother's role out of the performance. As a result, on tours of the ranch today, the bus drivers point out the half-car half-motorboat and explain how Johnson used it without any reference to Wilma Bullion's accident. People laugh at the story—or at least everyone but my wife, daughter, and I did when we took the tour in 1995. I suspect this laughter of unthinking folks was for Lyndon Johnson a distant second-best to playing his practical joke time and again.

So even on the ranch there were portents that things were awry, that luck was running against him, and that his ability to dominate

LBJ searches for answers in the corner, while Marvin Watson,
Waddy Bullion, Bill Moyers, Harry Macpherson, and (with
back to camera) Joseph Califano wait, May 11, 1965.
LBJ Library. Photo by Yoichi R. Okamoto.

people and control things was slipping away. I suspect this, as well as
his preoccupations with weightier affairs in the larger world, explains
the moodiness and the periods of silent, brooding concentration that I
observed in late 1965. What effect did these developments have on his
ability to lead and to govern?

At the conclusion of his biography of LBJ, Robert Dallek asked a
similar question, apropos of his subject's "irrational conviction that his
domestic opponents were subversives or dupes of subversives intent
on undermining national institutions." This "paranoia," he observed,
"raises questions about his judgment and capacity to make rational life
and death judgments." Dallek finally concluded that despite "the
cranky nonsense he espoused about his enemies," Lyndon Johnson
remained essentially in control of his faculties and more than capable of
discharging his duties.

I personally heard some of this nonsense at his dining room table.
I've never doubted that he was absolutely convinced *New York Times*
reporters were communists. I saw his reaction to my father's joke
about my draft card. I've never questioned that he despised protesters
against the war and regarded them as fundamentally unpatriotic and,

indeed, anti-American. In those cases, seeing and hearing were believing. To regard this as a sign of irritation or stubborn eccentricity, as pet peeves LBJ could easily set aside at more rational moments, is in my opinion to misunderstand how deeply he felt and how strongly he believed what he said. That he felt compelled to try to hide that feeling signaled the turning of his luck and the loss of his control, too. It marked the limits of power far short of where he felt they had to be in order for him to continue to achieve greatness. Like Dallek, I'm persuaded he remained fully capable of making decisions and being the president. I also think it was hard, oh so very hard, for him to do that. And I believe I understand part of the reason why.

★ ★ ★

Lyndon Johnson had been his mama's boy. That hadn't changed, though she'd died years earlier. The lessons she taught him, the confidence she gave him, had guided him to spectacular successes. Ironically, however, she didn't prepare him for what he faced now, and she had offered no clues for how to deal with his present situation.

LBJ's mother, like other mamas of that era and the succeeding one, simply didn't believe in blind luck or inescapable fate. I can recite the following axioms for you without any trouble whatsoever, because I heard them often enough from Mother. You make your own luck. Bad luck follows bad habits; it doesn't cause them. Good luck results from preparation, determination, intelligence, and, most of all, hard work; it comes because you deserve it. To be sure, God's grace is freely given. The Lord can, and doubtless does, save the most unregenerate souls when He chooses to. But success is earned. If you suffer a run of bad luck, find out what you are doing wrong, and stop doing it. Start working longer and harder and better. Impose your will on people and events. You'll soon see the results. Bad luck will change to good. Once that happens, nothing can keep a good man down.

Prior to his becoming president, all of Lyndon Johnson's experiences in life testified to the truth of these teachings. As years passed in the White House, though, new questions arose in his mind. What if you do all this, and your luck doesn't change? What if the harder you try, the more people and events elude your grasp? What if everything gets worse after your best efforts? Mama's examples and teachings don't provide these answers. They lose their potency to encourage perseverance. Her boy can't rely on them as confidently as before. But he can't turn loose of them either, because there's nothing to put in their place except complete reliance on dumb, blind luck.

When LBJ realized this, the sensation for him must have been akin to vertigo. He was looking down from the highest pinnacle of power and seeing the slopes and meadows below him blur and spin and the familiar dissolve into monstrous new shapes and realities. His mother's lessons helped him hang on. He didn't completely lose his balance and plunge to his doom. But he could no longer exercise sufficient power to control the whirling landscape and make it stable, predictable, comprehensible, and governable again.

For whatever reason—or for no reason at all—he'd become unlucky. He was learning that luck wasn't necessarily the residue of design and effort, as his mother had said. Nor could he change it by his own efforts, by helping himself, as she had promised. Bad luck is a horrible fate for anyone. It was infinitely harder on LBJ, because it refuted the verities his mother taught him and he had embraced as his own. Worse still, it left him faced with the possibility of taking the one option Rebekah Johnson would never, ever have advised him to take: he could quit. Ultimately, of course, that's what Lyndon Johnson decided to do. Then he spent the four unhappy years remaining to him living with that decision.

Those who want to experience vicariously LBJ's discontent during his last days need only scan the final passages in any one of the several studies of him. The most intimate and touching account is his own, as told to Doris Kearns Goodwin and published in her splendid work *Lyndon Johnson and the American Dream*.

This book shows him trying to confront what his childhood had been like and what impacts his father and mother had on him. Hard times play a role in these reminiscences as well. The subjects he had regarded as unimportant and irrelevant when he talked with my father had become highly consequential to him during his days of exile on the Pedernales. The man who insisted he could shape history now wanted to discover how history had shaped him. No longer did he feel that it affected only those not strong enough to master it. No more could he say he was immune from its contagions. The seas his boat rode on were swelling and pitching and heaving; their currents had torn the tiller from his hand. He had become merely a passenger, drifting where the tides took him. Could he get out and walk on home? He couldn't be

LBJ alone, *in extremis*, 1968.
LBJ Library. Photo by Jack Kightlinger.

certain, and the uncertainty must have chewed him up inside. Lyndon Johnson had learned this for sure: without faith in his power, he couldn't walk on water.

Though I can sympathize with LBJ when I think about him struggling against this fate, in my opinion his was not a sympathetic character. Did I like him? No. Did I think he was a good man? Again, my answer is no. I do not go so far as to regard him as an evil man, if that term is defined as someone uniquely and completely wicked. The years since the Bullions visited him on the ranch have convinced me that many people would be strongly tempted to be just as cruel as he was with the amphibious car if they had his power and enjoyed his freedom from any fear of reprisal. While I'm unwilling to forgive him for this joke, I believe his yielding to that and other temptations should be balanced against the good he did during his life. That brings up another matter. Did I think he was a great man? I have to say I didn't see any signs of greatness at the ranch, though I certainly respected and admired many of his accomplishments, then and now.

One last question: would I have gotten in the boat if he had asked me? That's impossible to answer without qualification or elaboration. I certainly understood the necessity of maintaining a degree of separation and independence from him. I saw how he coerced and bullied those around him. I remembered the sting of his criticism of me. I observed and experienced how difficult it is to correct or to say "no" to a president of the United States. Certainly I became aware that knowing the powerful and having their support can be a very mixed blessing, one which can leave their friends vulnerable to attack as easily as it can raise them up. But having said all that, I know I would have been tempted to answer "yes" and clamber aboard. Lyndon Johnson gave those close to him chances to try to change the world, and he promised he would give his all and demand their best in the effort. How seductive that would have been!

My head tells me it's best this didn't happen. I remember what Bill Moyers sadly said when he left the White House, how he had hoped to make Johnson more like Bill Moyers, but instead discovered to his anguish Moyers was becoming more like Lyndon Johnson. But when I let it, my heart wonders what I missed.

CHAPTER 18

Watches

Around Christmas time in 1972, the Johnsons invited Dad and Wilma down to the ranch for the usual mixture of business and pleasure. My father and LBJ talked about the Texas Broadcasting Corporation, the ranch, and adjustments and decisions that had to be made for tax purposes before the end of the year. Wilma and Bird chatted about life and the season. Although Johnson had been very ill during the summer and still looked unwell, there was no feeling that this might be the last visit. The only thing out of the ordinary during that day happened when LBJ autographed a picture of himself on the ranch. After thinking briefly, he inscribed it "For Waddy, from his friend through the years, Lyndon B. Johnson."

The photograph itself is one of Dad's favorites. Johnson is wearing a red-checked shirt, open at the throat. His Stetson is pushed back on his head, he has his glasses on, and his hair is long and curling around his ears and neck. Smiling and relaxed, he obviously is peering at something or someone that is pleasing him very much. One would be justified in thinking this is someone at peace with himself, and thus blessed, for that moment at least. Contemplating that picture, then glancing up at Dad and remembering the years since 1940, he wanted to acknowledge the friendship that had survived years in the boat together. Those words had significance then. They have even more in light of his impending death.

★ ★ ★

That night, my folks made their excuses and went to bed right after dinner. Their flight from Austin to Dallas took off first thing in the morning. To get to the airport on time, they would have to leave very early. LBJ agreed and made the arrangements for the helicopter. He also told them there'd be coffee in the kitchen, so they wouldn't have to face the ride from the ranch without any refreshment.

When Dad and Wilma went down to the kitchen at 5:00 a.m., they found him already there, preparing coffee. As it percolated, he told them how much he appreciated their friendship. With a grin, he hauled out two presents. "Open 'em now!" he insisted. As they did, he could barely contain his glee at their surprise. In each package, there was a gold Rolex watch. "Turn 'em over," he ordered. "Look what's written on the back."

On Wilma's watch was engraved,

> "To Wilma
> With Love
> LBJ"

Whether he felt real love for her is beside the point. This sentiment displays his heartfelt appreciation for what she had forgiven him and for how she participated so cheerfully in other adventures together.

My father's read,

> "To Waddy
> The Best
> LBJ"

These words were the highest praise imaginable for a man who ceaselessly demanded the best in effort and production from those who worked for him, and who was rarely totally satisfied with their attempts and the results.

As they thanked him for the watches and the thoughts, each had the poise not to dim the moment's glow by pointing out a mistake the jeweler made. The president's sentiments had been dated 1-1-72, rather than 1-1-73. Without speaking, they had simultaneously determined this would spoil the pleasure of pre-dawn fellowship and coffee with him in the kitchen. The watches were another flawed gift, like the lakehouse. Unlike it, though, they weren't apt to cause problems for their new owners.

The three drained their cups quickly. As they stood up from the table, LBJ laughed aloud. "Waddy," he said, "over the years I've given you a lot of cufflinks, pens, pencils, pictures, buttons, and a couple of books. With this watch, you've got one of everything I've got. Except, of course,"—here he chuckled—"my wife." Then he pointed out with a sly smile that it was time for them to go, putting enough emphasis on *time* to draw attention once more to the presents. A hug and a kiss for

Wilma, a handshake for Dad, and they moved out of the kitchen and through the still house toward the door closest to the runway. At the door, LBJ made his usual farewell to my father—"I'll see you again soon"—and then said, "Bird and I would like you two to go with us to Acapulco in February." As surprised as they had been by the news they were going to a football game, Dad and Wilma said they'd be delighted to come along. "We'll be in touch," LBJ promised. One more round of goodbyes, and they got into the car, leaving him behind.

★ ★ ★

On January 22, 1973, the final day of his life, LBJ spent most of the morning talking on the phone with various people about his firm intention to be more active and get out more during the coming year. He set the phone aside and had Jewell Malechek, the wife of his foreman, drive him around the ranch. He wanted to check the deer fences and make sure they were still keeping his whitetails enclosed. He must have been satisfied his property was safely confined, because he left no orders for repairs.

LBJ looking at deer fences, April 11, 1966.
LBJ Library. Photo by Frank Wolfe.

Just as he had on other recent days, LBJ tired swiftly. After a light lunch, he went to bed for a nap. When he woke up, he immediately called the Secret Service office for help. Before the agents could reach his bedroom, he had collapsed on the floor. He died quickly.

It snowed a couple of days before his funeral. Most of the snow melted overnight, but there were still dirty gray mounds on the north side of 290 as my sister and I drove west from Austin. The weather was cold and cloudy, and a sharp breeze made the temperature feel lower than the thirties. I wore my darkest suit and a pair of black wingtips I'd bought for the occasion. Ann had on a Sunday-go-to-meeting dress and high heels. We agreed we were wearing the sort of clothes you wore for a visit to the LBJ Ranch. I joked that I was ready to hunt; even though I preferred to shoot deer from a Lincoln, I guessed I could do it just as well from a Toyota. "I'm not opening gates," my sister replied. Then she closed her eyes and slept the rest of the way to Johnson City.

We had agreed to meet Dad and Wilma at a barbecue joint in town. They beat us there. When Ann and I came in, they waved us over to their table. Dad advised getting the chopped brisket without sauce, coleslaw, red beans, and a bag of potato chips. This was served cafeteria style, so my sister and I got in line and loaded our trays. The place filled rapidly with men and women dressed for the funeral. The Texans among them made their choices swiftly and decisively and didn't seem surprised or disturbed that customers got a slice of white Wonder Bread with their orders. Those from out of state stared at the steaming serving trays for a long time, then at the posted bill of fare and prices, then back again at the food before deciding.

I overheard one man reassuring his female companion that the *New York Times* had pronounced the barbecued beef here "very good" and praised the chicken fried steak with cream gravy as "excellent." "Don't believe what those Reds write," I muttered half to Ann, half to myself, "they're out to subvert us from within." She asked me what I was talking about, and I said, "Never mind." As I paid the cashier, I wondered how Lyndon Johnson would have reacted to the judgments of *Times* reporters on Hill Country cuisine. Would they have put him off his feed? Probably not.

There wasn't much talk at our table, or anywhere else in the restaurant. Dad was subdued. People who knew him stopped by to say hello, but he offered little in return beyond the usual courtesies. One man remarked, "Well, Waddy, you've lost a friend." My father didn't respond at all to this invitation to reminisce about LBJ. His friendship with Lyndon Johnson was too complicated to be described at this time and in this place with those who hadn't been in the boat.

I surveyed the scene to see if I recognized anyone famous among the politicians, lobbyists, and political hangers-on from Austin and Washington there. Suddenly, I realized none of them were working the room. They were sticking to their own tables and talking only to those sitting with them. LBJ, I was certain, wouldn't have approved of this reticence. He would have seen it as an opportunity missed. However much he might have respected the dearly departed, he wouldn't have passed by a chance to remind so many people about who he was.

After we finished eating, we agreed to return to Austin and Dallas right after the funeral. My father had no desire to go up to the house. He'd see Lady Bird and her daughters soon and often, as LBJ's will went through probate. At that time, he'd express his and our condolences privately and personally. There's no fun and not much point, he said, in struggling through hundreds of people in packed rooms to speak with family members for one or two minutes. Nobody argued with him. Ann had to teach school the next day; I had a meeting scheduled first thing in the morning with my dissertation director. We needed to get back as soon as we could. That settled, the four of us left for the ranch.

We parked in a field just off the state road. Her Toyota, Ann observed, looked out of place among the Continentals and Cadillacs. "Poor folks have poor cars," she pointed out. Then she added, "At least we'll have no trouble picking it out." We put on topcoats and walked up the road. Mercifully for Ann and Wilma in their heels, we didn't have far to go.

As we approached the Pedernales, Dad paused, watched for a moment, smiled, and then said, "See up there at the crossing. They're separating the sheep from the goats." A few folks were being ferried in government vans across the dam to the other side; most were milling about by the bank or drifting across the meadow toward a large tent. It was apparent dignitaries and those closest to the Johnsons would be under the trees right next to the cemetery. Everyone else would watch from the far side of the river.

"Which side are we on, Waddy?" asked Wilma.

"I guess this one," he replied, "I haven't heard anything else."

She looked closely at him, then quietly said, "Waddy, I believe the president would have wanted you close to him. I believe Lady Bird would want you there."

My father chuckled softly. "I don't think the president has any wishes one way or the other on that right now," he answered. The finality of that thought—LBJ at long last without wishes, desires, ambitions, demands, or commands—must have startled him. His mouth remained open for a long instant, he seemed ready to say something else, then he closed it and half turned away from us. Wilma reached out toward him, ready to comfort if comfort was needed.

That mood was swiftly broken. "Waddy!" boomed a familiar voice. "It's great to see you." We all broke into smiles. Irving Goldberg bustled up, full of good cheer, loudly praising Wilma's beauty, and enthusiastically remarking on how grown up Ann and I looked and the obvious promise we showed for great things. This done, he turned to his old friend, regretted for a moment their mutual loss, and then got down to what was on his mind.

"Waddy," he announced with mock solemnity "I have conceived a great desire to be on the other side of the river and, of course, to pay my family's respects directly to Mrs. Johnson after the service. As a mere federal judge, I am not on the cemetery list. So I want to ask you to use your influence to get me there." Then he winked and whispered, in a mock conspirational tone, "My wife and I could go as members of your family."

"Irving," Dad said, "I'm not sure my influence extends to getting any of us over there. I got no invitation or indication that I was supposed to be there."

"You should try, Waddy," interjected Wilma, "I really think you should."

"Wilma's right," decreed Judge Goldberg. "Go tell them who you are."

Dad smiled and obediently went over to talk to a sergeant who was standing by the low-water crossing. We trailed behind.

"I'm Waddy Bullion," Dad told the young sergeant, "and I wonder if my family and associates and I are on the guest list for the cemetery and the house."

"I'll check, sir," the sergeant said. He asked how our name was spelled, ran his eye down a list a couple of times, and said, "I'm sorry, sir, there's no Bullion here."

My father glanced at his friend and his wife, whose faces registered their keen disappointment. Then, in an act that had to be inspired by long friendship and deep love, he persisted, "Would you mind calling the house? I was President Johnson's friend and lawyer for thirty years."

"Of course not, sir," answered the sergeant. He hauled out a portable phone, dialed a number, and spoke briefly to someone. The answer was the same. There was no Bullion on the list, and no one who wasn't on that list could cross the river.

Dad thanked the sergeant for his courtesy and for making the call; the young man repeated that he was sorry. What solemnity the moment held was quickly dispelled, once more by Irving Goldberg. "Well, hell, you tried, Waddy! I thank you for the attempt on my behalf. Now, let's go over to that tent, where it's out of the wind and, I understand, we can get a drink!"

He was right. The atmosphere in the tent was less chilly. Its canvas blocked the breeze, and the press of bodies warmed its interior. A crowd gathered around tables stocked with orange juice, bloody mary mix, and vodka. John Hill, who ranched nearby in the Hill Country and owned an independent oil company, welcomed us at the entrance and claimed credit for the vodka. "Have some," he invited genially, "it'll warm you up on a cold day." We were all grateful for the relative warmth, but only the judge went over to have a drink.

LBJ with newly appointed federal judges from Texas, with
Irving Goldberg seated at the far right, July 21, 1966.
LBJ Library. Photo by Yoichi R. Okamoto.

Soon Dad looked at his watch and said, "It's about time." Either others reached the same conclusion at precisely that moment, or our departure sparked a general exodus out of the tent and into the field. Being among the first to leave shelter, we got a good place close to the bank, in front of a mott of live oaks, with a clear view of the cemetery.

As I peered across the river, I tried to pick out the trees I had wandered under seven years before, looking for the right spot. Then my gaze moved to the low-water crossing over the dam, where Wilma had leaped out and landed hard. On this day, the water was a frigid gray. We stood under the live oaks, trying to use them as a windbreak, and feeling the damp of the grass seep into our shoes.

As happens at funerals, people drifted from place to place until likes clumped with likes. Lawyers my father knew gravitated toward him, and judges as well. Hal Woodard, a federal judge from Lubbock, stood next to us and talked with Dad briefly about their law school days. Sarah Hughes came over. We congratulated her on her decision to wear lowcut boots. "I chose warmth over style," she replied.

Indeed she had. No one commented on the clear plastic covers she wore over her boots. These contraptions, which looked like she had tied large Baggies around her ankles, were the antithesis of fashion. Judge Hughes completed the effect by pulling a plastic rain hat out of her purse, unfolding it, putting it on, and tying its dangling straps loosely under her chin. Most of those around her were probably thinking they preferred discomfort to dis-couture.

Suddenly that familiar voice boomed out once more: "Sarah! It's great to see you." It was Irving Goldberg, rejoining us, and again altering the prevailing mood with his enthusiasm and his wonderful laugh. My father smiled. "Let me petition you, Judge Goldberg," he intoned, "to do something about the cold here."

"Waddy," his old friend replied, "I'm afraid my writ doesn't run here, in the fields outside Johnson City. You'll have to appeal to a much higher court."

Here he glanced upward and rolled his eyes. Everyone in the circle laughed, the judges most of all.

The funeral started. Like everyone else, we were still when Billy Graham prayed. While Anita Bryant sang "The Battle Hymn of the Republic," we resumed shifting from foot to foot and moving in small circles, in attempts to keep the blood flowing and to find a spot free from wind. Famous people; national reputations; careful choices. A prayer studiously nondenominational, delivered by a man whose very

LBJ and Judge Sarah Hughes, September 12, 1964.
LBJ Library. Photo by O.J. Rapp.

appearance and widespread fame denied the reality of a priesthood of believers. The country's hymn, belonging to everyone and therefore no one, rather than verses inviting us all to gather with the saints at the river, or one assuring Lyndon Johnson that he could lay down his sword and shield—right there!—down by the riverside, and comforting him with the knowledge he ain't gonna study war no more. No person, no prayer, no hymn spoke for Texas.

Then John Connally did. I remember his big, confident voice, tinted with a South Texas accent, as he answered outsiders who were scornful of his mentor. "Some people said Lyndon Johnson was insecure. Of course he was insecure!" Those who seek to change the world for the better, he went on, are never secure with the way the world is or their present place in it.

It was an interesting, even arresting assertion. I suspect his audience was too uncomfortable and too eager for the ceremony to end to think about it for more than a moment. Much more welcome, because they signaled that he was finishing, were Connally's eloquent words: "Along this stream and under these trees he loved he will now find rest.

He first saw light here. He last felt life here. May he now find peace here." The color guard proceeded toward the grave.

"Look over there," Judge Goldberg whispered in an excited tone. He grabbed my arm and turned me so I could see, behind us and to our left, Sarah Hughes. Somehow she had overcome the clumsiness of her footwear and climbed into the lower branches of a live oak that had spread outward close to the ground. Her left arm wrapped around its trunk, her right arm holding a branch above her head, she was looking over the heads around us toward the cemetery.

"What a great photograph that would be," my father's friend went on. "She swore him in as president, and there she is, watching him be buried. Where," he asked rhetorically, "are newspapermen when you need them?"

The answer unspoken by me was, "Watching LBJ, just like he'd want them to be doing."

I noticed my father and stepmother, my sister, and Hal Woodard had heard Irving Goldberg as well. We all were staring at Sarah Hughes, the judge who had legitimated his last great stroke of luck and now bore silent and dignified witness above the cold, wet grass to his final rites.

Then, as one, we turned away. Along with Judge Hughes and the rest of the crowd, we watched as Lyndon Johnson began his return to the soil of his beloved ranch.

Live oak near the LBJ Ranch House, December 12, 1965.
LBJ Library. Photo by Yoichi R. Okamoto.

If the Lord had not been on our side,
    let Israel now say;
If the Lord had not been on our side,
    when enemies rose up against us;
Then they would have swallowed us up alive
    in their fierce anger toward us;
Then would the waters have overwhelmed us
    and the torrent gone over us;
Then would the raging waters
    have gone right over us.
Blessed be the Lord!
    he has not given us over to be a prey for their teeth.
We have escaped like a bird from the snare of the fowler;
    the snare is broken, and we have escaped.
Our help is in the Name of the Lord,
    the maker of heaven and earth.

—Psalm 124

Honest Lawyer
    One Flight Up

    —sign in the stairwell
      at The Barn, W^2 Ranch

Coda

Soon after Winter Semester classes began in January 1999, the president of the undergraduate history association knocked on my office door. The UHA was having trouble finding faculty able to talk with them about issues in history during February. Could I make a presentation? "You can speak about anything," she added by way of encouragement. I agreed. Then, on the spur of the moment, I told her I'd talk about my experiences with Lyndon Johnson. She seemed pleased and pressed me for a title. "'Hunting Buddies: Personal Reminiscences of LBJ,'" I immediately answered. She thought that would do fine.

I chose the subject for the sake of convenience. I'd regularly given abbreviated versions of my trip to the LBJ Ranch to my classes in American political history as a personal supplement to others' comments about the character and personality of Lyndon Johnson. The students had been always attentive; in fact, after these lectures several invariably gathered around me to ask questions. This would be a perfect topic, I figured, for an audience hoping to hear something reasonably entertaining late on a winter afternoon. Best of all, I wouldn't have to prepare. No fear of contradiction or debate, either: this was, after all, my life, and I could narrate it as I damn well pleased.

To my surprise and my host's pleasure, "Hunting Buddies" was very well attended. Around thirty students came, one bringing her mother along, another, his wife. A few of my colleagues from history and other departments sat around the table. Enough people drifted in during my remarks to make the association's president hustle out and haul in more chairs. After I finished, I answered questions for over an hour and a half.

Some were straightforward, asking for factual information: What sort of rifle did LBJ give me? Others asked me to speculate about what Johnson was like as a human being. The most intriguing was posed by the director of the library. "John, did you see anything at the ranch that gave you any feeling for what the relationship between Lyndon and Lady Bird was like?" I had not even mentioned Mrs. Johnson in my talk, but the minute my friend asked her question, I remembered the scene described in Chapter 12. There, once more, was Bird, comforting the president in the hall. At that instant, I realized how much I had left out of this story every time I'd told it, whether to family, friends, colleagues, or students.

That realization inspired the thought that writing a book about my family and Lyndon Johnson might be a good project. I talked it over with my wife, whose strength and advice I have leaned on since we met. Laura was enthusiastic. Next, I spoke with Nancy Taube. She liked the idea, too. I asked her if she liked it enough to hire on to process and edit the various drafts in the evenings after the workday. When she said yes, I was in business.

★ ★ ★

My memory did not need much coaxing about the trip to the LBJ Ranch. Historians tend to have good memories; the demands of our craft force us to train them if we don't start out with better than usual powers of retention. My encounters with Lyndon Johnson were infrequent enough and sufficiently dramatic to stay vivid and detailed in my mind long after the events. Very few people, I suspect, forget very much about meeting the president of the United States under the most fleeting and banal of circumstances. I was with LBJ for hours on three consecutive days. During that time, I basked under his praise and shivered under his contempt. It doesn't surprise me I remember a great deal about our time together.

But I also believe that everyone's memory is better than he or she thinks. For me, the trick to recalling physical details, exchanges of words, and emotional moods was, first, to relax, and, second, to visualize appearances I could remember. When I did this, whole scenes would crystalize for me. At times, it also helped to pantomime physical acts I remembered doing. Once a colleague was startled to pass by my office and see me, left arm extended, left palm gripping an invisible object, left eye closed, and right finger curled in a half moon shape. I was perfectly still; I appeared to be holding my breath. When he learned I was preparing to fire a rifle and kill a deer, I don't believe he felt reassured about my mental state.

I don't recommend aiming imaginary deer rifles at co-workers to anybody. But I do think if people would apply the discipline of shooting to remembering, they would find their recollections improving. Find your target, relax, and slowly squeeze the trigger if you aim at recalling the past more fully. Succumbing to buck fever by furrowing your brow, gritting your teeth, tensing your muscles, and jerking the trigger, leads to misses in memory as well as in hunting.

Of course, there's the problem of having your scope properly sighted-in. In recalling Lyndon Johnson's conversation, I had the tremendous advantage of Michael R. Beschloss's *Taking Charge: The Johnson White House Tapes, 1963-1964* (New York, 1997). I have occasionally quoted from his transcripts in this book and relied on it for discussions of the Texas Broadcasting Corporation and the hunting experiences of John Kennedy on the ranch. My debt to this work, however, goes far beyond these specific references. *Taking Charge* refreshed my memory of the cadences, vocabulary, and pungency of LBJ's talk. It also provided a primer, in the words of the man himself, on the Johnson technique and treatment.

For matters relating to aspects of Johnson's life during the 1930s and afterwards, I dipped into books I have taught from before. The two volumes Robert A. Caro has produced so far in his study, *The Years of Lyndon Johnson: The Path to Power* (New York, 1982) and *Means of Ascent* (New York, 1990), are filled with fascinating detail about his relationship with his staff. They are enlivened throughout by a stringently critical view of the man. Caro would have been Mother's favorite historian of LBJ. He's not mine, though I certainly concede the power of chapters such as "The Sad Irons" in *The Path to Power*. The story of Jack Gwyn and shoe shining at midnight can be found in *Means of Ascent*. Robert Dallek's two-volume biography, *Lone Star Rising* (New York, 1991) and *Flawed Giant* (New York, 1998), is the best and most balanced narrative of Lyndon Johnson's life. Robert Kennedy's adventures at the LBJ Ranch are described in *Lone Star Rising*. Details about LBJ's last years are in *Flawed Giant*. My favorite work remains Doris Kearns Goodwin's *Lyndon Johnson and the American Dream* (New York, 1976; republished with a new introduction, 1991). She is one of the very few people with whom he discussed his early years in Johnson City, and probably the only one who heard him describe his terrible nightmares in the White House.

As I wrote, when I had questions about LBJ I looked up the answers in these books. At times, I have disagreed with their conclusions, though never so much as I did with the account of deer hunting on the LBJ Ranch in William Manchester's *The Death of a President* (New York, 1967). The discussion of the earlier drafts of that book in John Corry, *The Manchester Affair* (New York, 1969) was very helpful. I mined Laura Kalman's *Abe Fortas: A Biography* (New Haven, 1990) for information about LBJ's professional and personal relationships with another smart lawyer, one considerably more famous than my father. Finally, the August 2000 issue of *Texas Monthly*, with its striking photographic essay on "The LBJ Gang Today," includes the brief but important account of his relationship with Lyndon Johnson by A.W. Moursund, the man who shared the responsibility of being a trustee of the blind trust with Dad.

For the curious or the historian, my father's reminiscences about LBJ are in the Oral History Division of the Johnson Library in Austin. Since I know they are less colorful and more guarded—the former president, after all, was still alive at the time of the interview—than the stories Dad has told me over the years, I've never read them. The interested may find some of his meetings with LBJ listed in Johnson's calendars. They can look in Glenn Stegall's correspondence and discover how I got the job in Yosemite. I didn't search through either, and I doubt I ever will. LBJ did not record very many of his conversations with my father, yet another indication of his unwillingness to discuss personal business under circumstances where outsiders might witness it. He did tape four discussions with Dad in November-December 1963. The catalog at the Johnson Library indicates they talked about family business and the appointment of Sheldon Cohen as Commissioner of the IRS. I haven't listened in. Perhaps the records of the investigation of my father during 1964-65 may be found in the FBI Archives. I presume they might be retrieved if someone is willing to file a Freedom of Information suit in federal court. I won't, because I have no desire to read them. In all of these cases, I've stuck to my vow not to do the archival research that characterizes—indeed, dominates—formal, academic histories.

I've bent that rule only twice. I did consult at the Johnson Library LBJ's Daily Diaries for December 29-31, 1965. They helped me recall the sequence of events during my visit to the ranch, and I confess I was tickled to discover the president, Lady Bird, and Jesse Kellam spent ten minutes "looking at a new gun that he gave John Bullion for Christmas." Still, I must warn readers of any of these calendars against assuming they are unfailingly accurate. For instance, the entries for the days I was there incorrectly put A.W. Moursund rather than Jesse Kellam on my hunting expedition the first day, mis-state the purpose of the visit to the Johnson City bank, wrongly include Mrs. Johnson on the deer hunt the second day, and omit both Dad's meeting with the president on December 30 and the time we spent with him in his bedroom on New Year's Eve. All this bears out what that most helpful of archivists, Philip Scott, told me about LBJ's calendars while he was in Gillespie County: they are notoriously incomplete.

My second departure from my rule came when I looked for photographs at the Johnson Library to illustrate this book. Neither those pictures nor the Daily Diaries change *In the Boat with LBJ* from what I intended it to be: a memoir.

Thus the complete, detailed history of the partnership between Lyndon B. Johnson and J. Waddy Bullion remains to be written. It can't be done now, because many of the papers are closed. If and when they are opened, no doubt that history shouldn't be done by Waddy's son.

★ ★ ★

Mother died in 1983, the victim of a blood clot that reached her heart. I thought about her often as I remembered and wrote about the Bullions and the Johnsons. I owe a great deal to her habit of teaching morality by telling stories, and to her insistence that what had happened in the past was important to those who live in the present. I'm not sure she would have approved of either my ambivalent feelings toward LBJ or my attempts to see the good, bad, and mixed elements in his character and behavior. I'm confident, though, she would have forgiven me for any sins of omission or commission.

The hero of this book, and the teller of most of its tales, is still alive. His intellect is as keen as ever, though he is physically frailer. He no longer accepts new clients, but continues to advise some he worked with for years. Most of them are friends as well. Now they enjoy the same privilege Lyndon Johnson had: he doesn't charge them. The terms of his retirement from Thompson, Knight forbid him from competing with the firm, which he interprets as billing those he counsels. Dad enjoys reminding his friends that they shouldn't get too attached to free legal consultations. Given his age, they cannot expect to rely on his availability forever. "When you're old," he tells them, "you shouldn't even buy green bananas."

My father is also fond of warning his son, who is older now than Waddy Bullion was in December 1965, "Old age is not for sissies." Indeed, it is not. Nor is remembering events from long ago and responding to countless questions. Nor is painstakingly trying to be helpful to me without going beyond what's permissible to tell without violating the attorney-client privilege. Editing a long manuscript isn't, either. Dad read drafts of this book thoughtfully and thoroughly. His role, he informed me, was to check for factual errors and correct them. My conclusions were my own business.

It cannot have been easy for my father to read the thoughts of his son during years when the two of us spent most of the limited time we were together arguing about everything. Dad never complained; he just kept on reading carefully and making the occasional note in the margin. That he said he was pleased with the book means a great deal to me. So does the effort he put into his remembering, retelling, reading, thinking, and editing. It's yet more evidence that he's no sissy and that he loves me. I didn't need that additional proof, but I'm real grateful for it.

Waddy and John Bullion, February 2001.
Bullion Family Collection.

My stepmother and sister read portions of several drafts. Their memories of LBJ's funeral are particularly vivid. Ann's recollection of how Sarah Hughes dressed that day was so compelling that I appropriated it. Much of the narrative about Dad's effort to get us and the Goldbergs on the other side of the Pedernales I borrowed from Wilma. That we were not on the list still puzzles her. She remains convinced that President Johnson would have wanted my father close to him that day.

Mary Lewis Turner told me about LBJ's visit to my parents' apartment in Arlington when he played with me on the floor. It was the first time I'd ever heard it. I'm obliged to Aunt Mary for this rare glimpse of a relaxed, happy Lyndon Johnson.

I am also much obliged to Michael O'Brien for taking breaks from his duties as Associate Dean of the College of Arts and Science at my university and commenting on a draft of the book from the perspective of a Texan who happens as well to be an anthropologist. Once upon a time, Mike played bridge with Walter Jenkins. I owe him for that story.

Four of my colleagues have listened to me talk about LBJ for years. For their patience, encouragement, and criticism, I thank Richard Bienvenu, Gerard H. Clarfield, Robert M. Collins, and Steven Watts. In addition to The Gang of Four, my friends Martha Alexander, Robert Bender, and Felicia Bender have debated with me about politics, both university and universal, so much and so well that they shaped the way I interpreted the relationship between Lyndon Johnson and my father. A couple of extraordinary editors, Ginnie Bivona and Susan Malone, did the same. That they did so while persuading a stubborn author to tighten a gargantuan manuscript speaks volumes for their skill, their patience, and their commitment to getting this story told in the best way possible.

Two other friends made important contributions to my rendition of these adventures. Tony Taube gave me the single best line in the book, one that beautifully sums up Lyndon Johnson. Joe Taube was my color expert. He painstakingly created a spectrum ranging from purple to blue, with several varieties of violet in between. Thanks to him, I could see once more the exact shade of the haze that troubled my vision on the first day of hunting at the LBJ Ranch.

I can measure the Taube boys' contributions pretty precisely. There is no way I could do so for the third member of that family. Nancy Taube's imprint is indelible on every page of this book. Her love for the English language, her precise use of it, and her sure instinct for suggesting the right word or the most telling phrase improved passage after passage. She has been the perfect reader of a text, enthusiastic yet critical, encouraging but demanding. Every morning I could count on hearing her reaction to the material she'd read the night before. Every afternoon she asked with a smile if I had any additional pages for her. Nancy accomplished that most difficult of editorial feats: she improved my writing and sharpened my analysis, without slowing my progress. But important as this and other skills were, they are not what I treasure most about her. Nancy is my friend in the fullest sense of that evocative and ambiguous word. She did not merely strengthen passages in this book with her editing. She inspired them with her example. One of the most painful and consequential tragedies in Lyndon Johnson's life was his inability to be a true friend during the years he sought to preserve and extend his power. Writing about that has made me appreciate more fully the blessing of our friendship.

As with Nancy's friendship, so with Laura's love. My wife has commented so trenchantly for so long about my work and my life that I feel her deep and abiding influence on everything I think, or say, or do. This book is no exception. Like all "the other stuff" of mine that's been put into print, it's a product of my love, written to, for, and with her. As always, Laura's editing of drafts was sensitive and searching. Even more important, her impact on the conception and design of the book was crucial. From our earliest discussions of Lyndon Johnson to the ones during the final days of writing, Laura consistently and persuasively argued that this was a Texas story. I counted on her to know everything Texan: the words to second verses of fine old Baptist hymns, how live oaks grew, the shade of the mammoth mesquite in back of the lakehouse, and the differences between goatheads and sand burrs. If Nancy saw what was unusual, one of a kind about LBJ, Laura focused on what was Texan about him. "I'm your expert on Texas," she once joked to me. She certainly was and is. Probably that's why she smiles and shakes her head whenever her husband writes or says, "I'm a Missourian now." Laura doesn't believe people change what home is to them that easily. After so much time spent with Lyndon Johnson, I'm about ready to concede she's right.

The principal contribution by our children Jack and Chandler to the book was their love, most often expressed in the forms of forebearing acceptance of "Dad at his memoirs" and humorous asides about the work and its author. One dark time, when nothing seemed to be going right, Jack responded to my complaints about problems with the narrative by suggesting, "Maybe you should sneak in an evil communist on the trip who you have to dust with your rifle." From that time forward, whenever I felt discouraged, I'd remind myself that I could always slip in a Red—a *New York Times* reporter, perhaps?—and things would pick up.

In contrast, Chandler specialized in keeping me from being too puffed up on good days. After listening to me discourse endlessly on the differences between sheep and goats, she asked with a straight face, "Which was President Johnson? He must have been one or the other." So, when I was too full of myself, and pride was racing on ahead of the inevitable spill, I'd recall I'd expended a great deal of time on matters of distant relevance to LBJ and the Bullions. Furthermore, I still wasn't sure which type of animal Lyndon Johnson was. I finally decided he was all goat. You can figure out why for yourselves.

★ ★ ★

Little other than this book will ever inform Jack and Chandler about Lyndon Johnson and their Bullion relatives. The lakehouse has changed hands twice since Wilma's nephew sold it and moved to Alaska; the live oaks LBJ planted in its front yard died during one of several droughts that plagued Texas during the 1990s. Every picture the president gave me was lost during a move. The television gave up the ghost years ago. Almost all of "the other stuff" is gone too. I only have two souvenirs left from my visit. I have the 1965 inauguration medal. And, somewhere in our storeroom, in its original scabbard, is the deer rifle Lyndon Johnson presented to me on the second day I was at the ranch. There's no plaque on its stock. It has been sighted-in, and it has killed deer. I put it away when Jack started to walk. Not long after it was, so to speak, out of sight once more, I stopped hunting. LBJ's rifle has remained in storage ever since, never visible and mostly forgotten.

My most constant reminder of LBJ is the watch he presented to Dad the last time the two were together. Although he appreciated the gift, my father never really liked wearing it. After the president's death, he put it away in a safety deposit box. Dad is an unostentatious man; you may accurately infer his ideas about the proper limits of male jewelry from my telling you that his only accessories are his favorite Cross pen and pencil, the ones with the gold leaf worn off the barrels by years of pressure from his fingers. About five years ago, for reasons he's never told me, he took the Rolex out of his lockbox and gave it to me. I've worn it since, out of respect and love for the man it identifies as "The Best" rather than to memorialize Lyndon Johnson.

It's a fine watch, handsome to look at, with one defining characteristic. Fittingly, considering who gave it to Dad, it runs fast.

About the Author

John L. Bullion was born October 23, 1944, in Washington, DC. In 1947 his family moved to Dallas, where he was raised. He graduated from Stanford University in 1966. After a very brief and mostly unhappy time at Harvard Law School, he entered the doctoral program in history at the University of Texas at Austin and received his Ph.D. in 1977. By that time he had already been an instructor of History at Southwest Texas State University for three years. In 1978 he accepted a teaching position in the department of history at the University of Missouri-Columbia. He has taught there ever since, currently holding the rank of Professor of History. Dr. Bullion won the Burlington Northern Foundation Faculty Achievement Award as one of three outstanding teachers in the University of Missouri System in 1990. Between 1991 and 1996 he served a sentence as chair of the department. At the present time he is chair of the Executive Committee of the College of Arts & Science.

Dr. Bullion lives in Columbia, Missouri, with his wife, Laura, another expatriate Texan, whom he married in 1976. Their two children, Jack and Chandler, have both left the nest and migrated to universities south of the Red River.

Index